On Our Own Terms

THE NEW COLD WAR HISTORY

Odd Arne Westad, *editor*

This series focuses on new interpretations of the Cold War era made possible by the opening of Soviet, East European, Chinese, and other archives. Books in the series based on multilingual and multiarchival research incorporate interdisciplinary insights and new conceptual frameworks that place historical scholarship in a broad, international context.

A complete list of books published in The New Cold War History is available at www.uncpress.org.

SARAH FOSS

On Our Own Terms
Development and Indigeneity in
Cold War Guatemala

The University of North Carolina Press *Chapel Hill*

This book was published with the assistance of the Authors Fund of the University of North Carolina Press.

© 2022 The University of North Carolina Press
All rights reserved
Set in Arno Pro by Westchester Publishing Services
Manufactured in the United States of America

Library of Congress Cataloging-in-Publication Data
Names: Foss, Sarah, 1985– author.
Title: On our own terms : development and indigeneity in Cold War Guatemala / Sarah Foss.
Other titles: New Cold War history.
Description: Chapel Hill : University of North Carolina Press, [2022] | Series: New Cold War history | Includes bibliographical references and index.
Identifiers: LCCN 2022025067 | ISBN 9781469670324 (cloth ; alk. paper) | ISBN 9781469670331 (paperback ; alk. paper) | ISBN 9781469670348 (ebook)
Subjects: LCSH: Agriculture—Economic aspects—Guatemala—History—20th century. | Rural development—Guatemala—History—20th century. | Community development—Guatemala—History—20th century. | Indians of Central America—Guatemala—Economic conditions. | Indians of Central America—Guatemala—Government relations. | Indians of Central America—Race identity—Guatemala. | Economic assistance, American—Guatemala—History—20th century. | Economic development—Guatemala—Citizen participation. | Cold War—Influence.
Classification: LCC HD1531.G9 F677 2022 | DDC 338.1097281—dc23/eng/20220718
LC record available at https://lccn.loc.gov/2022025067

Cover illustration: Biology school (photographer unknown, 1990, CPR del Ixcán, El Quiché, Guatemala). Courtesy of Comité Holandés de Solidaridad con el Pueblo de Guatemala Collection, Centro de Investigaciones Regionales de Mesoamérica, La Antigua, Guatemala.

This book includes material previously published in a different form as "'Una obra revolucionaria': *Indigenismo* and the Guatemalan Revolution, 1944–1954," in *Out of the Shadow: Revisiting the Revolution from Post-Peace Guatemala*, eds. Julie Gibbings and Heather Vrana (Austin: University of Texas Press, 2020), 199–221; "Rumors of Insurgency and Assassination in the Ixcán, Guatemala," *Journal of Social History* 55, no. 1 (September 2021): 105–26, DOI: 10.1093 /jsh/shab038; and "Community Development in Cold War Guatemala: Not a Revolution but an Evolution," in *Latin America and the Global Cold War*, eds. Thomas C. Field Jr., Stella Krepp, and Vanni Pettinà (Chapel Hill: University of North Carolina Press, 2020), 123–47. All material used here with permission.

Contents

Illustrations

Acknowledgments

It was in a 2010 K'iche' Maya language course that I first developed an interest in Guatemalan history, thanks to the patience and dedication of my three teachers: Tat Wel Tahay, Nela Tahay, and Mareike Sattler. In 2012, I first traveled to Guatemala to participate in the K'iche' language school in Nahualá, where the Tahays welcomed me to their community. They allowed me to witness firsthand how Indigenous Guatemalans practice resilience in resisting outside efforts to change them, shape their cultures, and at times eliminate them. I saw how communities can simultaneously practice solidarity and navigate internal conflict, and how they rightfully insist on their centrality in Guatemalan history. They taught me how to center Indigenous history, actors, and perspectives in broader historical narratives, a lesson that has shaped this book and my scholarship. Tat Wel tragically passed away from COVID-19 as I finished this book, and I hope that in a small way, my work reflects his legacy and the impact that he had upon all his students. Sib'alaj maltyox che la, Tat Wel.

Also enrolled in the K'iche' class were three Guatemalan graduate students—Tatiana Paz Lemus, Ixchel Espantzay, and Felipe Girón—who became friends and who generously helped me during my stays in their country. They reassured me when I questioned the possibility of conducting research in Guatemala, and they facilitated important connections and helped me navigate everyday life. Thank you for making me feel at home.

Tatiana Paz Lemus deserves an additional thanks. She and her extended family invited me to Tactic; little did I realize the town's significance to my research when I visited during the *feria* to run in the local 10k race, which she joked was now an international competition. Once I recognized that Tactic featured prominently in my research, Tatiana made my fieldwork there possible. Beyond that, she included me in her personal and professional networks, taught me to love Guatemala City of all of its complexity, and helped me to locate a good IPA and the best coffee, which, in my mind, are two research trip necessities. Tatiana—you are a model of what committed scholarship looks like, giving back at every opportunity, even at personal sacrifice. Since I have known you, you've never given up hope for a more just Guatemala, even in the bleakest moments, and you fight every day for that future, inspiring and encouraging those around you. Thank you for your mentorship and friendship.

The 2012 trip became the first of several trips to Guatemala over the next decade. From the beginning, I benefited from the kindness and generosity that the Guatemalan academy extended my way. Thanks to Sandra Herrera at USAC, who in two phone calls connected me with the two living members of the IING, changing the trajectory of this project in the best way possible, to USAC's General Department of University Research, who welcomed me as a visiting scholar and provided important logistical support and office space, and to USAC's Department of History, particularly Edgar Mendoza and Regina Fuentes, who permitted me to use and digitize the *Archivo de la Oralidad*. To the working group *Cátedra Joaquín Noval*, in particular Isabel Rodas and Roberto Melville, whose commitment to locating personal archives and recording the history of Guatemalan anthropology allowed me to access incredible sources and provided a venue to share my work, a heartfelt thanks. And finally, a huge thank you to Silvia Méndez, the most talented and determined research assistant one could ever hope for. Your persistence and uncanny ability to track down sources and interview subjects never ceased to amaze me and brought a richness and depth of source material to this project. I hope we can continue to work together for many, many more years. If only everyone was lucky enough to have a researcher as brilliant as you on their team.

This project took me to several archives in Guatemala and the United States. To all the archivists who do the important work to preserve the historical record and make it available to researchers like myself, thank you. A special thanks to Thelma Porras, Reyna Pérez, and Anaís García at CIRMA for their expertise, patience, and many helpful suggestions over the years. Julia Morales helped me to access Tactic's Municipal Archive, Carolina Rendón introduced me to the ODHAG holdings, and the staff at the AGCA and the *Hemeroteca Nacional* regularly gave me leads and helped me to navigate their holdings—I am indebted to you all.

At an early point in this project, I realized that the written record could not answer all the questions I was asking. The generosity of nearly fifty people in telling me their stories added an invaluable component to this project that shaped the narrative in ways that the written record could not. There are three sets of people who helped with the oral history side of this project that merit a special thank you. First, Aracely Cahuec coordinated my fieldwork in Tactic and provided translation from Poqomchi', and several *tactiqueños* generously gave their time to share their experiences of the DESCOM with me. Second, Don Francisco Rodríguez Rouanet and Doña Hélida Esther Cabrera invited me into their respective homes on numerous occasions and patiently shared their life stories with me. They turned what would have been an erroneous and simplistic account of Guatemalan *indigenismo* into a much more complex and interesting history that took into account the multiple layers, meanings, and intentions of the historical actors. Finally, many people helped orchestrate the Ixcán leg of my fieldwork. The Maryknoll order in Guatemala, in particular Father Bill Mullan and Brother Marty Shea, first encouraged me to travel to the Ixcán to hear the local history from the people who lived it and then invited me along on their road trip to the Ixcán to commemorate the fortieth anniversary of Father Bill Woods's assassination, the most memorable part of my entire research journey. Padre Ricardo Falla, Eridenia Martínez, and Natividad Jiménez facilitated my Ixcán fieldwork and several Mayalán residents granted me interviews. These memories have had lasting impacts on my scholarship and my life, *mil gracias a ustedes*.

This book would not have been possible had I not been afforded the opportunity to study at Vanderbilt and Indiana University, respectively, and benefited from the mentorship and guidance of remarkable faculty at both institutions. At Vanderbilt, Marshall Eakin, Jane Landers, Eddie Wright-Ríos, Celso Castilho, and Frank Robinson introduced me to the discipline of history, patiently explaining what historiography was and how to do archival research and challenging me to read widely and think creatively. At Indiana University, I benefited from having an extraordinary dissertation committee. My advisor, Jeff Gould, pushed me to ask the tough questions and track down the hard-to-find sources in order to produce meaningful scholarship. Peter Guardino's generosity to his students, department, and community have benefited me every step of the way and have given me the best example to follow. Danny James and Nick Cullather pushed me to explore different historiographies and questions, which enhanced the project in amazing ways that I did not anticipate. You all cared about me as a scholar *and* as a person, an all-too-rare combination in graduate school. Your scholarship influences these pages, and I am grateful that you all formed the foundation of my intellectual development.

Colleagues have supported me and improved this project in many ways and have provided me with the best intellectual community. Rachel Nolan has shaped this book at every stage, from predissertation research when we were trying to figure out how to navigate an archive to reading a late draft of the entire manuscript. Thank you for your friendship, and I hope we can celebrate another milestone birthday at the lake, complete with fancy olive oil. To Dillon Vrana, who probably didn't realize that when they were assigned to mentor a first-year graduate student, it was more of a long-term commitment, for which I continue to be grateful. To the great cohort at IU for providing numerous rounds of comments and encouragement at each stage of this project, especially Denisa Jashari and Stephanie Huezo—you all are a big reason I got through the rough patches stronger than when I started and why I continue to love my profession today. Since joining the faculty at Oklahoma State University, I've benefited from the generosity of this community as well, especially the Faculty Writing Group that workshopped a chapter at a critical stage in this project. A special thanks to Richard Boles, Sarah Griswold, Emily Graham, Holly Karibo, and Doug Miller for reading and commenting on drafts and mentoring me through the publication process and through the early years on the job. Members of the Oklahoma Latin American History Workshop read and commented on the entire manuscript, in the middle of a pandemic no less—thank you to Sarah Hines, Adrián Lerner, Raphael Folsom, James Cane-Carrasco, and Drew Wood. Many thanks to other Guatemalanists and Latin Americanists who bring out the best in academia and have generously given advice, shared research materials, read drafts of this work, and provide me with the best intellectual community: Raquel Escobar, José Cal Montoya, Amelia Kiddle, Julie Gibbings, Lydia Crafts, David Carey Jr., J. T. Way, Thomas Field Jr., Betsy Konefal, Jim Handy, Eddie Brudney, Kirsten Weld, Carlotta McAllister, Abigail Adams, and Vanessa Freije. And a heartfelt thanks to Debbie Gershenowitz at UNC Press for taking this project on and patiently guiding me through the peer review and publication process and to the two anonymous reviewers whose comments, critiques, and ideas significantly improved the manuscript all while encouraging me of its potential and merit.

I am grateful to various institutions for funding this project: Oklahoma State University, the Oklahoma Humanities Council, Indiana University, the Fulbright-Hays Doctoral Dissertation Research Fellowship, the American Historical Association, and the University of Chicago. Thank you for your generosity in financially supporting this project.

The biggest debts I have incurred are unquestionably with my family. To my parents, Alan and Patti Lacy, and my in-laws, John and Beth Foss: you will never know how much it meant that you came to visit Guatemala to learn about the country that so intrigued me, and that you supported me at each stage of this long journey. I am particularly grateful to my mom, who meticulously proofread my entire manuscript, studied Spanish, and read several books about Guatemalan history all so that she could understand my research and learn about a place so meaningful to me.

Finally, my immediate family is my motivation, my refuge, and my joy. To Josh, who supported this project from the beginning and has stood by me at every step, celebrating the highs and encouraging me through the lows. You postponed your own goals to accompany me on my second extended research trip, and in doing so brought a piece of home to Guatemala. I am so lucky and grateful to have you on my team. And to my little girls, your entrance into our lives coincided with the beginning and the end of the book project, respectively, bringing necessary perspective and balance. Though preparing a book manuscript with two small children does not make for the most focused work environment, I would not have it any other way. Nora and Abbey, you are everything that is good about the world, and you have brought immeasurable joy to my life. I cannot wait to take you to Guatemala.

Abbreviations in the Text

APROFAM	Asociación Pro-Bienestar de la Familia
CAD	Comité Agrario Departamental
CAL	Comité Agrario Local
CAN	Consejo Agrario Nacional
CCII	Coordinadores Interinstitucionales
CEH	Comisión de Esclarecimiento Histórico
CHS	Comité Holandés de Solidaridad
CIA	Central Intelligence Agency
CNCG	Confederación Nacional Campesina de Guatemala
CNPE	Consejo Nacional de Planificación Económica
COCODE	Consejos Comunitarios de Desarrollo Urbano y Rural
CPR	Comunidades de Población en Resistencia
DAN	Departamento Agrario Nacional
DESCOM	Programa Nacional de Desarrollo de la Comunidad
DGAA	Dirección General de Asuntos Agrarios
EGP	Ejército Guerrillero de los Pobres
FAG	Fuerzas Aéreas Guatemaltecas
FAO	Food and Agriculture Organization
FTN	Franja Transversal del Norte
GMRR	Guatemalan Movement for Rural Reconstruction
HRAF	Human Relations Area Files
IBRD	International Bank for Reconstruction and Development
III	Instituto Indigenista Interamericano
IING	Instituto Indigenista Nacional de Guatemala
ILO	International Organization of Labor
INCAP	Instituto de Nutrición de Centro América y Panamá

INFOP	Instituto Nacional para el Fomento de Producción
INTA	Instituto Nacional de Transformación Agraria
JAD	Junta Agraria Departamental
MISEREOR	German Catholic Bishops' Organization for Development Cooperation
MLN	Movimiento de Liberación Nacional
ODHAG	Oficina de Derechos Humanos del Arzobispado de Guatemala
PAAC	Plan de Asistencia en las Áreas de Conflicto
PAR	Partido de Acción Revolucionaria
PAVA	Programa de Ayuda para Vecinos del Altiplano
PGT	Partido Guatemalteco del Trabajo
PMIT	Proyecto de Mejoramiento Integral de Tactic
PUAC	Partido de Unificación Anticomunista
SBS	Secretaría de Bienestar Social
SCIDE	Servicio Cooperativo Interamericano de Educación
SER	Socioeducativo Rural
SFEI	Servicio de Fomento de la Economía Indígena
SIL	Summer Institute of Linguistics
UN	United Nations
URNG	Unidad Revolucionaria Nacional Guatemalteca
USAC	Universidad de San Carlos
USAID	United States Agency for International Development

On Our Own Terms

Guatemala. (Map prepared by the Oklahoma State University Cartography Lab.)

Until the Indian Is Made to Walk

Of everything she had accomplished in her ninety-four-year life, Hélida Esther Cabrera claimed she was most proud of her development work with Guatemala's *Instituto Indigenista Nacional* (National Indigenist Institute, IING) from 1951 to 1956. Cabrera joined the IING as its first female ethnographer during the height of the Guatemalan Revolution (1944–1954). With the exception of a few brief democratic openings, military leaders had ruled Guatemala for almost the entirety of its independence from Spain in 1821, and the 1944 Guatemalan Revolution ushered in a new period of democracy and state-led efforts to integrate the diverse Guatemalan population, which included individuals from twenty-four distinct Indigenous Peoples.[1] Cabrera's work fit squarely within this project. When the IING reinitiated its fieldwork in 1955 after the Counterrevolution, fieldwork director Francisco Rodríguez Rouanet approached her with a difficult fieldwork assignment, one that her male colleagues had avoided: visit the Poqomam Maya and Xinca town of San Carlos Alzatate in the eastern department of Jalapa and report the town's infrastructure needs.[2] In 1947, San Carlos Alzatate had received the legal designation of a *comunidad indígena*, meaning that it operated as a distinct legal entity from the municipality. Though the record does not indicate why residents pursued this status, common reasons include the desire to afford Indigenous populations more clout at the municipal level, to protect communal land, and to retain some sense of autonomy.[3] Further, both Rodríguez Rouanet and Jalapa's governor warned Cabrera that San Carlos Alzatate was remote and dangerous, referencing it as a place "where they kill people," and perhaps not a suitable destination for a female ethnographer traveling alone. As a middle-class woman from rural Guatemala and, by this point, an experienced ethnographer, Cabrera did not shy away from this challenge and decided to fulfill her assignment, remembering, "Well, if it's my cemetery, then so be it."[4]

Cabrera borrowed the governor's horse to make the forty-eight-kilometer journey from Jalapa to San Carlos Alzatate, a feat of bravery in itself as she had been thrown from a horse not long prior while racing other IING ethnographers back to Jalapa after a day of fieldwork.[5] Upon arriving in San Carlos Alzatate, over 1,000 people had gathered in the main plaza, which she initially feared was a mob that intended to harm her. However, she soon realized that the town had actually surprised her with a large party, for she was their first official visitor in ten years. Townspeople had decorated the municipal building with pine needles, contracted a marimba band, provided liquor, shot off fireworks, and rang the church bells to celebrate her visit. Despite witnessing a deadly feud and arson during her ten-day stay, and after becoming incredibly ill to the point that she gave the local authorities her IING credentials so that they could properly record what she thought was her imminent death, Cabrera successfully completed her work and promised to relay the town's requests to the proper authorities.

On her return journey to Jalapa, she fortuitously stayed one night in the same hotel as Jalapa's education inspector, with whom she frankly shared her concerns about the infrastructure needs of the town, detailing the dismal status of the school's roof, inadequacy in educational supplies, and overflowing community latrines, relaying the town's desire to have the state address these problems.[6] Because Cabrera was concerned about the inspector's ambivalence, as he had never even visited San Carlos Alzatate, she also wrote a formal report and shared it directly with the minister of education, Enrique Quiñónez. Quiñónez traveled to San Carlos Alzatate and after his visit, the government built a new school and health center and repaired the main road to Jalapa.[7] Cabrera proudly referred to these accomplishments as "the best and the most historic" of all her work at the IING. Years later, long after leaving the institute, she saw a television news report praising San Carlos Alzatate's excellent health center, and she recalled, "I cried, I cried out of emotion because of my work."[8]

Cabrera and the IING's work in San Carlos Alzatate is just one example of outsider efforts to "improve" rural, predominately Indigenous towns in Guatemala during the Cold War, which in Guatemala included its ten-year democratic revolution from 1944 to 1954 and a thirty-six-year civil war from 1960 to 1996 that included rampant "disappearances," senseless executions, massacres—in sum, state-sponsored genocide. *On Our Own Terms* examines how development's complicated history helps explain why the Guatemalan state and the U.S. government came to view certain populations as subversive, which expressions of citizenship the state wished to foster and which it wanted to suppress, and how Indigenous people played a central role in Cold War history. The book's central argument is twofold. First, while for the Guatemalan state, development projects were intended to curb political instability and ensure national progress, this top-down, homogenizing project was not neatly implemented, as local-level staff and mid-level bureaucrats reworked it and applied it to different contexts. These individuals navigated the tricky intermediary role of both appeasing their employers while also applying their growing knowledge of local and material conditions. Thus, development was multifaceted; historical actors simultaneously framed it as a humanitarian endeavor, nation-building project, and preventative measure against leftist subversion. It functioned as a powerful tool of governance, a way for individuals to obtain material assistance, and as a site where individuals both perpetuated and challenged racism.

Added to this uneven application of programming were the actions of the intended recipients themselves, a heterogeneous set of actors with their own (and at times conflicting) ideas and practices regarding the type of intervention they would permit in their communities and the nature of their relationship to outsiders and to the Guatemalan state. This book's second main argument is that Indigenous people were central actors in determining the meanings that Cold War development acquired, actors that contemporaries and historians alike have often relegated to the margins of Cold War history. When experts and local-level staff allowed beneficiaries to shape the form that development took instead of imposing formulaic projects, such initiatives enjoyed more success.

Unfortunately, I have not located records that detail San Carlos Alzatate residents' views on Cabrera's visit because her late husband destroyed her field notes, and the IING's archive was destroyed in the late 1980s when the institute closed. However, the community-wide party that celebrated her arrival could suggest that townspeople welcomed her visit and perhaps hoped to obtain resources for projects that they desired, such as a new school. It mirrors the colonial *visita*, when colonists often extravagantly celebrated the arrival of Spanish officials in an attempt to garner favor, even if they actually despised colonial rule.[9] In the 1960s, San Carlos Alzatate participated in the literacy and public health campaigns of the National Program of Community Development (DESCOM), again signaling a willingness to engage with state-led development efforts.[10] In 1967, the town's alcalde, Juan Antonio Pérez Gómez, bragged in national newspaper *El Imparcial* that the town now had 300 students enrolled in school, had diversified its agricultural production, and was completing a new road that would facilitate farmers' ability to participate in regional and national markets.[11] Though these few records cannot represent the diversity of perspectives that surely existed among San Carlos Alzatate residents, it appears that retaining local autonomy did not mean that residents rejected all development initiatives; on the contrary, at least some seem to have welcomed projects they believed would improve their quality of life and allow them to better control their own futures.

Undeniably, development projects in Guatemala and throughout the world attempted to order society, make it legible to those in power, and homogenize a diverse citizenry.[12] They certainly did reinforce existing social hierarchies, extend capitalism's reaches, and promote political agendas. Within the context of the Cold War, development proved a powerful counterinsurgency tool that extended the state's presence in distant towns, theoretically permitting the close surveillance of any supposedly dissident activity. But in some instances, as seen in San Carlos Alzate and in Cabrera's own life, it also gave people a way to empower themselves through providing needed resources and helping to forge horizontal bonds of solidarity and community. Intermediaries like Cabrera mediated the imposition of development upon their host communities by reshaping state priorities, infusing their own convictions, and bending to local desires. And Indigenous recipients used the opportunities and discourses that development provided to challenge the state's modernization project and instead promote development on their own terms, proving themselves to be central actors in histories of Cold War development projects. My aim is not to evaluate the failure or success of development; what I am concerned with is the "social construction" of development and its intended and unintended consequences, how development programs served as "significant sites of state making," and the way that these projects shaped social categories and lived experiences in Guatemala during the Cold War.[13]

Development as History . . . But Whose History?

Hélida Cabrera and the IING's efforts are part of a longer history of development in Guatemala geared toward "making the Indian walk," to quote Cuban revolutionary and writer José Martí. Writing in 1894 amid Cuba's long struggle for independence, Martí grappled with issues of colonialism and identity for Cuba and, more broadly, Latin America. In denouncing colonial practices that repressed Indigenous populations, Martí directly linked the progress of the Americas to the well-being of Indigenous Peoples.[14] Forty-six years later in 1941, Guatemalan Consul to Mexico Carlos Girón Cerna used Martí's quote to refer to a different common goal for the Americas, that of economic development. He wrote, "Thirty million inhabitants living within our midst have a standard of life that is so low that it scarcely counts in the economy of the American continent. . . . In the words of José Martí, 'Until the Indian is made able to walk, America will not begin walking.'" According to Girón, what caused Indigenous marginalization was not just the legacy of colonialism but also contemporary and unacceptable socioeconomic conditions: economic development provided the solution for this crisis. Increasing the "purchasing power and productive capacity of these thirty million Indians" would foster American security and stability, and these goals remained consistent throughout the Cold War.[15] Instead of considering Indigenous populations as obstacles to progress, state builders like Girón now believed that Indigenous people could contribute to society, under the state's careful guidance. Increasingly in the post–World War II (WWII) world, state builders recognized that should Indigenous populations grow dissatisfied with their current situation and opt to join leftist organizations, they had the potential to challenge regional stability.

Efforts to "make the Indian walk" were not novel to Cold Warriors, nor to Girón in the 1940s or even Martí in the 1890s. Instead, these initiatives had characterized the relationship of Indigenous people to outsiders since the European invasion. Systems of forced resettlement and tribute; efforts at evangelization; and the imposition of new categories and meanings of race, class, and gender mirrored colonial practices in other parts of the world, as Spain worked to transform colonized people into its version of respectable, loyal subjects.[16] Even after Spanish America's independence, national elite replicated elements of this practice, only then with the goal of creating a controllable citizenry.[17] During the Cold War, notions of proper citizenship became entangled with ideas about international geopolitics and global security, as both superpowers ignored specific contents and contingencies and rather operated under formulaic, universalized assumptions of what steps and behaviors would yield citizens loyal to their respective causes. And as seen in the passive construction of Martí's quote, "until the Indian is made to walk," Martí, and then mid-twentieth-century state builders often failed to recognize the agency of Indigenous people in these processes. State builders, while perhaps well intentioned, viewed it as their responsibility to make "the Indian" walk, revealing their belief that "Indians" could not "walk" without outside assistance. And once walking, they believed it to be their responsibility to make sure Indigenous people learned to "walk" properly and to "walk" in the right direction. If they could guide them in this way, development practitioners often reasoned, they might create a notion of an abstract, universal modern citizen that, from their perspective, would allow Indigenous people to become tremendous assets and be easily appropriated as cultural symbols for the nation rather than derogatorily viewed as obstacles to progress.

However, Indigenous people did not blindly accept the development programs that the state offered them. Instead, they utilized the skills they had always employed when negotiating outside intervention to determine how to capitalize on the positive facets of such encounters while mitigating negative aspects. Again, this is not unique to the mid-twentieth century. For centuries, Indigenous populations in Latin America have negotiated with the ruling powers in a variety of ways, including violently rebelling; functioning as intermediaries who shaped colonial practices; operating within the global economy; forging strategic alliances with outside powers; shaping racial, class, and gender identity formation; and participating in local and national politics.[18] The intrusion of development experts at the mid-twentieth century marked only the latest effort to transform daily practices and relationships. What is significant about these Cold War development interventions is that they focus our attention on Latin America as a critical space where the global Cold War was literally and figuratively fought, and they highlight how development provided an arena not only for geopolitical objectives but also for the negotiation of identity and the simultaneous replication and contestation of social inequality.[19]

Development projects' planners, implementers, and intended recipients all debated the form that development should take. Individuals created and abided by different development models, which, following the definition of Erin Beck, consist of three components: a view of what constitutes and causes underdevelopment, a definition of the ideal condition, and an understanding of how best to transition from the former to the latter.[20] This book analyzes development not just as foreign and domestic policy but also as history and as daily reality, showing what the related concepts of development and modernization meant to historical actors living and working in Guatemala during the Cold War.[21] These concepts are historically contingent, highly contextualized, and constantly negotiated. As such, they prove difficult to singularly define. I follow Daniel Immerwahr's simple definition of development as "the increase of social capacity," understanding it to be a process by which some type of socially constructed entity attempts to "effect linked social and economic transformation" upon another entity, a concept that has long existed.[22] Modernization, then, is one approach to development. Though scholars use the term to broadly refer to tactics that historical actors utilized in pursuit of their vision of modernity, such as nineteenth-century efforts to industrialize or build transportation infrastructure, when used in this book it refers to its function as an ideological project of the United States in the mid-twentieth century.[23]

By the Cold War period, modernization certainly was a preeminent development model for the Western world and as such, was infused with an anti-communist political agenda and based upon a capitalist logic. Development experts viewed modernization as stagist, with countries passing through different points to the ultimate destination of a liberal democracy with an active citizenry, a capitalist economy, individual freedoms, and a strong sense of national identity. It operated as a top-down, universal program designed to satisfy the popular classes enough to prevent uprising but not significantly alter the status quo. While the U.S. State Department and Guatemalan elites were preoccupied with large infrastructure development in Guatemala, they also identified rural development as a central component to ensuring stability. In 1950, 75 percent of Guatemala's nearly 3 million population was rural, and 69 percent worked in agriculture.[24] Fearing a revolution of rising expectations, U.S. Cold War foreign policy had identified peasants—which they broadly defined as working-class rural populations—as potential revolutionaries.[25] Many Western development experts saw community-level development projects as ideal for guiding peasants toward democracy and capitalism, and in Guatemala, rural community development projects were designed according to the model of modernization with the intention of "transforming" the rural poor, specifically targeting the rural Indigenous majority.[26] However, as this book will show, modernization was never the only development model utilized in Guatemala, nor did its application go uncontested. This book explores these competing models alongside one another to render a more holistic analysis of the lived experiences of development.

Much scholarship on histories of development takes a top-down approach, prioritizing the stories of the people who designed the projects and predicted the outcomes of these initiatives. This focus reflects less a belief in the passivity of recipients than an issue of sources, a challenge I will discuss more in the methodology section. These narratives tend to center the perspective of the planners—their ambitions, influences, intentions, and complexity—and they are often critical of these historical actors, and rightly so. Because of this approach, we now have a better understanding of how the Cold War's two superpowers used ideas about development and modernity to discursively create the "Third World," and we can see how socioeconomic aid proved an important tool for various countries to employ during the Cold War in an effort to further their influence.[27] Development history from above has more recently moved beyond the confines of the nation-state to demonstrate the entangled nature of states, institutions, international organizations, and private individuals, revealing important networks between the public and private spheres. Together, this literature elucidates how world leaders and transnational institutions used development to underpin authoritarian regimes, shape civilians' psychology, integrate people into national economies, spread nationalism, create discourses about sustainability, and sometimes, meet very real material needs. Indisputably, these stories tell an important part of Cold War history.[28]

Left out, or at least relegated to the margins, however, are development's local-level project staff and intended recipients. While experts and politicians maintained visions for development's impact on the so-called Third World, it was at the local level that program staff put projects in action and where recipients imbued development with meaning. Recent scholarship has shown that these experts were "complex historical actors in their own right" that are too often cast aside as passive agents of the state or institution for which they worked.[29] This, however, is erroneous thinking. Using historian Sarah Hines's concept of "vernacular modernism," or the idea that a diverse group of actors called for some application of modernity but one that they described according to local logics and knowledge, we can understand the multiple ways that the actors of this history defined and desired development.[30] *On Our Own Terms* seeks to make sense of this complex intermediary role that development experts and local project staff played. Individuals who occupied this position of intermediary and expert were both "quixotic and indispensable" because they "could not escape prevailing paradigms and practices" but also often "constituted ethical responses to perceived injustices and attempts to forge partial consensuses."[31] This book applies this observation to the Guatemalan case, as the individuals whose lives I analyze thought in the realm of what they perceived to be possible in their own historical moment and had institutional parameters limit their actions, all the while hoping to make a tangible change in the social imbalances they viewed on a daily basis. At the same time, whenever possible, I analyze the voices and perspectives of development's intended recipients to understand how they utilized the opportunities, discourses, and resources made available through socioeconomic aid to pursue their own individual and collective needs and desires and how they negotiated the changing meanings of the social categories applied to them. Only in this way can we complicate the narrative of development's failure with examples of individuals capitalizing on the opportunities and resources that projects provided in an effort to assert their own power over their lives.

This history of development in Cold War Guatemala builds on scholarship about state formation that calls for "bringing the state back in without leaving the people out."[32] I employ Jan Rus's definition of the state as "both the apparatus of government and the economic and political elite whose interests it served."[33] Therefore, state building is a dynamic and contested process that takes place at all levels of society as individuals constantly redefine and renegotiate their relations of power to one another.[34] They do so through a "common discursive framework" that defines the language, concepts, and the "terms of which contestation and struggle can occur."[35] Ideas and practices of development functioned within this discursive framework and as a site for these power struggles, cementing development's role as an important part of state building. As this book argues, Indigenous communities saw development as a way to cement themselves as protagonists in state building and often sought to leverage state resources to further local interests. Viewing development as a dialectical process follows William Taylor's call to "expand the concept of the state beyond the usual meaning of centralized institutions of the sovereign authority to encompass a larger field of institutional expressions of social relationships that have to do with the regulation of public life."[36] Interrogating the perspective of intended beneficiaries alongside those of development actors creates a complicated and yet fascinating and necessary account of lived experiences of Cold War development.

By integrating a multiplicity of voices and perspectives into this history, *On Our Own Terms* interrogates not only the priorities emanating from actors working in offices in Guatemala City and Washington, D.C., but also those from local project staff and program recipients in predominantly Indigenous communities. As such, it is a layered history, one from above and below, as it seeks to understand development, in the words of historian J. T. Way, as a "dialogical and complex process."[37] Across political watersheds in Guatemalan history, such as the 1944 democratic Revolution, the 1954 Central Intelligence Agency (CIA)–backed military coup and subsequent Counterrevolution, and the 1960–1996 civil war, development projects simultaneously supported and undermined governance efforts. Therefore, development history permits us to move beyond a "crisis-driven narrative of inter-American affairs" and instead begin to understand how the global Cold War both shaped and was influenced by highly contextualized "identities and everyday practices."[38]

Placing Guatemala in the Global Cold War

Guatemala played a key but overlooked role in the global Cold War, and its history provides insight into the role that both Indigenous people and ideas about Indigeneity played in this international conflict. During World War II, Guatemalans participated in a hemispheric movement that linked the socioeconomic "improvement" of Indigenous populations with regional security, and after the 1944 Revolution, the Guatemalan state prioritized and funded programs designed to integrate the diverse population as active citizens, but on the state's terms. Some historical actors continued to call for the *ladiniza-tion* of the Indigenous population, or the contemporary notion that Indige-nous Guatemalans could shed their Indigeneity and become ladinos, simplistically understood as non-Indigenous.[39] However, others called for integration rather than assimilation in an effort to allow for cultural diversity within a broadly defined national identity, and in the mid-twentieth century, this integrationist position gained significant traction. State development pro-grams sought to "de-Indianize" the population, what Marisol de la Cadena de-scribes as the process by which behaviors perceived as problematic are replaced with acceptable, modern ones in a way that does not end in full assimilation but in a new, racialized identity.[40] Importantly, in Guatemala the process of de-Indianizing Indigenous people differed from ladinization because the former allowed for the retention of an Indigenous identity and thus opened space for development practitioners and recipients alike to both "reproduce[d] and contest[ed] racism." Although integration as de-Indianization provided a way for Indigenous people to improve their social status in Guatemala without needing to pass as ladino, it still left intact racist understandings of Indigeneity as an inferior mode of being. Additionally, de-Indianization in Guatemala did not suggest that non-Indigenous people adopt aspects of Indigenous cultures but rather that national identity embrace (and appropriate) certain aspects of Indigenous cultures as "shared cultural bonds," a process that Rick López refers to as "ethnicizing the nation."[41] As scholars have argued, revolutionary pro-grams such as literacy campaigns, expanded suffrage, public health initiatives, and land reform did provide Indigenous people with opportunities to chal-lenge structural racism and participate in national affairs, but these programs in many ways still sought to control individual actions.[42] Internationally, Guate-mala's revolutionary agenda inspired leftist social movements across the region but also worried anti-communist governments, especially in the increasingly polarized geopolitical environment of the escalating Cold War in the early 1950s.[43]

In 1954, the country witnessed the second act of U.S. covert interference in overthrowing a foreign government (the first had been Iran in 1953) and the first instance of CIA-backed coups in Latin America, dismantling the revolu-tionary government. In the immediate aftermath, a U.S. House of Represen-tatives special study mission identified Guatemala as "a political, social, and economic laboratory . . . the success or failure of this experiment by the first country in the world to overthrow the Communist yoke will be a major factor in determining the future course of Latin American affairs."[44] The Guatema-lan counterrevolutionary state found itself reliant on continued U.S. support in terms of aid and international legitimacy. Even as Guatemala experienced authoritarian military rule and an escalating civil war that unleashed profound violence against civilian populations, it continued to feature prominently in U.S. foreign policy toward Latin America. After the U.S. government cut off military aid to Guatemala in 1977, it continued to channel humanitarian aid to the country via the U.S. Agency for International Development (USAID). President Reagan praised Guatemalan military dictator Efraín Ríos Montt, later found guilty of crimes against humanity, as "a man of great personal integrity and commitment . . . [who] wants to improve the quality of life for all Guatemalans and to promote social justice."[45] Because the United States saw Guatemala as a strategic regional ally and feared the possibility of leftist insurgency, it supported repressive regimes and was complicit in the genocidal violence. Thus, from the immediate aftermath of World War II through the dissolution of the Soviet Union in 1991, Guatemala factored centrally in U.S. containment efforts and foreign policy in Latin America.

Race and Development

Just as Guatemala's international geopolitical significance makes it an ideal case for analyzing the history of Cold War development initiatives in Latin America, so too does its demographics make it an appropriate place to study the way that race and racism worked through development initiatives. A continuation across the various political ruptures in Guatemala during the Cold War was both the state's and international development experts' identification of the rural working class as the population that could either become the bulwark of the nation *or* the reason for its demise. And in Guatemala, this fear often became racialized, as many politicians and experts equated rurality with Indigeneity. Intended beneficiaries complicated international development experts' oversimplified and universal understanding of "the peasant" and challenged the meanings attributed to the broad category of "the Indian."[46] Project sites served as spaces where "racial struggles . . . [were] disinterred once again . . . reconstructed yet again and redeployed" and where elites could employ racialized social categories to maintain their own power while non-elites often challenged this racism and sometimes seized on these inscribed identities as a form of collective power that could alter the status quo.[47] Thus *On Our Own Terms* analyzes racialization, or the process of ascribing characteristics to people, practices, and places based on socially constructed notions of genealogical, biological, and cultural hierarchies.[48] As Laura Gotkowitz reminds, "racialization is not simply a discursive or cultural process. It goes hand in hand with the exercise of political and economic power."[49] This book utilizes this concept to analyze how historical actors racialized development programs, participants, places, and practices and in turn imbued ideas about race in Guatemala with notions of Cold War politics and competing ideas about modernity.

To historically contextualize the story this book tells, beginning in the sixteenth century Iberian monarchs and settlers created the juridical concept of "the Indian,"[50] a racialized category of Indigeneity defined first in opposition to Europeans, and then as one possible identity among a complex set of racialized categories based on lineage, concepts of blood purity, religion, behaviors and social norms, geography, and place within society.[51] Upon independence from Spain, national elites debated the place of "the Indian" in the state and nation, with some locating the national past in romanticized notions of Indigenous histories while others pointed to Europe as its point of origin. Despite these epistemological differences, Latin American elites consistently racialized Indigenous people in their contemporary condition as obstacles to modernity.[52] Thus I, like other scholars, argue that the category of "the Indian" is a racial category, "an object of knowledge that is constructed as a biological and social 'fact' grounded in what is taken to be empirical nature," and that is socially constructed "out of unequal power relations and discriminatory practices."[53] Rather than conflating the slippery concepts of race and ethnicity, I instead try to parse out how historical actors used the categories that they employed and thus reflect that in the terminologies this book uses. Thus, I use ethnicity to refer to a "shared group identity," so when I name specific Maya nations, such as Kaqchikel, K'iche', and Poqomam, for example, I am referring to ethnic categories.[54] Certainly, the concepts of race and ethnicity overlap, but by analytically considering "Indigeneity" as a racialized category, I intend to examine how "identity . . . is a process, not a thing, and is constantly under renegotiation" and how its various meanings shaped interpersonal interactions and politics in the historical context of development projects.[55]

In Guatemala by the 1870s, the numerous racialized identities that individuals used to describe the diverse population had begun to crystallize into a false dichotomy of ladino and Indigenous. Contemporaries began to racialize Indigeneity both in cultural and economic terms; it described a non-Spanish (or nonfluent) speaker, an illiterate person, one who did not use Western clothing or shoes, one whose diet heavily revolved around corn, and one who typically, but not always, worked as a rural laborer. Ladino, on the other hand, also collapsed significant diversity into a singular racialized category and was constructed in opposition to that of "the Indian," broadly referring to a non-Indigenous person, including anyone of Asian or African descent.[56] These categories were fluid and relational, based more on behaviors and status rather than physical appearance, thus affording one the opportunity to adjust one's practices to fit the social criteria for a particular category. The very process of categorizing people and places also replicated the racialism inherent in the "power of naming."[57] Similarly, categories are constantly changing to better reflect social realities, to strengthen solidarities, or to obscure diversity and facilitate exclusion.[58] Thus, I use these labels according to the categories that contemporary actors attributed to the person, place, or practice under question in order to historicize how race worked in Guatemala via development projects.

Scholars of Guatemala have underscored how processes of state building and elite ideas about who constituted the nation operated alongside popular interpretations of nation and society.[59] Racism in Guatemala has always blended biological and cultural explanatory factors to the point that the two cannot be neatly disentangled and "this synthesis almost makes racism more versatile and gives it a greater capacity to transform itself and survive."[60] One dominant discourse of elite racism in Guatemala is the idea of Indigenous degeneration, defined in terms of behaviors and practices and the related notion of the tutelary state, tasked with "civilizing" the country's "backward" population.[61] In midcentury development initiatives, these concepts gained new meanings as experts took the lead in pursuing the regeneration of "the Indian" through modernization. Importantly, as scholars have shown, racialized identities and racism and their relation to broader historical processes like the construction of time, the definition and pursuit of modernity, the development of liberal democracy, and the growth of the capitalist economy were not just elite ladino impositions upon the rest of the Guatemalan populace. Instead, an array of historical actors who spanned class, racial, and ethnic divides contested these social categories, making them ever evolving and always historically defined.[62] For example, K'iche' elites in Quetzaltenango and Kaqchikels in Comalapa challenged ladino racism through employing concepts like regeneration and *superación* (overcoming) to argue that Indigeneity coupled with behaviors they marked as modern was not incompatible with Guatemala's national progress but actually could serve as the nation's cornerstone.[63] *On Our Own Terms* joins this conversation, arguing that development initiatives, too, were spaces where individuals both reproduced and challenged the meanings and racialization of different subjectivities and the ways in which they were historically constituted and highly contingent upon contemporary events and ideas.

With the 1944 Revolution, state builders wished to incorporate Indigenous people into the nation, yet on specific terms. What resulted was a revision of the construct of "the Indian" into new categories of a racialized social identity, ones that did not neatly fit within the preexisting Indigenous-ladino divide. Building on a concept first discussed by Bolivian sociologist Silvia Rivera Cusicanqui at a workshop, anthropologists Charles Hale and Rosamel Millamán have called this construct the "*indio permitido*," or the "permitted Indian," which is a sociopolitical category that defines certain claims and behaviors for Indigenous empowerment as acceptable while deeming others as impermissible, signaling, as the authors point out, ongoing subordination.[64] Hale and Millamán argue that the construct of the "permitted Indian" is a product of multicultural neoliberalism in the postwar era of the 1990s.[65] In the same vein, historian Jennifer Schirmer argued that the military state created the category of the "sanctioned Maya," but she dates its emergence to the genocide of the early 1980s as the military state began pursuing policies aimed at "rehabilitating" people it classified as subversives and thus established the parameters for "appropriate" expressions of Indigeneity.[66] While these authors all provide persuasive arguments and applications of this concept in their respective historical moments, I instead follow Amy Offner, whose scholarship on midcentury development and the welfare state in the United States and Colombia compellingly argues that practices categorized as neoliberal did not necessarily emerge as novel phenomena in the late twentieth century but were actually revisions based on the direct experiences of midcentury policies.

Accordingly, I argue that this practice of designating "acceptable" expressions and practices of Indigeneity and of categorizing Indigenous people as "permitted" has much earlier roots that were significantly reconceptualized in the mid-twentieth century within the context of the Cold War.[67] The emergence of these constructions also signaled a departure from ladinization as the state's defining approach to Indigenous populations because in ladinization, the question of permitted versus prohibited is made obsolete by virtue of "Indians" no longer existing. However, in midcentury Guatemala, the construct of the "permitted Indian" and its counterpart, the "prohibited Indian," aligned with what María Josefina Saldaña Portillo referred to as "the two manifest subjects: the modern, fully developed citizen and its premodern, underdeveloped counterpart."[68] However, these two subjects did not exclusively exist as a strict dichotomy but rather served as ends of a linear spectrum. Thus, in extending back the concept of the "permitted Indian" and viewing it as synonymous with constructs of the modern Indigenous citizen—and adding in the "prohibited Indian," or the premodern, underdeveloped Indigenous citizen—we can begin to understand how state builders and popular actors alike coded some behaviors as appropriate and productive and others as unacceptable, backward, antithetical to national progress, and, at times, even dangerous and subversive.

These theoretical concepts provide a framework for interrogating how development projects powerfully combined with international geopolitics to provide an arena for replicating and contesting racism and negotiating different ideas about modernity, thus underscoring development's dialectical nature due to the various positionalities of its participants. The layered framework that this book employs, which moves between the micro and the macro, the individual and the collective, and the local and the international helps to explain why, for example, residents in San Carlos Alzatate welcomed their IING visitor despite oversimplified critiques of the institute's assimilationist mission. It allows for examination of the reasons the colony of Ixcán Grande in the Guatemalan jungle received USAID and Guatemalan state funding in its early years as a showcase for cooperative agriculture, only to be targeted for eradication a mere decade later by the Guatemalan military. It reveals how a program like Guatemala's National Program for Community Development could be unabashedly anti-communist, according to program training materials, and yet remembered as completely apolitical by farmers in Tactic who received program assistance. And it elucidates how international geopolitics and local political rivalries manifested themselves and became entangled in debates over a henhouse and school lunch program in Magdalena Milpas Altas. Showcasing the interaction between the ideas of the project planners, staff, and recipients demonstrates the historical contingency of these moments, challenging teleological or predetermined notions of modernization. Development intervened in the most private aspects of individuals' lives and, in doing so, reshaped local social relations, political ideologies, and cultural norms. Centering these stories helps us to better understand these processes as they relate to the ways that individuals redefined their sense of self and their solidarities with others during the Cold War in Guatemala.[69]

Methodological Considerations

Just as development projects were multilayered and transnational, so too did the research for this book require a wide array of sources and various methodologies. In each chapter, I utilize a "zoom lens" approach to examine specific case studies and to emphasize the importance of local histories, which reveal the variability in how individuals utilized development and emphasize their different experiences in navigating these interventions.[70] Several factors impacted case study selection: availability of sources, the historical significance contemporaries attributed to specific projects, a desire for wide geographic coverage and discussion of multiple ethnic groups, and a balance between private and public initiatives. Practical issues also shaped my options, as professional networks in Guatemala facilitated research in some locales, like Tactic and Mayalán, whereas at other moments, insufficient time to build relationships, inadequate skills in local languages, or little to no local interest in my project prevented me from utilizing local sources. These case studies are not meant to be in-depth, ethnographic studies but rather snapshots of development that emphasize "how local, regional, and international processes intersected on the local level."[71]

The search for archival materials for *On Our Own Terms* took me across Guatemala and the United States to national and local government archives, personal homes, institutional archives, and university collections. Casting this wide net for materials was further necessitated by the absence of institutional archives for the IING and other state programs that I studied, such as the National Program of Community Development and the Poles of Development. Often, the types of records I located in governmental archives revealed the perspective and goals of project managers or the policy goals of specific administrations. These documents tended to be project proposals, summary reports, propaganda, news reports, or ephemera used in the projects themselves, such as literacy tracts or training materials. On the surface, these sources help explain planners' priorities and political objectives and material outcomes of projects. A closer analysis also reveals the ways planners and experts framed the places, projects, and participants with whom they interacted, thus allowing for inquiry into how ideas about race and citizenship factored centrally in development initiatives.

Government agencies often relied on private institutions and individuals to actually program and implement development projects, and because I wanted to interrogate the perspective of intended recipients and project intermediaries alongside program directors and foreign policy makers, I used written records like unpublished anthropologists' field notes and correspondence, priests' journals and reports, budget spreadsheets and accounting logs, land titling and survey records, and newsletters and pamphlets to gain further insight into this history. In reading these sources, I carefully considered purpose and audience, as many of these sources were not written for the public or even for more than a select readership. Thus, they often reflect a less filtered perspective or combine professional and personal matters, giving important insight into the personalities involved in development programs.

Obtaining the voices of intended beneficiaries was trickier, a challenge that constantly confronts historians studying subaltern populations. Anthropologist papers and ethnographies proved valuable, as at times I glimpsed the perspectives of their informants as reported or retold through these records, though still always mediated by the document's author. In other moments, sources such as municipal archives in Tactic or the records from the agrarian reform of the 1950s provided me with documents that the intended recipients of development aid had more directly authored, either through penning the records or signing a document via thumbprint that claimed to speak on their behalf. I had to carefully consider the power relations at play in the creation of these sources, but these records permitted an analysis of how recipients framed their petitions, rationalized their actions, and engaged with discourses of development.

Oral histories also significantly shape the histories this book tells, as this methodology enables the inclusion of voices omitted or obscured in the preserved written record. I conducted over sixty interviews, asking former IING employees; residents from Tactic and Mayalán, Guatemala, two of the book's case studies; Guatemalan and U.S. anthropologists and social scientists; community development practitioners; and retired military officers to recount their lived experiences and perspectives on development. Most interviews were conducted in Spanish, though I hired a Poqomchi' Maya research assistant in Tactic to assist with language barriers and to mitigate my presence as a curious foreigner. These interviews captured the complexity of development in ways that the written record could not but also introduced their own set of challenges, such as the relationship between memory and oral history, issues with recollection and conflation of episodes in the past, and hesitance to discuss certain themes. Oftentimes, as I built relationships with these individuals, they also generously shared their personal archives that contained documents like institutional records, field notes and correspondence, newspaper clippings, military records, and photograph collections. I also utilized oral history collections, such as those that Edgar Mendoza conducted and archived as part of the Universidad de San Carlos's *Archivo de la Oralidad* and written summaries of interviews that the *Oficina de Derechos Humanos del Arzobispado de Guatemala* conducted during its Truth Commission investigation.

Through placing these various types of sources and perspectives into conversation, and by carefully analyzing the provenance and politics of the source—who wrote it, why, with what intended outcome, in what context, and, in the case of oral history, in what ways both memory and the present influenced its retelling—I have attempted to reliably reconstruct a multilayered account of the intended and unintended consequences of community development in Cold War Guatemala. And in doing so, I have also been forthcoming about moments when I have been unable to access the perspective of recipients, and I have used pointed language where the historical evidence has led me to a particular interpretation, though an absence of more substantial proof has disallowed for a strongly argued claim. Still, the corpus of research that informs this project, both material and oral, shows how the encounters that development projects facilitated led to a critical reconstruction of social categories and identities that had real and lasting consequences for Indigenous Guatemalans.

Outline of Chapters

Taken together, this book's seven chapters show that questions of modernity, race, citizenship, and development lie at the center of state efforts to shape a manageable citizenry in the midst of the Cold War's international political turmoil. Chapter 1 analyzes the ways in which state builders throughout the Americas reconceptualized state policies toward Indigenous populations and began suggesting the use of anthropology and socioeconomic development projects as ways of integrating Indigenous people into the state. The democratic opening of Guatemala's 1944 Revolution allowed Guatemalan revolutionaries to try to remake the nation into one that was at once modern, according to their definition, and more inclusive, though their proposals never fully stopped replicating the "tutelary state" that saw outside intervention as the solution for instilling modernity and extending the offer of citizenship.[72]

Chapters 2 and 3 address the tension between remaking the nation and reinscribing racialized identities in the revolutionary state building project. Chapter 2 centers on state efforts through IING investigations and literacy campaigns to create the concept of the "permitted Indian" and thus establish the state's model for the modern Indigenous citizen. Chapter 3 examines how Indigenous people responded to subsequent development initiatives like nutrition campaigns and agrarian reform that intended to transform them into modern citizens. Individuals utilized their understandings of Cold War geopolitics and ideas about development to frame demands and complaints, carefully evaluating these intrusions that outsiders had designed to "improve" their lives and defining the terms of their participation as citizens.

The 1954 coup ushered in an authoritarian counterrevolution that attempted to limit opportunities for organic, localized development initiatives and instead began to use development as a means to control and monitor the population. The new regime feared the consequences of letting Indigenous Guatemalans define the terms of their political participation and social relations at the local level, precisely what Revolution-era development initiatives had supported. Chapter 4 examines this transition through the history of the IING's short-lived community development initiative in Tactic, Alta Verapaz, and the subsequent defunding of the institute.

The remaining chapters take place against the backdrop of the violent civil war, as the military state increased its counterinsurgency efforts to defeat guerrilla insurgency. Chapter 5 analyzes Guatemala's DESCOM, a centralized program intended to function as a counterinsurgency tool in regions of recent unrest and as a preventive measure in places where the guerrilla presence was not yet strong. However, at the local level, project staff and recipients utilized the opportunities and resources that development initiatives provided to pursue their own agendas that at times directly challenged the state's modernization project. Although the Guatemalan government intended DESCOM to directly administer all of the country's community development projects, private initiatives such as religious organizations often received official approval and then exercised significant autonomy in practice. Chapter 6 tells the story of the Maryknoll Order's Ixcán Grande colonization scheme and traces how a project the state once touted as a successful endeavor quickly became one of the bloodiest theaters of its genocidal civil war, largely because the state no longer allowed alternate versions of development and citizenship.

Chapter 7 explores the use of development in the aftermath of the genocide of the early 1980s as a means to control and a means to resist. Methodologically, it differs from earlier chapters in that I use photographs and visual analysis to understand competing ideas of development as seen in the military's Poles of Development project and the Communities of Population in Resistance (CPRs), communities that internally displaced people clandestinely formed. Though visual analysis still examines this traumatic past, it avoided the potential harm that any attempt on my end to collect oral histories may have had for survivors. In contrast to the Poles of Development, which institutionalized modernization and revolved around the capitalist economy and strict allegiance to the centralized state, the CPRs established a more egalitarian and decentralized model that presented alternative ideas about modernity, development, and citizenship. Finally, a brief conclusion examines the way that discourses of development and Indigeneity permeated the drawn-out peace negotiations of the 1990s and continue to shape Guatemala to the present.

The history this book tells, at once highly localized and intrinsically global, reveals how people shaped the way that states used development during the Cold War and, in turn, how these interactions revised ideas about race and citizenship in Latin America. Clearly, for the Guatemalan state, rural development meant not only improving living conditions but also integrating diverse Indigenous populations into the national economy and fostering a collective sense of Guatemalan national identity. These goals would prove ever elusive in the face of continued Indigenous resistance to state efforts. Rarely did the intentions of project planners and the actions of recipients align, yet it is precisely within these disconnects that the politics of development can be understood and in these moments of contestation that individuals reshaped their relationships with one another and the state. Analyzing this process helps explain why efforts to alleviate poverty often simultaneously occurred with increased repression, elucidating the impact of development's failure. At the same time, it also sheds light on individual efforts to define development, and in essence, their own futures, on their own terms.

CHAPTER ONE

A Beautiful Laboratory

Pan-American Indigenismo *and the Guatemalan Revolution, 1940–1945*

In July 1945, thirty-four Indigenous schoolteachers from across Guatemala gathered in the departmental capital of Cobán, Alta Verapaz, a city surrounded by lush mountains and cloud forests. Once a key site for religious instruction in the colonial era, in the nineteenth century, Cobán transformed into an important economic center, as German immigrants poured into the region and began cultivating coffee. During World War II, the Ubico regime deported some of these German and German-descendant growers and nationalized their land, but Cobán remained an important center for regional governance, for international trade, and, it turned out, for hosting an unprecedented conference in Guatemala's history. This select group of Indigenous teachers met in Cobán's municipal theater at the direct invitation of Guatemala's new minister of education, Manuel Galich, to critique, advise, and form state policy toward Indigenous populations. For several days, these teachers informed state officials about the towns where they worked and the people whom they served, a diverse population that the state singularly categorized as Indigenous. Occurring only eight months after the 1944 Guatemalan Revolution, this often-overlooked meeting marked a moment where the state requested, and then listened to, a critique of government programs from Indigenous people themselves. One by one, the teachers demanded that the state provide towns with the necessary resources to improve socioeconomic conditions while leaving decision-making to local leaders. In other words, the teachers wanted aspects of modernization but on their terms.

In the aftermath of this meeting, the government created the *Instituto Indigenista Nacional de Guatemala* (IING) and tasked it with creating knowledge about and bringing resources to rural Indigenous Guatemalans, all in an effort to theoretically integrate them as equals into the nation.[1] The IING was part of a broader movement called *indigenismo*, "a field of dispute over national identity, regional power, and rights that places 'Indians' at the center of politics, jurisprudence, social policy, or study."[2] Once rejected as simply a racist and paternalistic movement, recent scholarship analyzes indigenismo's complexity and historical significance while not absolving it of its problematic renderings of Indigeneity, also drawing attention to the ways Indigenous people interacted with the movement.[3] As this chapter discusses, Guatemala's indigenismo by the 1940s most closely resembled that of postrevolutionary Mexico, where *indigenistas*, or adherents to this philosophy, "desire[d] to incorporate Indians into the modern nation, in which living Indians were treated with respect and dignity" but were also understood to be in desperate need of outside intervention to guide them toward being productive citizens.[4] This chapter historicizes the creation of the IING in an effort to understand how revised notions of indigenismo became enmeshed in discussions about development and citizenship at a key political juncture in Guatemalan history and in the context of WWII politics.

This chapter argues that indigenistas across the hemisphere began to identify state-led socioeconomic development as the foundation for the state's approach to improving material realities and fostering nationalism in predominantly Indigenous regions. In taking this developmentalist approach to addressing socioeconomic conditions, they reconceptualized understandings of citizenship and society, firmly pinning the obligation for resolving exploitation and poverty upon the government and not dismissively explaining these conditions on racist portrayals of innate inferiority. Despite the hope and optimism for social equality that the Revolution introduced by implementing vast changes across Guatemalan society, we must be mindful of its unintended consequences and continuities. As scholars have argued, in many ways, revolutionary development remained a high modernist project that called for outside intervention to paternalistically transform these populations into "human beings, citizens, and people of integrity."[5] While the changes intended to address structural inequalities did usher in new opportunities for the pursuit of social justice and solidarities, at the same time they also reinforced racialized paternalism through introducing development as a key tool for remaking the Indigenous population and for assuming that people categorized as Indigenous needed remaking in the first place. Revolutionary developmentalism expanded the notion of ladino nationalism that emerged as a more inclusive project under the Estrada Cabrera regime in the early 1900s by intentionally including Indigenous people—on certain terms—into this vision of the Guatemalan nation while also collapsing racial categories into the simplified dichotomy of ladino and Indigenous.[6] And just as ladino nationalism provided opportunities for lower-class, mixed-race people to claim their place within society as citizens, so too did revolutionary development projects allow for Indigenous people to continue to confront structural racism.[7]

Founding the Inter-American Indigenist Institute and Revising Indigenismo

In 1933, at the Fourth Pan-American Conference in Montevideo, Uruguay, Mexico's delegates proposed a meeting for the hemisphere's experts on Indigenous cultures. This meeting never occurred, yet the desire for new studies on Indigenous Peoples did not wane, and at the 1935 meeting of the Pan-American Institute of Geography and History, participants suggested that a hemispheric institute be founded for the scientific study of Indigenous populations.[8] Again, nothing materialized, and at the Eighth Pan-American Conference in 1938, delegates once again called for a Continental Congress of Indianists. This time, they framed their petition in terms of hemispheric solidarity and security, positioning their initiative within the growing concern about the threat of Hitler's Nazi Germany. They named a conference planning committee and scheduled the event for 1939 in La Paz, Bolivia.[9] Moisés Sáenz, Mexican ambassador to Peru and a prominent indigenista who had long been interested in establishing a "clearing house of Indian data," took the lead in fostering hemispheric support for this meeting.[10] However, due to Bolivia's growing opposition to Mexican president Lázaro Cárdenas's leftist politics, the conference went unfunded and unorganized, so the planning committee rescheduled it for 1940 in Pátzcuaro, Mexico.[11] While traveling from Peru to Mexico to plan the meeting, Sáenz stopped in Guatemala and met with President Jorge Ubico. Despite these overtures, Ubico refused to send an official delegation to Pátzcuaro, but he did agree to allow Carlos Girón Cerna, the Guatemalan consul to Mexico, and David Vela, a lawyer and prominent journalist, to unofficially attend the meeting, with the Mexican government financing Vela's participation.[12]

Understanding David Vela's intellectual community and its conceptualization about race and nation is critical for analyzing the importance that the 1940 Pátzcuaro conference had for him and other intellectuals. Vela was a student leader in what scholars now refer to as the Generation of the 20s. Largely comprised of classmates from the *Instituto Nacional Central para Varones* and known for their participation in the 1913 strike that protested President Manuel Estrada Cabrera's dictatorship, this group continued to object to undemocratic rule, called for Central American unification, and fostered a strong anti-imperialist mentality.[13]

The majority of the Generation of the 20s understood modernity to include a strong belief in science, a linear understanding of national progress, and a commitment to democracy. Many also held a positivist-influenced eugenicist view of race, believing "the Indian" to be the cause of Guatemalan underdevelopment, with "whitening" through immigration posited as the solution.[14] However, by the late 1920s, some had begun proposing integration based on neo-Lamarckian ideas of racial improvement via environmental and behavioral improvement and "soft" or "preventative eugenics" as a solution for Guatemala's underdevelopment, a turn that aligned with revisions in racial thinking taking place across the hemisphere.[15] For example, in a series of 1929 newspaper debates, Miguel Ángel Asturias stopped advocating for European immigration and subsequent "whitening" of the Indigenous population, as the idea of the "improved race" via European (mainly German) miscegenation fell out of vogue in an increasingly anti-fascist atmosphere.[16] Instead, Asturias and others called for an incorporation of "the Indian" that would preserve elements of Indigenous cultures that he believed formed the "spirit" of the nation, thus laying the foundation for a growing turn to integration, rather than assimilation, as the recommended path to nation building.[17] Like Asturias, Vela was a significant proponent of this integrationist position, though his more inclusive vision never escaped the "racialized paradigms that ascribed inherent biological and cultural characteristics" to the Indigenous populations in Guatemala and established non-Indigenous men like himself as the decision-makers that dictated the terms and meanings of integration.[18]

The 1940 meeting would not be Vela's first trip to Mexico. In 1926, he had traveled there amid the institutionalization of the Mexican Revolution, and he witnessed how the revolutionary government's nation-building project had incorporated the Indigenous populations in Mexico through development initiatives in ways that at least initially "began as a radical, antiracist critique of the status quo" and "treated [Indians] with respect and dignity."[19] Inspired by these observations, Vela regularly began to publish articles relating to Indigenous rights, race, and nationalism in *El Imparcial*, a leading Guatemalan daily newspaper.[20] However, when General Jorge Ubico took power in 1931, Vela was forced to resign from *El Imparcial*, so that he could continue to live and work in Guatemala and not go into political exile.[21] While prevented from publishing newspaper articles about Indigeneity, Vela's interest in these themes did not waver. He likely became aware of the Pátzcuaro congress through his brother Arqueles Vela, who lived and worked in Mexico and had become closely linked to the Mexican Revolution. Arqueles, along with Sáenz, invited David to participate in the congress, and David successfully got Ubico's permission to visit Mexico, which for Ubico represented a significant threat due to the socially progressive aspects of the Mexican Revolution.[22]

Finally, in April 1940, David Vela and representatives from most of the American nations, including some Indigenous delegates, held the inaugural Inter-American Conference on Indian Life, which resulted in the founding of the *Instituto Indigenista Interamericano* (Interamerican Indigenist Institute, III).[23] The U.S. Office of Inter-American Affairs financed the III despite an initial rejection by Coordinator Nelson Rockefeller on the grounds that it had no immediate bearing on U.S. national defense. He claimed that his office wanted to tread carefully on sensitive topics such as this, because "anything done in relation to Indians might offend the powers that be in many Latin American countries."[24] However, President Franklin D. Roosevelt disagreed and appropriated $32,400 for the III, most likely due to the urging of John Collier, the commissioner for the U.S. Office of Indian Affairs.[25]

The historical contingency of this process of redefining indigenismo, both in the Americas and in Guatemala, meant that indigenistas intentionally framed their efforts within the global geopolitical context of World War II, a trend that would continue into the Cold War. German fascination with Native Americans translated into Nazi propaganda efforts among Indigenous populations in an attempt to gain support in the Western Hemisphere and to facilitate access to important natural resources for the war effort. U.S. reports likely overexaggerated the actual Nazi influence in Indigenous communities. Still, this fear of infiltration shaped the creation of the III and subsequent efforts at integration, both to counteract Nazi claims of Indigenous exploitation and to transform the hemisphere's Indigenous populations into consumers.[26] Supporters of the III, such as Mexico's undersecretary of foreign affairs Torres Bodet underscored how America (broadly defined) "does not accept racial discrimination or the supremacy of a caste that seeks to sink mankind to the lowest forms of mechanized barbarism" and argued that the III was proof of this fact.[27] Clearly, Torres's claim of racial equality completely failed to match any reality in the Americas. But in positioning indigenismo as evidence that the hemisphere was distinct from the fascism plaguing Europe, III members were able to secure some degree of state support for socioeconomic policies designed to "help" rural Indigenous populations in the name of national security and solidarity.

At the Pátzcuaro congress, this redefinition of indigenismo as an antidote to fascism became clear in discussions on integration. For example, Professor Luis Chávez Orozco, director of Mexico's Department of Indian Affairs, stated, "In these moments of unfortunate events that on other continents are disturbing the happiness and the tranquility of men, you all, as delegates of

North, Central, and South America, are making a work of peace and of praise out of one of the most profoundly human resources of our hemisphere: the American Indians, who constitute an ethical reserve, a reserve of creative work and a reserve for the brotherly linking of the American continent."[28] In other words, Chávez conveniently ignored long histories of settler colonialism and violent dispossession of Indigenous Peoples throughout the Americas, presenting the contemporary issue of governing and managing Indigenous people as a unique opportunity for the hemisphere's nations. While critiquing fascist social policies, he still dehumanized Indigenous people by labeling them as a resource to deploy in the face of international instability and uncertainty.

Chávez's counterpart in the U.S. Office of Indian Affairs, Commissioner John Collier, similarly referenced the violence wrecking Europe in his call for "continuous and inter-racial international exchanges, that should contribute in part to the slow but incremental and ultimately victorious democracy. . . . This is our possible gift to the world, that surely will exist as the sum of our efforts, and will need the indigenous race, and [will live on] when the darkness of this actual historical moment on our planet is only remembered as a story for some tale."[29] Democracy via social integration was this gift, with development providing the means for stable, democratic, and capitalist countries to define and control this project. Integration also called for an involved, centralized national government responsible for meeting the basic needs of all citizens and ensuring that all people of the hemisphere, Indigenous people included, could participate in the market economy and have representation in the government. In other words, for Collier, Indigenous people needed to modernize to ensure the security of the Western Hemisphere and safeguard democracy. In the context of World War II, then, delegates positioned themselves as a welcome alternative to Nazism as they advocated for racial and ethnic diversity and thus offered a bold counterargument to fascist ideas of racial purity. It is likely that in other historical circumstances these indigenista programs would have been a much tougher sell, as they threatened to alter the national status quo.

With war raging in Europe and military dictatorship at home, Vela carefully reported on the Pátzcuaro conference, recording the debates that delegates had as well as the resolutions they passed. Repeatedly throughout the proceedings, in discussions on topics ranging from literacy campaigns to unionizing, delegates emphasized the idea of racial equality and blamed exploitative socioeconomic conditions—not supposed innate racial qualities—for what they still perceived to be Indigenous "backwardness."[30] Delegates held the state responsible for remedying this situation, calling for interventions that would not only improve each member nation but the hemisphere as a whole. Recommendations included the creation of national institutions to protect and promote Indigenous art, investigative research into medical and nutritional problems confronting Indigenous populations, infrastructure improvements and urbanization projects, and educational initiatives designed to teach the national language to Indigenous people.[31] Integration into the nation, on these delegates' terms, remained a central preoccupation of discussions, yet undergirding these conversations was the consistent conviction that socioeconomic development projects provided the key to solving inequities confronting Indigenous populations.

Guatemala's *Grupo Indigenista*

Vela feared that the Guatemalan government would not commit to seriously considering how to address socioeconomic inequality and racism. He felt that the national government did not know much about the Indigenous population, nor did it have any "interest in attracting them to national life" beyond using them as a labor force and as a base for political support.[32] However, from frequent correspondence with III director Manuel Gamio, Vela knew that many Guatemalans were interested in indigenismo and III activities. A December 1944 III subscription list of the 197 Guatemalan individuals and institutions receiving the III's quarterly publication, *América Indígena*, confirmed this assumption. Although such a list does not exist for 1941, it was likely that many of these subscribers signed up when the III first began publishing its bulletin in that year, as the government would not have promoted it on a national level. Guatemala did not yet have a formal indigenist institute, but Guatemalans closely followed regional conversations and activities and thought about how they could best apply these principles and programs when the national political scene might make such visions tangible possibilities.[33]

Vela and other prominent professionals formed the *Grupo Indigenista* and developed a crucial transnational network that would reinforce their work. After Pátzcuaro, Moisés Sáenz scheduled a layover in Guatemala City during his travel back to Peru. Though he failed to gain an audience with Ubico, he reported to Cárdenas that he met with a small group of Grupo Indigenista members, including Manuel Galich, Jorge Luis Arriola, and J. Epaminondas Quintana. Though Sáenz could not have known it at the time, these men would go on to be influential in the Guatemalan state, as Galich would become minister of education and Arriola and Quintana each would serve as directors for the IING.[34] Based on the types of programs the Grupo Indigenista later pursued, it also seems likely that Sáenz's cultural pluralism helped guide their philosophy further away from ladinization and toward integration.[35] Later, in December 1941, U.S. Indian Affairs field representative Emil Sady hosted a meeting of this informal group at his hotel in Guatemala City. In his work, Sady collaborated with national indigenist institutes throughout Latin America and was in Guatemala to visit the public health campaign taking place at the Finca Las Delicias in Chimaltenango to treat and prevent filariasis, a parasitic disease. The Grupo Indigenista took advantage of his short trip to arrange this meeting, formalize the structure of their project, and hopefully gain the support of the U.S. Office of Indian Affairs.[36]

Grupo Indigenista participants elected Vela as president and decided to focus on problems of an immediate, practical nature.[37] Vela reported the group's philosophy to the III's quarterly publication, defining the members as people "interested in the actual conditions of the Indian and the integral activities necessary to improve them, which lie within the scope of continental efforts toward solidarity and the strengthening of one and all the nations of the New World."[38] Though certainly gentler than the conquistador trope, this mindset still positioned the Grupo Indigenista as the architect of this project, placing it in a long line of European-descended colonizers set on transforming the so-called New World and the people who lived there with the goal of creating loyal and productive citizens.

Citizenship is made and is not fixed but is always in negotiation. Actors and institutions debate, perform, and fashion citizenship and in doing so, they make and unmake notions of belonging.[39] But like elsewhere in Latin America, in Guatemala the actual exercising of one's citizenship was largely viewed as a privilege rather than a right.[40] Guatemalan indigenistas grappled with *de jure*, or legal, and *de facto*, or practiced, notions of citizenship and the various constructions of national identity as these pertained to Indigenous people, questioning the latter's marginalization with an outsider's perspective.[41] A newspaper article explaining the purpose of the Grupo Indigenista quoted Flavio Herrera, a member who became a famed author and Guatemalan diplomat. Herrera clarified how the concept of indigenismo had shifted philosophically in recent years, as previously it was focused on "sentimental declarations or literary essays." Now indigenismo had taken on a much more material dimension, demonstrating a "serious and constant effort whose results will be reaped later in the form of practical solutions and effective improvement of the social condition of the Guatemalan indígena."[42] Vela himself reiterated this redefinition of indigenismo in a 1990 interview where he said that indigenistas strived to help "the indígena get to know himself, to have an understanding of himself and to have at the same time a notion of his role as a citizen, not as a protected child or as a folkloric race useful for tourism."[43] While rife with racialized paternalism, since Vela audaciously suggested that he, a ladino, could help Indigenous people understand themselves, he did recognize how legislation prevented many Indigenous people from exercising the rights accorded to Guatemalan citizens and how ideas about Guatemalan national identity largely excluded Indigenous people, except for some Indigenous elite, from the vision of the national community.[44] The Grupo Indigenista, and later the IING, in spite of its paternalism and shortcomings, worked to remake citizenship in a way that included Indigenous Guatemalans as political actors and critical members of the nation, but still in need of the state's tutelary guidance.[45]

Vela's transnational collaborations led him to tour the United States in February 1942. In the press release about the visit, the U.S. State Department referenced Vela's newspaper articles that called for "the necessity of wholehearted cooperation among the Americas in defense of democracy" and his "considerable attention [given] to the customs and history of the Central American Indian." Mr. Charles Thompson, from the State Department's Division of Cultural Relations, helped to organize several tours of museums and universities as well as a special tour to the U.S. Southwest to see indigenista projects in action.[46] This trip likely influenced the types of projects that the Grupo Indigenista undertook during the last years of the Ubico dictatorship and helped to solidify linkages between anthropologists, government officials, and Guatemalan indigenistas.

Although Grupo Indigenista members were prominent professionals and intellectuals, lack of official support limited their private efforts and resources. In 1941, members sponsored research on onchocerciasis (river blindness) and malaria; in 1943, they distributed iodine to Indigenous communities to combat endemic goiter; and in 1944, they collaborated on additional onchocerciasis research and preliminary experiments for controlling its spread with DDT, a pesticide later found to be carcinogenic.[47] Vela also recalled a failed effort to convince residents in Nahualá, a K'iche' Maya town, to remove wood-burning stoves from areas where people slept. Vela traveled to Nahualá and met with local leaders, explaining how smoke inhalation caused pulmonary disease. Vela proposed that the Grupo Indigenista and *nahualeños* collaborate to build a model home that separated the stove from the sleeping quarters. Local leaders readily concurred, supposedly recording an agreement in the municipal record book. However, shortly after beginning construction, the men assigned to the project were called to build roads, and because this unpaid work was a legal requirement under the Ubico regime's exploitative vagrancy law, the model home was left unfinished. When Vela returned to Nahualá, leaders told him that they had destroyed the municipal records that noted their collaboration with the Grupo Indigenista because it was no longer possible for them to uphold their commitment.[48]

While limited, Grupo Indigenista efforts established an important network of like-minded Guatemalans who began developing a coherent indigenista policy for Guatemala to adopt once the political environment became more receptive to such a program. Their work cultivated ties to outside institutions like the Office of Indian Affairs, the III, and other philanthropic institutions. Most significantly, the Grupo Indigenista also redefined Guatemalan indigenismo to adhere to the III's philosophy of taking a developmentalist approach to the countryside in an effort to expand notions of citizenship even further to include Guatemala's Indigenous population in a way that allowed for cultural differences while remedying what they perceived to be socioeconomic problems.

The Rise of Guatemalan Action Anthropology

Overlapping chronologically with the developments in hemispheric indigenismo at Pátzcuaro and the organization of the Grupo Indigenista, the early 1940s also saw Guatemalans paying increased attention to the idea of applied anthropology and pursuing the professionalization of the discipline. The expansion of coffee capitalism and the arrival of German immigrants led to much German-led investigation into Indigenous populations in Guatemala and natural landscapes earlier in the twentieth century. By midcentury, Guatemalans were seeking training in anthropology and were paid employees of anthropological investigations, thus joining in this knowledge creation effort.[49] In the 1940s, Guatemalans utilized their ties to U.S. scholars and institutions to establish a homegrown network of anthropologists and ethnographers that began to study their own country in an effort to create effective plans to integrate diverse populations into the nation and in 1946 established the Faculty of Humanities at the *Universidad de San Carlos* (USAC), the national university.[50] Anthropologists served as important intermediaries between communities, politicians, and outside experts, helping to craft initiatives that they believed to be appropriate given local culture, beliefs, and practices. At the same time, these projects brought rural communities into closer contact with outsiders who increasingly became interested in local politics and social structures. At a time when progressive politicians, professionals, and intellectuals throughout the Americas advocated for the expansion of citizenship, anthropology proved critical in understanding these important constituencies of Indigenous citizens.

University of Chicago anthropologists Robert Redfield and Sol Tax heavily influenced the development and professionalization of Guatemalan anthropology. Despite the common scholarly critique of their influence as imperialist, it is well recognized among Guatemalan social scientists; renowned Guatemalan sociologist Carlos Guzmán Böckler joked with me that "Al Capone is not the only one from Chicago," emphasizing the relative fame that Redfield and Tax had in the Guatemalan academy.[51] Historians point to Redfield as the scholar who first theorized the process of modernization, as his "folk-urban continuum" and the distinctions he made between what he termed primary and secondary urbanization conceptualized a linear progression through various development phases. For Redfield, secondary urbanization resulted in complete modernization and loss of cultural traditions. Primary urbanization, in contrast, kept the "little traditions" and instead molded modernity to fit within existing social structures. Redfield became a firm advocate for primary urbanization, arguing that it was essential for "folk cultures" not to abandon the historic foundation of their societies in favor of Western sociocultural values, though he still suggested that Indigenous Peoples would culturally evolve in some way as they urbanized.[52] In 1934, Redfield received funding from the Carnegie Institute to conduct a sociolinguistic project in Guatemala, and he heavily relied on the ethnographic research of his students, Sol Tax and Alfonso Villa Rojas, and the linguistic research of his colleague, Manuel Andrade. Intermittently over the next six years, Tax and his wife Gertrude lived in Guatemala, spending their first year in Chichicastenango and then relocating to the lakeside town of Panajachel.[53] They began to embark on ethnographic research that asked similar questions to Redfield's work on Mexico a decade prior, namely how small, predominantly Indigenous communities were navigating the changes he believed capitalism had introduced and how social relations transformed, as a result.

During this time, Tax hired local Indigenous men as translators and trained them in ethnography so they could conduct their own research. Juan de Dios Rosales, a Kaqchikel Maya schoolteacher from Panajachel, began working for Tax in March 1936. Tax found Rosales to be intellectually gifted despite only having the equivalent of a junior high education. Tax wrote to Redfield, describing Rosales as "very wide-awake and intelligent; above all he seems to be one of these natural-born scientists. He seems entirely honest, with a penchant for exactness and thoroughness both."[54] Tax and Gertrude formed a deep friendship with Rosales: they hosted him in their Chicago home when he studied English in the early 1940s; they served as godparents for one of Rosales's children, Roberto, named after Redfield; and they sent Christmas cards to Rosales's relatives for over thirty years after their fieldwork concluded. The Taxes also helped Roberto rebuild his house after the devastating 1976 earthquake and provided financial assistance to Juan's daughter when she immigrated to Canada in 1972.[55] Through Rosales, Tax also met Agustín Pop, a Tz'utujil Maya court record keeper from San Pedro La Laguna, remarking that his assistance, language skills, and connections to municipal records were a "fortunate opportunity."[56] Both men would eventually become two of the IING's first ethnographers.

In addition to translators, Tax also relied on the local travel agency Clark Tours for transportation, where he met Antonio Goubaud Carrera. Goubaud, a Guatemalan ladino who had attended high school in California, quickly connected with Tax due to a shared interest in anthropology.[57] Immediately, Tax noticed Goubaud's potential and capacity for understanding ethnographic techniques and theory. Wishing to hire Goubaud, Tax wrote to Redfield, "I think you agree that part of our business is to develop natural resources, so to speak."[58] Eventually, Tax and Redfield secured funding for Goubaud to enroll at the University of Chicago. Goubaud completed a master's degree in anthropology and completed fieldwork in New Mexico, where he met Vela during the latter's 1942 U.S. trip.[59] In earning this advanced degree, Goubaud Carrera became Guatemala's first professionally trained anthropologist.[60]

During his studies at Chicago, Goubaud adhered to Tax's evolving idea of action anthropology. Although Tax did not coin the term until 1951, his ten years of experience in Guatemala shaped his critique of applied anthropology and the distinction he made between it and action anthropology. For Tax, applied anthropology was a top-down project that reinforced state policies of assimilation, giving communities little voice. Tax's increased discontent with U.S. assimilation policies and his belief that anthropologists should actively collaborate with communities, not apply broad theories to specific locales, led him to propose an alternative method of anthropological research, that of action anthropology.[61]

Action anthropology's central tenets of nonassimilation and self-government embrace a "decolonization political alignment."[62] In challenging applied anthropology's assumption that Western values were universal and should be replicated throughout the world, Tax instead insisted that action anthropologists work as equals with their host communities and allow local residents to dictate the changes they wanted to effect, if any. Tax's philosophy of anthropology shaped the way that his students understood the discipline. It also reconfigured how Chicago-trained Guatemalan anthropologists would utilize development projects as part of their anthropological research by stressing the importance of mitigating unequal relationships of power by recognizing subjects' agency and respecting local decision-making.

Goubaud's master's thesis reflects his understanding of action anthropological tenets. As mentioned, he conducted fieldwork in Cundiyo and Canyon de Taos, New Mexico, writing about nutrition in local Hispanic communities. He argued that Canyon de Taos residents were more malnourished than those in Cundiyo because Canyon had comparatively urbanized and acculturated into Anglo-American society. In contrast, residents of Cundiyo had not acculturated and therefore maintained a nutrient-rich diet consisting of atole, milk, and fruits.[63] During this project, Goubaud worked closely under Michel Pijoan, the director of the health committee for the U.S. National Indian Institute, thus developing another connection to the transnational network of indigenistas.[64] Based on Goubaud's findings, he and Pijoan developed a project to study local dietary customs in Guatemala with the hopes of creating programs to address nutritional insufficiencies.

Goubaud became convinced that increasing protein intake would improve the health of Indigenous Guatemalans by reducing stunted growth, endemic goiter, and anemia and would also strengthen immune systems against other diseases such as malaria. Because Goubaud found that Cundiyo residents had comparatively better nutrition eating traditional diets that he believed mirrored those in rural Guatemala, he sought to introduce a protein supplement in rural Guatemala without significantly restructuring consumption patterns. Dried fish became Goubaud's proposed solution. In a series of letters that Goubaud sent to Redfield and Tax in the spring of 1942, he proposed the creation of small fish protein cakes, telling Redfield, "The cake is simply dried fish, including fish bones, head, and tail, perhaps with a slight addition of iron. Since the Indian is already familiar with the dry fish sold in the markets, probably not much worrying would have to be done about changing his food habits." Despite Tax's critique that fish was a costly source of protein compared to other meats, Goubaud insisted that utilizing fish would provide the quickest and most culturally appropriate protein. Goubaud even drew a blueprint for a protein concentrate factory, established a budget, and predicted the project's extended impact into rural areas. His passion for the protein project is undeniable; in one letter he even utilized the metaphor of birthing and raising a child.[65]

As the ever-practical advisors, Redfield and Tax encouraged Goubaud's ideas but urged him to conduct feasibility studies before presenting the project to the Guatemalan government. Redfield wrote Goubaud, stating, "I am not used to seeing anthropological interests translated so rapidly into practical achievement." Without denying the importance of applied work, Redfield urged Goubaud to conduct a dietary survey in the highlands to gauge the project's appropriateness and effectiveness. He encouraged Goubaud to "be cooperative, but let us not allow these specialists in action push us into taking steps with the Guatemalan government before the steps should be taken." Goubaud's response to this advice was positive; he wrote to Redfield that "I would much rather have considered first—before bringing it [the protein project] to life—whether it was practical and economically sound to father it. That seems to be the job now."[66] Thus, Goubaud halted his nascent negotiations with contractors for the construction of the protein plant and he did not present his proposal to the Guatemalan government.

In 1943, Goubaud and Tax's two other main assistants, the aforementioned Juan de Dios Rosales and Agustín Pop, embarked on fieldwork in rural Guatemala as employees of the Carnegie Institution's dietary survey project.[67] The project goal was simply to record consumption patterns in rural Guatemala, and resulting data would serve as preliminary evidence to determine the efficacy of any subsequent food supplement program, such as Goubaud's protein project.[68] Goubaud, a member of Guatemala's National Committee on Food under President Ubico, easily secured letters of introduction from Guatemala's health department to pave Pop's and Rosales's entry into communities.[69] For several months in 1943–1944, these men visited fifteen towns, and Goubaud worked independently while Pop and Rosales traveled together, as Rosales had also received some training, though no degree, from the University of Chicago. Goubaud even wrote to Redfield that Rosales would pass as ladino while Pop would wear his "Indian costume," as they clearly believed that the cultural marker of Indigenous clothing might generate stronger rapport between Pop and Indigenous residents, while Rosales's utilization of Western clothing and Spanish would facilitate dialogue with the town's ladino residents.[70] This action demonstrates the fluidity of racial categories in Guatemala and how individuals strategically deployed them given the demands of the situational context.

In every town, the men collaborated with local leaders to find informants willing to allow the researchers to measure and record meal content and quantities for one week, a task that included careful notation of food preparation methods and consumption traditions. In an attempt to gather data on a wide range of families, the researchers also noted each informant's occupation, religion, literacy, primary language, landownership, housing conditions, social positions, and economic status.[71] To share their research, all three men sent field diaries to Tax; Goubaud collected the food data and eventually turned it over to Emma Reh of the Nutrition Division of the Food and Agricultural Organization (FAO) of the United Nations (UN).[72] In total, these researchers gathered data from 148 families from fifteen communities. The percentage of Indigenous to ladino families surveyed (64 percent to 36 percent) mirrored the demographics in Guatemala, according to official census records.[73]

As intermediaries, Goubaud, Rosales, and Pop provided numerical data for analysis and helped mediate cultural misunderstanding through providing detailed accounts of varying local practices and customs. The FAO's report identified the most serious dietary deficiencies as riboflavin, vitamin A, and protein, especially from animal sources. Due to the anthropologists' explanations of local practices, this report proposed solutions based on local realities. For example, attempting to increase livestock and milk consumption was not realistic; families could not afford to keep cattle, feed was scarce, and inadequate land holdings prohibited grazing. Similarly, a chicken distribution program was impractical because locals would simply sell the eggs for extra income, as was customary. The report suggested increasing fat intake by augmenting production of avocados and peanuts, two locally grown products, and it also called for investigation into the possibility of using more lowland for corn cultivation, thus freeing highland farms for agricultural, and theoretically, dietary diversification.[74]

The Food Survey Project was the first anthropological investigation in Guatemala that was conducted solely by Guatemalans and could immediately inform practical development projects. By the survey's conclusion, Goubaud had established himself as a capable anthropologist, carefully utilizing ethnography to diagnose what he perceived to be problems and investigating potential solutions. Goubaud's professional training combined Redfield's theoretical questions on how modernization affected traditional societies with Tax's call for action anthropology, shaping his ideas on indigenismo and the role of the state and intended recipients in improving rural socioeconomic conditions.

On October 20, 1944, far from Goubaud's fieldwork location, machine gun bursts interrupted the tranquility of the early morning hours in the capital. After months of protests and uncertainty, students, workers, and some young, disillusioned military officers were overthrowing the final remnants of military dictatorship in what became known as the October Revolution.

When the violence stopped and the democratic movement emerged victorious, the leaders installed a temporary three-man junta to rule until presidential elections could be held later that year to formally and finally return Guatemala to democratic rule.

Goubaud immediately sensed an opening for the inclusion of indigenista programs in an official capacity, an option that had not been available under the Ubico regime. The Grupo Indigenista had helped establish connections and had introduced the idea that Indigenous people could and should be considered equal citizens who would help advance the nation. Though not formally part of the Grupo Indigenista, Goubaud's own work put into practice the technical solutions that the Grupo and the III envisioned, thus cementing socioeconomic development as the preferred means for addressing inequality. Seizing the opportunity that the Revolution presented, Goubaud left the field and returned to the capital to convince the new regime of the important role that anthropology could play in defining a place for Indigenous people in the nation-building project, excitedly writing to Tax that "bright days are ahead for Guatemala!"[75]

Institutionalizing Indigenismo in the Revolutionary Government

However, the days immediately following the Revolution were not bright but dark and violent, reaffirming the racialized fear of Indigenous people that many non-Indigenous Guatemalans had long internalized.[76] Forty miles west of Guatemala City, in the predominantly Kaqchikel Maya community of Patzicía, newspapers reported "a horrifying massacre and pillage" among descriptions of similar uprisings elsewhere in the country.[77] When Ubico resigned in July 1944, he named General Juan Ponce Vaidés as his replacement to guarantee the continuation of military rule. Amid popular protest against his undemocratic rule, Ponce acquiesced to holding elections and apparently promised to give state-owned land to the Indigenous population if he won the upcoming election, hoping to secure their votes. As election day approached and it became obvious that he would not win, Ponce supposedly encouraged his supporters to "take action" if they wanted to obtain land.[78] When the October Revolution described above abruptly ended his rule, uncertainty about these promises of land factored significantly into rural responses to the news; in some places, like Patzicía, these responses turned violent.

There are two competing versions of the Patzicía violence. Kaqchikel oral history testimonies and local history emphasized the violence ladinos committed against Kaqchikel residents. They maintained that military troops and ladinos from the nearby town of Zaragoza came specifically to kill Kaqchikel townspeople, murdering 400 to 900 people. This number's imprecision is due to a lack of documentation and to the use of mass graves to hide the atrocities.[79] However, newspaper accounts told a different story, reporting that the town's Kaqchikel residents perpetuated the attack and targeted ladinos who, from the Kaqchikel perspective, were withholding access to the land that Ponce had promised them. This account of Patzicía confirmed many ladinos' worst nightmare—namely, a reckoning by the Indigenous majority holding the ladino minority to account for centuries of exploitation and abuse.

Patzicía, and the memories the violence generated, complicated indigenista attempts to include Indigenous people in the nation, as the popular interpretation of the massacre solidly reinforced an irreconcilable racial difference and a fear of the "Indian other." The very thought of developing programs to integrate the Indigenous population into national life and give them equal rights was repugnant and implausible to even some of Guatemala's more progressive revolutionary leaders. Undoubtedly, one of the major initial challenges confronting revolutionary leadership was how to assuage these tensions and institute policies that would reduce socioeconomic barriers for Indigenous participation as full citizens without greatly antagonizing the elite who did not support this project.

A little over a month after the massacre in Patzicía, Guatemalans voted and elected Juan José Arévalo as president. In January 1945, President Arévalo requested a meeting with Goubaud, Guatemala's only professionally trained anthropologist with a university degree and thus a person Arévalo likely perceived to be the nation's foremost expert on Indigenous cultures. In this meeting, Arévalo requested that Goubaud draft a proposal for a Guatemalan Office of Indian Affairs. For the Revolution to foster a unified nationalism, Arévalo's government had to effectively communicate and work with Indigenous communities.

Excitedly, Goubaud wrote to his Chicago advisors, stating that he would have to postpone pursuing his PhD because "I find myself in the midst of a remarkable political and social change occurring in Guatemala now, and somehow I feel that there are possibilities of fruitful work for me in the immediate future." He reported that Arévalo had stated, "Truly this department is of tremendous significance for Guatemala, and it will have to provide scientific data concerning the Indian population on all phases of government, education, the army, public health, economics, social organization." Goubaud wrote that he was studying the structures of the U.S. Office of Indian Affairs and Mexico's National Indigenist Institute to see how these organizations functioned but that he primarily envisioned the Guatemalan institute as a "field organization" that would directly report to the executive about all aspects of rural life.[80]

Before Arévalo could create an indigenist institute, he had to be inaugurated as president, and for that to happen, Guatemala needed a constitution. For forty-five days between January 9 and March 11, 1945, fifteen men met, debated, and wrote Guatemala's revolutionary constitution, which would remain in effect until the 1954 coup. Then, the National Assembly debated the proposed laws and voted on whether to pass, revise, or reject each article. Particularly during the respective debates on voting and workers' rights, the larger, looming question of citizenship was raised.[81] Though legally citizens through Guatemala's birthright citizenship policy, secondary laws like literacy skills and property requirements hindered full participation and rendered many Indigenous people as second-class citizens.[82] In the aftermath of the Patzicía violence, many delegates were leery of extending full rights to Indigenous people, arguing that they were unprepared for the responsibilities of citizenship.

The first place in the constitutional assembly's minutes that invoked this fear of Indigenous uprising occurred in the suffrage debate. While discussing the possibility of keeping literacy requirements for voting in place, constitutional committee members racialized illiteracy as Indigenous and indicated their belief that Indigenous Guatemalans were incapable of exercising democratic rights. José Rölz Bennet even blatantly stated, "The vote of the indigenous masses only has served to consolidate tyranny."[83] However, others maintained that suffrage for illiterate citizens was an issue of social justice, as Julio Antonio Reyes Cardona declared that "there exists a great quantity of illiterates that yes, have a civic capacity."[84] Rubén Luarca Duarte even rebuked his fellow commission members, arguing that the "enemy is hidden under a hypocritical cloak of indifference." He continued his diatribe, raising rhetorical questions that clearly tied his understanding of nation building to social integration, positing, "As a nation, what have we done for the *indígena*? What have we done for the conquered race? Degrade it, enslave it, intoxicate it." In positioning the "we"—in this case the ladino elite—as the historical agents, Luarca recognized himself and his peers as the perpetrators of injustice. At the same time, in relegating the contemporary Indigenous population to "the conquered race" and as passive victims, he still failed to see Indigenous compatriots as equals. Luarca concluded with strong words: suppressing the illiterate vote was "illegal, anti-democratic, unjust, anti-revolutionary, and dangerous." The record indicates that his speech was met with thunderous applause.[85] The very next day, the National Assembly voted 42–14 in favor of extending suffrage rights, thus incorporating universal male suffrage (over eighteen) and voting rights for literate women.[86] Illiterate women did not receive the right to vote, so many Indigenous women remained disenfranchised.

Debates about Indigenous rights and citizenship emerged again just over a week later in discussions about workers' rights. Once again, some delegates expressed fear of Indigenous uprisings that would ruin the country, a theme underlying the heated conversations. Carlos Pellecer Durán argued in favor of workers' rights, stating that this measure would create a national culture and elevate political participation, thus allowing Guatemala to avoid succumbing to the totalitarianism and fascism that had engulfed Europe.[87] However, another delegate, Roberto Guirola Leal, challenged Pellecer's notion that workers' rights would bring immediate stability, suggesting that suddenly giving "*nuestra raza indígena*" too many rights, without helping them to first understand what these rights entailed, would "raise tremendous chaos in the country." Continuing, Guirola stated that he "want(s) to make the Representatives see the danger that could arise in the spirits (*ánimos*) of our Indigenous race." He referenced a recent failed uprising in his home department of San Marcos, where he claimed that his intervention helped to avoid what "could have been translated as a series of 'Patzicías' for Guatemala." Emphasizing that he was not against gradually extending rights to the Indigenous population, he called for the representatives to think clearly, arguing, "We have to do something better, we have to establish the foundation for effective social justice, so that afterwards our indigenous race will not cause disturbances, because in a country like ours they would ruin it in a moment."[88] Clearly, Guirola cast the Indigenous population as second-class citizens who had a role to play in the revolutionary project, but one that elite non-Indigenous people dictated in order to largely preserve the status quo.

David Vela was both a representative and a member of the Constitutional Commission, yet to this point he had remained largely silent during these debates despite his unofficial role as Guatemala's leading indigenista. Perhaps due to his new job as the editor of *El Imparcial*, he felt a need to remain neutral and not make enemies of powerful men. However, Vela was wholeheartedly committed to seeing Guatemala adopt the 1940 Pátzcuaro Accords, and he drafted a special constitutional article that would specifically address Indigenous rights, titled *El Estatuto Indígena* (the Indigenous Statute).[89]

Vela's statute revealed the contradictions inherent in the integrationist position by proposing legislation to address systemic racism ingrained in Guatemalan society while also suggesting that remedying these conditions would

"Guatemalanize" the Indigenous population. On the one hand, the proposal called for the preservation of Indigenous arts, languages, and cultural practices, the legalization of Indigenous marriage practices, the extension of suffrage and workers' rights, and the improvement of *finca* (agricultural estate) laborers' living conditions. On the other hand, Vela's statute claimed to have the ultimate goal of fostering a homogenous sense of national identity that would resonate with all Guatemalans, regardless of ethnicity. Knowing (and perhaps feeling himself) that the events of Patzicía consumed the representatives' thoughts, Vela did not articulate a version of indigenismo that promoted autonomy but rather proposed a state-directed project that strove to get the Indigenous population to identify with the Guatemalan nation.[90]

However, Vela's statute met stiff opposition. The most vehement opponent, Clemente Marroquín Rojas, stated that "indigenous cultures are useless; to the contrary, they are a burden (*un lastre*) for the nation."[91] Further, he declared that the "indigenista campaign" wanted to revive past civilizations in order to destroy Latin culture; "if it was in my hands, I would destroy all indigenous tendencies to avoid having in our country two cultures in clear opposition."[92] Vela quickly interrupted Marroquín Rojas's ethnocidal remarks by clarifying that indigenismo did not call for the abolition of ladino culture. On the contrary, it wished to extend state services to Indigenous populations with the goal of integrating them into the nation.[93]

In the end, the members of the National Assembly voted against the statute, instead dispersing a few of its articles to other sections of the constitution. For example, they included an article protecting popular industries in the culture section, moved an article calling for improved housing for finca workers to the labor section, and placed an article calling for the creation of an indigenist institute under the executive section.[94] In my 2015 interview, Jorge Mario García Laguardia, a leading scholar on Guatemalan legal history, explained that Vela garnered only slight support from a group of revolutionaries who wanted to enact limited changes to Guatemalan society. At its core, he argued, these leaders "were making a revolution, but a revolution that was urban and mestizo, not an Indigenous revolution that would rescue the rights of the Indigenous."[95]

Despite the dissolution of the statute, the passage of the 1945 Constitution was a watershed moment in Indigenous-state relations. Goubaud excitedly wrote Redfield that "Guatemala right now is a beautiful laboratory. . . . The trend of the social change may be gathered from what *El Imparcial* published in its editorial last night, which reads more or less as follows: 'the political fetters and economic and cultural neglect which has weighed heavily on Guatemala in the past must go.'"[96] For Vela, Goubaud, and other like-minded Guatemalans, the 1945 Constitution created possibilities for more equitable social relations by extending voting rights and legal protections to a large segment of the Indigenous population and through beginning conversations about future actions that would drastically alter the fabric of Guatemalan society.

Despite the indigenistas' setback with the statute's dissolution, Arévalo's government did follow through in creating an indigenist institute. In May 1945, Vela and Goubaud met with Manuel Galich, the newly appointed minister of education and member of the Grupo Indigenista.[97] The men discussed the likelihood that the government would finally sign the Pátzcuaro Accords, formally join the III, and establish a national institute. Galich wholeheartedly supported this proposal, but instead of simply modeling the Guatemalan institute after similar organizations in other countries, he called for a conference with Indigenous teachers to discuss the future institute's structure and mission. Such a move marks the revolutionary government's recognition that the category of "the Indian" varied widely, so applying the Mexican or Peruvian model to Guatemala, for example, would be neither appropriate nor effective. However, the IING did utilize some similar methods to the Mexican institute, namely, the use of Indigenous *promotores*, or field agents, in an attempt to mitigate cultural and linguistic barriers.[98] Instead of simply relying on Guatemalan and foreign anthropologists and experts to design the institute, the government turned to Indigenous Guatemalan schoolteachers, albeit an educated minority, to ask what types of progress they desired in their communities.

The July 1945 Cobán teachers' meeting took place within this historical context of official interest in indigenismo, perhaps modeled on the regional congresses of Indigenous leaders that Mexico had held.[99] Of the sixty-five teachers that the government invited, who were from twenty-one different municipalities, thirty-four attended, with the government covering their travel and lodging costs.[100] Over the course of the two-day conference, participants discussed rural education, agriculture, and health, and participants met with several representatives from the national government, including Galich, Manuel María Ávila Ayala from the Ministry of Public Health, and representatives from the Ministry of Economy and the Ministry of Agriculture. Also present were Dr. William Griffith, a professional historian serving with the Inter-American Education Foundation, Goubaud, and Vela. The teachers concluded that while it was easy to speak in general terms about problems facing Indigenous people, it was problematic to collapse such a diverse population into a single category of "the Indian." To truly understand the challenges facing rural Guatemala, the new institute needed to systematically study rural towns and identify local needs, as defined by residents, not bureaucrats and outside experts.[101]

Schoolteachers were community elites who were experienced in navigating between their local cultural practices and ladino culture, perhaps fluidly moving between the two categories as Juan de Dios Rosales often did. All the delegates to the Cobán meeting were male, and as intermediary figures, they candidly advised state officials about effective solutions to confront problems facing their communities. Unsurprisingly, they saw education as a critical means to teach rural Indigenous communities about modern agricultural methods and health and sanitation practices, but they emphasized that teachers must use local languages and demonstrate respect and knowledge of local cultures. Professor J. Luciano Tahay proposed a model of development that shared the revolutionary government's goal of integrating Indigenous communities into the nation. However, while the government positioned state authorities and outside experts as those responsible for defining how this integration should tangibly take place, Tahay inverted this model, attributing agency to local residents. He held the state responsible for providing resources to all Guatemalans, but he deviated from the idea of a standardized, universal path to integration via state-defined modernization. According to Tahay, top-down development had been failing since the arrival of the Spanish, so for effective development to occur, the state must surrender control over how Indigenous communities would define modernity, how they would utilize resources, and to what degree they would choose to integrate themselves into the nation. To Tahay, the state's top-down programs reduced the Indigenous population to passive recipients, a subjectivity the people had been resisting for nearly 450 years.

It is difficult to know to what degree other delegates shared Tahay's model of development because newspaper accounts are the only written source that include interviews with delegates. However, the teachers' suggestions indicate the problems they saw and the local projects they envisioned, and through this, we can interpret their understanding of the central issues they believed to be confronting Indigenous populations. For example, Lorenzo Carchaj from Nahualá suggested that the government support local industries like weaving in order to improve local and regional economies. Francisco Abel Motul and Jorge Rabí Motul from Quetzaltenango and Hipólito Menchú from San Cristóbal Totonicapán emphasized the need to improve rural nutrition and sanitation, citing examples of animals roaming freely in homes and infrequent clothes washing, two practices that they believed to transmit preventable disease. Several teachers noted that the lack of potable water or outhouses caused the rapid spread of disease; others mentioned how seasonal migration to agro-export plantations exposed townspeople to hazards, including venereal disease, malaria, tuberculosis, and alcoholism.[102] Martín Ordóñez and Julio César Petz, both from Sololá, and Juan Alejandro Peneleu from San Pedro La Laguna also suggested improving crop diversity and establishing more effective cultivation techniques.[103] At least in the newspaper's reporting of these conversations, delegates never pointed to structural inequality or racism as the underlying reason for these issues but rather framed them within the state's explanation of socioeconomic conditions.

In the final report, teachers organized their recommendations under four subsections: economy, health and public services, literacy, and education. Like Tahay, they called for some state intervention, but only involvement that the town's representatives requested and approved. In other words, the question was not whether the state would maintain a presence in Indigenous communities but rather one of power, and these delegates inverted existing relations by making the state subservient and accountable to local leadership. For example, in the first point in the economy section, teachers mandated that "the intervention of the State in resolving problems should be active." More specifically, they called for the state to create diets based on local customs and products, establish experimental agricultural stations, study soybean production and possibilities for consumption, and construct rural houses that met local preferences while providing security and comfort. Regarding public health, the teachers called for the state to study the causes of common illnesses and design culturally appropriate solutions, build public latrines and piped water systems, provide crematoriums and landfills, and initiate reforestation. Pertaining to education, the teachers mandated a complete revision of literacy programs, focusing on literacy in local languages first, then the introduction of Spanish. Furthermore, the resolutions requested drastic improvements in educational infrastructure and in teacher training, suggesting a residential normal school for rural teachers.[104]

While by no means representative of all Indigenous Guatemalans, clearly these teachers did not oppose integration into the nation, nor did they wish to remain isolated from state services. This is one of this book's recurring arguments: development's intended recipients did not reject all characteristics of modernization but rather parts of the process like top-down impositions and the hierarchies that it imposed. These teachers took full advantage of the stage provided to them in Cobán to demand an increased state presence in their communities. At the same time, they also wanted to dictate the terms of this integration, and as these resolutions repeatedly emphasized, they took care not to surrender local autonomy or alter local beliefs and customs. In other words, the teachers were willing to integrate into the nation on their own terms but under no circumstances willing to assimilate and abandon their Indigenous identity. The Cobán meeting had given these intermediaries an important voice in the formation of Guatemala's indigenist institute.

On August 28, 1945, a little over a month after the Cobán meeting, the Guatemalan government issued a presidential decree that officially created the IING.[105] Goubaud was named director, and Tax wrote that he and Redfield were "pleased as punch" and that the IING "will have one of the most important functions of any branch of government."[106] The inauguration ceremony took place at USAC on September 26 in conjunction with the opening of USAC's Faculty of Humanities. In his speech, Minister of Education Galich remarked that the IING could become an "authentic laboratory" that the government could use to establish development programs "for the good of the *patria* (homeland) and for the relief of two million of our fellow citizens, left until today in age-old obscurity."[107] Framed in this paternalistic way, Galich committed the state to investing in rural Guatemala, but at the same time, he objectified Indigenous people and portrayed them as scientific human subjects that the state could use as it wished. It denied the contributions that Indigenous people made to the Guatemalan state and did not acknowledge the demands of the teachers from the Cobán meeting for local autonomy and control over development initiatives. His vision for the IING seemed to be one that would reinforce a top-down model of modernization.

Director Goubaud Carrera gave brief remarks at the inauguration, where he discussed the same revolutionary principle that Vela had articulated with the Indigenous Statute, namely that the government had the dual (and seemingly contradictory) goals of recognizing Guatemala's ethnic diversity *and* creating a homogenous and unified national identity. He recognized that solving Guatemala's national identity crisis could be perceived as insignificant when compared to global issues, which he described as the "uncertainty of international anarchy." Still, he argued that Guatemala's future depended on the resolution of the "two distinct systems of life in the country, the Indian and the non-Indian" to establish a nation where all people proudly identified as Guatemalan and shared a mutual definition of what constituted Guatemala. The following excerpt communicates Goubaud's tension in resolving both the question of nation and of diversity:

> How many Guatemalans would think that Guatemala is not just what is enclosed by the four walls of a lawyer's office, or a medical clinic, a business building, or by a stall in the capital's market? On the other hand, how many Guatemalans would there be speaking languages different from the national language, dressing in fancy *trajes* that set them apart from the rest of the population, tortured by beliefs that an average amount of enlightenment would eliminate, tied to technology that dates back to thousands of years, how many, one might ask, would think that Guatemala is not just that which is marked by the mountainous borders of their social community?[108]

In his vivid statement, Goubaud clearly associated non-Indigenous life with modernization, referencing urban infrastructure and legal and medical institutions. He used the word "walls" to reveal an understanding of the designated non-Indigenous space as man-made. In contrast, Indigeneity seems to naturally occur in the existing landscape, demarcated by natural structures such as mountains. In these communities, Goubaud painted life as static, utilizing the same type of clothing and tools for centuries, speaking languages that are incomprehensible to anyone beyond the confines of the village. For Goubaud, Indigenous belief systems revealed their ignorance, and he used language like *tortured* to reflect their need for salvation, not with faith, but with education.

As discussed, Goubaud spent over a year living in rural communities during the dietary survey, but despite his knowledge of the country's diversity, he still depicted Guatemalan national life in these strict binaries of rural versus urban and Indigenous versus ladino. Goubaud likely used hyperbole to get his point across to an urban audience who would have thought in terms of these dichotomies. However, the condescension in his description of Indigenous Guatemala does reveal a tendency toward modernization, according to non-Indigenous standards. Perhaps this can be attributed to a desire to gain support for the new institute; this attitude certainly would have resonated better with residents in Guatemala City than the suggestion that they adopt Indigenous practices. However, as the IING diversified its personnel and gained experience in fieldwork, projects became more collaborative between institutional employees and rural communities, and as future chapters discuss, the IING never fully embraced state-led modernization as its desired outcome.[109] Goubaud's speech, however, reveals once again the constraints that indigenistas felt as they revised their own understandings of race and nation, sought broad support for their projects, and hoped to instill meaningful societal changes.

The structure of the IING clearly demonstrates the linkages between Guatemalan indigenistas, and Goubaud and Vela drafted a proposal that detailed the desired structure for the institute, which the Ministry of Public Education largely approved. The original staff was small and were all ladino/a, with Goubaud serving as director, Alberto Arriaga as secretary, María Ortega as typist, and Joaquín Noval and Francisco Rodríguez Rouanet as officials.[110] The Grupo Indigenista maintained a presence in this new institute as members Epaminondas Quintana and David Vela served on the IING's board of directors. Jorge Luis Arriola and Manuel Galich, both Grupo Indigenista members served respectively as the IING's fourth director and as the minister of education, who oversaw the IING. Members from Guatemala's Association of Landowners (*agricultores*) and Ministries of Public Education, Work and Labor, Agriculture, Public Health, and Governance each had a delegate on the board of directors, cementing the formal ties between the IING and other branches of government.

There are two deviations, however, between the proposed board and the actual board. Vela and Goubaud had called for a representative from the Carnegie Institution and at least one Indigenous representative. These two positions were omitted from the final version. It is likely that Goubaud, out of courtesy for Carnegie's generous funding of his education at Chicago and the dietary survey, wished to extend a formal invitation for it to participate in the IING, perhaps also with the intention of continuing to benefit from Carnegie's financial resources. Though sources do not reveal the rationale behind rejecting a position for Carnegie, the revolutionary government's strong nationalistic tendencies likely saw the participation of a U.S. philanthropic organization in a state institute as meddling and unnecessary. The omission of Indigenous representatives on the board is also revealing of the continued paternalism and perhaps distrust that continued to influence even more progressive Guatemalans. Unfortunately, the historical record does not provide any details on this decision, nor any indication of how Indigenous Guatemalans felt about this exclusion. While the revolutionary government wished to "improve" the lives of the Indigenous population, it was not willing to give an equal, participatory voice on the board to an Indigenous person.[111]

However, a handful of Indigenous teachers found employment with the IING as Goubaud, following Redfield's advice, hired several participants from the Cobán teachers meeting, though IING publications do not detail the selection process. These teachers-turned-ethnographers comprised the institute's fieldwork team, as Goubaud recognized the need to have staff who were fluent in both Spanish and Indigenous languages and cultural practices. Almost immediately, Goubaud hired and trained Rosalio Saquic (hometown: Santa Lucía Utatlán and Nahualá, language: K'iche'), Luis Felipe Utrilla (San Bernardino Suchitepéquez, K'iche'), José Botzoc (San Juan Chamelco, Q'eqchi'), and Agustín Pop (San Pedro La Laguna, Tz'utujil), suggesting a prioritization of ethnographers from larger linguistic groups. After completing approximately six weeks of training with Goubaud in Guatemala City, the men returned to their hometowns to practice interviewing informants, mapping towns, recording family census cards and genealogies, and keeping a fieldwork diary.[112] Soon after, the IING hired additional fieldwork staff from the pool of Cobán meeting attendees, including Martín Ordóñez (Sololá, Kaqchikel), Hipólito Menchú (San Cristóbal Totonicapán, K'iche'), Ricardo Ixcol (San José Chacayá, K'iche'), and Pablo Morales Alonzo (San Juan Ostuncalco, Mam). After one year, the IING promoted Rodríguez Rouanet to the head of the research division. He supervised the men's work and noted that all came from rural families, which made it easier for them to understand local rural conditions. For example, Ordóñez's mother raised pigs and sold sausages and other pork products, Saquic came from a family of farmers, and Pop's family worked as fishermen. The IING recognized that these men, in the words of Rodríguez, "as teachers, had local leadership, at least within their community, for no matter how small the community was, a teacher always had power there."

By 1946, the IING was fully functioning and working toward completing its mission of researching and producing knowledge about Guatemala's diverse population, and Indigenous ethnographers were part of this knowledge production. Receiving a daily stipend of three *quetzales* ($3) while traveling and an annual salary of Q800 ($800), these men conducted ethnographic research and wrote monographs, which the next chapter will discuss in more detail. The ethnographers mainly worked in towns that spoke the same language they did and regularly sent reports to the office on a wide range of topics, including agriculture, religion, daily life, and social relations.[113] As Goubaud had learned during his own education and fieldwork, the IING first emphasized systematic data collection before making practical recommendations to the government. In the uneven production of knowledge that followed, Indigenous people contributed, both as informants and as IING employees, but ultimately the non-Indigenous directors and the revolutionary state determined how to present, release, and use this knowledge. Through this national goal of integration, the revolutionary state hoped to foster a stronger sense of nationalism, win the support of the Indigenous majority, and incorporate Guatemala into hemispheric efforts to improve socioeconomic realities for Indigenous people. One consequence of these efforts was that notions of acceptable versions of Indigenous citizenship became defined within contemporary discourses of development and modernity.

Conclusion

In the WWII moment, Guatemalans displayed an interest in joining hemispheric indigenista efforts to promote socioeconomic development among Indigenous populations as a means to strengthen their respective nations and the region as a whole. Though not a state project in Guatemala until after the October Revolution, individuals such as David Vela, Antonio Goubaud Carrera, and Juan de Dios Rosales capitalized on opportunities to build international networks and collaborations that would prove instrumental in convincing the revolutionary government to adopt the integrationist indigenista position as state policy through the newly formed IING. Exhibiting what A. S. Dillingham has referred to as the "double bind of indigenismo," IING members sought to create national inclusivity by reconfiguring citizenship as a right and extending that to Indigenous populations, but they were careful to do so in a way that would not significantly alter racialized power relations.[114] Still, in these formative years, there were instances where Indigenous leaders used the opportunities they were afforded, such as the Cobán teachers' meeting, to express what they considered to be acceptable forms of development and what integration looked like on their terms.

When Robert Redfield visited Guatemala in June 1945, he was impressed with the proposed structure of the IING and with nascent state efforts to foster cohesion across racialized societal divisions. In a public address at USAC he confidently stated, "Guatemala will undoubtedly form a unified nation, but a nation made up of regional cultures, of groups whose members will conserve admirable traits of the traditional cultures and whose members will be accepted as full members of the Guatemalan nation."[115] His remarks echoed what would become the goal of many of the IING's employees, namely to achieve integration without assimilation and what they understood to be a higher level of socioeconomic development that was unaccompanied by the cultural loss that modernization would trigger.[116] At the same time, both Redfield and the IING positioned outside experts as the arbiters of what constituted "admirable traits" destined for preservation and which "traits" could be lost or changed, though a select group of Indigenous men did participate in this knowledge creation process as low-level, but significant, employees. As the Guatemalan revolutionary state began partnering with outside institutions and actors to implement development projects intended to integrate and modernize rural Indigenous people, the IING strove to inform these decisions through its investigations. But in the process of introducing outside intervention into the daily lives of Indigenous citizens, these collaborations revised notions about Indigeneity and citizenship and began to impose a definition of exactly how the construct of the "permitted modern Indian" should think and behave.

CHAPTER TWO

Sons Like Juan Are the Pride of Guatemala

Creating the Permitted Indian, 1945–1951

In the months leading up to the 1944 Revolution, Juan de Dios Rosales (Kaqchikel Maya) worked for the Carnegie Institute, under the supervision of Antonio Goubaud Carrera and Sol Tax.[1] He lived in Aguacatán, a diverse municipality in the department of Huehuetenango and spent most days completing dietary surveys. The majority of Aguacatán's population was Awakateco Maya, though individuals tended to identify in one of two groups depending on whether they lived in the eastern or western part of the municipality. Aguacatán also had a sizable ladino population and a small K'iche' Maya community.[2] One day, a man invited Rosales to meet with him on his house's patio. Before long, a crowd of curious onlookers gathered, so Rosales took the opportunity to share the nature of his work with the townspeople. However, the man, who goes unnamed in Rosales's field notes, expressed resistance to participating, arguing that when government employees had visited Aguacatán in the past, they never brought resources or good opportunities for the community.[3] These concerns about outside intrusions had become even more prominent at the local level after the 1943 completion of a road that had made Aguacatán accessible by truck and bus.[4] Despite the fact that Rosales was working for an international organization, not the government, this man's position indicated that he—and perhaps other *aguacatecos*—considered outside intervention and interest to be detrimental.

In the immediate aftermath of the Revolution, Rosales noted that aguacatecos gathered in the central plaza to listen to radio reports and expressed much uncertainty and trepidation about the political changes taking place in the distant capital.[5] In addition, the community's *zajorines*, or the Maya spiritual authorities, conducted Maya ceremonies in their sacred places, burning incense, lighting candles, likely sacrificing a chicken or turkey, and praying that "the country's political disturbances would quickly end to calm the people." Rosales was likely familiar with these ceremonies, regardless of whether he regularly participated in them. He would have realized their significance as well as their cost, and he took care to note that the zajorines conducted these ceremonies on their own accord for the well-being of the town.[6] Clearly, Indigenous aguacatecos felt a sense of insecurity about the political changes

and the presence of outsiders like Rosales, and they questioned how their relationship to the state might change given these events and interactions. Rosales
left Aguacatán soon after these events and began employment at the IING,
and available records about IING activity do not inform us about any subsequent development efforts in the town. While aguacatecos' thoughts and emo-
tions certainly are not representative of those of other Indigenous Guatemalans,
this brief episode provides a glimpse into the reality that Indigenous communities across Guatemala faced with the change of government, as they recognized that a regime change would likely reshape their relationship to the state.

This chapter focuses on the top-down view of this change, examining the
revision of the notion of Indigenous citizenship. It argues that the revolutionary state created and solidified the prototype for the ideal Guatemalan, and
more importantly for the "permitted Indian." To do so, it utilized the IING to
create knowledge about Indigenous people and towns in order to more effectively define what it perceived to be "problems" and thus develop "solutions" that both supported its high modernist civilizing mission and facilitated
state governance across national territory. Though this project introduced
legislation that included a large segment of the Indigenous population as active citizens—those who could vote and hold office—it had clear limitations.[7]
The revolutionary years were a time of democratic opening and increased
inclusion in the nation, but it was an inclusion that the state always defined,
ensuring the preservation of the status quo. While it invited exciting new
opportunities for Indigenous participation in the nation as subjects, it also
limited the expressions of these new rights to ones that coincided with state
interests and ones that the political elite deemed to be appropriate. However,
before the revolutionary state began pursuing applied projects in Indigenous
communities, it first sought to render the population legible, defining who
it considered Indigenous and, in turn, deciding upon the "acceptable" parameters of Indigenous identity. In this moment of extending a more active
citizenship role to the illiterate male population, the Guatemalan state relied
on the IING to create knowledge about these potential citizens and guide it
in defining the model for the permitted modern Indigenous citizen.

Defining Indigeneity

In 1945, the newly created IING sent surveys to the directors of national schools
in sixteen of Guatemala's twenty-two departments, selecting those with substantial Indigenous populations. Because a large majority of responders were
ladino, the IING phrased questions to explore perceptions of what characteristics

these responders used to define someone as Indigenous. Guiding all survey questions was a central preoccupation of the revolutionary government—who exactly was "an Indian"?[8] Antonio Goubaud Carrera, the IING director, insisted that society needed clear definitions of ethnic groups in order to function efficiently and peacefully, citing the United States' one-drop rule for determining African ancestry as an example of a clear-cut measure. At the same time, Goubaud did not understand race to be biological; as he wrote, the survey's purpose was to "crystallize in the public opinion" what "sociological characteristics" identified a person as Indigenous.[9]

This goal proved impossible. Of the 1,248 surveys that the IING disseminated, it received 881 to use in its analysis. Unfortunately, no original surveys exist, but the aggregate data does allow us to draw some conclusions about how midcentury Guatemalans defined Indigeneity. Instead of producing a simple definition of a "Guatemalan Indian," the data stressed the fluidity and diversity within this category, emphasizing its contingency on place, socioeconomic status, and cultural practice. For example, while 86 percent of surveys identified cultural behaviors (*costumbres*) as a key determinant, the IING could not concisely define these because they differed widely by department. For example, 72 percent of survey replies from Suchitepéquez identified *traje*, or Indigenous dress, as a key indicator while only 48 percent of replies from Jalapa deemed it significant.[10] Across all departments, physical appearance was the least important factor. Goubaud concluded that "there does not exist in the country a uniform and general criterion" for defining "the Indian."[11]

Given this predicament, the revolutionary state tasked the IING with creating more knowledge about Indigeneity in Guatemala. If it could not neatly categorize people, at least it could produce experts on Indigeneity, according to the state's logic. Low human development indicators revealed numerous social "problems" that the state wished to solve; illiteracy levels were 72 percent, life expectancy was forty years, and the International Bank for Reconstruction and Development determined that Guatemalan children were malnourished and thus had stunted development.[12] Both statistics and popular stereotypes positively correlated these indicators with rural Indigenous populations. But according to the state's logic, without first understanding this diverse population, it could not possibly devise effective solutions to socioeconomic problems. Despite their progressive proclivities, revolutionary state builders still believed Indigenous "improvement" to be a prerequisite for an offer of full citizenship. With trepidation, the revolutionary government had abolished legislation that had served to render Indigenous people as secondary citizens, but it also called for increased state presence and activities in rural communities with the intention of "civilizing" and guiding Indigenous populations toward the "proper" expressions of citizenship.

Indigenista efforts via the IING shaped the revolutionary state's efforts to understand the diverse group of people the state collectively defined as Indigenous. Anthropologist James Scott argues that legibility is a "central problem of statecraft," or the process by which state builders take complex, local customs and behaviors and fit them into "a standard grid whereby it could be centrally recorded and monitored."[13] This process serves noble and ignoble purposes at the same time; it is "as vital to the maintenance of our welfare and freedom as [it is] to the designs of a would-be modern despot."[14] By standardizing Guatemala's diverse cultures and conveniently, if not always accurately, fitting them within clear, defined categories, the state hoped that the population would gradually become more governable and socioeconomic problems easier to diagnose and solve.

When it became clear that rendering the diverse Indigenous population legible would be quite difficult, historical actors from Guatemala and abroad formed a new conceptualization of the "permitted Indian." Imposing this idea of "permitted" and "prohibited" behaviors upon Indigenous bodies at once allowed for increased participation in the nation but also took measures to protect elite rule by expressly forbidding actions that could challenge existing power relations. The desire to be more racially inclusive while still maintaining the status quo became a key paradox of Guatemala's Revolution, as the revolutionary leadership pursued a high modernist agenda of engineering its version of a modern Guatemala while simultaneously attempting to mitigate some degree of structural inequality.[15]

Ethnography as a Tool of Governance

Ethnography served as an important tool of governance, helping the state to diagnose "problems" that it could hope to solve through modern development initiatives. In the first years of the IING's existence, staff members dedicated themselves to creating knowledge about Indigenous communities for primarily non-Indigenous audiences. The IING's fieldwork staff initially had four ethnographers, all bilingual schoolteachers, and by 1951, the institute had hired four additional ethnographers, including the first woman, Hélida Esther Cabrera, a ladina woman from Santiago Atitlán who spoke Tz'utujil Maya fluently.[16] Using an adaptation of George Murdock's cross-cultural survey, IING ethnographers traveled throughout the highlands and compiled their data into community monographs in order to depict the people and places they encountered in terms that made sense to policy makers in Guatemala City.

Murdock originally titled his survey the "Outline of Cultural Materials," and he developed it for Yale University's Human Relations Area Files (HRAF) project. HRAF served to collect an abundance of "cross cultural" data with the goal of standardizing the study of foreign cultures. One of HRAF's directors, Mark May, wrote in 1971 that the purpose of this data collection was "to make greater progress in the understanding of human life from the biological, psychological, and sociological points of view."[17] However, historian David Price's work on Cold War anthropology gives a less generous interpretation of HRAF's function, referring to it as the "wartime era military intelligence brainchild" and emphasizing its purpose in supplying information for the nonclassified portions of the U.S. Army's country handbooks in the 1950s.[18] Within these conflicting interpretations of HRAF's historical significance, we clearly see the divide between the intentions of the project's creators of expanding knowledge of "foreign" cultures and the (un)intended consequences that HRAF had upon foreign societies and U.S. foreign policy, as this knowledge at times informed military operations and counterinsurgency measures.

The cross-cultural survey was comprehensive: 557 questions spanned an array of topics from religion, local political structures, child-rearing, sexuality, and the acquisition of honor and respect.[19] Ethnographers created maps, noting the existence and placement of various buildings and telegraph, telephone, and electrical lines. They categorized people according to the census's two broad racial categories—indígena and ladino—designating how many people of each group worked certain occupations, wore shoes, or used furniture, for example. More intimate questions about religion, interpersonal relationships, and parallel governance structures helped ethnographers communicate more unfamiliar aspects of local cultures to readers.[20]

Beyond the voluminous data collected, this methodology marked the professionalization of anthropological studies under the IING. In selecting the IING as the institute to scientifically collect information to guide state policies, Guatemalan policy makers revealed their profound trust in social science and in the role of experts, which they prioritized over local knowledge. This decision also reinforced the coloniality of the process of knowledge production, as ethnographers used a survey created with Western categories of behaviors and social organization to help the state "govern beneficiaries."[21] At the same time, they functioned as "local brokers" who could determine the contents of the reports and take into account voices and perspectives that the institutional expert focus had ignored.[22]

Ethnographers visited households in each town to get an array of perspectives and responses, spending a few hours with each informant.[23] After completing the surveys, ethnographers compiled a report based on their data that also made suggestions to government ministries about the towns' various needs. The IING never formally published these reports, and with the institute's closing in 1988 and the destruction of its archive, this fascinating data was lost, for which former fieldwork director Francisco Rodríguez Rouanet "cries tears of blood." Therefore, it is impossible to know how many reports the IING authored; Rodríguez estimates that by 1975, he and his colleagues had surveyed over 150 towns.[24] Luckily, the IING did publish eight community monographs in its first decade, assisted by funding from the *Servicio Cooperativo Interamericano de Educación* (SCIDE) as part of the teacher-training program that the Arévalo government developed.[25] SCIDE helped fund the IING monographs with the intention that these publications could inform teachers-in-training about the towns where they would work.[26]

In 1945, the Guatemalan government signed an agreement with SCIDE to build a rural normal school in the Kaqchikel region around Chimaltenango, and project leaders selected the Finca La Alameda as the site for this school.[27] The Guatemalan government had given the finca to two U.S. Americans in 1877 to conduct agricultural experimental fields and train locals in new techniques, but this project never materialized, so the development of the normal school fulfilled this intent to use the land as a training center.[28] By July 1947, an educational pamphlet described La Alameda as "the country's first gain in modern education," citing the school's focus on primary academic subjects and hygiene, agriculture, and cultural education.[29] Harvard University anthropologist Benjamin Paul was a SCIDE consultant, and he helped IING staff adapt George Murdock's cross-cultural survey to the Guatemalan context so that it could be used to create these monographs, further cementing this connection between expert knowledge and governance.[30] Beyond educational purposes at La Alameda, Rodríguez recalled that bureaucrats from state ministries and members of the national university frequently visited the IING's library to consult these studies, gathering the necessary information to justify their projects and programs for the countryside.[31]

The IING monographs are quite formulaic, but close readings of these documents reveal how the ethnographers served as intermediary figures that simultaneously provided clear and oversimplified data to the revolutionary state and used this opportunity to voice their own perspectives and perhaps those of their informants. Similar to the K'iche' elite in Quetzaltenango or Kaqchikel intermediaries from Comalapa that historians have studied, these IING ethnographers straddled Indigenous and non-Indigenous societies and skillfully used their positions of power to simultaneously serve the interests of both.[32] Importantly, in creating new knowledge about these communities, ethnographers heavily relied on the information that their informants provided. Thus, informants could choose what to divulge about their communities, and ethnographers included or omitted the information and then categorized it, at their discretion, but in accordance with the survey's centralizing categories. Eventually, this knowledge production "composted back" to local communities through the applied efforts of various state institutions that experts developed based on local conditions, as understood from these reports.[33] While the monographs reinforced unequal power relations by positioning outsiders as experts of local cultures, we must also recognize the spaces available for Indigenous ethnographers to act as intermediaries and for informants to choose what information they disclosed.

For example, in December 1946, IING ethnographers Agustín Pop (Tz'utujil) and Simón Otzoy (Kaqchikel) spent eight days in San Bartolomé Milpas Altas, a town approximately eighteen miles west of Guatemala City. This was not the first study or monograph that either man had written, and it was the eighth one that the IING had published. Further, all the IING's monographs focused on municipal centers in Chimaltenango or Sacatepéquez, with the one exception being Chinautla, a municipality in the department of Guatemala, located just north of the capital.[34] The San Bartolomé monograph rigorously followed a standard format that the other studies also used, touching upon many subjects and carefully elaborating upon those that the IING deemed particularly important to report to government ministries. By focusing on municipal centers, what we can infer is that the state viewed these urban populations to have the potential to rapidly modernize and become contributing members of society, as it hoped to convert these Indigenous populations into "permitted modern Indians."

Like the other publications in the series, San Bartolomé Milpas Altas's fifty-nine-page monograph opened with a detailed map of the town. The grid-like streets presented a sense of modern organization to the community, and a meticulous key explained the numbers and abbreviations used to designate schools, governance buildings, churches, and stores. Pop and Otzoy placed emphasis on roads and infrastructure, with no attention given to natural geography or landmarks, demonstrating an understanding of space as man-made and relatively recently constructed. Without physical infrastructure, the space around the mapped town appeared blank on the white page, void of meaning and civilization.[35]

In the pages that followed, Pop and Otzoy explored several themes of San Bartolomé's community life, including the local economy, infrastructure, political and religious hierarchies, and integration with the nation. The 1950 Census estimated that 72 percent of the municipality's 1,240 people were Kaqchikel, and the ethnographers relied on nineteen informants' testimonies to shape their information.[36] While the authors never used their informants' names, they did identify each person by initial and a series of characteristics, including age, ethnicity (indígena or ladino), marital status (single, married—with distinctions between common law, civil, and ecclesiastical—and widowed), occupation, and literacy status. All nineteen informants were male, Kaqchikel, and were or had been married. Only three were illiterate, and their average age was 54.89 years.[37] Though we cannot be certain, these indicators would suggest that Pop and Otzoy focused on interviewing the elders and leaders of San Bartolomé's Kaqchikel community.

In discussing local power structures, the ethnographers described the content of three municipal meetings held in 1946. On each occasion, town leaders discussed local development projects such as expansion of communal pasturelands, distribution of cement tubing for piped water, and bridge repair on the main road that connected San Bartolomé with the departmental capital. By emphasizing these topics, Pop and Otzoy argued that local residents were indeed concerned with what the revolutionary state would perceive to be modern development initiatives, and they also emphasized that residents were not "backward" or "uncivilized" by choice but rather were constrained by their socioeconomic status.

While Pop and Otzoy had to closely abide by the structure established by the Cross-Cultural Survey, they found several opportunities to draw attention to the material poverty and structural inequalities confronting San Bartolomé's Indigenous residents. For example, when noting the amount of land necessary to sustain a family of five, the authors stated that while most residents did own some land, few had a sufficient amount for subsistence and thus were forced to either rent land or work as day laborers for low wages.[38] Similarly, when describing the adobe houses common to the town, the authors wrote, "most indígenas prefer sleeping in beds but lack the money to buy them."[39] The ethnographers reported that the town's few ladinos all wore shoes while the majority of Indigenous people did not own shoes for lack of financial resources.[40] By including these examples of material poverty, Pop and Otzoy revised interpretations of Indigeneity that had posited alcoholism and ignorance as reasons for these behaviors.[41] Instead, these ethnographers strongly refuted such assertions and offered an alternative understanding of local conditions that they believed emanated from the state's neglect to address economic exploitation and unequal access to resources.

Accompanying the text is also a detailed chart of the variety of agricultural products grown in the community, debunking the misconception that Indigenous people only ate corn and beans. Farmers in San Bartolomé cultivated other crops such as cabbage, cauliflower, carrots, beets, and several kinds of fruit. However, in order to supplement familial income, farmers often sold these products at markets in nearby Guatemala City and Antigua.[42] Thus, the authors suggested that malnutrition and a diet limited to a few agricultural staples was not due to an unwillingness to cultivate alternative crops nor was it based on an ignorance of other types of foods. Rather, it was a direct result of local socioeconomic conditions.

IING ethnographers were instrumental in returning Guatemalan indigenismo's focus to legal protections for Indigenous peoples and socioeconomic initiatives to address state neglect of contemporary Indigenous towns. This focus had briefly occurred during the Reina Barrios presidency in the 1890s but had reverted to "fix[ing] Mayas in the past in folkloric traditions and rendered other aspects of Maya culture threatening in the present" during the Ubico era of the 1930s.[43] Through presenting local problems as lack of access to resources, notably land and money, and local leaders as agents of change who collectively sought development projects for their communities, IING ethnographers helped to reshape the way that the social category of "the Indian" was understood in Guatemala. They revised the idea of the "indolent Indian," and passive citizens, instead presenting engaged citizens who only needed financial resources to "improve" their lives. And they positioned these practices and behaviors as determined by class, not by race, indirectly also suggesting that the adoption of new behaviors would not make one less Indigenous. Additionally, this reconceptualization placed the responsibility for providing the means for this improvement upon the state, not upon Indigenous populations themselves, and served to justify the state's designation of acceptable forms of Indigenous citizenship.

However, even though IING staff challenged existing racialized understandings of Indigeneity, this transformation of the relationship between Indigenous citizens and the revolutionary state also fortified existing ideas about the utility of a citizen, making claims about "who counts" in their exclusion of populations living outside municipal centers, rendering them incapable of participating in the nation.[44] The IING's work also reinforced the colonial practice of minimizing local knowledge and assigning new taxonomies and categories, labels that fit the mentality of the state and not necessarily of the people now expected to embody them. While IING ethnographers did not have this intention and did not recognize their role in this process, it is important that we recognize one of the unintended consequences of their work in that they aided the revolutionary state in attempting to shape Guatemalan society sometimes against the desires of some of its inhabitants.

The revolutionary government recognized the challenges that governing a marginalized and diverse population entailed, and for it, the social sciences provided a means to create the knowledge necessary to govern effectively. As historian Christy Thornton has argued for 1920s Mexico, "development was not an outside imposition, but a necessary international program for overcoming the dislocations that unfettered capitalism had brought to their region."[45] Guatemalan revolutionary state builders shared this sentiment. Through the IING, the state received the information it deemed essential to design programs that would instill the patriotic values, behavioral characteristics, and new priorities that it wished the Indigenous population to adopt. State builders saw education as the primary vehicle through which to transform the countryside, but illiteracy was a central obstacle preventing its success. As the next section discusses, education and literacy campaigns became vehicles for instructing Indigenous Guatemalans in how to be "permitted Indians."

Revolutionary Literacy Campaigns

President Arévalo was a professor before he became a politician, and for his government, education was a key means to bring the values of the Revolution to the people. Born in the southeastern department of Santa Rosa in 1904, Arévalo studied in Argentina and in 1934 received a doctoral degree in philosophy from the Universidad de La Plata.[46] In his writings, he referred to literacy campaigns as "a duty with which the men of the revolution have been charged" and suggested that schools "would not just bring hygiene and literacy: they would bring the doctrine of the revolution."[47] For Arévalo, the Revolution exemplified what he termed spiritual socialism. As journalist George Black described it, "this was capitalist development shot through with a strong dose of nationalism, but stopping short of major structural reforms."[48] Arévalo emphasized the psychological liberation of spiritual socialism, arguing that a focus on "civil and moral virtues" would restore individual dignity, thus permitting the individual to "integrate himself into the atmosphere of society's values, needs, and goals."[49] Though abstract and vague, Arévalo promised a democracy that included individual rights but also emphasized "some form of economic justice, equality, and security."[50]

The use of the school as a site for citizen formation was not unique to Arévalo's Guatemala or to the 1940s. The Spanish American empire relied on schools as sites of colonialism, training Indigenous youth in Catholic practices with the hope that they could become important intermediary figures between Crown and community. Education functioned as a key tool of empire throughout the modern world. For example, the U.S. Bureau of Indian Affairs used Native American boarding schools as a means of forced assimilation, and the British Empire developed a colonial education system designed to foster loyal but subordinate subjects. Revolutionary Mexico utilized the school as a site to impart the revolutionary ethos. And schools also sometimes served as sites of empowerment and opportunity, as literacy and the social capital acquired through formal education permitted some individuals additional prospects and mobility, such as the Indigenous schoolteachers that the IING hired as ethnographers.[51] In line with neo-Lamarckian ideas about race, literacy and education could "rehabilitate" the Guatemalan population through "control of the social milieu."[52]

Educational efforts had long focused on reaching Guatemala's rural population, specifically the Indigenous population, and this emphasis became a cornerstone of the Guatemalan Revolution.[53] State spending on education increased 800 percent and the number of rural schools grew by almost 90 percent.[54] Major newspapers regularly released statements about the inauguration of schools and literacy programs throughout the country. In 1946, a major national newspaper, *La Hora*, published a short article paying tribute to the inauguration of a school in Jalapa, claiming that it would help the "Indians of the mountain" to incorporate into the national environment of progress.[55] A 1945 newspaper advertisement echoed this idea, claiming that literacy was the only path toward democracy and progress, stating, "Our people have to be taught to read, only in this way can they progress and stop being the victim of tyranny and exploitation."[56] Clearly, literacy campaigns were a means to teach people to read but more importantly to instruct Guatemalans, particularly those who had just received voting rights, how to portray patriotic fervor on the terms of the political elite. Further, literate Indigenous Guatemalans could read materials such as newspaper coverage of current events and manuals that included information about modern hygiene and agricultural methods. They would be able to read ballots, thus to some degree alleviating electoral

¡El Analfabetismo es una Vergüenza Nacional!

Hay que combatirlo, evitándolo ante todo, y para evitarlo es preciso establecer Escuelas en número suficiente, para que todos los niños de edad escolar tengan oportunidad para instruirse.

El Censo Escolar que se levantará en enero de 1946 será la base para la creación de las muchas escuelas que hacen falta.

Coopere usted, en los trabajos que en tal sentido ha iniciado la Dirección General de Estadística

FIGURE 2.1 "Illiteracy is a National Embarrassment!" (*El Imparcial,* December 13, 1945. Courtesy of AGCA.)

fraud and manipulation. In sum, the revolutionary government believed that creating a literate Indigenous population would strengthen its popular base of support and foster a collective sense of national identity.

While the government admitted that improved education was only one advancement Guatemala needed, it understood literacy to be a prerequisite for other programs of socioeconomic development, as learning about agricultural techniques or public health, for example, required one to be able to read instructional materials. This ordering of social projects explains the revolutionary state's insistence on literacy as a means of disseminating modernity; the country could only be redeemed from its disjointed state "when the large majority of its children learn to write, to read, and to feel the word **homeland**" (bold in original).[57]

Promotional materials reveal the racialized nature of Guatemalan society and of revolutionary programming, as they invoked the discourse of degeneration and the idea of the tutelary state to promote a more grassroots level civilizing mission.[58] A December 1945 newspaper advertisement entitled "Illiteracy is a National Embarrassment!" pictured a light-skinned couple seated next to one another reading a book (see figure 2.1). In the advertisement, the man's wedding ring is prominently visible as he affectionately embraces his wife, establishing the heterosexual and legally married couple as the ideal standard. Both individuals are well dressed with manicured nails and sparkling white smiles. This propaganda positioned women alongside men as important contributors to the literacy project but still as collaborators with men, not as wholly independent actors. The Guatemalan government called on couples like this one to educate the dark-skinned rural masses that, in its opinion, would continue to embarrass the nation until they were literate.[59] The image also reveals the paradox of social integration, for, on the one hand, revolutionary actors called for recognition of Guatemala's diversity as long as all citizens expressed loyalty to the Guatemalan nation, but it also held up couples such as this one as emblematic of the national image.

Newspaper advertisements used military euphemisms to present illiteracy as a national enemy, and it encouraged literate Guatemalans to give financially or volunteer as teachers in the "Army of National Literacy," targeting white, middle- to upper-class Guatemalans as potential volunteers or short-term paid staff.[60] The government believed this demographic to be equipped with the necessary skills and civic knowledge to educate the rest of the population and framed these calls to action as a way for one to express dedication to the revolutionary cause. For Guatemalans, volunteering in a literacy campaign was often simply a gratifying way of participating in the Revolution and working in one's community. One clear example of this is evident in the oral history of IING ethnographer Hélida Cabrera. Cabrera belonged to a middle-class ladino family, but as a young child, she spent time in the market with Tz'utujil women in an effort to learn their language, an unusual desire for someone of her class and race, and an endeavor that her mother surprisingly encouraged. Cabrera was twenty-three years old when Arévalo assumed the presidency, and she actively began to participate in literacy work in Santiago Atitlán. With her mother's blessing, she conversed in Tz'utujil with young men as they came home from work, offering to give them classes in Spanish, and soon she began teaching almost thirty students. The local schoolteacher provided a classroom; the Ministry of Education sent her literacy pamphlets. For six months she taught this class for two hours a day, five days a week.[61] While aware of the existing social hierarchies in her community and the fact that she held a privileged status, Cabrera maintained the belief that all Guatemalans deserved an education, and she considered it a source of great pride that she helped Tz'utujil youth become literate.

Between 1944 and 1951, hundreds of Guatemalans like Cabrera participated in literacy work, with the funding for these campaigns largely coming from national lotteries. Campaigns typically ran for six months, and teachers received a monthly stipend between Q20 and Q30 (1:1 with the U.S. dollar) and taught children in the morning and adults in the afternoons. At the end of the course, examiners administered tests to determine whether students could be considered literate in Spanish.[62] The Ministry of Education recommended the same pedagogy for children and adults, instructing teachers to start first with learning the vowel sounds and then learning short syllables.[63] After a few lessons that focused on letters and short words, the primer introduced short phrases. It is with this step that the ideological work of the campaigns began to feature more prominently through primer content, which the next section will analyze in detail.

Despite these efforts, illiteracy rates did not diminish.[64] By 1960, illiteracy still hovered between 60 and 70 percent, demonstrating no decline from the rates reported in 1950.[65] One explanation is that early campaigns generally focused on the capital and only later extended to rural areas. Literacy campaigns were easier to organize in the capital, with its adequate buildings and resources. When literacy campaigns extended outward from Guatemala City, they still often focused on departmental and municipal centers, the urbanized rural spaces depicted in IING monographs. Another important variable is that efforts to create literacy materials in Indigenous languages were still in nascent stages when the 1954 coup occurred. Nor were there significant numbers of bilingual teachers, although the state was making strides in this area through the La Alameda Normal School. Further, rural Indigenous Guatemalans likely faced other barriers to participation, such as lack of time, the need to seasonally migrate for work, and discrimination within the school setting, all of which diminished these campaigns' overall effectiveness at improving literacy rates.

But statistics do not tell the whole story. While significant numbers of the population may not have learned how to read, those who participated certainly learned what kind of citizen the state wished them to be, as the messages and lessons conveyed through literacy campaigns transcended basic reading skills. An analysis of literary materials reveals exactly how this ideal citizen would look and behave, which mapped onto ideas about race as the "permitted Indian." Anything outside of this mold during this period would be considered detrimental to national progress and would be seen as opposing the Revolution's goals.

Citizenship Lessons in Literacy Primers

The first campaign's primary, *A.B.C.*, included a lengthy section named "*Eres Ciudadano*" (You Are a Citizen) that taught students what rights and responsibilities accompanied this status.[66] The first sentences clearly defined the broad parameters for citizenship, designating anyone reading this primer who was over the age of eighteen and who had "normal use of your faculties." The primer asserted that economic status, skin color, first language, or level of formal education did not affect one's citizenship status. It even emphasized that citizens could go barefoot, a key racialized marker of Indigeneity, thus implying that people who Guatemalan society placed at the very bottom of the social hierarchy still had the same rights and responsibilities as everyone else.[67] This depiction of the national community is paternalistic and patronizing, but unlike earlier, more inclusive versions of the nation, such as the ladino nationalism of the Estrada Cabrera presidency (1898–1920), it specified a place for Indigenous people, regardless of class, in the nation. As historian Julie Gibbings has explored, ladino nationalism did allow for participation of Indigenous elite by defining ladino identity in terms of "honor and social standing" rather than race, and it marked a clear departure from creole nationalism of the mid-nineteenth century. However, it made little space for Indigenous commoners. Revolutionary nationalism, at least discursively, sought to remedy this exclusion.[68]

According to the primer, with citizenship came the great responsibility of voting. The primer instructs its audience to carefully consider candidates and to vote for the person who is the most honorable and capable, warning that "your vote can serve for the good and the enrichment of the Republic or for its ruin and humiliation."[69] The very creation and inclusion of this material in the first literacy campaign conveys the trepidation that many Guatemalans felt about expanded suffrage. As seen in the debates during the Constitutional Assembly, some Guatemalans believed that extending suffrage to illiterate people—particularly Indigenous people—would foster tyranny. They believed that a larger voter base was necessary for democracy but feared that if illiterate people did not use these new rights in the desired way, they would destroy the nation.

A 1946 primer called *Nuevo Día* used the character Juan Chapín as the prototype Indigenous citizen. His last name, Chapín, is a popular slang term simply denoting "Guatemalan." Juan first appeared in *A.B.C.* and resurfaces in several primers from the era, always exemplifying the character qualities that the Guatemalan state wished to instill in the hearts and minds of its new citizens (see figure 2.2). In the images that illustrate the accompanying text, Juan and his son wear Western clothing while his wife and daughter wear a more ambiguous blouse and skirt, one that easily could be considered a *huipil* and *corte*, Indigenous dress, or one that could adhere more to ladino style. This ambiguity allows for the primer's messages to resonate with a broader rural

14

Juan

audience. Juan's family instructs ladinos on civics and modern life while also embodying the modern Indigenous family that the state desired and illustrating the state's idea of social integration without ladinization, or full assimilation. Furthermore, it elevated civic virtues and identity markers over ethnic signifiers, not necessarily erasing difference but certainly relegating it as a clear second to national identity. As such, this family's depiction serves as a guide, urging Indigenous people to transform themselves in the same way and reap the same benefits.[70] Juan is what historian Heather Vrana calls a "peripheral protocitizen," an individual who, from the perspective of Guatemalan state builders, could grow into the full rights and responsibilities of citizenship through following the state's careful guidance and instructions.[71]

Juan's family symbolizes the type of interpersonal relationships that Guatemalan state builders wanted to see exhibited between citizens of the nation. Juan is happily married to Juana and they have two children, a boy named Manuel and a girl named María.[72] According to the primer, Juan and Juana

FIGURE 2.3 Juana Chapín. (*Nuevo Día* Literacy Primer, 1946. Courtesy of AGCA.)

never get into arguments and are faithful to one another; "Juana is young, is good, she doesn't like luxury. Juan will never leave her" (see figure 2.3).[73] Reinforcing patriarchy, the primer makes Juan's faithfulness contingent on Juana's daily behavior. There is no indication in the primer that Juan or Juana desire to have more children; in contrast, they seem content with the size of their family, and everyone's needs are met. Although development experts would not begin advocating for nationwide family planning projects for Guatemala until the 1960s, they believed that large populations put a tremendous strain on a nation's resources, particularly in terms of food supply. However, U.S. foreign policy recognized the problem of overpopulation. In 1953, the National Planning Association, an organization based in Washington, D.C., that proposed solutions to the United States' problems, which at that time included communism, published a pamphlet entitled *Communism in Guatemala*. Though this pamphlet was published seven years after the primer, these concerns did not materialize overnight. The author, Theodore Geiger, asserted that Guatemala's population had increased 120 percent between 1920 and 1951.[74] At a time when experts believed high population growth rates contributed to global poverty and hunger, this primer subtly suggested that modern families maintain a small nuclear family for the sake of the nation.[75]

The primer describes Juan as possessing five general traits that define him as a "good Guatemalan": he is healthy, honorable, hardworking, Christian, and patriotic. A large portion of the text is spent unpacking this first criterion of health, and the state reinforced this idea through other types of materials as well. For example, public health campaigns worked in tandem with literacy campaigns, reinforcing ideas of modern hygiene and sanitation practices in rural communities. At the Escuela La Alameda, teacher-training materials included a magazine called *Alfabetización Higiénica*, or hygiene literacy, and regularly included pedagogical articles about how to properly bathe, boil drinking water, defecate in outhouses, and brush teeth.[76] The 1952 literacy campaign distributed small posters that "underscored modernization and communal responsibility" and warned of the dangers associated with public urination and defecation, walking barefoot, and not using disinfectant.[77] One poster depicted monster mosquitos attacking an innocent, sleeping man and commanded viewers to "Use mosquito spray. Destroy puddles." Another depicted a man squatting and defecating under a tree, flies landing first in his excrement and then on food, contaminating it. Unknowingly, a second man consumed this food, becoming gravely ill. The looming specter of a bright orange skull lingered over his sleeping figure, indicating his fate (see figure 2.4). Still another poster provided detailed instructions for how to construct a latrine, including diagrams with exact measurements, trying to convince the viewer of the ease and reasonable cost of this necessary project.[78] These types of materials complemented literacy classes in hopes of instilling knowledge about public health and prevention measures, and assuredly, Juan and his family readily accepted and practiced the depicted behaviors.

Through literacy primers, the Guatemalan revolutionary state revealed its belief in the common stereotype that Indigenous people were dirty, so Juan Chapín's behaviors provide a model for how to overcome this condition. First, the family lives in a clean, modern house constructed with wooden boards and a pitched roof. It has a front door and a window, and a wooden fence carefully demarcates the lot as Juan's privately owned property, as opposed to some form of collective ownership. A sidewalk leads visitors to the front door, and around the house grow various shrubs and trees.[79] Juan and his family never permit any animals to enter their home, instead keeping them outdoors in

FIGURE 2.4 Public health campaign poster. (Educational Poster from Third Regional Literacy Campaign, 1952. Courtesy of AGCA.)

clean, fenced pens to battle infestation by fleas, ticks, and other disease-bearing insects. Juan also uses modern medicine, like quinine, to help fight malaria, taking advantage of the free pills that the Ministry of Public Health offers.[80] And when his son Manuel breaks his arm, Juan does not use a local bonesetter but instead takes him to the hospital, where two doctors examine him and place his arm in a cast, free of charge.[81]

Juan's home is immaculate, and his family's hygiene habits are above reproach. Juan and his entire family bathe daily and use soap, because as the primer instructs, "a bath without soap is not a bath." Family members also carefully clean their hair, nails, and teeth and change their clothes at least once a week, regularly washing them (see figure 2.5).[82] These standards mirror those displayed by the middle-class couple in the propaganda advertisement; Juan and his family likewise adopt and practice habits that will render them clean, neat, and tidy like the urban, literate, ladino couple. The primer does not push Juan's wife and daughter to abandon Indigenous dress, nor does it indicate that

33

FIGURE 2.5
Depicting modern
hygiene habits.
(*Nuevo Día* Literacy
Primer, 1946.
Courtesy of AGCA.)

Juana ☐☐☐ *a su hija.*
₂ ₁ ₁₇ ₁

Juan y Manuel se bañan solos.

baña - niña - mañana - muñeco
baña - niña - mañana - muñeco

Vamos a baño papá - dijo Manuel -
Sí, sí papaíto, la mañana está linda.-dijo Maruca-.
Vamos pues, el baño es bueno. ☐e pasada cor-
taremos piñas, cañas y leña. ₅

¡Ah!, pero no se olviden del jabón; el baño sin jabón no es baño.

La familia de Juan se baña todos los días. ☐or
eso, todos son sanos. ₁₉

☐uatemala tiene miles de ríos como
₈
éste.

Juan and his family should migrate to the city. Instead, it portrays them as a rural and potentially Indigenous family who, through careful hygiene, can maintain good health and have the energy to positively contribute to the nation. They are capable of socially integrating into the nation without complete assimilation; through them, the state acknowledged the possibility that families like Juan's can be both Guatemalan and Indigenous.

Not only do Juan's personal hygiene habits qualify him as a modern citizen but his economic activities also reach the state's high standard of participating in the market and point to the state's erroneous assumption that this was a novel practice.[83] Through his hard work, he meets his family's subsistence needs and cultivates excess crops to sell at market, transporting these with a cart, not his own body.[84] In doing so, he debunks racialized stereotypes that Indigenous people were "incapable of entrepreneurial spirit."[85] Juana, however, does not participate in capitalist economic activities but remains relegated to the domestic sphere, where she proudly keeps her home clean and orderly, prepares delicious food, and regularly washes the family's clothes.[86] The primer remarks that when she does leave the home, she and Juan always travel together, indicating that this pattern of behavior is respectful, proper, and admirable.[87] The primer does not mention the children partaking in any economic activities, suggesting that they attend school and do not need to contribute to familial labor or income. Both Juana's and the children's lack of economic activity do not match the reality that scholars have documented in rural Guatemala, where women and children played crucial parts in accruing familial income.[88] Instead, their family is highly patriarchal, with Juan providing for the family economically and serving as the bridge to the community while Juana remains at home dutifully supporting her husband's activities. These defined gender roles indicate that the revolutionary state positioned the nuclear family unit with a male head of household as the ideal social unit. This male leader would participate in the national economy, vote in elections, and obtain resources outside the home, while the female would serve her family and by extension, her country, through maintaining an orderly, healthy, and virtuous home. Even with the social changes that the Revolution introduced, individuals still had an expected place and role to play.

Beyond being economically productive, Juan's behavior symbolizes the types of virtues that the revolutionary state wished to see exhibited in all rural Indigenous citizens. Juan never drinks liquor, nor does he engage in other social vices, challenging a long-held stereotype that Indigenous people were by nature alcoholics.[89] Juan's reputation for honesty has gained him the respect of the community. He represents a younger generation of modern leaders who are formally educated, as opposed to traditional authorities who ascended the cargo system. As the primer indicates, the times were changing in Guatemala, and Juan was a central part of that change in his town.

The primer emphasizes that Juan faithfully serves not just his community but, perhaps more importantly, his country. He loves his country and knows its geography even though he has never traveled beyond his department's confines. He recognizes that the government needs the help of each of its citizens to strengthen the nation, so Juan dutifully commits his time and resources to public projects, such as construction of hospitals and roads. He pays his taxes with great joy and enthusiastically collaborates with local officials in order to maintain "the peace, tranquility and harmony between all Guatemalans." Most importantly, Juan participates in and loves democracy. The primers never indicate Juan's political affiliation, but they do state that he enthusiastically votes for and supports candidates he believes will improve Guatemala. As the book section concludes, it reiterates that Juan is the ideal modern Indigenous citizen, conveying that "sons like Juan are the pride of Guatemala."[90]

Juan Chapín represents the "permitted Indian," illustrating the behaviors that Guatemalan state builders wished to see the Indigenous population adopt and the ways that Indigenous people could "de-Indianize" and thus improve their status without shedding their ethnic identity. He knows his place within Guatemalan society, and he happily accepts it. It is important to also recognize what behaviors Juan does *not* exhibit, as these represent his opposite, the "prohibited Indian." Juan votes, but he never holds office nor does he have any aspirations to do so. He does not challenge existing legislation nor does he try to change the status quo. He participates in the market economy and spends his earnings on consumer goods, and he does not participate in economic exchanges outside of the cash economy, thus disrupting other co-existing economic systems and relationships. Juan practices hygiene habits and medical treatments that correspond with those that the Ministry of Public Health advocated, instead of refusing these changes and continuing to utilize local healers and remedies. While he is more economically stable, his social mobility is limited to his small town, where he is a modest farmer. For the Guatemalan elite, creating citizens like Juan was ideal; theoretically, it facilitated a significant base of support for the current political regime and expanded Guatemala's economy. However, it would not significantly alter existing hierarchies or remove power from those who currently enjoyed it. In practice, and as the next chapter will discuss, Indigenous people did not readily accept the permitted Indian model and instead used opportunities that state development efforts accorded to pursue their own interests and preserve practices they deemed important.

Conclusion

When the 1945 Constitution extended suffrage rights to all Indigenous males over the age of eighteen and to literate females, Guatemalan state builders immediately recognized the need to first understand and then be able to conveniently categorize and transform the Indigenous population into modern citizens. The IING's primary objective was to provide carefully researched studies of Indigenous people and places. To facilitate this undertaking, the IING hired Indigenous bilingual schoolteachers as ethnographers who prepared the type of information that policy makers wanted to know but also emphasized ways that the state had failed to provide for rural Indigenous communities.

While the IING worked to make the diverse Indigenous population legible to state builders, Indigenous people now equipped with voting rights presented a serious challenge to Guatemala's elite, as the expression of citizenship rights could potentially alter societal hierarchies. The democratic participation of Indigenous people certainly could challenge the status quo because it permitted the possibility of the election of new power brokers to political office. However, the permitted Indian model as detailed through literacy campaigns sought to structure this participation in a way more palatable to the elite because it clearly defined the acceptable attitudes and behaviors of Indigenous citizens. Further, this model did not threaten the agro-export economy but rather required Indigenous people to continue modest livelihoods and depend on state-provided resources, leaving it in the hands of political elite to determine what kinds of opportunities for socioeconomic improvement to extend into the countryside. However, as the chapter's opening anecdote detailed, Indigenous Guatemalans' actions revealed the fictitious nature of the "permitted Indian," as they did not passively accept outside intervention but rather expressed concern about how the Revolution would reshape their relationship to the state and their daily lives. They understood these changes as challenges to navigate, potential opportunities to seize, and as threats to mitigate. The next chapter elucidates examples of Revolution-era community development initiatives that intended beneficiaries actively shaped through their actions.

CHAPTER THREE

Hen Houses and Hectares
Making Productive Citizens, 1951–1956

Due to their proximity to the national capital, Kaqchikel Maya citizens in Magdalena Milpas Altas regularly dealt with outsiders coming to their town, and this was no exception during the Revolution. Macario Pérez recalled that when "the men" brought DDT to treat homes and people, he felt it benefited the town because it "even killed all the lice on the women's heads." Accordingly, "he said thank you and was very grateful" but others, whom he called ignorant, did not allow their homes—or themselves—to be sprayed.[1] Mariano Bautista remembered when an IING ethnographer visited the town while residents were dealing with a rat infestation and suggested that they store their corn by hanging it in its husks, rather than dehusking and stacking it. Bautista appreciated the visit but found the advice impractical, as their homes were too small to store corn in this new fashion. Plus, rats could climb and still access the corn, thus not eliminating the problem.[2] And while villagers did show up to view the U.S.-produced Walt Disney educational films that the cultural missions circulated, they did not praise all aspects of the content. For example, Ignacio López enjoyed the film about vaccinations but did not trust the one about hens because it used accelerated recording to show hens rapidly laying eggs, a feat he believed to be impossible. Augustín Zamora did like the hen film but found the one on corn impractical, because while the use of mechanized agriculture functioned well on corn plantations in the United States, he reasoned, it would "never be good for Magdalena, because the land is much too mountainess [*sic*]."[3] Each of these anecdotes reveals different types of development interventions—public health and sanitation, agricultural, and cultural—and each also emphasizes how magdaleños thoughtfully engaged with these interventions, accepting programs and suggestions that resonated with them while rejecting others.

It is tempting to read these episodes as novel, as moments when a progressive government looked to the countryside with a benevolent but paternalistic eye, viewing people and places as key repositories of national wealth if properly guided by outside mediation. And while midcentury development initiatives did reshape Guatemala, we would be mistaken to conclude that these development programs presented clear and neat ruptures with past relations of racist exploitation. And we would be wrong to assume that Indigenous Guatemalans viewed them as part of a linear historical narrative or to extract these twentieth-century moments of intervention from a deeper historical context of contact and conflict with outsiders.[4]

Take, for example, the story of the Spanish conquest that a carpenter named Narcicio Lobos from nearby Santo Tomás Milpas Altas told anthropology student Raymond Amir in 1951. According to Lobos, when the Spaniards arrived to what is present-day Guatemala and Central America, only people he called *Jicaques* lived there. They fought the Spanish by putting "poisoned sticks" in the paths, and they hid on Volcano Fuego and shot flaming arrows dipped in sulfur at the Spaniards, allowing them to kill and capture several. The Jicaques were cannibals, according to Lobos, and they skewed the captured Spaniards by "passing the spit through the mouth and anus," then roasted and ate them one by one, causing the Spanish commander to request permission to return to his king and insist that the Spanish immediately vacate the region. The Jicaques agreed, but the king of Spain instead responded by sending more men "with machines" who defeated the Jicaques, made some into "*salchicho*" (sausage), and initiated the "time of *esclavitu* [*sic*]" (slavery). Pointing in the direction of nearby Antigua, the colonial capital, Lobos informed Amir that the reason so many good buildings still existed from this period was because of the forced labor of the Jicaques, who he emphasized were not protected by any labor laws. Lobos ended the story by recounting how priests arrived soon thereafter and "civilized" the Jicaques by providing them with "clothes, soap, combs, [and] mirrors."[5]

First, Lobos refers to inhabitants of the valley of Guatemala as Jicaques. Though the present-day Jicaque People reside in Honduras, the term "Jicaque" seems to be one that Nahua interpreters in the early colonial period used to describe a region's "former inhabitants" and thus "applied to the people upon whom the Mexican colonists [referring to the Spaniards' Native allies] were encroaching or whom the newly arrived Spaniards were conquering."[6] Both Pedro and Jorge de Alvarado relied on Native allies during their campaigns against the K'iche', Kaqchikel, and Poqomam Maya during the early sixteenth century, and many of these Indigenous allies settled in the Valley of Guatemala near the colonial capital.[7] Perhaps Lobos used this term to distinguish himself from the people that used to reside in the region, or perhaps he employed the term as it was used in the late colonial period, to refer to "all non-Christian Indians."[8] At any rate, his retelling emphasized aspects that appear in pictorial accounts, such as the *Lienzo de Quauhquechollan*, and he portrayed the eventual Spanish occupation as arduous, violent, and ongoing, as evidenced through the infrastructure. Blending the forced labor of the colonial period with the recently passed 1947 Labor Code, Lobos's account portrays exploitative labor conditions as both past and present, indirectly pointing hopefully toward a better future with some protection against maltreatment. For our purposes, his discussion of the Jicaques' mixed reactions to outside intervention illuminates contemporary challenges that development practitioners faced in the region. It emphasizes a longer and ongoing history of intrusions of various scales, portraying recipients as anything but passive and easily malleable. In his narrative, some efforts, like the priests' introduction of clothing, were accepted, while others were violently rejected. Jicaques—and mid-twentieth-century Indigenous Guatemalans—drew on ancestral knowledge and experience to carefully consider and engage with development efforts.

In the early 1950s, official indigenista efforts proved to be an essential link between the state and rural Indigenous communities. Indigenismo functioned as a tool of social engineering, as it helped craft the permitted Indian model as evidenced through the character of Juan Chapín (discussed in the previous chapter), an active and patriotic citizen who proudly identified as Guatemalan and worked to serve his country through his everyday actions. As the second government of the Revolution under President Jacobo Arbenz prioritized the capitalist development of the countryside, efforts such as a nutrition program and the agrarian reform supported this agenda.[9] In tracing the local histories of these two initiatives, this chapter argues that, like the Jicaques in Lobos's narrative, Indigenous people did not enthusiastically accept all programs nor did they have a unified response to these development efforts, despite the state's characterization of them as a singular entity. Their varied responses shaped the efficacy of state-sponsored projects and reveal important, and often minimized, local histories of engagement with outside efforts to mold them into model citizens and "permitted Indians" according to top-down international development plans, which the next section details.

Planning Development during the Second Revolutionary Government

From May 1950 to August 1951, University of Saskatchewan economics professor Dr. George E. Britnell led an International Bank for Reconstruction and Development (IBRD) mission to Guatemala at the invitation of President

Arévalo to analyze the comparative advantages and the weaknesses in the Guatemalan economy.[10] In a letter that accompanied the final report he submitted to IBRD president Eugene R. Black, Britnell remarked how well received he and his team had been by Guatemalan officials and expressed his hope that "our Report will contribute, in some measure at least, to the further development of the Guatemalan economy and the improvement of the living standards of the Guatemalan people."[11] In the report itself, Britnell called for increased agricultural production and improved highway networks throughout the country, and he remained optimistic that Guatemala could overcome what he called its "underdeveloped economy."[12] In fact, in a conference presentation that he gave at the American Economic Association's meeting in 1953, Britnell proclaimed that a "Brave New World is well on its way to Guatemala."[13]

However, Britnell also cautioned that one crucial obstacle could hinder Guatemala's ability to improve economic conditions—nationalism. In this conference paper, which was subsequently published in the organizational journal, he argued that Guatemalan nationalism was "inflamed by the arrogance of North American capitalism and fanned by a well-entrenched local communist movement."[14] While the IBRD report never mentioned the word "nationalism" or "communism," clearly Britnell shared the same concern that the U.S. State Department had with regard to local politics in Guatemala, as CIA and State Department officials began corresponding as early as 1952 about supporting an armed overthrow of the Arbenz government and its supposed communist infiltrators.[15] While both Britnell and the U.S. government certainly wished to see Guatemalan standards of living improve and the economy grow, they only desired a version of development compatible with their own understandings of modernization and progress.

Specifically concerning the Indigenous population, Britnell wrote that the "cultural isolation and defensive attitude of the Indians" was certainly justified given the legacies of colonialism and continued discrimination into the present. However, this isolation posed a significant problem for Guatemalan development, one that the state needed to immediately address.[16] Clearly, the revolutionary governments agreed through their continued support of the IING's work. During the administration of Juan José Arévalo, the IING fulfilled its investigative role by surveying numerous Indigenous communities, studying various definitions of "the Indian," and ultimately, helping the state craft the model for the ideal modern Indigenous citizen, the "permitted Indian." The second government of the Revolution, under President Jacobo Arbenz, focused on improving economic production, particularly in rural regions. These efforts were multifaceted, as the government sought to improve immediate issues like per capita income and public health concerns while also addressing structural inequality, such as land tenure patterns.

The second presidential elections of the Revolution were held in November 1950, and a peaceful transition from Arévalo to Arbenz took place, though not without controversy and amid increased political polarization.[17] In terms of national development, what Arbenz envisioned was not all that different from what Britnell proposed in his official IBRD report. His administration also pointed to continued exploitative and unequal economic relationships that prevented Guatemala's poor majority from productively contributing to the nation as a key obstacle to economic progress and national identity formation. Development projects in the Arbenz era sought to create a new rural middle class that could produce for the national and international market *and* become consumers that would support national industry. Unlike the Britnell report, which identified Indigenous people as obstacles to progress, the Arbenz regime saw them as the country's greatest resource and as potentially a key set of producers and consumers for the nation.

Nutrition and Communism in Magdalena Milpas Altas

Across twentieth-century Latin America, revolutionaries linked citizenship with nutrition and economic productivity, believing that only healthy citizens could fortify the nation.[18] The belief that a government should actively invest in improving nutrition and health echoed throughout the world and increasingly became framed in the Cold War language of anti-communism, democracy, and modernization. What transpired in this moment was "an emergence of a worldview in which hunger and poverty were no longer seen as the universal human condition but as a danger to international stability."[19] With better nourishment, development experts and politicians reasoned, the individual could work harder and longer, thus increasing one's capacity for economic production. Then, with increased wages, individuals could improve their standard of living and participate as active consumers in the national capitalist economy. By improving their material conditions in this way people would theoretically be less likely to seek nondemocratic, noncapitalist political alternatives, instead facilitating stability and modernization.[20] Development experts like Britnell, Guatemalan state officials, and U.S. diplomats adopted this mentality and hoped that better nutrition would create conditions where rural workers had more energy to participate actively in the national market economy. Through nutrition programs, this conglomeration of state and private actors, as well as their intended recipients, created new knowledge and new relations and forms of power.[21]

The revolutionary state's focus on nutrition did not escape the purview of the IING. At the time, the Smithsonian Institution had an exchange program that sent U.S. anthropologists to Latin American countries at their request to help train social scientists in anthropological methods. Upon being named Guatemalan ambassador to the United States in December 1949, Goubaud (the former IING director) requested an anthropologist for Guatemala, and the Smithsonian hired recent Yale doctoral graduate Richard Adams for this job. Even after the Smithsonian contract ended in 1951 and Goubaud's untimely and mysterious death in 1951, Adams remained in Guatemala and continued his close collaboration with the IING.[22]

The IING and Adams also partnered with the relatively new Nutrition Institute of Central America and Panama (INCAP). Founded in 1946 by Central American delegates to the Third Inter-American Conference on Agriculture in Caracas, Venezuela, the INCAP maintained the institutional goal of defining and researching the region's predominant nutrition and health problems and developing solutions to combat these issues.[23] The INCAP, headquartered in Guatemala City, was officially inaugurated on September 15, 1949. With funding from member nations and the Kellogg Foundation, it sent Central American doctors and scientists to U.S. universities, notably Harvard and Massachusetts Institute of Technology, to receive nutrition training.[24] At the same time, the INCAP began conducting fieldwork in rural communities, and with this research, scientists hoped to identify nutritional insufficiencies and create programs to combat rural malnutrition. In sum, the making of health and nutrition standards in Guatemala involved collaboration between local, national, and international actors and entities.[25]

In May 1950, the INCAP began working in Magdalena Milpas Altas, a town and municipal center of 1,092 people located eighteen miles west of Guatemala City in the department of Sacatepéquez. Ninety-two percent of magdaleños (residents of Magdalena Milpas Altas) were Kaqchikel Maya, but its two aldeas, or villages outside the municipal center, were more divided; Buena Vista was 70 percent Kaqchikel and San Miguel Milpas Altas was entirely ladino.[26] Most residents engaged in small-scale agriculture and owned small plots of land, ranging from ten to thirty *cuerdas* (roughly one to three acres). Some supplemented this income with seasonal labor on coastal plantations, and magdaleños regularly participated in regional markets.[27] As noted in this chapter's opening, this was not an isolated or insular community but rather one marked by mobility and interaction with nearby urban centers.

Initially, the INCAP tried to collect biological samples like blood and to start a school lunch program, but magdaleños resisted these efforts, a tendency that historians have also noted occurred contemporaneously in Mexico.[28] Adams led a small team of ethnographers that included Berkeley anthropology student Raymond Amir, Betty Hannstein (a German-Guatemalan woman and Adams's fiancé), INCAP staff members Berta Pineda and Ana Díaz, and IING ethnographer Rosalio Saquic (K'iche'). Once fieldwork began, these ethnographers recognized that the INCAP staff's actions had unintentionally violated cultural beliefs about the body and blood and fueled local rumors about child theft and cannibalism. These ethnographers created an extensive corpus of field notes, relaying their daily activities, conversations with local informants, and observations about Magdalena. While we must remain mindful that all local voices are mediated through these ethnographers, these notes do provide an avenue for accessing Indigenous voices and perspectives as magdaleños navigated the arrival of the INCAP and, more broadly, the revolutionary moment in Guatemala. These field notes are replete with examples of informants invoking various explanations for rejecting INCAP efforts.[29] For example, Saquic recorded in late April 1951 that some mothers from Magdalena traveled to Antigua to consult ladinas there about INCAP's lunch programs (he recorded no additional information about who these ladinas were) and some fathers called upon the departmental governor, as they feared that INCAP doctors only wanted to fatten kids up and then sell them for consumption in the United States. In both instances, their fears were assuaged, and Saquic notes that many began to participate after these reassurances.[30] From these actions, we might surmise that magdaleños at least respected the opinion of governmental authorities and other outsiders with whom they likely had long-term relationships, like the trusted ladinas in Antigua.[31] Eventually, INCAP programs saw more success, although resistance and controversy continued over the cultural meanings associated with projects or the political implications these projects unintentionally embodied.

As discussed in this chapter's introduction, Jacobo Arbenz had just been elected president, defeating opposition candidate Miguel Ydígoras Fuentes in November 1950, and at the local level, Magdalena's elections for mayor (alcalde) were scheduled for November 1951. Thus, the INCAP entered Magdalena amid an increasingly polarized political scene. Early on, Adams and his team became aware of a local division that was spatially articulated and that the 1950 elections had greatly exacerbated and politicized. Magdalena had two main neighborhoods, which ethnographers referred to as *arriba* (above) and *abajo* (below). According to various informants, everyone living arriba was Catholic and all leaders in the local *cofradías* (religious societies) came from arriba while the abajo neighborhood had a mix of Catholics and Evangelicals.[32]

Arriba residents used Kaqchikel more widely than abajo, and one informant, Vicente Rivera, told Adams that some people arriba did not understand "castillo," referring to Spanish. Santiago López also informed Adams that the abajo women wore Western blouses while those arriba used huipils.[33] While magdaleños and the ethnographers seemed to suggest that residents arriba maintained Indigenous cultural practices more than those from abajo, they did not allude to any clear class divisions between the neighborhoods, nor did they suggest that one living abajo ceased to be Indigenous. And, since the 1950 elections, this spatial divide also defined political affiliation, as those from abajo were largely *arbencistas* because they supported Jacobo Arbenz and the *Partido Acción Revolucionario* (Party of Revolutionary Action, PAR) and those from arriba tended to be *ydigoristas*, backing Miguel Ydígoras and his *Partido de Unificación Anticomunista* (Party of Anticommunist Unification, PUAC).[34]

Much debate appears in the field notes over local uses and meanings of the label "communist." It served as a convenient insult for one's rivals and fueled existing divisions. For example, Adams detailed one occasion when an arbencista man referred to the ydigoristas as communists, ironic as Ydígoras was the right-wing candidate. This man had even named his pig General after Miguel Ydígoras to further insult the opposition candidate.[35] Adams's documentation of the deployment of the term "comunista" demonstrates how magdaleños utilized the language of national and international politics to pursue their own agendas at the local level, and, as it turns out, to navigate the INCAP's intervention in their town.

The field notes make clear that magdaleños on both sides of the division viewed communism as a negative, foreign intrusion that provoked insecurity. In one conversation with ydigorista Macario Pérez, Adams noted that he praised the authoritarian military regime of Ubico from the 1930s because of its strict disciplinary laws, stating (as recounted by Adams) that "people need that, to be dominated" and likened it to Ydígoras's political platform.[36] Historian David Carey Jr. found a similar sentiment in his oral histories in Chimaltenango, namely, that despite Ubico's discriminatory laws that perpetuated regimes of forced Indigenous labor, some Kaqchikels preferred a recognizable system of domination over one with more uncertainty, changing norms, and unpredictability.[37] Pérez—and perhaps other ydigorista magdaleños—felt similarly.

In Adams's field notes, three themes recur that pertain to the uses of the term "comunismo": religion, family, and property. For example, residents, especially Catholics, tended to equate religious adherence with anti-communism, as they believed that communism did not allow for belief in God.[38] Many magdaleños also thought that communists opposed the family unit and threatened the decency of women. María Mixtun told Hannstein that she believed the communists were foreign men who would take the town's girls away and mistreat them.[39] Ricardo Escobar also alluded to sexual violence, asserting that "women would become free game . . . a man's wife would become available to anyone."[40] Macario Pérez even told Adams that there was a man in town who reportedly had children by his daughter; Pérez concluded that this man must be a communist because he neither respected his family nor the laws of God.[41] Not only did communism supposedly threaten his religion and family but Eulogio Martínez told Adams that he understood communists to also be against private property, so he feared they would seize his land, house, belongings, and clothing.[42] Though different informants emphasized various components of their definition of communism, likely due to the context of the conversation, what is consistent in all these explanations is the idea of communism as ushering in a period of instability and danger that would threaten the town's social structures. We should not dismiss these various interpretations of communism as ignorant or provincial. They are neither. Rather, we must seriously analyze how they feature within a longer history of awareness of international political changes and tensions and careful negotiation with new intrusions, all for the sake of maintaining individual social status and collective autonomies.

Many magdaleños also seemed to believe, at least initially, that INCAP staff were communists. They thought that the ethnographers were gathering information about household demographics, cultivation patterns, and land tenure to "have accurate facts (*los datos cabales*) about the town and turn these over to their communist companions."[43] Thus, when magdaleños began to hear the unfounded rumor from nearby towns that INCAP workers were communists who had infiltrated Magdalena, they were appalled and worried about their town's future and their reputation. Raymundo Velásquez reported to Adams that people in Antigua said INCAP was communist and was trying to win Magdalena over to the cause.[44] Socorro Hernández also reported to Adams that the nearby towns of Santa Lucía Milpas Altas and Santo Tomás Milpas Altas were embargoing Magdalena due to its alleged communist affiliation.[45]

Collectively, magdaleños worked to amend their reputation. Saquic noted a conversation in late July 1951 among several magdaleño men where they collectively decided not to allow any "communist propagandizers" to come to Magdalena and were willing to violently prevent their entry, if necessary, preferring death to a communist takeover.[46] Just a few weeks later, around 200 residents from both neighborhoods, Catholics and Evangelicals, traveled in five trucks to attend an anti-communist rally in Antigua to showcase Magdalena's anti-communism to the rest of Sacatepéquez.[47] Socorro Hernández, a father of a child in the school lunch program, even approached nutritionist Ana Díaz at a party and, referencing the departmental capital, remarked, "The people of La Antigua are saying: 'Poor Magdalena, the gringos have entered there, now there are communists there.'" Surprised that anyone would associate U.S. Americans with communism, Díaz reminded Hernández of the newspaper reports that explained how "the gringos are fighting with the Russians because they don't want Russian communism, because of this there's war, so they [the gringos] aren't communists."[48] Though the record does not indicate who the architect of these rumors was nor why they were created, their deployment allows us to consider why certain rumors gained widespread credibility and to what effects.[49] It is clear that these rumors widely circulated throughout Sacatepéquez and affected the credibility and efficacy of the INCAP and damaged Magdalena's reputation. This also points to a hesitation on the part of many rural and Indigenous Guatemalans to accept the revolutionary government's message of inclusion and programs intended to foster rural development, a trend that Carey Jr. also noted in other Kaqchikel regions.[50]

This accusation of communism certainly played a role in the nutrition program despite INCAP personnel's ability to persuade many magdaleños that they were not communist, and the INCAP's presence continued to exacerbate political divisions. When women from abajo began helping with food preparation for INCAP's school lunch program, families from arriba refused to participate.[51] Similarly, when INCAP wanted to sponsor the construction of a hen house to provide the town with eggs as a source of protein, ydigoristas from arriba threatened arbencistas from abajo who supported the project. Antonio Pérez, an arbencista from abajo, explained that ydigoristas refused to support the project because, from their perspective, it was a gift from the president, whom they deemed to be communist. These ydigoristas interpreted the hen house as a clientelistic gift from Arbenz for his supporters in Magdalena; as members of the opposition party, they could not be involved in the project nor reap its benefits. From their perspective, doing so would violate their commitment to the opposition party and enter them into a social contract with President Arbenz. Pérez insisted that he tried to convince ydigoristas that they no longer should think in terms of political parties, that this "was only for the elections, that now there is a President and we should now work together for the good of the town." INCAP workers attempted to foster collaboration by circulating a volunteer sign-up list to encourage ydigoristas to help, either financially or with labor or building materials, but to no avail.[52]

However, the ethnography team's field notes reveal a more complex picture about why magdaleños hesitated to support the hen house. INCAP, recognizing the town's division, asked community members to form a hen house committee, comprised of men from both neighborhoods, and magdaleños complied.[53] However, problems arose once the committee began creating tangible construction plans. Although residents had expressed willingness to the committee to give two days' labor, Saquic later reported that many resented this request, noting that they felt behind in their own work and were concerned about the free labor that the INCAP was requesting for a project that they were not enthusiastic about in the first place.[54]

Then, problems arose between the committee and the mayor's office when the committee requested permission to cut down an additional tree for lumber for the project. Apparently, the mayor and on-duty village official—both arbencistas—were drunk and angrily denied the committee's request and verbally insulted committee members. One member challenged this ruling and asserted that in 1945, when he was a municipal employee, he had even given the seeds for the tree that they were requesting. Then, a physical fight broke out in the courthouse hallway, and several committee members immediately resigned.[55] In the aftermath, Gregorio Lobo García told Saquic that many residents felt INCAP had caused significant problems and complained that the program was always wanting to start new projects without finishing ongoing ones. It always requested collaboration from the town, leaving magdaleños wondering what INCAP would next demand of them.[56] For two weeks in August 1951, the hen house's future seemed jeopardized, and residents paused all work on the project.

INCAP staff member Ana Díaz recorded individual conversations she had with committee members during these two weeks, as she tried to salvage the hen house project. Municipal officials apologized for their poor behavior, blaming their inebriation, and they agreed to allow the committee to cut an additional tree for lumber. Committee member Alberto Bautista asked other members to forgive the officials for their bad behavior and not let this unfortunate episode prevent Magdalena from acquiring a valuable community resource.[57] After two meetings with the municipal officials and committee members, INCAP staff convinced all but one of the original members to rejoin and continue the project.[58]

While this resolved the issue of reorganizing the committee, the hen house remained controversial, and residents seemed concerned with the project's monetary costs. In early September, committee member Raymundo Velásquez told Díaz that one member was resistant to the request to contribute Q2 toward covering carpentry costs. Others worried that committee members would have to continue paying the maintenance costs even after construction finished, so Velásquez had suggested that the project utilize fewer chickens to keep expenses lower.[59] Some expressed concern over who would pay to feed the chickens, noting that "51 chickens' corn would cost $11.00 every 20 days."[60] It appears that the INCAP was insensitive to the economic burden that the project placed on the community and was unwilling to continue supporting the project beyond some of its initial costs.[61]

As the mayoral elections neared, political tensions escalated to the point that some ydigoristas reportedly levied death threats against arbencistas. As discussed, this division predated the INCAP and the hen house, but both became embedded and manifested these deeper and historical tensions. In November, the departmental governor of Sacatepéquez visited Magdalena to end the dispute. Upon his arrival, Magdalena's mayor, an arbencista, denounced all the ydigorista PUAC members to the governor, using this hen house debate as an opportunity to weaken his political rivals' relationship with the higher authority and perhaps exact revenge on those who publicly humiliated him after his inebriated attack on the hen house committee. The governor admonished the ydigoristas, even declaring that they had illegally formed their political party. Various informants did tell the INCAP ethnographers that the ydigorista mayoral candidate, Cipriano Sas, had failed to turn in the correct paperwork to register for the election, and Magdalena's PAR mayor did not inform him of this failing, so Sas was ineligible to run.[62] Sas had also reportedly been jailed the previous year for spreading ydigorista propaganda, so he was clearly a political rival of the current mayor and perhaps also of the governor.[63] In response to the governor's rebuke, the ydigoristas feigned ignorance, stating that they had no idea that their party was against the government. While they had supported Ydígoras, they claimed to now fully back "our government" and pled ignorance if their actions had led the governor to think otherwise. They claimed to be "ignorant" and "misinformed" and emphatically declared that they would never intentionally thwart a state project. The only reason, according to the ydigoristas, that they maintained their political party was to "defend their religion . . . defend the Church." The governor told them that a commitment to the Church was not related to a political party and with that pronouncement he suspended Magdalena's PUAC chapter.[64]

These chastised ydigoristas employed a common stereotype of Indigenous ignorance and used it as their defense in the face of punishment from regional authorities. Playing on the idea of the premodern, undeveloped subject, ydigorista magdaleños insisted that was precisely what they were and why they could not be held accountable for their actions.[65] On election day, many ydigoristas cast null votes as their candidate was not allowed to run, begrudgingly participating in electoral proceedings while still expressing their opposition.[66]

Clearly, they were anything but unaware. Magdaleños had utilized the new voting rights they received under the Arévalo government to build important local networks, and some did accept INCAP assistance. Yet they also made strategic decisions about when participation would improve their lives and their local position of power and when it would not, and they felt no obligation to the state to readily accept all aspects of outside intervention. As this example demonstrates, during the Revolution and against the backdrop of the Cold War, even everyday actions such as whether to support a local hen house were deeply politicized, and people recognized this and acted accordingly.[67] Magdaleños knew the political language of the time, and even if they did not fully understand the ideology of communism, they recognized the controversy and significance behind leveraging this term. They did not interpret development efforts as a sure way to bring economic prosperity nor did they pliably adopt the behaviors and mentalities of the permitted Indian model; rather, they interpreted them within a localized context of power structures and cultural meanings. In order to justify their actions to outsiders, they used international political discourse to frame local politics and their responses to development efforts and, in so doing, helped shape the successes, and failures, of these projects.

In the end, the INCAP did construct the hen house next to the municipal building in Magdalena. However, it was largely a failure. Instead of distributing the eggs to community members, the committee sold them. Several chickens died, and in general, Hannstein noted a general lack of enthusiasm for the project in June 1952.[68] Still, in February 1953, Díaz noted that the project "was proceeding" and that the yard had been fenced and that they had borrowed chickens from Xenacoj, suggesting that perhaps the INCAP restarted the project in 1953 after its first failed attempt.[69]

The school lunch program continued to meet resistance as well. On one instance in February 1952, schoolboys told Hannstein that they were not participating because they believed INCAP staff wanted to fatten them up, then draw their blood and sell it. When Hannstein challenged the veracity of these

rumors, one boy reportedly said, "We are no lyers [*sic*], we are 'Magdaleños,' and we don't need the strangers. 'Que vive Magdalena' (long live Magdalena)."[70] By June 1952, however, the INCAP seemed to fade from public
scrutiny as magdaleños had a new point of political discussion: the agrarian
reform.

Magdaleños occasionally engaged with INCAP staff about the agrarian reform. Though we must recognize the incomplete nature of the archive, the
mediation of local voices through the ethnographer, and the unequal power
relations inherent in these relationships, none of the recorded conversations
expressed support for the agrarian reform. In fact, Calixto Pérez claimed that
everyone in Magdalena was against the law "except the most poor ones and
the drunkers [*sic*]."[71] Eulogio Martínez commented that it was natural for
there to be rich and poor and that a government should not alter this. Employing racialized stereotypes, he asserted that he and his neighbors, as Indigenous people, were physical workers; in contrast, "there are other men, they
don't have the courage to work with the hoe or in rain and mud." Magdaleños
were "wealthy in health . . . and are satisfied in that."[72]

Others remarked on the uncertainty they felt the law introduced into society. Alberto Pérez emphasized economic issues, claiming that the law would
cause wealthy landowners to store their crops in order to drive up prices of
commodities like sugar, corn, and coffee, allowing them to later sell at higher
prices.[73] Juan Velásquez told Díaz that he did not like the uncertainty of the
law nor the insecurity of the general political situation. He preferred the old
system of renting land to cultivate his family's food commodities because he
felt certain that he would be able to make ends meet in this way.[74] Later, commenting on an expropriation that took place nearby on Finca Bárcenas, Ignacio
López told Díaz that the recipients from Buena Vista had "become real slaves."
In addition to receiving land, they also accepted loans of Q100 for cultivation
costs, which he claimed they instead spent on fine clothing and liquor during
Magdalena's annual festival. He reasoned that without this money, they would
not be able to cultivate their land, so the government would seize their land,
leaving them once again landless and now indebted. Díaz (or Hannstein, who
often typed up the field notes) roughly translated López's final comment on the
matter to English, recording that he stated, "It is better to be poor than to have
so much money in the pocket that is not of the [*sic*] own."[75]

These responses debunk notions that rural Guatemalans enthusiastically
accepted a law intended for their benefit. Perhaps this was because many
magdaleños did own some land and feared its expropriation or believed
redistribution to be unfair. Maybe residents did not wish to damage their

reputation again, or perhaps many found the opposition's propaganda convincing. What is clear, as this chapter's opening anecdote elucidates, is that some magdaleños found development efforts like INCAP programs and state-sponsored land reform to be a part of the same historical pattern of outside intervention and thus hesitated to quickly accept it, despite its alluring promises. They also knew how to deploy the "language of power" to pursue their goals.[76] The next section zooms out from our close analysis of Magdalena to first situate the passage of the agrarian reform within the context of indigenista efforts and international development experts' visions for Guatemala, then it will zoom back in to the departmental level of Sacatepéquez, a department where the IING was most active during the Revolution.

Indigenista Involvement in the Agrarian Reform

While the IING became involved in public health efforts, it also indirectly supported the state's efforts at agricultural modernization and reform. Joaquín Noval was director of the IING during the Arbenz administration. He was born in 1922 and raised in Ayutla, Guatemala, a town on Guatemala's western border with Mexico, and he migrated to Guatemala City in the 1930s to pursue his education.[77] Though he dropped out of school before completing the equivalent of high school, his intellectual curiosity did not waver, and he read widely, particularly Marxist and anthropological literature. He also became a prolific writer.[78] He was not directly involved in the 1944 October Revolution but enthusiastically supported the revolutionary governments.

Noval began working in the IING's fieldwork division in 1948, which brought him into close contact with rural communities.[79] He understood the inequalities he saw facing Indigenous populations mostly as a question of class, though he did not reduce Indigeneity to a class identity.[80] For Noval, the Indigenous populations' precarious economic situation was based on three aspects: shortage of accessible land, low agricultural salaries, and difficulty in gaining employment in the nonagrarian sector. Arguing that the Indigenous populations and regional markets were critical elements of the national and international economy, what he believed Guatemala needed most were programs aimed at improving economic stability, not just alleviation of social ills like illiteracy.[81]

Starting in the late 1940s, the IING conducted studies of land tenure patterns, seasonal migration, and rural credit in an effort to guide the state in developing effective rural development programs. In February and March 1949, IING ethnographers analyzed land tenure patterns, visiting 170 predominantly

Indigenous municipalities in thirteen departments. After compiling the data, they determined that 62.9 percent of surveyed families either lacked land altogether or had less than an adequate amount for subsistence farming.[82] The IING reported these results to the *Instituto para el Fomento de Producción* (Institute for Economic Development, INFOP), thus making the administration aware of the pervasiveness of this issue and supporting calls for nationwide agrarian reform.

In 1952, the IING began researching seasonal migration to the coastal plantations, and this effort marked the first time a state institution paid attention to the human cost of this migration instead of simply analyzing gross export statistics. Based on data collected in fifty-two towns, staff estimated that 46,651 people seasonally migrated. The report identified three repeated reasons that individuals and families migrated: lack of land, few economic resources for cultivation, and insufficient harvests, thus necessitating cash to buy additional food. The IING also determined that the Indigenous population suffered the most from internal displacement through migration.[83]

Finally, beginning in 1949, the IING collaborated with the INFOP, the FAO, and the International Organization of Labor's Commission of Experts on Indigenous Labor to research rural credit access in predominantly Indigenous areas, surveying thirty-seven municipalities.[84] This research demonstrated that rural credit was largely inaccessible to Indigenous people and exploitative when available. For example, the monthly interest rates ranged from 35 percent to an incredible 175 percent, with payment demanded every 150 days. Few formal agencies existed, and only 8–9 percent of applicants could get access to credit through private means.[85] Britnell's 1951 report detailed similar findings, concluding, "Agricultural credit for the Indian is practically nonexistent."[86]

No wonder, then, that IING ethnographer Juan de Dios Rosales argued that "bank credit is something unknown and outside the radius of the social life" for Indigenous communities.[87] Rosales argued that ladino discrimination factored into this unequal access to credit. Though Rosales was Kaqchikel Maya, in this article Rosales positioned himself as ladino, perhaps believing that his readership would not pay attention to scholarship written by an Indigenous person. Additionally, Rosales argued that ladinos caused the social problems because "we," the ladinos, assume Indigenous people are obstacles to progress instead of seeing them as "esteemed and valuable elements to mankind (*la estructura humana*)." Rosales's solution was to make rural credit culturally relevant, understandable, and available to Indigenous populations who had never seen it as a viable option.

To accomplish this vision, Rosales recommended that rural bank branches have an anthropologist or sociologist on staff to help mitigate cultural misunderstandings and to train bank staff in aspects of local culture and social networks. He also suggested that bank employees patiently work on an individual basis with applicants to help them complete paperwork and understand repayment schedules.[88] In October 1953, the Arbenz government created the National Agrarian Bank with the explicit goal of providing farmers with affordable credit, and by April 1954, it had approved loans for the equivalent of approximately $6.5 million.[89] It is not clear if the bank heeded Rosales's recommendations, but the sheer number of loans indicate that unlike before, rural credit was more readily accessible and easily understood by Indigenous populations. As these studies demonstrate, the IING helped inform the Arbenz government about rural conditions through its analyses of land tenure patterns, seasonal migration, and rural credit in an effort to foment national development.

Noval and the IING were not alone in suggesting changes in land tenure practices, credit availability, and agricultural modernization but shared these concerns with international entities like the IBRD, as expressed in Britnell's 1951 report. The final report detailed seventy-seven recommendations for the Guatemalan government, including the modernization of agricultural techniques. Specifically, it identified the Indigenous population as isolated and as using "antiquated" cultivation techniques. Although not calling for comprehensive land reform, the report did suggest a reorganization of the national *fincas*, or farms, and a carefully orchestrated coastal colonization program that would voluntarily resettle highland populations to state-owned land along the Pacific Coast.[90] The Arbenz government significantly expanded on these measures from the IBRD report, and the president's speeches articulated his overarching goal of improving Guatemala's economic productivity. The agrarian reform, he claimed, would serve to "distribute these riches so that those who have less—and they are the immense majority—benefit more."[91]

In late 1951, President Arbenz asked leaders of the Communist Party, the *Partido Guatemalteco de Trabajo* (Guatemalan Labor Party, PGT), particularly José Manuel Fortuny, to help him draft the agrarian reform.[92] Noval joined the PGT in 1952 but because he was a junior member, he did not directly help draft the reform. However, he would have made Arbenz aware of the IING's findings, and these studies likely helped the reform's writers understand the reality for rural Indigenous people.[93] Given the PGT's reputation among Guatemalan and U.S. politicians as honest, hard workers who readily engaged with the rural population, the PGT architects of the legislation likely took the IING's findings seriously because of its emphasis on rural realities.[94]

On June 17, 1952, the Arbenz government passed its most controversial piece of social reform legislature: Decree 900, the agrarian reform. The opening sentence of this law clearly cited the goals of the Revolution as they pertained to rural economic development in Guatemala: "One of the fundamental objectives of the October Revolution is the necessity of realizing a necessary and substantial change in property relations and the forms of farming the land, as a means to overcome Guatemala's economic backwardness and sensibly improve the level of life of the large majority of the population."[95] A 1947 Ministry of Agriculture survey had revealed that only 11.8 percent of privately owned land was cultivated and only 20.3 percent served as pastureland. Recognizing that landowners were not efficiently using Guatemala's land, the agrarian reform intended to "inspire both more productive and more equitable agricultural enterprises."[96] It sought not only to expand the number of Guatemalan landowners but also to transform their agricultural methods and daily lives.[97]

Practically, the law approached national fincas and privately owned land differently. Regardless of size, national fincas were to be divided and redistributed as small parcels. In contrast, size and use of land mattered with private holdings. The law dictated that the state could expropriate uncultivated land on private fincas over 672 acres whereas it would only take uncultivated land on fincas between 224 and 672 acres if less than two-thirds of the entire holding was uncultivated. Any finca smaller than 224 acres did not qualify for expropriation.[98] Written into the law were various exceptions intended to promote conservation and agricultural modernization. Thus, land that was considered a forest reserve, had a steep grade, or was utilized for production of essential commodities could receive an exemption.[99] Landowners would receive compensation for any expropriated land through agrarian bonds, with recipients typically obtaining land in lifelong usufruct.[100]

Individuals claimed land through a bottom-up hierarchy of agrarian committees (see figure 3.1). Starting at the local level, individuals filed denunciations with their *Comité Agrario Local* (Local Agrarian Committee, CAL), which in turn completed an investigation and made a recommendation as to whether the disputed land qualified for expropriation. This recommendation passed to the *Comité Agrario Departamental* (Departmental Agrarian Committee, CAD), and depending on the CAD's decision, involved parties could appeal to the highest office, the *Consejo Agrario Nacional* (National Agrarian Council, CAN), the advisory component of the *Departamento Agrario Nacional* (National Agrarian Department, DAN). This hierarchy encouraged

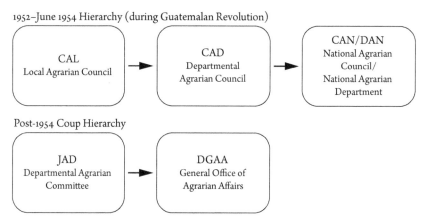

1952–June 1954 Hierarchy (during Guatemalan Revolution)

CAL
Local Agrarian Council

→

CAD
Departmental
Agrarian Council

→

CAN/DAN
National Agrarian
Council/
National Agrarian
Department

Post-1954 Coup Hierarchy

JAD
Departmental Agrarian
Committee

→

DGAA
General Office of
Agrarian Affairs

FIGURE 3.1 Institutional hierarchy of the agrarian reform in the Revolution and Counterrevolution. (Chart prepared by author.)

rural organizing and directly involved potential recipients in the process; nationally, Guatemalans formed over 3,000 CALs.[101] After the 1954 coup, when the counterrevolutionary government began reversing Decree 900 rulings, it used a similar hierarchy, with revocation requests first going to the *Junta Agraria Departamental* (Departmental Agrarian Committee, JAD) and appeals going to the *Dirección General de Asuntos Agrarios* (General Office of Agrarian Issues, DGAA).

Documentation also reveals the ways that individuals deployed different types of identities based on the type of labor relations they had with the finca owner, their membership in a rural community, or their ethnic identity. In this historical moment, Guatemalans appeared to use the overarching category of *campesino* to refer to a member of the rural working class who was generally tied in some way to agricultural activities, and this is how I have used it here. As scholars have argued for elsewhere in Latin America, campesino identity operated independently from ethnicity and increasingly became a politicized identity within revolutionary movements.[102] But within the Decree 900 archival records, individuals also referred to themselves based on the type of labor relation they had with the finca owner, using terms that roughly translate to sharecropper, renter, or wage laborer. It was often these types of different identities that created division among rural people hoping to acquire land through Decree 900, a phenomenon that I and other scholars have analyzed elsewhere.[103] Labor and political organizations such as the PGT and the *Confederación Nacional Campesina de Guatemala* (National Confederation of Guatemalan Campesinos, CNCG) actively visited communities to encourage landless campesinos to file denunciations with their CAL. In the process they often helped local people organize as campesino unions, providing important mechanisms at the local level for pursuing land reform. At the same time, CALs also exacerbated divisions into local communities, as not all members wanted to join these politicized organizations. In this way, campesinos could democratically participate in the Revolution and in the state's goal of extending a nationalist capitalism throughout the countryside.[104]

The effects of the agrarian reform were felt throughout the nation. In fact, President Arbenz declared in early 1953, "There is no family, there is no class, there is no person now in our country, who has not felt, in one form or another . . . the impact that the agrarian question has caused in Guatemala."[105] During the eighteen months that the agrarian reform transpired, agrarian committees approved 794 expropriations for a total of 900,896 acres, with some scholars estimating the expropriated acreage to be higher, closer to 1.4 million acres.[106] Despite this discrepancy, scholars and contemporary diplomats agree that during the years of the agrarian reform, agricultural production in Guatemala improved. An August 1953 U.S. Embassy report indicated that Guatemalan corn production increased 15 percent in 1952. Likewise, it also indicated that "rice and wheat production had increased by 74 percent and 21 percent respectively over 1952, and bean production had remained the same." In 1953–1954, Guatemalans witnessed the second highest coffee harvest in the country's history.[107] A September 1953 educational pamphlet titled *Boletín Agraria* proudly marked the passage of Decree 900 as the date of Guatemala's economic independence, and in early 1954, the country seemed on its way to achieving this goal.[108]

Despite these positive economic impacts, several sectors of Guatemalan society reacted negatively to the agrarian reform program. Affected landowners protested these measures, and as the next section will discuss, they repeatedly protested CAL and CAD decisions. The national leadership of the Catholic Church, particularly Archbishop Mariano Rossell y Arellano, publicly characterized the agrarian reform as a scheme to gain votes and framed it as a communist law incompatible with Christianity, a claim that powerfully resonated with many Indigenous campesinos, as we saw in INCAP's experience in Magdalena.[109] Clemente Marroquín Rojas—congressman, journalist, and staunch antagonist of the Revolution—referred to the agrarian reform as seductive and deemed the government's promises to be "hollow."[110] The *Asociación General de Agricultores* (General Association of Agriculturalists), an organization comprised of conservative landowning elite opposed to the Arbenz regime, published an advertisement in a national newspaper, asserting that the law was antithetical to democracy: "Can a cow give lemonade? The communists cannot make a democratic law."[111] These elite protests captured the attention of the U.S. State Department through their insistence on communist infiltration, despite the clear capitalist intentions behind the reform. After all, Decree 900 closely followed the recommendations outlined in the Britnell report. But within the context of growing Cold War tensions, U.S. foreign policy often reinforced existing social hierarchies to maintain the status quo and thus ensure political stability. It also sought to eliminate all possibilities of leftist intervention *before* they took root, so it began to pay particularly close attention to the growing social changes in Guatemala.

Local Histories of the Agrarian Reform

The implementation of the agrarian reform generated a thorough paper trail, as each affected finca has a file containing a record of correspondence, denuncias, and claims of the involved parties. After the 1954 military coup that overthrew Arbenz and abruptly terminated the Revolution, the counterrevolutionary government under Colonel Carlos Castillo Armas quickly overturned Decree 900 and reversed many of the expropriations that had occurred; the finca files also document this process. In some instances, campesino perspectives appear in these records, though their voices were often mediated through a representative or are recounted by a committee member. Notably, just as nineteenth-century Indigenous campesinos utilized the language of republicanism, equality, and citizenship in post-Independence Latin America, so too did mid-twentieth-century Guatemalan campesinos use the language and terms most pertinent and influential in their time.[112] These records provide unique insight into the ways that campesinos and landowners alike utilized development discourse, ideas about justice, and the theme of national progress and modernity in tandem with the legal stipulations of the law to pursue land and frame demands that they hoped would resonate with the authorities.

The following illustrative examples how campesinos justified their requests for land and how owners challenged expropriation. I focus here on the department of Sacatepéquez, where initial IING ethnographic work, literacy campaigns and rural education initiatives, and public health projects tended to focus. According to the 1950 Census, the department of Sacatepéquez was 52 percent Indigenous (largely Kaqchikel Maya). However, the ladino population was mainly concentrated in the departmental capital of La Antigua and

nearby Ciudad Vieja, so the remaining municipalities had a much higher Indigenous population.[113] The 1950 Agrarian Census reported that 69 percent
of renters and 61 percent of mozos colonos in Sacatepéquez were Indigenous,
making clear that people characterized as both Indigenous and ladino were
campesinos and comprised the rural lower classes.[114] Thus, in reading these
records, rarely can I definitely conclude that individuals would consider
themselves Indigenous, but last names and municipality of residence can provide some indication as to whether we might reliably conclude that their contemporaries understood them as such. In analyzing these records, I have
organized the discussion around four recurring themes that frame the use of
development discourse by participating parties: nutrition and food politics,
infrastructure, notions of justice, and ideas about national progress.

The case of the finca Nacimiento El Hato illustrates both the way that
some rural people organized and promoted participation in the agrarian reform and how they utilized contemporary preoccupations with nutrition
to justify their demands. Enrique Otzoy from the *Unión Campesina* of Chimaltenango visited the town of San Jacinto on August 24, 1952, to encourage
residents to petition the CAL for land from Nacimiento El Hato.[115] Otzoy
explained his understanding of the intentions of the agrarian reform, plead-
ing with his audience to "take advantage [of the agrarian reform] so that the
campesinos that don't have [land] or have very little" could obtain this important resource. Referencing national well-being, he explained that they lived in
a current state of exploitation that "directly harms the economy, development, and health of the campesino because of feudal methods." In focusing
on the development of the individual as a means of strengthening the country, Otzoy argued that the acquisition of land would permit a revision of the
feudal relationship that campesinos had with the landed oligarchy and instead position them as the foundation upon which the country could be built.
In conclusion, he argued that locals should claim land from Nacimiento El
Hato "for the benefit of the poor campesinos of the community, for the Revolution of October, for the Patria."[116] Though the record does not contain
paperwork of San Jacinto's denunciation, documentation from April 1955 indicates that residents had denounced the finca and did receive land, as they
were imploring the counterrevolutionary government to allow them to finish
cultivating their current plantings before relinquishing their holdings to the
former landowner.[117]

Petitioners from the town of Santa María de Jesús also denounced Finca
Nacimiento El Hato, and they emphasized public health in their request,
claiming they desired land to "plant cereal grains that would serve in the

nutrition of their children." In underscoring their plan to grow grains instead of corn, they signaled a departure from the cultivation of a dominant staple in the rural Guatemalan diet. In reality, rural diets were much more diverse than contemporary stereotypes assumed; for example, campesinos in the nearby department of Chimaltenango had cultivated wheat since the 1870s.[118] Notwithstanding this history, and despite the FAO's synthesis of Goubaud's 1944 nutrition surveys that deemed rural Indigenous diets to be more balanced and nutritious than previously thought, racialized stereotypes still associated Indigeneity with corn consumption and malnutrition. As one reporter derogatorily put it, Guatemala needed to have "indios" with better nutrition than just corn tortillas and salt.[119] A 1945 newspaper article had even stated that the rural diet's two central components—corn and liquor—weakened rural workers by lowering red blood cell counts. Instead, rural Guatemalans should strive to be like Italian workers, who, according to the author, were more muscular due to their diversified consumption that included polenta, meat, garbanzos, and just a little wine.[120] Thus, when Santa María de Jesús residents clearly specified that they wished to grow cereal grains, this was possibly a real desire that they collectively had. At the same time, it is also likely that they emphasized this aspiration—real or not—to demonstrate their awareness of these condescending views of rural diets and to clarify that their cultivation plans fit neatly within national efforts to diversify diets and agricultural production. Their petition was successful, and records indicate that the CAD approved the expropriation of a *caballería* (~990 acres). However, after the 1954 coup, the counterrevolutionary government returned this land to the original owner.[121]

Like campesinos, landowners faced with pending expropriation also utilized food politics to justify their arguments, but unlike campesinos who asserted that land would improve their nutrition, landowners emphasized their finca's contribution to national food supplies. For example, when residents in Sumpango denounced Finca Las Flores, owner Carlos Herrera argued that his finca's uncultivated land was covered in forests or had a steep grade, conditions that the law stipulated would disqualify land from expropriation. The rest, he insisted, was planted with corn and beans, "which are articles whose production is destined to satisfy the needs of the internal market." Historically, government officials regularly struggled to balance their desire for expanded export agriculture with the need to support domestic-use agriculture, and periodic food shortages coupled with a growing population kept this issue at the forefront of public food policies.[122] Herrera hoped that by claiming his finca provided the country with its two primary staple crops the CAD would reconsider the expropriation order. It did not.

In addition to nutrition, claimants also capitalized on the state's preoccupation with rural infrastructure to frame their expropriation requests. For example, in the municipality of La Antigua, Miguel Rosales led twelve families in petitioning their CAL for thirty-nine acres of land from the El Portal finca that they believed qualified for expropriation. Their denunciation, dated January 5, 1953, rationalized this choice by stating that the claimants were developing the land in question, as they had built thirty-four houses on the property. They wished to create a hamlet (*caserío*), complete with streets, avenues, parks, a public plaza, school, market, and churches so the people "can enjoy all the benefits of urbanization." The petitioning families emphasized their material poverty; their homes had dirt floors, and they did not have electricity, running water, or latrines, desired modern conveniences. Reflecting their understanding that the state prioritized the modernization of rural infrastructure, these claimants likely hoped that through framing their request in this way, the CAD would approve it and that their case would be airtight. And quite possibly, they actually desired to have some or all of these things as well.

The CAD approved this request, and on November 13, 1953, expropriation took place. In a rare case where he did not fight the denunciation, the same Carlos Herrera agreed to the expropriation, provided he was justly compensated. However, once the counterrevolutionary government reversed Decree 900, Herrera petitioned for his finca's return. In December 1956, the government complied and provided him with over Q3,000 in damages (=$3,000). According to the records, the inhabitants had voluntarily left after 1954, likely fearing expulsion, or worse, arrest, if they did not.[123] In the coup's aftermath, the U.S. Embassy reported that landowners used widespread arrests as a convenient way to remove "troublesome employees," giving the example of an owner bragging how he loaded eighty-two campesinos into a truck and turned them over to local police as communists.[124] While records do not indicate what happened to El Portal's residents, newspaper, radio, and word of mouth reports of similar incidents likely scared many people into abandoning land they had acquired to avoid extreme retribution. Despite this unfortunate outcome, the case of El Portal reflects the ability of claimants to frame successful petitions in the language of development, knowing full well the priorities of the revolutionary state and the type of infrastructure it desired.

Located on the other side of a river from El Portal was Finca La Azotea, which became the subject of denunciations by campesinos from Jocotenango who coupled infrastructure development with historical claims to the land. Many Jocotenango residents worked on El Portal, and they accessed the finca by a road that ran through La Azotea. According to the petitioners, landowner J. Alberto Orive del Pando annually required the town to clean out the sand and mud from the river's irrigation channel, at their expense. In May 1947, Jocotenango issued a municipal decree, stating that this exploitative practice began during the government of Manuel Estrada Cabrera (1898–1920). Referencing the 1945 Constitution, they argued that this qualified as forced labor and violated their rights. They asked the government to require Orive to pay them for this labor, and they pledged to use the money to improve the municipal school and government buildings. In retaliation, Orive closed the access road that ran through his finca. Residents accused him of "tyranny and despotism" and of "trampl[ing] on the Constitution." Not only could they no longer access El Portal but he had also cut them off from their main water source. They implored the CAN to reopen the road, writing, "The people of Jocotenango should be able to also participate in the conquests that it has achieved through the 1944 revolution and through Decreto 900."

To defend his actions, Orive wrote that he had cultivated coffee trees along the road. Further, he had Herrera write in on his behalf, and the latter noted that residents could enter El Portal through the main entrance instead of through this access road, which he preferred as it allowed him to control the movement of people in and out of his finca. Both owners also reiterated that the denunciation did not even pertain to agrarian reform. In April 1953, the CAN ruled in favor of Jocotenango. A letter a few months later indicated that jocotecos did indeed reopen the road. Orive complained that a great number of armed residents cut down many trees and created a road "whose width does not equal any in all of Antigua." In response, the CAN informed Orive that he was mandated to cut down the necessary trees to clear the road and that he could keep half the wood; he had to donate the other half to the municipality.

Immediately after the coup, Orive filed for a reversal. When the evaluating agronomist, Ramiro Leiva López, arrived to complete the inspection, he found that Orive had closed the road off with barbed wire just two days after the fall of Arbenz, and he had also planted it with legumes. Leiva, despite being an employee of the counterrevolutionary government, often wrote sympathetic reports about the plight of campesinos, and in this instance, he insisted that the road was necessary for residents to access El Portal and the river. Initially, the DGAA ruled that Orive could cultivate the legumes but then had to reopen the road by 1955; a later document from June 1955 indicated that the Ministry of the Interior (*Ministerio de Gobernación*) reversed the earlier ruling and allowed Orive to permanently close the road. The documentation ends there, failing to provide us with campesino responses to this decision.[125] Though jocotecos did not successfully maintain access in the postcoup moment, the La Azotea case does demonstrate how some predominantly Indigenous communities at least discursively used infrastructure development alongside revolutionary promises, as they interpreted them, to pursue justice against historic grievances, a pattern that I and other historians have noted took place elsewhere and that the next case will also elucidate.[126]

Campesinos from Sumpango denounced Finca Las Flores, and after waiting over a year without notification of a decision, they wrote directly to the CAN, demanding a resolution in their favor. Like those from Jocotenango, they invoked a longer history of dispossession and ideas about justice. In this instance, they abandoned framing their demand within the legal framework of the agrarian reform, instead invoking their concept of revolutionary justice. First, they noted that "the patrón [Herrera]" has "lots of fincas," a considerable understatement, given that Carlos Herrera and the Herrera Brothers company were among Guatemala's wealthiest landowners and had accrued an estimated sixty-five fincas across six departments.[127] In doing so, they invoked a notion of justice as prioritizing equitable distribution over the protection of private property. Then, they shared their exasperation with waiting for months without a decision, possibly reflecting how some community members had likely been waiting for generations to receive this land they believed rightfully to be theirs. In concluding the letter, they powerfully claimed, "We are the legitimate owners of this land." In a moment of heightened tension and emotion, Sumpango campesinos revealed that this was land they and their families had likely cultivated for generations and to which they felt deeply connected. In November 1953, the CAN favorably responded, giving Sumpango residents land. However, the majority of the expropriated land was returned to Herrera after the 1954 coup.[128]

Campesinos and occasionally agronomists also referenced notions of justice through citing abusive labor conditions both before and after the coup. Though they never directly stated that experiencing exploitation justified expropriation, they certainly implied it, and in doing so, called for a development model that focused not only on production statistics but also on human well-being. For example, agronomist Ramiro Leiva cited Herrera's "system of exploitation" across all his properties in his postcoup inspection of Finca El Tigre y Pachali, referring to it as "slavery." He reported that the Herreras made campesinos work on coastal plantations to "pay" for the land they rented, where finca supervisors "paid them, fed them, and worked them as they pleased." Campesinos reported that to cultivate one *manzana* (1.7 acres) of land at El

Tigre, Herrera required them to labor unpaid and harvest thirty *quintales* of coffee (3,000 pounds), a task that required about three months of work, in conditions they called "very onerous and unfavorable."[129] Similarly, sixty-six campesinos from Finca El Pilar explained in their 1952 denouncement that owner Julio Herrera (of the Herrera Brothers) required those who planted land in this Antigua finca to seasonally migrate to Escuintla and work there for nine days for each *cuerda* (~0.3 acres) that they had rented. After the 1954 coup, campesinos continued to denounce labor conditions; for example, Regino Bautista boldly claimed before the departmental committee that for twenty-five years, he had rented land at El Pilar that he "paid" for with his labor at the coastal plantation, where "they paid us a salary that could not sustain a family." The JAD returned part of the expropriated land to Herrera. However, it gave the rest to the campesinos because the Herreras engaged in exploitative labor practices, requiring renters to labor unpaid on their coastal plantations and providing them with a meager salary of ten cents per day and an inhumane ration of only twelve tortillas and one pound of beans per week.[130] In this case, this appeal to unlawful labor practices as counterproductive to Guatemala's pursuit of modernity resulted in campesinos partially retaining the gains made under the agrarian reform.

While campesinos deployed notions of justice as a means to pave the way toward a modern future, landowners commonly insisted that their finca's production supported national progress through modeling modern agriculture. As the following examples show, some landowners explicitly juxtaposed their practices with what they believed to be the primitive methods of campesinos, questioning why the state would seize their modern establishments in favor of methods they viewed as premodern. Héctor Francisco Pérez Mollinedo, owner of Finca San Francisco Las Flores in Sumpango, claimed that his important dairy farm serviced nearby towns, including the capital and the La Alameda normal school. He positioned himself as a small landowner whose commitment to modern agricultural and husbandry techniques could improve the national economy. In a letter dated October 13, 1953, he vehemently wrote that he did not "deny for a moment" that the CAD would reverse its expropriation ruling because he knew that Decree 900 did not wish to "harm the true agriculturalists" like himself who used their "small extension of land" appropriately. He regularly cited the high quality of his cows and detailed their diet of mixed grains and his use of a partial free-range grazing system, a practice he suggested was innovative for the time. After 1954, Pérez wrote to the JAD to argue that "small anticommunist landowners" like himself suffered from injustice and that he hoped that the new government would quickly reverse this unfair ruling. Less than two months later, it did precisely that.[131]

Though the Herrera brothers did not position themselves as small landowners, they, too, claimed that the superiority of their agricultural techniques protected their fincas from expropriation. Never one to mince words, Carlos Herrera described the conditions in his coffee finca, El Potrero in Ciudad Vieja, as "magnificent" and boasted that the shade-grown, arabica, bourbon coffee had some of the country's best yields. As he expressed to the JAD, the expropriation of this finca was detrimental to national economic development because the recipients caused erosion through their planting techniques and harmed coffee production. Though both Herrera and the aforementioned Pérez did cite some of the legal provisions to argue that expropriation had been illegal, they emphasized the modern nature of their agricultural operations and situated these as more important for national development than campesino cultivation.

Filadelfo Salazar Suárez, owner of Finca Florencia in Santa Lucía Milpas Altas challenged the CAN's expropriation ruling by claiming that his finca was a "model farm." While he did not explain what he meant by this, he utilized the same term that agricultural extension agents in Guatemala and abroad used to describe experimental plots that showcased what they believed to be new and improved cultivation techniques, including the use of hybrid seeds, insecticides and fertilizers, irrigation systems, and mechanized equipment.[132] Besides serving as a self-proclaimed example for the region, Salazar even offered to contribute 3,300 acres (thirty *caballerías*) from a finca he owned in Alta Verapaz to demonstrate that he was not opposed to the spirit of the agrarian reform. However, he included a condition with this donation; Salazar would only donate this land if "they [the recipients] truly wanted to work and progress; but if what they are going to pursue is the destruction of what is already formed, soon they will be tricked into working sterile lands."[133] In making this statement, Salazar positioned himself as a modern agricultural entrepreneur that understood the best cultivation techniques, which is ironic, given that Salazar was a lawyer in Guatemala City. In contrast, he revealed his belief that Indigenous cultivation patterns were primitive and would not take full advantage of the land's potential, in actuality causing its ruin. This argument maintained that Indigenous campesinos' "backwardness" hindered Guatemala's agricultural development and that by giving land to people characterized as Indigenous, the government was removing land from a responsible owner—himself—and erroneously allotting it to new stewards who would mismanage it, and thus hinder Guatemala's development.

In the coup's aftermath, campesinos deployed the tactic of emphasizing their commitment to the new government and referenced national progress, often citing their poverty and the threat of hunger if the state took away their newly received land. While this framing might have realistically reflected their material conditions, campesinos also strategically invoked a racialized trope of Indigenous poverty and apolitical tendencies and appealed to the paternalistic nature of the presidency. For example, when Finca Los Tulipanes owner Carlos Herrera argued that Arbenz did not have the national economy in mind when he passed the agrarian reform, the recipients responded, reasoning that without land, they would return to extreme poverty. At the very least, they needed to keep their land through the current harvest, as the new law stipulated, because they had taken out loans that they could only repay with the profits from their crops. Filing an appeal to the revocation order, they wrote, "We are a group of campesinos that are really poor and far removed from any political influence." Across the bottom of their stationery, in the format of a footer, they included the slogan of the counterrevolutionary government: GOD, FATHERLAND, LIBERTY, TRUTH, JUSTICE, WORK (capitalization in original). By including this tagline, the campesinos predominantly displayed their supposed allegiance to the new regime in the hopes of gaining its favor. The framing of this petition also reflected their understanding of the counterrevolutionary state's ongoing prioritization of economic production and repayment of loans, as they stipulated that these two activities were precisely what they would do if allotted an extension on landownership. Despite this overture, the government decided against them on February 23, 1956, and returned the land to Herrera.[134]

Similarly, campesinos from Sumpango directly appealed to President Castillo Armas in October 1955 after the Ministry of the Interior issued a final ruling that returned all expropriated land from Finca El Rejón #4 to the landowner. These campesinos, self-described as poor, illiterate, and Indigenous, remarked that they "had seen in newspapers and heard on radios the new measures taken by the supreme government to give land as private property" to people like themselves. Using almost religious language, they "beg that the President of the Republic hear their humble petition" as they lack "the most sacred thing, which is daily bread for our children." Castillo Armas did no such thing, and the state returned the land to the landowner.[135]

Instead of stressing the negative outcomes that would result if rulings did not favor the petitioner, some campesinos and landowners instead emphasized how they would contribute to national well-being, if given the opportunity. These cases also provide glimpses into what was at stake for campesinos in this historical moment and what possible violent ramification they might face should they continue to exercise persistence as a tool of their political agency. After denouncing Finca Monte María in Alotenango, the CAN awarded 159 campesinos a combined total of 550 acres (five caballerías), despite owner Carlos Matheu's vehement protests that his farm was a productive dairy farm. After the coup, when the JAD summoned the three campesino leaders to Antigua to give their accounts of the former proceedings, Victor Dondiego Pumay gave an account but also reported that the other two leaders were unable to testify; Samuel Cojolón was in jail for personal assault, and Ignacio Pashel was imprisoned in the capital because "he was the president of the *Comité* (CAL)." He also reported that many of the recipients had abandoned their land, and though he did not directly tie it to Pashel's imprisonment, it is possible that the others also feared violent repercussions for participating in the agrarian reform.

The JAD determined to return the land to Matheu, but in a common practice, it required him to submit a plan of finca improvements. These types of documents are often disparaging and dehumanizing, and they emphasize the superficial nature of counterrevolutionary development efforts. On paper, elite Guatemalans made minor concessions to workers' well-being but in no way implemented measures to actually change the status quo or redistribute wealth. For example, Matheu pledged to give a ten-cent bonus for each completed workday as a Christmas bonus and give workers' children toys, clothes, and sweets as Christmas gifts; maintain his company store, which he claimed sold items under market value; hire a doctor to attend to workers and establish a local hospital; and screen films regularly to provide wholesome entertainment options. The plan does not discuss improved wages, better working conditions, or land access. In response, the campesinos asked the DGAA to intervene on their behalf, implicitly implying their dissatisfaction with the improvement plan. They wrote that they believed the "Liberation Movement (*movimiento libertador*)" had come to free the poor like themselves and not the wealthy from communism. Taking away their lands would "cause serious harm to the nation, which we give our support, because it would not be the rich that at a moment's notice would jump to its defense but had always been us the poor." In framing their demand in terms of national defense, these campesinos point to themselves, the rural working class, as the backbone and sole defenders of the nation. In doing so, they subtly threaten national stability and invoke the peasantry's potential power, playing on fears of rural unrest. The DGAA did not return their lands, but they did mandate that Matheu pay the campesinos for their crops, which lamentably only accrued to a few quetzales for each individual.[136]

Like campesinos at Monte María, a group from Sumpango also framed its denunciation of Finca El Naranjo in terms of national well-being, identifying the "improvement" of the campesino as the cornerstone of national progress. After the counterrevolutionary government reversed the expropriation decree, the campesinos appealed to the president and asked him to oblige the owner to rent them land so they could harvest their crops. Understanding that they now had to separate themselves from the social justice discourse of the revolutionary law, they wrote that returning the land would "harm the development of agriculture in our country." In a separate letter, they took the strategy of detailing potential negative outcomes, claiming that without this land and thus, their harvest, their families would "be condemned to be hungry" and would no longer be able to diligently work for the good of the country in their weakened state. They went so far as to accuse the agrarian inspector of delaying his survey until after the planting period ended, which would jeopardize their ability to grow crops for that season. In February 1955, the counterrevolutionary government ruled to return the land to the landowner but mandated that she rent out unused land to local campesinos. A letter from mid-October 1955 indicates that the owner did not comply with this request, and the last piece of documentation in the file implied that the campesinos had appealed directly to the president for his intervention. Because no response is included, it is likely that their plea was ignored.[137]

The final case discussed here, Finca San Rafael, encapsulates many of these themes, capturing various usages of development discourse alongside violent encounters as campesinos struggled against landowners for control of the land. Though several groups of campesinos denounced the finca, Martín Pec Batocic, self-identified as an Indigenous farmer from Sumpango, continued the struggle for land into the late 1950s. In October 1955, he wrote to the Ministry of Agriculture claiming that his group of recipients had a valid expropriation accord that allowed them "to cultivate the land and with them contribute to the growth of the national economy." When no resolution was forthcoming, Pec and two other men, Francisco Chicop and Manuel Eulalio Culay, wrote directly to Castillo Armas, asking him to rule in their favor so that they could harvest their crops and, more ominously, so that Guatemala "could have tranquility in the countryside." A later agrarian inspection reported that the campesinos had planted a variety of crops, such as cauliflower, beets, spinach, cabbage, broccoli, soybeans, basil, and lettuce, products that would diversify their own diets and provide them with items to sell at market. Thus, they claimed that their efforts would not only improve the national economy but also prevent Indigenous rural uprisings, a constant fear of the landed elite.

Brothers from the Aparicio family owned the finca, and they constantly wrote to the DGAA that members of Pec's group were not *parcelarios* (individuals who had received parcels of land) but rather invaders who were squatting on the finca and "causing irreparable harm" to the forested landscape. He accused them of cutting and trading the finca's lumber in Mixco for "octavos" (liquor) and argued that in trying to solve one problem, Arbenz had created another ("*se dedicó a desnudar santos para vestir a otros*"). Their wives even wrote that they hoped to establish a dairy (*lechería*) on the finca and build houses there, but that at present, they could not do so with people nearby that they considered "enemies," "dangerous," and threatening to their children. While the campesinos presented themselves as guardians of the peace, the landowners instead suggested that they caused instability in the countryside.

While waiting on a ruling in early 1957, both parties reported armed threats against the other. In January 1957, Gervasio Chacón, the finca's security guard who described himself as a sixty-seven-year-old Indigenous man, testified that Pec and fifty others had arrived to the finca with Colonel Antonino Alonso, who claimed he was the owner and was there to expel those living there and reallocate all land to Pec's group. Pec's account differed; he explained that the campesino union at San Rafael had discussed the possibility of the colonel purchasing the finca from the Aparicios, and so on that day they had simply gone to see the land. The agrarian inspector concluded that no damage had been done. Still, and perhaps in retaliation, Pec reported directly to the president that two of the Aparicio brothers came to the finca, threatened the campesinos, asserted that they were even going to assassinate the president, and burned down several buildings. The inspection supported this account, informing that the Aparicios had burned two unoccupied huts, a communal kitchen, and a crop storehouse. They were ordered to pay for damages. Finally, in May 1957, the campesinos' persistence was somewhat rewarded when the Aparicios conceded and gave each person 1.74 acres (a *manzana*) to cultivate for free, provided that they planted grasses there after harvesting their milpa. Though nowhere near the quantity of land the campesinos had originally received, they were not fully dispossessed like many others. The one exception that the Aparicios made was that Martín Pec could not be one of the recipients. Instead, the DGAA gave him a small plot at the nearby finca Pachali.[138]

When considered as a corpus of material that gives incomplete glimpses into the lived experiences of the agrarian reform in Sacatepéquez, these cases demonstrate how campesinos and elite landowners alike recognized the Guatemalan state's preoccupation with developmentalist policies. They effectively used this language to shape their demands and justifications for their actions and opinions both during the Revolution and in the Counterrevolution. Indigenous campesinos who decided to participate in the agrarian reform utilized the state's depiction of the "appropriate" expressions of Indigeneity to argue that their lack of land kept them from embodying this identity, and elite landowners' unwillingness to cede their excess holdings reminds us once again of the controversial nature of Guatemala's nation-building project that mandated the inclusion of Indigenous people, even if on high modernist terms.

Conclusion

As this chapter has shown, during the politically charged Arbenz government, the state emphasized development via economic productivity, public health, and integration into the capitalist market in the hopes of creating the "brave new world" in Guatemala that Britnell and other development experts believed to be possible. The state's permitted Indian model positioned Indigenous citizens as politically active and readily accepting the state's assistance by utilizing new channels, such as INCAP's nutrition program or the CALs, to improve their situation. However, despite the revolutionary state's overtures, not all rural Indigenous people welcomed these projects and the accompanying identities and discourses. When individuals at times refused these projects' provisions, such as rejecting a hen house or declining to participate in denouncing uncultivated land, in the state's eyes, they behaved as prohibited, nonmodern Indians. However, this did not mean that they were politically inactive or apathetic to change. Instead, as this chapter argues, in challenging these intrusions into their lives, they helped to reconceptualize the meanings of citizenship for Indigenous people in Guatemala and showed their intention to critically analyze their choices, however limited, and pursue the path that made the most sense for them.

While the revolutionary state certainly maintained a high modernist vision for development, efforts to accomplish this vision were largely decentralized, allowing for individuals to reject various aspects without considerable fear of violent consequences. Similarly, the state did not use development to extend its gaze into the countryside in the same authoritarian way that it would in the upcoming years. As the Cold War heated up in Guatemala, the opportunities for individuals to dictate the terms of their development in state-sponsored projects would become increasingly slim in the years that followed. Similarly, the IING's ability to foster this type of development and mediate between Indigenous communities and the counterrevolutionary state would also be drastically lessened, as the next chapter will show. Still, just as Indigenous people actively shaped the successes and the failures of the revolutionary state's development project, so too would they play central roles in the developmentalist projects during the Counterrevolution.

CHAPTER FOUR

Indigenista Community Development and the Counterrevolution, 1954–1960

In a little over a week at the end of June 1954, Joaquín Noval went from being the director of the IING to a prisoner and enemy of the state. On June 18, 1954, Guatemalan colonel Carlos Castillo Armas crossed the Guatemalan-Honduran border with his CIA-trained rebel army, initiating a successful coup d'état. Accusing the Arbenz regime of communism, Castillo Armas ended the democratic revolution with the support of Guatemala's landed elite, the Church, and the U.S. State Department. To consolidate rule, the counterrevolutionary government imprisoned approximately 4,000 political dissidents upon taking power in Guatemala City.[1]

One of these political prisoners was Joaquín Noval, a member of the PGT, the communist party. After taking office, Castillo Armas quickly outlawed the PGT and imprisoned many of its members, like Noval. Those who eluded capture were forced into exile or clandestinity.[2] After six months of imprisonment, the government unexpectedly released Noval, possibly due to his personal connection to prominent lawyer and right-wing politician Jorge Skinner Klee, a known indigenista.[3] While Noval never resumed work with the IING, he continued teaching at the USAC and maintained his political activities with the PGT, all while living clandestinely until he died of lung cancer in 1976. His writings continued to influence Guatemalan revolutionaries and their understandings of the relationship of Indigeneity to political and class identities.[4]

In addition to imprisoning Noval, the counterrevolutionary government immediately suspended all activities of the IING, jeopardizing its future. Just a few months later, the government reopened the institute and rehired many of its former employees, including Juan de Dios Rosales, Francisco Rodríguez Rouanet, and Hélida Esther Cabrera. In 1956, the IING launched its first comprehensive community development project in Tactic, Alta Verapaz, the *Proyecto de Mejoramiento Integral de Tactic* (PMIT). In some ways, the counterrevolutionary government continued the high modernist tendencies of official revolutionary indigenismo, using development as a means to redefine Indigenous people as either "permitted" and modern or "prohibited" and detrimental to national progress and stability. The Castillo Armas administration also used rural development to foster political support.

Despite these continuities, what is different about the state's programming in Indigenous regions is not so much its content but the manner in which involved institutions could implement their projects. Under the revolutionary administrations, the IING functioned with relative autonomy, partnering with other institutions as it saw fit and carefully implementing detailed studies prior to enacting any practical programs. This changed with the transition to authoritarianism, as the counterrevolutionary state sought to oversee all development efforts, confine institutional independence, and eliminate—or at least severely restrict—freelance or private programs and collaborations.

Historians have emphasized various aspects of the complex 1954 moment, and more recent scholarship has revised earlier debates that largely mirrored popular contemporary discussions of whether the Guatemalan Revolution was a communist or a nationalist movement. This new body of scholarship moves past this dichotomy by exploring the importance of understandings of ideology, the use of psychology and public opinion, the entanglements between U.S. business and political interests, the actual role of U.S. actors as recently revealed through declassified documents, and the actions of Guatemalan actors in the events surrounding the 1954 coup.[5] Still others have sought to decenter the military coup and the Cold War altogether. Within this revisionist literature, some scholars, particularly within the Guatemalan academy, have made efforts to analyze how this pivotal moment affected race relations in Guatemala.[6] Others, like Gibbings and Vrana, argue that not one but many revolutions occurred, requiring scholars to examine "what was being fought over" in order to grasp the making and remaking of revolution across Guatemala's history.[7] Grandin's examination of the 1978 massacre at Panzós argues that revolutionary democracy in Guatemala was based on "insurgent individuality and social solidarity," and he examines how individuals and collectivities forged new notions of self and society through their lived experiences.[8] For some of his historical actors, the 1954 coup strengthened their commitment to organizing, but for others, it signaled an end to their political activism.[9]

This chapter joins this recent trend to focus on lived realities of the Guatemalan coup and Cold War through local and individual histories, and it seeks to situate these within the larger context of international geopolitics. Recent scholarship emphasizes the historical agency of the various types of experts that prominently featured in programs on the ground, shaping the cultural meanings given to Cold War politics and facilitating material and intellectual exchanges. They put into practice the plans and ideologies emanating from the offices of governments and philanthropic institutions, and their relationship with their host communities deeply informed the trajectory of their work.[10]

Thus the Cold War frame is necessary and relevant, but it remains in the background against the foregrounding of individual and collective histories. In doing so, this chapter analyzes how trends in international development influenced practices in the Guatemalan countryside that directly contributed to revisions of the state's ideas about acceptable expressions of Indigeneity. It argues that the counterrevolutionary state's increasingly close relationship with U.S. advisors led to the official adoption of modernization as the ideological model it would follow for state-sponsored development projects. Because of this, official community development changed from being a model of careful collaboration with host communities that allowed for local agency in modernizing to one that only required the imposition of standardized programs with the idea of minimally addressing material needs, establishing new forms of dependency, and creating opportunities for state surveillance.

As the previous chapters have argued, IING programs sought to modernize Indigenous people, meaning that development practitioners wanted to alleviate poverty and improve economic realities, positioning themselves as intermediaries who could guide this process. The PMIT was no exception. But this process can be distinct from modernization because it allows for local agency and flexibility in project plans and is tailored to specific contexts. This more organic form of development saw Indigenous people as capable citizens who only lacked material resources as opposed to potential citizens that required lengthy state efforts to prepare them for the responsibilities of such a status. And importantly, for the IING, though perhaps not for broader Guatemalan society, whether an individual chose to embrace modernity did not affect one's Indigenous identity.

The remainder of the book explores how ideas about development and Indigeneity shifted under the weight of successive counterinsurgency regimes during Guatemala's long civil war, understood within the context of the global Cold War. I argue that counterrevolutionary state development programs sought to "de-Indianize" the population and began to situate that process within a strategy to contain the appeal of leftist politics, broadly labeled communism. Both the PMIT's model of modernizing Indigenous people and the state's de-Indianization via modernization operated under the dichotomy and spectrum of the "permitted" and "prohibited Indian," but as later chapters demonstrate, the counterinsurgency regimes increasingly labeled individuals that aligned with the prohibited Indian model as subversive, dangerous, and in need of elimination. This chapter shows that the state's embrace of modernization as development policy, its abrupt cancellation of the PMIT, and its defunding of the IING resulted in the foreclosing of officially sanctioned development initiatives that granted local actors considerable autonomy in defining the shape and terms of development projects.

The Post-1954 Modernization Turn in Guatemalan Development Planning

The United States supported the Castillo Armas government from the outset, viewing Guatemala as "a continental guinea-pig."[11] Building on the momentum gained in Iran in 1953, the CIA covertly supported Castillo Armas's Army of Liberation, providing necessary logistic help, recruiting and training rebel troops, and launching a propaganda campaign that undermined the Arbenz regime.[12] The U.S. government and conservative Guatemalans justified the coup in terms of hemispheric security. Both asserted that the Arbenz government was a Soviet puppet, basing this assumption on the legalization of the PGT and the arrangement Arbenz made with Czechoslovakia to buy weapons. The agrarian reform fueled this accusation, as the program redistributed nearly 1 million acres of land, angering the landed elite and, importantly, the United Fruit Company.[13] In a last effort to raise widespread popular support, Arbenz gave a radio broadcast during the coup, declaring, "Our crime is our patriotic wish to advance, to progress, to win economic independence to match our political independence. We are condemned because we have given our peasant population land and rights."[14] On June 27, 1954, he resigned and sought political asylum at the Mexican Embassy while Castillo Armas's regime inaugurated the Counterrevolution.

In the coup's immediate aftermath, Richard Adams (discussed in previous chapter) and fellow anthropologist Manning Nash conducted 267 interviews with political prisoners in order to ascertain the actual influence that communist ideology held throughout the country. Published under Stokes Newbold, a penname that combined their middle names, their report showed that the majority of these "dissidents" had instead experienced a "sociological awakening."[15] Interviewees repeatedly indicated how they had come to a realization that they no longer had to accept their subordinate roles and statuses within the social system and that "new channels were suddenly opened for the expression of and satisfaction of needs."[16] The U.S. Embassy in Guatemala cited this report in a dispatch to the State Department as evidence for its skepticism that the majority of political prisoners had any understanding of communism, claiming that most prisoners "were unable to distinguich [SIC] correctly between Leonardo CASTILLO Flores, Communist-line ex-Secretary

General of the Confederación Nacional Campesina de Guatemala, and Colonel Carlos Castillo Armas, President of the Junta of Government. To them, they were both somehow connected with 'the government.'"[17] But despite this rather tacit admission that the United States had overplayed accusations of communism, the embassy also recognized that the military coup provided an opportunity to ensure that Guatemala not be removed from the path of First World modernization.

The abrupt transition to authoritarian rule once again limited the ways in which Guatemalans could pursue social justice. It also changed the organization of the national government and its affiliated institutions, including the IING. At first glance, counterrevolutionary indigenismo does not seem to widely diverge from the Revolution's agenda. It continued to pursue the transformation of Indigenous people into "permitted Indians" in an attempt to socially engineer a population that would support the current administration. What is different about counterrevolutionary indigenismo was its focus on quick applied programming, as opposed to knowledge creation, its insistence on avoiding property redistribution, and its framing of problems and the appropriate solutions as technical and thus solvable by expert intervention instead of recognizing that they were political problems that required structural change.[18] The state sought to implement programs that could be quickly and easily measured and whose results would be widely disseminated as a testament of its commitment to its Indigenous majority and of its successful interventions in the countryside.

These changing ideas about programming in Indigenous communities were part of Guatemala's larger shift toward the model of modernization as the key framework for socioeconomic development. The U.S. State Department understood its commitment to Castillo Armas's success as extending beyond the coup, and a classified memorandum dated a week after the coup detailed how the new president needed clear guidance on "how to win and maintain popular support." Further, the document suggested that U.S. advisors give "every kind of practical encouragement to the development of prosperity in Guatemala so that the people are increasingly content."[19] The idea emanating from the U.S. State Department that Guatemala was a "laboratory" for showcasing the successful overthrow of a communist regime exemplifies historian Greg Grandin's argument that Latin America served as the U.S. "empire's workshop," a testing ground for foreign policy. In the mid-1950s, the U.S. government saw Guatemala as a potential showcase for the merit of First World modernization, that is, if the U.S. could guide the fledgling and unprepared Castillo Armas regime in successfully consolidating power and achieving positive socioeconomic indicators.[20]

As the United States began to pursue development via modernization in Guatemala, it established what historian Stephen M. Streeter has called a "parallel government" through the *servicio* system, a model that created a U.S. administrative equivalent for each sector of the Guatemalan government. Though some servicios briefly operated in Guatemala during the revolutionary years, the scale of operations drastically expanded under Castillo Armas. Nor was the application of the servicio system unique to Guatemala; scholars have explored how it occurred throughout the Americas, allowing the United States to directly shape public policies and intervene into the daily lives of Latin Americans.[21] This shadow government officially served an advisory role, but in reality, U.S. officials dictated the terms of aid and the structure of new programs, effectively keeping a close watch on the authoritarian regime it had helped to install.[22] For the United States and the Guatemalan government, the coup provided the opportunity to change Guatemala's path to development away from redistributive policies and toward capitalist modernization. Guatemalan officials realized they needed U.S. support—material and symbolic—to acquire grants and loans, maintain infrastructure projects, increase standards of living, and fulfill the promises they had made to the Guatemalan people. Indeed, between 1954 and 1959, the U.S. government gave Guatemala $110 million in foreign aid.[23] This close networking of Guatemalan officials with U.S. experts firmly embedded the United States into Guatemala's national policies and economic decisions.

However, U.S. efforts to dictate Guatemala's development model encountered disinterest from the Castillo Armas administration. For example, a declassified September 1954 U.S. State Department letter details a conversation between Samuel Waugh, the assistant secretary of state; Henry Holland, the assistant secretary of state for Inter-American Affairs; and Robert L. Garner, the IBRD vice president, about U.S. efforts to secure IBRD funding for large-scale infrastructure projects in Guatemala. However, Castillo Armas had exhibited unwillingness to create such a plan during his first few months in office. Waugh and Holland voiced concern that Castillo Armas's nationalistic tendencies would prevent the U.S. Embassy from being able to closely monitor his cabinet's actions. Garner pointed out that the IBRD would be unable to bring "a loan project . . . to the point of final action" until Guatemala had a clear national development plan.[24] On September 17, 1954, diplomat Thomas Mann wrote from the U.S. Embassy in Guatemala to Raymond Leddy, director of the

State Department's Central American and Panamanian Affairs, reporting that Castillo Armas supposedly had three people working independently on a national economic strategy, but no national plan had been publicly released. Mann wrote, "The fact that confusion exists imposes greater rather than less responsibilities on us to act promptly and decisively, for it is literally true that economic stability and progress, on the one hand, and political stability, on the other, are indivisible."[25] Mann suggested hiring a financial advisor to work directly with the Guatemalan government to both advise them on economic development *and* report back to the U.S. Embassy.

Initially, the IBRD sent David Gordon to Guatemala in late 1954 to join the newly formed *Consejo Nacional de Planificación Económica* (National Council of Economic Planning, CNPE) as a permanent board member.[26] In 1955, the CNPE created the first of Guatemala's five-year development plans with Gordon's direct assistance, to the point that Guatemalan critics, including Castillo Armas, referred to it as "Gordon's Plan."[27] These critics were not the only people who were discontent with the close collaboration between the IBRD and the CNPE. The U.S. Embassy expressed dismay that the IBRD advised the CNPE without first consulting Embassy staff, and as a result, Ambassador Sparks recommended that the State Department hire a consultant from the economic consulting firm Klein & Saks to come to Guatemala and join the CNPE. Klein & Saks had experience working in Latin America and, according to an Embassy memo, had reportedly "done an 'outstanding job in Peru.'" Their presence on the CNPE, therefore, could allow them to "act as watch dog to help the new and inexperienced administration avoid making serious blunders in the economic field" and to "get closer to the Guatemalan government."[28] Importantly, the U.S. Embassy mandated that Klein & Saks discuss any recommendations for the CNPE with the embassy before presenting plans to the Guatemalan government.[29] Clearly, the United States hoped to use development experts as part of its intelligence apparatus in Guatemala. Despite protest from the IBRD, Klein & Saks representative Mr. Quinn gained a seat on the CNPE, thus serving as a conduit for suggesting U.S. development priorities to the planning council.

The CNPE's 1955–1960 Economic Development Plan prioritized the integration of the rural Indigenous population. First, it emphasized the goal to complete the Pan-American highway, as these planners believed that such a road system would connect Guatemalans that "have different traditions in their economic practices" and thus increase participation in the national economy.[30] Second, it mandated agricultural training in new cultivation techniques to "transform [the rural community] into an effective market for industrial products."[31] Like the revolutionary governments, the counterrevolutionary government also prioritized the creation of an agricultural middle class, as a U.S. State Department memo revealed the opinion that the creation of such a class "was the foundation stone of the Guatemalan Government's policy."[32]

Further, Guatemalan officials believed they could "derive political advantage" through basic rural development. Citing a potable water project in a town that supposedly still had a "pro-communist" mayor, the national government aimed to demonstrate that the "government really could do something for them."[33] Development served as a vehicle for fostering political clientelism, providing just enough material support to prevent uprisings but not enough to effectively restructure society. The CNPE saw community development projects as cheap and effective ways to transform the countryside, and in the process, socially engineer a population of "permitted Indians" who supported the Counterrevolution.

Immediately postcoup, the IING's role in these development programs remained unclear. After its reopening, IING staff faced the practical problem of ensuring that its programming and relationships with Indigenous communities could continue despite the political instability. Again, the lack of an institutional archive makes it difficult to evaluate exactly how the 1954 coup affected the IING. However, oral histories provide insight into how the Counterrevolution reshaped the role of IING staff members within state bureaucracy, elucidating the intersections between their personal and professional lives as they navigated this shifting political scene. These testimonies reveal memories in flux and narratives that are subject to change, as realities in the moment of recounting always give new meanings to the past. However, when analyzed within the context of a larger life history, they provide insight into the changes in official indigenismo during the tumultuous first years of military rule.

Competing Memories of the 1954 Coup's Impact on the IING

When Castillo Armas temporarily suspended the IING via presidential decree in August 1954, he justified this decision by saying that the institute had failed to provide solutions for the problems confronting the Indigenous population. This statement signaled his disagreement with the IING's model of action anthropology that called for careful study and collaboration with host communities prior to beginning applied programs. The decree stripped the IING of its budget and appointed a special committee within the Ministry of Education to do a full study of the institute and determine whether to reopen it under new leadership.[34]

About six weeks later, the *Consejo Técnico de Educación* wrote a favorable report about the IING's work, calling for its reopening. It cited examples of existing international agreements between the IING and foreign entities: its agreement with the Musée de l'Homme in Paris, France, to conduct archaeology, ethnography, and linguistic research in Huehuetenango; another agreement with the United Nations to study Indigenous economic activity; a partnership with the Pan-American Union to continue research with the cross-cultural survey for the Human Relation Area Files; and an agreement with the International Organization of Labor to conduct research on the salaries of Indigenous wage laborers. Further, in 1952, Guatemala had signed a contract with the University of Oklahoma and the Summer Institute of Linguistics to create bilingual literacy primers in several Indigenous languages. Finally, the 1940 Pátzcuaro Accords committed Guatemala to providing a national indigenist institute as part of its membership in the III. In conclusion, the report remarked that with the "resignation" of Noval, the IING no longer had personnel problems and recommended that to avoid future issues, all current and future employees should regularly complete disclosures about their "civic activities (actuación cívica)."[35] On October 7, 1954, through *Decreto-Gubernativo* 105-27, the Guatemalan government reopened the IING.[36] In all, the IING was closed for only two months and had a change in director, but the first bulletin it released after reopening gave the impression that the institute was otherwise unaffected by the Counterrevolution.

However, oral histories complicate this simplified narrative, "point[ing] to how people create their consciousness and subjectivity given the material, intellectual, and social resources at their disposal."[37] In 2015, Francisco Rodríguez Rouanet and Hélida Esther Cabrera were the only living IING employees who had worked at the institute in 1954, and they were ninety-four and ninety-three at the time, respectively. Their oral life histories provide a record of the IING at this historical juncture, and they embedded the IING's history within a narrative that more holistically also incorporated their personal and familial lives.[38] Beyond their histories, the physical spaces of their homes bore testimony to the fact that while their lives extended beyond their careers in the IING, their fieldwork in rural Guatemala had profoundly influenced them.

Over his long career with the IING, Rodríguez collected figurines and other handicrafts that filled his living room, often placed alongside family photos. The multiple crucifixes and nativity scenes reflected his adherence to Catholicism, and portraits of him and his son with their instruments made his love for music apparent. On the wall hung his framed honorary doctoral

degree awarded by the *Universidad del Valle de Guatemala*, a proud testament
to the academic merit of his work despite never formally completing higher
education. Rodríguez shared his life history with me, all while sipping sweet-
ened coffee out of porcelain cups that he claimed had once belonged to Justo
Rufino Barrios's wife, a nineteenth-century Guatemalan first lady, and that
his mother-in-law had purchased at a rummage sale. His library had a few remaining volumes of his field notes, along with numerous publications of the
IING and the Center of Regional Artisanry and Folk Art (*Subcentro de Arte-
sanías Regionales y Artes Populares*), where he spent the latter part of his career.
Interspersed among the documents were his personal and professional writings, numerous family photographs, and aged newspaper clippings and announcements from significant life moments. His home as archive reflected his
personal values of family and tradition, dedication to one's profession, and ap-
preciation for the arts.

Cabrera lived in her family home in Santiago Atitlán, which her grandparents purchased when they migrated from Germany in the nineteenth century.
While she no longer enjoyed the same elite political position and financial
stability that her grandparents had acquired, her home's central location in
Santiago Atitlán facilitated regular visits from Indigenous and ladino neighbors from all social classes. The upper floors of her home had been converted
into guest rooms, where I stayed, and her granddaughter ran a restaurant out
of the front room, where I ate almost all my meals. Cabrera remains a respected member of the community and continues to use her knowledge
about natural medicine to attend to sick people that visit her, selling herbal
remedies and her homemade yogurt and admonishing children for drinking
Coca-Cola, which she refers to as "criminal." While we shared meals, watched
telenovelas, and did daily errands, she shared aspects of her life story, often talking well into the night. Unlike Rodríguez, Cabrera did not have a substantial
personal archive, and she carefully stored her few remaining books and papers
in an antique armoire. With tears in her eyes, she repeatedly lamented that her
late husband burned all her fieldwork notebooks, a spontaneous act of jealousy
that she still struggled to forgive.

The central goals of these oral histories were to elucidate the impact that
the 1954 coup had upon the IING and to learn how the state's approach to
integrating Indigenous people changed in this moment. But initially, their accounts seemed more contradictory than similar, necessarily complicating a
simplistic understanding of 1954 as a defined, temporal moment. Instead,
Rodríguez and Cabrera attributed meanings to the coup based on life experi-

ences that occurred on either side of this pivotal political moment and with the hindsight that the present afforded. Scholar Alessandro Portelli reminds us that the subjectivity and the messiness of oral history is its greatest strength; as he writes, "errors, inventions, and myths lead us through and beyond facts to their meanings."[39] Recounted sixty years later, Rodríguez's and Cabrera's oral histories depict how two middle-class Guatemalan ethnographers experienced the transition to authoritarianism, both in their personal lives and in their professional work at the IING. While the significance that they attributed to the coup itself differs, they both clearly indicated that the Counterrevolution reduced the IING's influence on development initiatives in predominantly Indigenous regions, thus ending the possibilities of creative and flexible collaboration with local communities as official state projects.

Rodríguez confirmed the IING's official retelling of the immediate impact of 1954, insisting that the change in government was insignificant, and like before, the work of the institute remained apolitical. When asked how the IING changed after the 1954 coup, he simply stated, "Well, very little." Upon further prodding by asking what IING employees thought of both the Revolution and then the Counterrevolution, he told me a bit exasperatedly, "Look, as I've told you since the beginning [of our interviews], the *Indigenista* [referring to the IING] didn't get involved at all in anything political." At another point he remarked that he did not like to discuss politics or religion, because these topics only divided people, and that it was better to keep these opinions to oneself. Thus, Rodríguez refused to directly identify the 1954 coup as significant in the IING's history.[40] Conversely, Cabrera remembered this moment quite differently. She recounted that Castillo Armas accused the IING of being communist and arrested the director, Joaquín Noval, whom she greatly admired. She dramatically recalled, "We suffered, they suspended the institute . . . we suffered, we suffered the change that happened [referring to the coup], my outlook (*mi panorama*) changed, my thoughts changed."[41] For Cabrera, the coup marked a sudden and pronounced watershed moment in the history of the IING.

The construction of these different narratives is revealing of the interviewee's subjective self, and the information that narrators choose to include and that which they omit reveals cognizant choices in their constructions of the past. Historian Daniel James's theoretical framework proves useful for thinking about how oral history reveals different levels of memory: (1) the episodic present, based on the mundane, daily experience, (2) the performed memory that is based on stereotypes and generalized ways of seeing the world, and (3) the hymnic moments, which the narrator recognizes perhaps for the first time as a moment of special significance in his or her life.[42] This framework allows historians to interrogate why certain moments retain personal significance within the narrator's broader life story. And for the present purposes, this analytical frame provides a means to examine apparent discrepancies that appear in various accounts of a single historical event, such as the 1954 coup.

Rodríguez's interpretation of 1954 represented a performed memory. Despite, or perhaps because of, my repeated questioning, Rodríguez maintained that he was not a political man. He loved his country, he proudly voted (he showed me his inked index finger during our meeting the Monday after the 2015 presidential elections, where he had sealed his ballot with his fingerprint), and he worked hard to serve his nation during his forty years with the IING and the Center of Regional Artisanry. He attributed his lack of interest in politics as one reason why he was able to work for so long in these postings despite the numerous political shifts in Guatemala; employees with known political views were often dismissed with regime changes, so neutrality—performed or not—was important for job security. Rodríguez maintained the conviction that the IING was an apolitical institute, without a partisan or a religious agenda. Thus, 1954, while a date he knew and remembered, did not mark a moment in which his life drastically changed. This memory was not part of the episodic present, for nothing about the 1954 coup was a normal part of life, but neither was it a hymnic moment, for it held no special meaning for him. Instead, it was a performed memory.

Key to understanding Rodríguez's narrative is the context of the rest of his life history. His girlfriend's father served as a member of General Ubico's cabinet, and when Ubico's government fell in 1944, her family feared possible repercussions. In that moment, Rodríguez traveled with their family to the Black Christ in Esquipulas, a wooden crucifix that over time has darkened and serves as an important religious relic and pilgrimage site. There, his girlfriend's mother prayed for her husband's safety, and Rodríguez took the opportunity to pray that his girlfriend would accept his upcoming marriage proposal, which she did. While her family remained tied to Ubico's government and thus very critical of Arévalo, his own family had connections within the revolutionary government. Manuel Galich, the minister of education, was Rodríguez's godfather, and he helped Rodríguez attain a job in the newly founded IING. Additionally, it was Galich who loaned Rodríguez a pair of suit pants to wear for his wedding, much to his mother-in-law's dismay, as Rodríguez needed to coordinate with his father-in-law's army uniform but did not have his own. Thus, within his own family the potential for politically inspired conflict loomed large, and perhaps this explains Rodríguez's stance that political opinion needed to remain private to ensure peaceful familial relationships.[43] Beyond this personal aspect, also important to note is the fact that with the restructuring of the IING, Rodríguez received a promotion to head of the Fieldwork Division.[44] Thus, professionally, Rodríguez benefited with the postcoup restructuring, and he carefully managed any personal feelings he had about the political change for the sake of his personal relationships and his career.

On the other hand, 1954 represented a hymnic moment in Cabrera's life. Only weeks before the coup, Cabrera coincidentally encountered her first serious boyfriend, Manuel "Meme" Castañeda de Castillo, at a bus stop in downtown Guatemala City. They had dated ten years prior, when Meme was stationed with Ubico's army in Santiago Atitlán. She fondly told me about the love letters he used to secretly pass to her through her family's maid and how he would frequent their restaurant in order to catch a glimpse of her working in the kitchen. However, her mother disapproved of their relationship and managed to have Meme transferred from Santiago Atitlán to San Lucas Toliman, thus ending his relationship with her daughter. This unexpected meeting in the capital marked the first time Cabrera had seen Meme for ten years. She related that she felt thrilled to see him, and when he got off the bus, he told her that soon he would have a surprise for her.

Just a few weeks after this encounter, the coup transpired. At that point, Cabrera learned that Meme was closely connected to Castillo Armas and had helped orchestrate the coup, which greatly disillusioned her. She commented that perhaps she would have dated him again had he not been involved with Castillo Armas, but this association she could never overcome. However, she never shared her disappointment with him because of the delicacy of the political situation.[45] Years later, Cabrera married Edgar Bauer, and she spoke less fondly of this relationship, characterizing their marriage as one filled with hardship and difficulty. With the hindsight of sixty years, she marked the 1954 coup as the moment that robbed her of her first love and ruined her chance at a romantic, fulfilling marriage.

Further, Cabrera's professional life also suffered as a result of the IING's restructuring. Unlike Rodríguez, who received a promotion, Cabrera was demoted from being a full-time ethnographer to an auxiliary researcher.[46] She had greatly admired Noval and was personally loyal to him, as he had taken a significant risk in hiring her, a woman, for a traveling ethnographer role. The new director, Juan de Dios Rosales, had once been her colleague, and she had personal conflicts with him and thus was greatly dismayed to learn he would now be her superior. In recounting her story, she identified 1954 as the moment that transformed the IING and forever changed the work that gave her a sense of purpose and confidence. Thus, Cabrera positioned the coup as a hymnic moment, one that profoundly reshaped her professional options and altered her personal life.

Cabrera's oral history undeniably positions 1954 as a pivotal moment in IING history; at first glance, Rodríguez's account seems to argue the opposite. Yet when I reframed the question in less overtly political ways, simply asking instead about the institute's historical trajectory, Rodríguez also marked post-1954, just not the coup itself, as the beginning of the IING's decline, explaining how the government repeatedly defunded projects and made significant budget cuts. When asked if the government in the 1960s and 1970s still had interest in Indigenous issues, he sarcastically replied, "Yes, but only to obtain votes."[47] Comments like these, while not expressing a direct position on particular leaders or on the 1954 coup, did communicate his disenchantment with the low status to which the Counterrevolution relegated the IING. Taken together, and with careful recognition of the fictious nature of the personal-professional divide, these two oral histories do suggest that in the longer aftermath of the 1954 coup, the IING became a backwater institution, one that the state did not prioritize or adequately fund, resulting in its inability to continue being an institution capable of effecting any meaningful change.

What these oral testimonies still do not make clear is precisely why the counterrevolutionary state stopped prioritizing the work of the IING and what this decline meant in terms of how the state understood Indigeneity and its relationship to Indigenous Guatemalans. The history of the PMIT—the short-lived community development project that the IING briefly conducted postcoup—adds another layer of evidence to support the interpretation that the institute's significance slowly declined during the Counterrevolution. More importantly, it also helps to contextualize why this transpired, what aspects of the IING's agenda fell out of line with governance under authoritarian rule, and how this reshaped the construction of the permitted modern Indian citizen.

The Proyecto de Mejoramiento Integral de Tactic

In counterrevolutionary Guatemala, economic development took on various forms, and while extant scholarship has explored the state's large-scale infrastructure projects of the 1950s, it has given less attention to Guatemalan community development projects of this decade.[48] Elsewhere in the world, particularly with India's 1952 model village project, community development initiatives became what historian Nick Cullather called "one of the leading strategies of rural modernization."[49] Guatemala also received U.S. aid and recommendations for community development. In the early Cold War moment, and in the aftermath of President Truman's 1949 "Point Four" speech that called for "the improvement and growth of underdeveloped areas," community development shifted from a domestic strategy of urban renewal to an important component of U.S. foreign aid for rural development.[50] Importantly, as many scholarly discussions of community development focus on its practice during the so-called Decade of Development of the 1960s, over a decade earlier, Truman's Point Four program precipitated this turn toward community development as a viable strategy for improving rural life and thus quelling discontent.

As the idea of community development gained traction as a legitimate project, "a strange pattern thus emerged within the foreign aid apparatus" as adherents to modernization theory, the modernizers, "gravitated toward centers of power." Those more supportive of a communal, localized approach, the communitarians, worked at "the sites of implementation."[51] This dichotomy that Daniel Immerwahr proposes between modernizers and communitarians is productive in unpacking the layers of meaning and intentionality that occur within a single community development project. However, in its focus on development experts, it minimizes the agency of recipients. When combined with Tania Murray Li's distinction between the practice of government, or the state's objective with a program, and the practice of politics, referencing the local responses to the program, this distinction between communitarians and modernizers allows for the examination of project planners' intentions, the actions of the project's local staff, and the agency of recipients.[52] By putting into conversation the visions of institutions and individuals we might categorize as modernizers with those of communitarians, and through examination of sources that provide glimpses into the lived experiences of a development project, we can better understand how official community development projects shifted toward modernization and in doing so, cemented the idea of a state-sanctioned version of Indigeneity that rendered all autonomous expressions to be antithetical to national progress and, eventually, subversive.

The IING's first decade of work focused on compiling data and writing monographs on Indigenous communities. By the mid-1950s, however, it entered into more practical work, and in 1957, the Institute launched the PMIT.[53] IING staff chose the municipality of Tactic in the department of Alta Verapaz to serve as the program's site because its population of nearly 10,000 people was 76 percent rural and largely identified as Indigenous (~85 percent).[54] The Poqomchi' Maya were by far the largest ethnic group, but the villages (*aldeas*) of El Manantial and La Cumbre were Q'eqchi' Maya and the village of Chalcalté was Achi Maya.[55] However, the PMIT only worked in the municipal center and in Poqomchi' villages such as Pasmolón, Tampó, Chiacal, and Tzalam. Furthermore, the IING wanted this project to be a shining example of a successful community development project, so it strategically chose a visible location.[56] Tactic is an important transit center, located on the main highway that connects Guatemala City to the department capital of Cobán.[57] Thus, the community was easily accessible to state officials wanting to visit the project and to the many ordinary travelers who would have witnessed this showcase of community development.

The PMIT briefly appears in limited primary and secondary sources. Historian Claudia Dary mentioned the project as an example of an assimilationist project of the Counterrevolution, citing one of the PMIT's official objectives which gave the goal of "assimilating the *indígena* to our nationality," and historian Olga Pérez Molina similarly described the PMIT as evidence for her claim that the IING pursued more applied projects after 1954.[58] Contemporary IING publications contain brief summaries of the project, but like the aforementioned scholarship, these provide little analysis of the local history of the PMIT or insight into the interchanges between project staff and recipients. To reconstruct fragments of this history, I relied on oral history interviews with Rodríguez Rouanet, his field notes, and published reports from affiliated institutions. Given that local voices are all mediated through these outside actors, I carefully examined these materials for moments when Indigenous agency and autonomy were exercised and recorded, or when informants' voices do speak through these records. I attempted to interview Tactic residents who remembered the PMIT, but unfortunately, those who were alive during the 1950s were too young to remember the project; only Miguel Peláez Morales, whose father was mayor during the PMIT, had any recollection of the program. Tactic's municipal archive contained a few mentions of the PMIT, and these records, though often recording only the actions of the leadership, help capture a sense of the ways that rural people engaged with the program. Despite these source limitations, I argue that what becomes clear in this reading of the PMIT is how the IING's vision for community development clashed with the state's adoption of modernization, particularly in how it allowed for participants to usurp the official mandate of de-Indianization in order to define modernity that was compatible with their understanding of Indigeneity.

Each local PMIT staff member oversaw an aspect of the project, and these included a professor, an obstetrician, two linguists from the Summer Institute of Linguistics (SIL), a health inspector, a social worker, an agronomist, an anthropologist, an administrator, a chief of audiovisuals, a chauffeur, and several assistants who helped organize social events. They lived in Tactic and worked there for nearly a year and a half before the program ended in 1959.[59] Despite never having completed a project of this nature, years of fieldwork in rural communities had taught IING ethnographers about the importance of local collaboration. And the IING had previously worked in Tactic; municipal records from July 1955 detail how Cabrera and Rodríguez visited Tactic to organize a local weaving committee and distribute tags of authenticity as part of a textile protection program.[60] PMIT staff recognized that rural Indigenous communities often had dual power structures via the civil-religious hierarchy, so they directly collaborated with both the political and the religious leadership. Prominent local citizens often accompanied PMIT employees as they interviewed local people and set up their projects, and their presence gave PMIT staff credibility in the town but also may have inadvertently coerced participation, if clientelist relationships existed. PMIT leaders also collaborated with the governor of the Department of Alta Verapaz, who occasionally lent logistical support.[61] Over the course of the eighteen months that the PMIT was in effect, Tactic experienced infrastructure and programmatic changes most notably in education, public health, and agriculture, and at least one PMIT staff member, Rodríguez, came to understand the challenges confronting Tactic's socioeconomic development as political, not technical.

Even before the PMIT arrived in Tactic, village leadership requested educational opportunities and supporting infrastructure from the municipal government. In his analysis of the history of another Guatemalan municipality—Comalapa—Edgar Esquit argues that many Kaqchikel saw education as a means to "improve oneself" (*superarse*) and challenge racism. Perhaps the same held true for Tactic's Poqomchi' residents, based on this pattern of petitions. For example, in May 1955, sixty-one residents from the village of Pasmolón requested that the municipality fund the construction of a new school. Over two-thirds signed with a thumbprint, indicating their inability to sign their names. Though the entry is brief, it is plausible that Pasmolón residents wished for the next generation to have access to an opportunity that they had not but needed the municipality's fiscal assistance in building the necessary infrastructure.[62] Parents from the village of Tzalam appeared in municipal records in February 1958 when they requested that a new teacher be appointed, as the previous teacher had left for Cobán and failed to return, thus abandoning the students.[63] In both instances, residents seemed to prioritize education and desire a local school.

School construction factored centrally in the programming that the PMIT oversaw, and local residents collaborated on planning and at least partially constructing schools in Tampó, Pasmolón, and Tzalam, respectively. In late September 1958, PMIT staff met in Tzalam with Tactic's mayor, the new Tzalam teacher, and the majority of the village's adult males to discuss the school construction project. The major challenge confronting residents was acquiring land, as one man, Francisco Xoy Cho from Pasmolón, privately owned the land in the town center. In the discussion that the PMIT mediated, Xoy agreed to give them his lot for the school in exchange for a plot of Tzalam's communal land that measured over twice as large.[64] What the record leaves unclear is Xoy Cho's position: Was he an upper-class landowner? Was this unequal exchange of property exploitative and one more example of the erosion of communal land, or was it a fair exchange in terms of the location and quality of the two plots? The Xoy family in Tactic historically had counted among the Poqomchi' elite, but the archival record does not detail whether Francisco Xoy continued to enjoy this position.[65] However, the record from the Pasmolón school request hints that he did not. In a rare instance, the municipal secretary listed the sixty-eight participants from Pasmolón by name in the meeting minutes themselves, and he attributed the honorific "Don" to only five of them, indicating their higher status. Francisco Xoy's attendance is noted, but "don" does not precede his name. However, he was one of the few who did sign in neat cursive script rather than with a thumbprint, thus indicating that he had obtained some degree of education, likely a status symbol.[66] Reasonably, then, Xoy was a local elite in Pasmolón but perhaps not recognized as a municipal elite, and this exchange might have allowed him to further solidify his position. Thus, while we cannot determine the nature of this exchange, we do know that Tzalam residents agreed, provided that Xoy allow them to first cultivate the milpa they had planted on their communal land. Forty people signed the agreement, and thirty signed with their thumbprints, indicating their willingness to part with communal land in exchange for a new school for the village's youth.[67]

Additionally, the PMIT's collaboration with the SIL resulted in Guatemala's first bilingual education program in the local language, Poqomchi'.[68] SIL linguists Margarita Wendell and Rubi Scott arrived in November 1958, but only a month later, the government revoked PMIT funding. Still, by that time, Wendell and Scott had written two primers and a book of short stories.

With funding from the SIL and the Inter-American Education Foundation and IING support, they continued the bilingual education program, creating five primers and two workbooks.[69] On February 17, 1959, SIL and IING staff introduced the new materials and methodology to Tactic's schoolteachers. Initially, some teachers resisted this new approach because the Ministry of Education's exams required student proficiency in Spanish. However, after months of discussion, the Ministry of Education decided to allow Tactic's students to be tested in Poqomchi', and the final exams reveal the program's success: of the 165 students tested, 96 percent passed the exam.[70]

In her report, Wendell recounted an example that demonstrated the personal impact that literacy in Poqomchi' had for *tactiqueños* (residents of Tactic municipality). One day, a young girl named María Vicente Cáceros, whom Wendell described as barefoot and Indigenous, came to Wendell's office and asked to be taught to read. Although María never explained why she was not attending school, the two linguists surmised that as Indigenous, female, and poor, she felt unwelcome and feared ridicule. Perhaps, also, her family needed her labor and prioritized her economic contributions to the household over her formal education.[71] Over the next few months, the linguists taught María how to read Poqomchi', and they even invited her to read before the Peruvian delegation at the III's 1959 IV Inter-American Congress on Indian Life, held in Guatemala City, to demonstrate the success of Guatemala's pilot bilingual education program.[72] María had the opportunity to demonstrate literacy in her own language at an international convention, but SIL linguists used a child and showcased her poverty to prove the success of their program. In doing so, they racialized Indigeneity to connote poverty and illiteracy and Indigenous people as objects of Western benevolence. Without sources that explain María's perspective, it is impossible to know if this experience made her feel emboldened or exploited—or a combination of the two.

As a methodology, *castellanización* emphasizes literacy in one's first language based on Spanish phonetics, believing that this skill could easily transfer to Spanish literacy and facilitate assimilation into national culture and eliminate, or at least minimize, the use of Indigenous languages.[73] In the PMIT project, the SIL linguists seemed to model the same program that the Mexican *Secretaría de Educación Pública* used in the 1930s, which involved "harmonizing their practices with local cultures and conditions, and using local idioms as a means of communication and teaching."[74] The state linked Spanish competency to national progress, as evidenced through countless literacy campaigns and education reforms. This practice of government certainly suggests the goal of gradually reducing difference among Guatemala's diverse population by fostering linguistic unity in Spanish, as discussed in the Juan Chapín primer. Official castellanización did not establish multiple national languages, nor did it restructure educational curriculum to have a multicultural perspective. However, the PMIT's bilingual education program undermined the assimilationist goal of castellanización because eradication of Poqomchi' was never the PMIT's objective.

The practice of politics through castellanización in Tactic reveals ways in which local people used the opportunities that this program provided to become literate and bilingual and to further solidify their position as Indigenous citizens, on their own terms. Students spoke and studied their own language in a national school. The program acknowledged that Poqomchi' was a language in its own right, with its own internal grammar, structure, and complexity. At the same time, such a program facilitated Spanish competency, but as used in Tactic, this did not necessitate erasure of Poqomchi'. With Spanish literacy, one could understand written contracts and titles, one could read newspapers and connect to print society, and one could more easily navigate complex bureaucracies such as the national education and health system. Though the PMIT's literacy program did not change the state's prioritization of Spanish, it did partially subvert the state's intentions by both instilling the national language into the community while simultaneously promoting the use of Poqomchi'. The meanings attributed to this project at the local level were not ones of cultural assimilation but instead ones that promoted engagement with the nation, on the participants' terms.

In addition to its focus on literacy, the PMIT also worked in local health care but never attempted to eliminate forms of Maya medicinal practices or the role of *curanderos* (healers). Once again, the practice of politics differed from the practice of government, which aimed to replace "traditional" practices with modern medicine. Prior to the PMIT's arrival, the Guatemalan Ministry of Public Health conducted immunization campaigns in the local schools, vaccinating schoolchildren against diphtheria, whooping cough, typhoid, and smallpox, but this was the extent of state public health initiatives.[75] The Red Cross's local chapter remained the primary option for medical care, and its presence predated the PMIT. Supported by donations and local fundraising such as ticket sales for basketball games and marimba concerts, this center operated as a basic dispensary and vaccination center.[76] At first, Poqomchi's in Tactic had rejected the Red Cross. However, by the time the PMIT arrived, many people were using their services, buying medicine for parasite prevention and participating in vaccination campaigns. According to one local ladino and simultaneously revealing his ideas about modernity and his own sense of perceived cultural superiority, the Indigenous population had further "civilized themselves," as they now built more modern houses and even used toothpaste.[77]

However, the Red Cross often lacked the necessary resources and the technology to assist in medical emergencies. The PMIT filled this need and improved tactiqueños' access to health care through establishing a dispensary in the municipal building that held medical equipment and a variety of medicines. Over the course of the PMIT, dispensary staff treated 1,145 people and took medicines and vaccinations to the nearby village of Pasmolón. In the case of extreme medical emergency, PMIT staff used their connections in the departmental capital of Cobán to call an ambulance.[78] The PMIT also built latrines in the municipal market to combat the spread of disease and improve public sanitation, and the staff nurse trained local midwives so that they could receive a certificate noting they had met the Ministry of Health's licensing requirements.[79] Clearly, a central part of integral development was creating healthy citizens by establishing adequate and sanitary infrastructure. At the same time, and as scholars like David Carey Jr. have shown, the state's effort to push populations away from non-Western medical practices were "as much about maintaining social order as it was about public health."[80]

However, PMIT staff members like Rodríguez did not view their actions in the arena of public health in this way. From their perspective, through providing medicines, basic health care, and sanitation services, the PMIT gave medical services to a town that had previously received very little in terms of public health. Unlike medical campaigns on coffee and banana plantations that reportedly made employment contingent on consenting to vaccinations, or the horrific experimentation that the U.S. Public Health Service conducted in Guatemala from 1946 to 1948 that intentionally infected at least 1,300 people from vulnerable populations with syphilis, gonorrhea, or chancroid, the PMIT never forced health services upon people and carefully explained procedures to each recipient.[81]

Rodríguez recalled that when the PMIT arrived, many residents remained wary of new health care practices. For example, he recounted that people feared the hospital, believing that only those who were dying went there. Similarly, many community members believed vaccines to be cures that one should inject in the place where one was hurt.[82] Thus, they believed it to be irrational to inject healthy children in the arm when they felt no arm pain. Perhaps applying lessons learned during the IING's collaboration with the INCAP in Magdalena Milpas Altas, PMIT nurses held meetings with schoolchildren's parents to explain the preventive nature of vaccinations and the importance of hospital services. According to Rodríguez, the PMIT never sought to forcibly convince people to participate; as he simply stated, "If they didn't want it, they didn't want it."[83] PMIT staff did not racialize Poqomchi's as unsanitary or unhealthy but rather sought to extend and explain these optional services and allowed individuals to exercise bodily autonomy and decide what—if anything—to accept. They viewed all tactiqueños as rational citizens capable of making decisions regarding their health and bodies, a position that the state certainly would not have shared. Once again, this disconnect between the modernizers' practices of government in terms of public health interventions and the communitarians' practices of politics on the ground in Tactic discloses differences in philosophy and in the implementation of development agendas that shaped the complex meanings and the outcomes of community development.

The PMIT also prioritized agricultural development, although the program did not last long enough for the IING to make serious advancements in this sector. Rodríguez's field notes indicate the PMIT's interest in townspeoples' access to credit via the *Banco Agrario Nacional* (National Agrarian Bank). Since opening in 1950, the Tactic branch had given out 354 small loans: 302 had been paid in full, 32 were current and only 20 were defaulted.[84] The bank always gave individual loans that never exceeded Q300 or a three-year term, which underscores the state's objective of quickly transforming subsistence farmers into an agricultural middle class.[85] These loans helped farmers cultivate land that they either owned or rented, providing them a more stable alternative to working as day laborers where payments were incredibly low. For example, day laborer Juan Suc informed Rodríguez that he only received fifty cents per day without food or twenty-five cents per day with food.[86] In Tactic, basic necessities like powdered milk cost seventy-five cents per packet, unscented soap was five cents per bar, and sugar was ten cents a pound at the local market, so clearly, these low wages were insufficient.[87] Loans helped provide additional opportunities besides wage labor to farmers, but they also indebted people and tied farmers to another system of economic dependence, the Agrarian Bank.

Rodríguez witnessed this dependence firsthand on April 24, 1957, when Francisco Jor Chococ, an illiterate Poqomchi' farmer, requested an extension on his loan because of the exceptionally poor corn harvest. The bank agent agreed to file his petition with the national branch, but Rodríguez's records do not indicate whether it granted Jor's extension.[88] Uncontrollable factors like weather often determined farmers' ability to repay loans, and while many found loans appealing because of the potential financial independence they promised, poor harvests forced farmers like Jor into increasingly precarious situations, ones that development projects tried to mitigate, but could not entirely prevent.

To help farmers avoid defaulting on their loans because of poor harvests or low crop yields, the PMIT worked with the bank and the Ministry of Agriculture's Office of Indigenous Economic Development (*Servicio de Fomento de la Economía Indígena*, SFEI) to introduce farmers to new cultivation methods and technologies, providing borrowers with seeds, insecticides, and fertilizers. PMIT agronomist Rodolfo Lizama gave demonstrations about how these products might help increase crop yields.[89] While the archival record does not indicate how many of Tactic's farmers adopted these new techniques, historians like Patrick Chassé and David Carey Jr. have demonstrated that elsewhere in Guatemala, many Indigenous farmers hesitated to embrace chemical inputs and new cultivation techniques, as they questioned the environmental conse-quences.[90] Development experts, like PMIT staff, often emphasized the po-tential short-term gains of new technologies like fertilizers, insecticides, and modified seeds, but they did not always anticipate or question the long-term consequences that these changes might have for farmers.

Through these practical programs in education, health care, and agriculture, the state's intention with the PMIT was to address President Castillo Armas's 1957 mandate that Guatemalans "awaken" to the "new life" the Counterrevolu-tion provided.[91] The U.S. State Department was more explicit in identifying Indigenous people as those that needed to "wake up," stating that the "illiterate Indian majority . . . live[d] separated from the main currents of modern life, en-trenched in the ancient customs of the Mayan era."[92] Thus, the state and its U.S. advisors intended for the PMIT to instruct one municipality in how to behave in accordance with this new vision for the nation based on the promises of modernization. Through bringing democracy and capitalism to a rural com-munity, the PMIT would theoretically work to remove any remnants of the leftist ideology of the prior revolutionary government and would transform the population into the counterrevolutionary state's idea of the modern permit-ted Indian citizen. Instead, the practice of politics through the PMIT yielded a collaborative effort at development according to the community's terms; tac-tiqueños received education in their own language and participated in health services whenever they wanted. Though their experiences are mediated through an IING ethnographer's field notes, it seems clear that community members were free to reject any of the PMIT's modernizing instruments *and* their accom-panying ideologies, and PMIT staff on the ground found tactiqueños to be capable and motivated partners in improving their community.

Rodríguez's field notes underscore his own humility and willingness to critique the state's development program when he felt it to be inadequate. Unlike the indigenista figures in Chiapas who historian Stephen Lewis has studied, whose efforts disbanded an exploitative alcohol monopoly, Rodríguez's critiques were more careful and subtle, understandable in the counterrevolutionary political environment.[93] In these notes, he never suggested courses of action or behaviors that residents should adopt. For the most part, these notes are strictly ethnographical, systematically categorized with key words or phrases. On three occasions, Rodríguez used the category "social problems," but in each instance, his critique was not of tactiqueños but was directly aimed at the Guatemalan state's failure to meet citizens' basic needs.[94] An analytical reading of these instances provides a glimpse into the mentality of this intermediary figure, allowing us to understand what he viewed as problematic and underscoring that he did not fully buy into the state's modernizing project.

The first two entries categorized in this manner resulted from a single home visit with José Joaquín López y López. López was currently unemployed due to a heart condition he sustained while working for the Tactic branch of the liquor company *Licorera San Jerónimo*. One day, López caught a box of aguardiente bottles against his chest when it fell from a delivery truck, and he claimed this had caused a heart condition. Doctors in Guatemala City failed to cure him, and the liquor company refused to recognize the injury as workplace related, thus leaving López destitute and barely surviving by cultivating a small plot of beans on rented land. López's brother-in-law also suffered from a workplace injury at the brewery *Cervecería Centroamericana de Castillo Hermanos* in Guatemala City. While working, he fell down a staircase and hit his head, leaving him totally deaf and with mental disabilities that included violent mood swings. López and his wife had considered institutionalizing him but had decided against it, as "nobody gets out [of the asylum] until they have died."[95] The company offered no compensation or assistance. Though Rodríguez offered no potential solutions in his field notes, his decision to classify both episodes as "social problems," seems to indicate his displeasure at the lack of responsibility that both companies took for their injured workers and their complete impunity in totally dismissing these men's claims. In doing so, Rodríguez seems to be indirectly arguing for better state accountability in enforcing labor laws and workers' rights. Additionally, in directly quoting López's belief about the horrific conditions of the asylum, Rodríguez also indicated his dissatisfaction in the options that the state made available for citizens with mental disabilities.

The third instance of a "social problem" entry occurred less than a week later, on May 17, 1957, when Rodríguez wrote about a visit he made with the bank agent to a nearby village. The agent went to inform a client, Francisco Buc Isem, that the bank had approved his loan, and he offered Buc a ride to Tactic to collect his money. Buc readily agreed, and he and his son accompanied Rodríguez and the bank agent on the nearly half-mile walk back to the road where they had parked their car. Rodríguez noted that Buc was completely blind, yet his seventeen-year-old son provided him with no assistance. When asked, the son explained that his father did not like to be led nor did he need it; he could travel to and from the municipal center hauling a heavy load on his back. Rodríguez took care to note that the path from the village to Tactic required one to traverse a small river, with a fallen tree trunk serving as the only bridge. Again, Rodríguez made no policy suggestion, nor did he insist that a more structurally sound bridge be built. But by including this detail after remarking on Buc's regular need to travel by foot to Tactic, and through labeling the moment as a "social problem," Rodríguez seems to suggest that neither the municipal nor the national government were adequately addressing this man's needs.[96] In all three cases, Rodríguez was careful not to criticize the government, but he intentionally recorded situations he felt needed remedying and clearly did not find fault with the victims. And, it is telling that these entries are the only instances in his daily fieldwork diary that he classified as "social problems."

The Guatemalan government suddenly terminated the PMIT at the end of 1958, and municipal records reflect the community's disappointment, solidifying the claim that the program was something that at the very least the local leadership desired.[97] On January 12, 1959, local authorities met with the governor of Alta Verapaz and the departmental public health inspector to write a report that the governor could use to detail the problems resulting from the PMIT's suspension. In the resulting document, participants expressed their anger that individuals that the PMIT hired were suddenly unemployed and projects like Pasmolón's new school were unfinished, even though the original one had already been demolished. They expressed dismay that tactiqueños would forfeit all the money and time invested in these projects and that the PMIT's agricultural and health programs ceased operations. They declared that the PMIT was "absolutely necessary" as it was "a formula that Guatemala could use to address problems." Clearly, they understood the state's intention to use the PMIT as a pilot project and a model for a larger, nationwide initiative of community development, and they were willing to label it as such. Furthermore, they argued, the PMIT could potentially be "a plan for the rest of the countries in Latin America," again expressing their understanding of the project within the context of hemispheric geopolitics and growing concerns about rural instability. They asked for the plan to be restarted as soon as possible because it was of "great importance" for their community.[98] For local residents, the PMIT had been instrumental in providing much-needed infrastructure and had acted as a bridge to secure government funding for community-dictated projects.

National newspapers also admonished the national government for ending PMIT. Under the editorial direction of prominent indigenista David Vela (discussed in chapter 1), *El Imparcial* lamented the abrupt end of this program that provided development "without uprooting individuals from their community."[99] IING staff member Jaime Búcaro published a 1959 article that criticized the central government for reneging on its commitment to Tactic. His scathing critique argued that this decision had reinforced Indigenous communities' distrust of outsiders because tactiqueños now felt "defrauded" and "deceived."[100] In his own history of the project, Rodríguez wrote that tactiqueños "had found in the PMIT an institution that understood them and helped them to solve all types of problems, not just through their own means but with collaboration from other official and private institutions."[101]

The Ministry of Education cited a lack of funding as the official reason for terminating the program, despite having recently signed a multiple-year contract with Peruvian-born and Mexican-trained anthropologist Carlos Incháustegui to advise the PMIT, a contract which it then terminated.[102] Though I was unable to locate the Ministry of Education's budgets for the 1958–1959 fiscal year, records from congressional sessions revealed that in October, the Guatemalan Congress allotted an additional $105,000 to the Ministry of Education with funds from an IBRD loan.[103] If the PMIT had been a high priority, surely this funding could have further supported it. Financial issues seem to have been a convenient but inaccurate excuse for terminating a successful program. Additionally, the date that the program ended, December 31, 1958, occurred when Congress was not in session; it did not reconvene until February 1959. Thus, the decision could not be discussed or debated among representatives, and it is possible that few of them were even aware that the program had ended.

While not clearly stated in the archival record, it is reasonable to suggest that the PMIT had begun to venture into unacceptable territory because it allowed a rural community to pursue development in a way that enabled participants to create alternatives to the state's permitted Indian model and challenge modernization with local interpretations of what modernity meant. In a brief history of the PMIT that Rodríguez wrote in 2002, he stated that "the principal reason for the disappearance of the PMIT was that the high authorities of the government, starting with President Ydígoras, did not believe in the utility of the *Instituto Indigenista* and much less in its development projects."[104] Because IING staff largely let the community dictate the terms and the priorities of its projects, it unfolded in a much more organic way that deviated from the citizenship mold that the state wished to force upon all Indigenous Guatemalans. Instead, the PMIT's communitarian structure introduced the possibility of citizens challenging the status quo and upsetting existing social relations that rarely worked in their favor. Particularly in the national context of the Counterrevolution and against the international backdrop of the Cold War, the state found this possibility dangerous and unacceptable.

Despite the formal closure of the PMIT, the IING leveraged its existing resources and institutional networks to preserve its relationship with tactiqueños and at least finish projects that were underway. In June 1960, IING representative Jaime Búcaro traveled to Tactic and met with municipal leadership regarding the Pasmolón school and the PMIT dispensary. Through connecting the municipality with the Ministry of Education's *Socioeducativo Rural* (Department for Rural and Social Education, SER), Búcaro successfully negotiated increasing the pay for the school's carpenter and mason and thus helping the project resume. He also signed an agreement to turn over the PMIT dispensary to the municipality, including a considerable amount of medical equipment and medicines, in exchange for the municipality's commitment to pay the rent and salary of the dispensary nurse. In this way, the school project continued, and the dispensary reopened while the IING unburdened itself of financial commitments it could no longer keep.[105] Miguel Peláez, whose father was mayor for the PMIT's tenure, and who later served as mayor in the 1970s, recalled that despite its limited resources, the PMIT positively impacted the community, gained the support of residents, and helped to establish an effective pattern for future programs to follow, as the next chapter will discuss.[106] Though we cannot extrapolate more broadly than Tactic, it is clear that many tactiqueños—Poqomchi' and ladino alike—were upset by the PMIT's abrupt closure and desired development projects of this nature.

The IING after the End of PMIT

Returning to the chapter's broader question of what the 1954 political rupture meant for the state's policies toward the Indigenous population, both the PMIT's history and the IING staff's oral histories suggest that the 1954 coup itself was less significant than the years immediately following it in terms of histories of development. As the Guatemalan state, with direct U.S. assistance, centralized economic development and more directly monitored local politics, the new authoritarian government foreclosed the possibility for autonomous, organic development projects like the PMIT. As soon as the practice of politics began challenging the practice of government in Tactic, the executive branch of the Guatemalan government abruptly terminated the project and significantly decreased the IING's funding for all future work.

The archival record for IING activities post-1954 is scanty, and annual reports from the Ministry of Education indicate that it ceased being a key institution that the government used to help shape state policy. At the Second National Congress on Education in October 1956, a resolution defined the IING's primary function as a dependency of the Ministry of Education that could advise rural teachers on how to best interact with the towns where they worked, not as an institution that created knowledge about Indigenous communities and carefully orchestrated plans to address a wide array of local needs.[107] While neither the Guatemalan national archives nor those of the Ministry of Education hold the Ministry's annual reports for 1954–1965, the 1966 report indicated that the IING had become a dependency of the SER, further solidifying its primary role in teacher training.[108] The IING remained part of the SER until 1971, when it was transferred to yet another Ministry of Education branch, the Office of Culture and Fine Arts.[109] By 1971, the IING focused the majority of its studies on folklore, a seemingly less political avenue that the state deemed to be an acceptable form of cultural expression.

In addition to being shuffled around within the Ministry of Education, the IING also suffered drastic budget cuts. The Ministry of Education's 1970–1971 annual report noted that the IING's most pressing obstacle was the "surprising and unexplained reduction of Q25,000," which left the Institute with only Q13,075 to use toward its projects, as the rest of its Q56,495 covered operating costs and employee salaries. This significant reduction left the fieldwork budget with only Q6,000, an amount that would only cover a total of sixty days of investigation. Because the IING had six ethnographers on staff, this meager amount only provided for a mere ten days of fieldwork per individual, hardly sufficient for any type of quality investigation.[110]

The same report implied that the government cut these funds due to the false assertion that the IING had not been completing its assigned research. The report's author (who goes unnamed) claimed that this simply was not true; the IING had continued its labors but had been unable to formally publish its findings since 1945.[111] The IING actually regularly published monographs and the institutional bulletin until 1954, so this claim makes clear the author's hesitation to mark the change in government as the reason for the lack of publication funding. Instead, the author chose to indicate that the IING's work had not been published since the time of the revolutionary administrations rather than risk appearing critical of the authoritarian regime.

In concluding this report, the author implored that the next budget be significantly more substantial because "in view of the fundamental problems of integration and national development, the IIN[G] can offer valuable collaboration in those cases where, if it could count on available funds, it would have the ability to provide information outside the purview of other institutions and could suggest applicable solutions to the problems of the Indigenous population and the interrelationship between it and the ladino group, which coexist in the national territory."[112] Clearly, the IIING staff wished to be more than an expert advisor on questions of folklore and education: practicing action anthropology remained the IIING's goal, but the national government did not support this goal, as first evidenced in the cessation of the PMIT.

A 1970 USAID report supported the main points in the IIING's annual report. The author, USAID mission director for Guatemala Robert Culbertson, explained that the IIING had received "less and less money each year. Due to lack of funds, this formerly well-respected institute has not been able to carry out research for the past several years." He suggested that $10,000 could financially support the IIING (considerably less than what the IIING's operating budget had been), and he called for any leftover funds from fiscal year 1970 to be given to the institute. Records do not indicate whether USAID provided this funding to the IIING, but Culbertson's suggestion does indicate that the Guatemalan government no longer prioritized the IIING and that its minuscule budget severely hindered its efficacy.[113]

Despite the small budget and lack of official support, the IIING managed to collaborate on a few small-scale development projects after the PMIT. Anthropologist Jaime Búcaro served as IIING advisor to the 1964 National Program of Community Development, but after the PMIT, the IIING never administered another integral development project. Between 1966 and 1967, they helped five villages in Sololá acquire piped water, schools, and access roads; from 1971 to 1972 they studied highland seasonal migration, traditional medicine, the basic needs of a rural family, and the efficacy of castellanización programs; and from 1974 to 1975 they helped the communities of San Pedro La Laguna and Chuarrancho acquire potable water systems and collaborated with Jacaltenango to reconstruct their colonial-era church.[114] Additionally, in the aftermath of the devastating 1976 earthquake, the IIING conducted studies about local earthquake reconstruction needs and processes.[115]

Many of these projects were collaborations with the National Program of Community Development and SER, top-down, centralized entities that answered directly to the president or to one of his ministers. This shift is significant, as it coincides with the beginning of Guatemala's efforts to centralize economic planning through the five-year plans and use community development as a tool of counterinsurgency.[116] No longer could small state institutions like the IING create autonomous development projects intentionally structured in a communitarian way. Instead, all development projects were now, at least officially, structured according to the state's plans for modernization. Projects first had to meet approval from their respective government ministry, and all ministries had to justify their decisions and expenditures in light of the National Council for Economic Planning's plan, priorities, and categories. This allowed the state to directly oversee development projects, supervise personnel, receive progress reports, and extend its reach into the countryside. Just as development served to further the agenda of the democratic Revolution, so too did development help to consolidate and strengthen the authoritarian state.

Conclusion

The 1954 moment signified the waning importance of the IING, and the next decade reduced it to a severely underfunded research institute and a virtually insignificant actor in community development projects. However, there are continuities across this political rupture, particularly in the way that indigenista projects emphasized changes in educational, agricultural, and health practices. Revolutionary indigenismo had introduced the idea that socioeconomic development provided the state with a means to attempt to integrate Indigenous populations into the nation as modern "permitted Indians," and this continued to be a central tenet of the authoritarian regimes of the Counterrevolution.

Amid these continuities are also important changes. Under the Arbenz government, the state promoted integration through horizontal organizations such as unions and local agrarian committees, resulting in more communitarian initiatives, and the PMIT attempted to foster this same type of horizontal structure. Though some of revolutionary indigenista programs certainly sought to homogenize and flatten Indigeneity, the IING had come to recognize and appreciate the diversity within Guatemala. Through the PMIT, it promoted the paternalistic modernizing of the Indigenous population in a way that did not racialize Poqomchi's nor attempt to alter one's ethnic identity. However, as clearly exhibited in the Ydígoras government's decision to terminate the PMIT, this focus changed during the Counterrevolution. The authoritarian regimes foreclosed the era of careful and deliberate collaboration between the state via the IING and Indigenous communities and incorporated the goal of a state-defined de-Indianization. While socioeconomic development continued to be a key strategy during the years of nearly uninterrupted authoritarian rule between 1954 and 1985, this development was highly centralized. It was controlled by the highest echelons of government and adhered to an "antipopulist modernization model," with technocrats defining and implementing all changes instead of a communitarian approach.[117] Further, "permitted Indians" were now expected to fully support the government and oppose anything that could be characterized as leftist political action or ideas, including any efforts to restructure political power or change enduring socioeconomic inequalities and structural racism. The confines of this citizenship model became increasingly narrow and inflexible after the Counterrevolution.

This chapter has argued that the counterrevolutionary government viewed communitarian projects that allowed recipients to dictate the terms of the development projects, like the PMIT, to be dangerous and unacceptable because it gave too much autonomy to local leaders. As the IING faded from view, new actors and institutions emerged as more prominent players in this story. Particularly in terms of transforming the Indigenous population, the state began to cast its efforts less under a discourse of indigenismo and more as containment of communism. As the state increasingly used violence to quell discontent, the stakes for practicing development in a way unlike that which the state intended became framed as subversive. However, despite these higher stakes and top-down efforts to manage community development projects, recipients and local project staff continued to interpret and apply these efforts at modernization in unpredictable ways. Even as the Guatemalan and U.S. governments began to utilize community development as a critical part of a broader containment strategy, on the ground, individuals still took the risk of utilizing the opportunities that projects offered to pursue an alternate vision modernity and citizenship.

CHAPTER FIVE

Operation Awaken

Guatemala's National Program of
Community Development, 1960–1975

In 1963, the Guatemalan government created the National Program of Community Development (DESCOM), also called *Acción Conjunta*, and the DESCOM received aid from USAID to support these endeavors.[1] As the previous chapter discussed, the Counterrevolution centralized development efforts and framed these as technical, not political problems. In the mid-1960s, the state institutionalized this framework via the DESCOM and positioned Guatemala's "underdevelopment" as an issue of rural "underdevelopment."[2] For both Guatemalan and U.S. development experts, "'the village' contained all of the dangers and possibilities" that confronted the world, and the DESCOM's purpose was to "engineer 'modernity'" and, in Indigenous regions, transform the population into the racialized construct of the permitted Indian.[3]

At the DESCOM's 1964 inauguration, Director Elisa Molina de Stahl called the newly created program *Operación Despertar* (Operation Awaken), reflecting her conviction that through development, the government could magically "wake up the sleeping giant that is the people."[4] Molina's speech paralleled U.S. foreign policy, whose architects also imagined a "global Rip Van Winkle moment," calling for community development initiatives to "awaken" rural people to the freedom and prosperity that democracy and capitalism offered.[5] Referring to all rural Guatemalans as "sleeping" and in need of outsiders to "wake them" revealed her ignorance of the ways popular classes mediated outside intervention, and her assumptions racialized Indigenous Guatemalans as existing temporally outside of modernity.[6] Whereas during the Revolution more flexibility existed that allowed for the designing and implementation of projects at the local level, this chapter argues that the DESCOM centralized state efforts to chart the "appropriate course" for rural development. In doing so, it racialized and homogenized the rural poor as obstacles to progress due to socioeconomic status, and it categorized the Indigenous rural population as doubly "backward" due to cultural practices as well. Instead of relying on decentralized approaches and indigenista networks to study and transform the countryside, the state now promoted what historian Michael Latham has termed the "right kind of revolution," one that remained firmly grounded in capitalist relations and modernization.[7]

This chapter analyzes the history of the DESCOM within Guatemala's official transition to militarized development and the ways that Guatemalan and U.S. development experts and politicians envisioned the program's goals and intended outcomes. However, it also argues that a disconnect existed between the DESCOM leadership and local staff, as the latter did not see the containment of leftist subversion as directly related to the poverty alleviation measures they were implementing on the ground. Returning to Tactic, this chapter also maintains that recipients' interactions with the DESCOM remained ambivalent; while they did accept some forms of development aid that they found beneficial, they wholeheartedly rejected others that they found incompatible with their culture or daily life practices. To reconstruct this history, I rely on municipal archival records and oral histories with the few living participants from Tactic's various aldeas, municipal leadership, and program staff. These sources allow for an analysis of local agency and history from the perspective of various types of participants, complicating the state's narrative of the history of the DESCOM.

Guatemala in the Decade of Development

For the United States, the geopolitical importance of Latin America significantly increased in 1959 with the successful Cuban Revolution and the ensuing declaration of Cuba as a communist state two years later, the first in the Western Hemisphere. Suddenly, U.S. politicians and right-wing Latin Americans saw the small island of Cuba as a physical threat to the hemisphere's safety. Cuba was just over 100 miles from the U.S. coast, and U.S. politicians began to highly prioritize the containment of communism in Latin America, not just in Southeast Asia and Eastern Europe. Discursively, Cuba came to stand in as a metonym for this fear of communist infiltration and the possibility of the exportation of revolution elsewhere in the so-called Third World.[8] In fact, Adolf Berle, who would become an architect for Kennedy's Alliance for Progress, revealed in his diary in January 1961 that "eight governments may go the way of Cuba in the next six months unless something is done."[9] Guatemalan leaders also used Cuba as a metaphorical straw man to justify repressive actions while revolutionaries touted Cuba as an inspirational example to follow.

On November 13, 1960, a rebellion gave start to what would become the front bookend of a thirty-six-year civil war and caused concern in Guatemala City and

Washington, D.C., that Guatemala might just become a second Cuba. A group of young military members, disenchanted with the government's corruption and inability to improve living standards, launched an attack on the Matamoros Barracks in Guatemala City. While the government successfully stopped this uprising, those remaining from the rebelling faction founded the *Movimiento Rebelde 13 de Noviembre* and continued the insurgency in the eastern part of the country, primarily in the departments of Izabal and Zacapa.

Guatemalan president Miguel Ydígoras Fuentes was anti-communist to the point of obsession, and he played on the U.S. government's fear of a "second Cuba" constantly in his correspondence with Kennedy. On July 4, 1962, Ydígoras wrote to Kennedy to ask for support of the newly formed Central American Common Market, arguing that Central America was vital for the hemisphere's security. In supporting this economic integration, Ydígoras continued, the United States could show Central Americans that unlike the communism in Cuba, "the democratic system is the only one which, while guaranteeing liberty, meets the needs of the peoples."[10] In the aftermath of the Cuban Missile Crisis in November 1962, Ydígoras congratulated Kennedy, sending a telegram that began with "Hip Hip Hurrah" and celebrated how "the muscovit [*sic*] pride and Khrushchev's political career experienced its first spectacular failure." Continuing, his tone shifted from jubilant to grave, stating that as long as Castro remained in power, Cuba continued to threaten Guatemala and all Latin America.[11]

Kennedy and his administration shared these concerns about the Cuba phenomenon spreading across Latin America. At the 1961 Inter-American Conference in Punta del Este, Uruguay, participants created the statutes that formed the basis for the Alliance for Progress, committing to use socioeconomic development to strengthen hemispheric security. This agenda aligned with U.S. foreign policy toward Latin America, which identified social discontent as a key precursor to revolution.[12] A 1962 secret Department of State file suggested that the United States guide Latin American governments in "satisfy[ing] basic human wants," which in turn would "isolate and promote the downfall of the Communist beachhead in Cuba." Recognizing that in the hemisphere were "two continents whose security was interdependent," this document reemphasized the central tenets Kennedy's March 13, 1961 speech to Congress and the members of the Diplomatic Corps from Latin American nations, where he had insisted that the Americas needed to "demonstrate to the entire world that man's unsatisfied aspiration for economic progress and social justice can best be achieved by free men working within a framework of democratic institutions."[13] Infused with a Cold War flavor, the undertones suggested that development functioned as a "peaceful" means of counterinsurgency.

Though the Kennedy administration presented the Alliance for Progress as a novel approach to U.S.-Latin American relations, just over a decade earlier in 1949, President Harry S. Truman had called for similar measures on a global scale in his Point Four program, firmly defining development aid as a U.S. foreign policy. A key shift with Kennedy's Alliance for Progress plan was the earmarking of development funds for counterinsurgency operations, such as training of police forces or investment in surveillance technologies. The Alliance for Progress plan, a ten-year project that would foster economic development, promote regional integration, and improve social conditions, was based on collaborations between host countries' institutions and U.S. programs like USAID and the newly formed Peace Corps. It promised to focus on both large-scale infrastructure and on community development projects, as many development experts on the international scale promoted the latter as the best means to efficiently and cost-effectively improve rural life.[14] Ydígoras Fuentes formally replied to this endeavor, using the opportunity to point out how Guatemala remained "*muy amigo*" with the United States despite the previous sins committed by U.S. businesses such as the United Fruit Company. Still, he assured Kennedy that Guatemala would enthusiastically participate in the Alliance for Progress in order to improve the nation's well-being and to contain communism.[15]

A little over six months later, on September 25, 1961, President Kennedy addressed the United Nations in New York City, declaring the 1960s as the Decade of Development. He proposed, "Development can become a cooperative and not a competitive enterprise—to enable all nations, however diverse in their systems and beliefs, to become in fact as well as in law free and equal nations."[16] Again, this discursive framing of development was ironic, as Kennedy positioned development as cooperative. In reality, the United States was engaged in a significant competition with the Soviet Union to shape the nonaligned world and draw additional countries into close allegiance with what the United States termed the Free World. For the countries of Latin America, and particularly those the United States considered to be its own backyard in the Caribbean and Central America, development via the Alliance for Progress was a critical foreign policy strategy to ensure U.S. national security and to keep friendly Latin American leaders in power.

From the U.S. perspective, investing in Guatemala's security under the guise of development aid seemed extremely urgent in 1962, as popular protests against the Ydígoras government became more rampant and guerrilla activity in the east simultaneously escalated. In March 1962, the highest echelons in the U.S. government briefly considered invading Guatemala because they worried that Ydígoras was incapable of handling the growing threat of leftist insurgency, but by mid-month, they determined this course of action to be ill-advised.[17] Still, with the upcoming elections, former revolutionary-era president Juan José Arévalo announced his candidacy and his intention to return to Guatemala, triggering concern from the Guatemalan right and the U.S. Embassy. The Embassy warned in a January 1963 classified memo that Arévalo would jeopardize Guatemala's close relationship with the United States and the Alliance for Progress. It also reported that protestors linked support for Cuba, Arévalo, and anti-U.S. sentiment in their cries for political change; in one particularly dramatic instance, anti-communist women "hurled buckets of urine at heckling arevalistas."[18] So, when the State Department received word from the CIA that Guatemalan military officers were going to overthrow Ydígoras at dawn on March 30, the State Department did not warn Ydígoras but instead believed that a military regime might help to stabilize the country. The military coup occurred as the intelligence sources had reported, and on March 31, 1963, the U.S. Embassy cabled that "the President of Guataamala [*sic*] has been ousted, Peralta, Mindez (sic) has taken over. All is quiet at present in Guatemala."[19]

Just two weeks after Colonel Enrique Peralta Azurdia assumed the presidency, the United States officially recognized his regime despite the notable absence of democratic elections.[20] Peralta wasted no time in turning to community development as a means to gain popular support and to extend the state's control. He established a committee of nine experts to study the 1961 Punta del Este statutes and create a plan to apply them to Guatemala, recognizing that adherence to these recommendations would shape how the United States distributed Alliance for Progress funds. In contrast to Guatemala's prior emphasis on export agriculture, the committee's report called for "direct promotion of agricultural activities that traditionally have tended to stagnate" and "a sensible improvement of agricultural extension services and development for Indigenous communities that the Government would provide," bringing Indigenous campesinos' livelihoods and bodies to the forefront of the development agenda. This nationwide plan for community development via regional centers sought to guide the rising expectations of the countryside toward supporting the governing regime, one strongly aligned with the United States.[21] From the military state's perspective, such a program could be presented under the auspices of decentralization and local empowerment while being carefully orchestrated and fully controlled from above.

The U.S. government was much more explicit in positioning community development as an effective tool of counterinsurgency, one that would remove the conditions it believed to foster support for leftist organizations. A secret action memorandum addressed to James R. Fowler, the deputy U.S. coordinator for the Alliance for Progress, commented on the need to improve the acquisition of intelligence in rural regions and asserted that USAID-supported rural community development projects might provide "collection nets" for this critical information.[22] In 1966, Charles R. Burrows, director of the State Department's Central American Affairs, wrote to Lincoln Gordon of the Alliance for Progress and remarked that Guatemala's development endeavors "are motivated by political necessity," which was to preclude anti-government sentiment and revolt.[23] Finally, a 1966 U.S. Embassy report to the State Department warned that without improved conditions, the Guatemalan countryside would have "serious vulnerabilities which can be exploited by insurgents, including the potential for social explosion among some peasant sectors."[24] These examples expressed the U.S. government's willingness to support authoritarian military regimes in order to contain communism, masking this disregard for democracy by positioning foreign aid as humanitarian and as a remedy for socioeconomic problems.

While improving infrastructure was certainly a central objective of the DESCOM, changing the recipients' psychology was key. As historian J. T. Way writes, this model sought to "surgically modify their [the recipients'] entire way of being, from their habits to their deepest thoughts," not only shifting behaviors and actions but the very way in which people understood their world and its social relationships.[25] A 1962 article by Ernest F. Witte in *Community Development Review* stressed this psychological component of community development. Framing development as a "self-help process," Witte paternalistically explained how U.S. aid had effectively helped the "little people" by "bridg[ing] the gap that often exists between villagers and government" and by allowing "villagers [to] participate in determining how and by what means they can improve themselves and their communities."[26] This position is marred with assumptions. First, Witte racialized foreign governments of the Global South by positing them as incapable of interacting with their rural populace without the United States' help. Second, he presumed that all "villagers" were homogeneous and that universal solutions existed to resolve all problems, regardless of cultural or geographic context. Third, he took for granted that "villagers" wanted to participate in state projects in the first place. The discursive framing of development as a "self-help" process underscores how some experts began to recast poverty as a technical and not a political problem, one that called on rural people to be responsible for their own conditions and did not demand that the state restructure unequal relationships.[27]

Another article in the same volume built on President Franklin D. Roosevelt's famous 1941 declaration of the four freedoms: the freedoms of speech and worship, and the freedoms from want and fear. The author insisted that U.S. community development aid provided a "fifth freedom" that communism could not, namely the freedom for "every man to have a voice in the affairs of his community."[28] From U.S. development experts' perspective then, the psychological shift remained a key component of U.S. Cold War foreign policy and perhaps the most important dimension of the community development project, helping to explain USAID's insistence on only funding projects that were "self-help" in nature. Here is a clear departure from revolutionary-era programs like the IING that positioned the state as the party responsible for addressing socioeconomic injustice. The counterrevolutionary government in Guatemala refused to recognize the structural causes of poverty that would require a political solution and a reshaping of Guatemalan society. Instead, they positioned individuals as responsible for taking advantage of opportunities presented to them via modernization. Finally, these experts believed the psychological component to community development to be novel. However, changing a population's mentality had been a goal of the literacy campaigns and nutrition project, part of the CALs during the agrarian reform, and a key component of PMIT. In the Cold War moment, this two-pronged approach to development built on earlier ideas about integrated development, but now was strongly infused with an anti-communist flavor.

The DESCOM ascribed to this dual emphasis of development, using the underlying assumption that practical projects not only would propel a community toward modernization but also would achieve the mental transformations necessary for forging political stability. Through inculcating communities with a sense of social responsibility and the tools to effectively organize themselves, the government believed that the DESCOM could, as its foundational document asserted, "help people to acquire the necessary attitudes, habits, and points of view to effectively and democratically participate in the solution of problems for the local, regional, and national community."[29] Guatemala's diversity presented an additional challenge to this development model, and the DESCOM continued to build upon the idea that through development, Indigenous people would begin to identify with the larger nation and exercise their citizenship in a way that the state promoted.

The U.S. State Department also recognized that race played a huge role in shaping the success of Guatemalan state development efforts. Noting that Guatemala was "a country of two cultures and of two peoples," a 1966 report termed Guatemala's current economic situation as "layered under-development."

Blaming the inability of people to "improve their situation" on the lack of governance and infrastructure in rural regions, the report indicated that this inability was not innate but rather a result of inadequate access to resources and leadership. The report also recognized that U.S. foreign development aid had to be channeled "through an upper layer of society which resists social change not only to maintain the symbiotic relationship between itself and the underprivileged majority, but also because of a belief in the inherent superiority of its own culture." Clearly, the report's authors recognized Guatemala's structural racism and the fact that many social programs failed due to a lack of elite commitment and a fear of altering the status quo. Devising any type of program that the Guatemalan elite would accept required leaving existing power hierarchies in place.

Yet convincing the ruling sector of the necessity of community development was only part of the challenge; the other, the report indicated, was convincing Indigenous Guatemalans of the altruistic nature of outside development assistance. The report explained, "Having inherited a position of inferiority through military defeat and subsequent economic exploitation, the Indian is suspicious of outside interference and presently fears change as the prelude to a new form of bondage."[30] It recognized exploitation without clearly calling for its end or disagreeing with the implied premise of Indigenous "backwardness," and it suggested that training Indigenous people to work within the prevailing system was the means to ensure the program's success. This summarizes the very essence of this model of community development's appeal, as it would theoretically ensure the status quo while helping those most negatively affected by it to figure out how to alleviate their sufferings. Therefore, in adopting this approach to shaping recipients' bodies and minds, the U.S. and Guatemalan governments hoped that a comprehensive community development program would prevent leftist insurgency while simultaneously molding the diverse population into manageable citizens.

Various layers of racism exist in this model of community development. First, the United States remained skeptical of Latin Americans' capacity for expertise based on long-standing racialized assumptions of Latin Americans as inferior. Second, the U.S. experts discussed above enacted a paternalistic racism toward Guatemala's Indigenous people, problematically viewing them as a singular entity whose exploitation only the United States could remedy, an ironic position given the U.S. government's treatment and policies toward Native Peoples. Third, the Guatemalan state viewed the rural poor as racial others, at once fearing their potential power if left unguided but also viewing them as easily manipulated and thus needing outside guidance. Lastly, it saw rural Indigenous Guatemalans as doubly unmodern, both as a class condition and due to cultural practices. It was not until later that the Guatemalan military state would racialize the Indigenous population as subversive (as later chapters will explore), but the DESCOM program laid the foundation for development as a practice of counterinsurgency and as a means to promote integration according to the state's vision of modernity and acceptable forms of citizenship.

Institutionalizing Community Development

On November 24, 1964, *Decreto-Ley 296* ratified the DESCOM's creation and gave it the authority to approve, oversee, and coordinate all programs taking place in Guatemala to purportedly avoid duplicating efforts.[31] Though the military regime and the U.S. government touted the DESCOM as democratic, in actuality they used it to consolidate authoritarian rule under the guise of humanitarianism, a process I have analyzed in more detail elsewhere.[32] However, one overarching dilemma the Guatemalan government faced was where exactly to house such a program, as various ministries had specific programs, but to date, only the IING had attempted a more holistic development project with the PMIT. U.S. public affairs officer Taylor Peck referred to the new program as potentially "effecting an experimental plan for social engineering," and suggested the *Consejo de Bienestar Social* as an institutional home, as it engaged in child welfare and family services.[33] Records do not indicate if the U.S. Embassy influenced the Guatemalan government's choice, but in 1964, the military government placed the DESCOM under the *Secretaría de Bienestar Social* (SBS), which had replaced the *Consejo*, and allocated it a monthly budget of nearly Q7500 (Q1= $1) and a regional center in Chimaltenango. This institutional choice framed the DESCOM in gendered terms, as a program under the purview of a "motherly, state-based charity" that, following the analogy, would teach her most vulnerable children how to better care for themselves with minimal material assistance.[34]

Elisa Molina de Stahl served as director of the SBS during the Peralta administration. As a member of an elite family from Quetzaltenango, Molina had received a degree in social work and maintained a reputation in Guatemalan society for her charitable activities, particularly in children's services and education for the blind and deaf.[35] Journalists referred to her as a "strong woman of the Bible" and as "a cistern of altruistic abundance (*caudales altruistas*)."[36] Richard Waverly Poston, a professor from Southern Illinois University, described her in his book *Democracy Speaks Many Tongues*, writing, "Deep in the coffee and banana country of tropical Central America, in the Republic of Guatemala, lives a tall, dark-haired woman of aristocratic Spanish descent whose personal attack on the ancient forces of poverty has become a demonstration of the kind of leadership that must be found and supported if democracy is to succeed in this underdeveloped world. Her name is Señora Elisa Molina de Stahl."[37]

Beyond exoticizing Guatemala, Poston remarked on Molina's fitness for leadership based on her class status and her whiteness as evidenced by her direct European descent. Poston also framed the objects of Molina's passion as static and passive, captive to their socioeconomic status. For Poston and other contemporary development experts, the "underdeveloped world" directly threatened democracy, and the world could only emerge unscathed from this moment through partnership with people deemed capable based on racialized assumptions. By placing an upper-class, ladina, urban woman in charge of development projects aimed at lower-class, rural, and predominantly Indigenous populations, the state again revealed its unwillingness to allow development's intended recipients a voice in determining communal affairs for fear that doing so would threaten the status quo. Certainly, Molina had ample experience in social work and in donating money to charitable causes, but neither she nor the SBS had experience working in the countryside or in designing, planning, and implementing practical development projects.

Despite this inexperience, the SBS became the institutional home for the DESCOM. While Molina directed all the SBS's programs, DESCOM director Salvador Hernández Villalobos, professor of social work Arcadio Ruiz Franco, and agrarian engineer Rodolfo Martínez Ferraté worked on a more daily basis with the DESCOM.[38] Martínez Ferraté estimated that he traveled between 1,000 and 2,000 kilometers weekly with these men to the regional centers, where coordinators hired local people to provide the labor and equipment to accomplish DESCOM projects.[39] For example, the Chimaltenango center had hired fourteen local carpenters by July 1965, in addition to day laborers and night guards, and in April 1966, it hired twenty-six workers as laborers to construct latrines, drainage, and roadways.[40] During the first three years of the DESCOM's existence, regional offices established over 400 centers for adult education and completed projects such as kitchen and latrine construction, house painting, bridge and roadway development.[41] During these early years, Martínez Ferraté remembered that the DESCOM enjoyed a budget higher than many government ministries and gradually established a widespread network of projects throughout a few departments, all in an effort to help who he referred to as Guatemala's "forgotten people."[42] A June 1965 newspaper article bragged that the DESCOM's goal was to have the entire republic covered in projects by 1972.[43]

By 1966, although nowhere close to covering the entire country, the DESCOM had rapidly expanded, with centers in Chimaltenango, Jalapa, and Zacapa. It collaborated with several Guatemalan and outside institutions, including US-AID, the Organization of American States, the Interamerican Development Bank, the *Instituto Nacional de Transformación Agraria* (National Institute for Agrarian Transformation, INTA), and the Cooperative for Assistance and Relief Everywhere.[44] The year 1966 also brought a return to democracy with the surprise electoral victory of the *Partido Revolucionario*'s candidate, Julio Méndez Montenegro, after the two right-wing parties split the vote. However, the army prevented congressional ratification of this unexpected result until Méndez Montenegro signed an accord with the military that allowed it to name the minister of defense, maintain executive control over the armed forces, and continue, without oversight, the war against the guerrillas.[45] Under the guise of democracy, military control ran unchecked and state repression escalated, particularly in eastern departments, where Colonel Carlos Arana Osorio's special forces and extrajudicial death squads killed an estimated 10,000 people between 1967 and 1968.[46]

A change in the DESCOM's directorate and institutional home accompanied this shift in national leadership. While rural development initiatives continued, and the DESCOM had a 1967 operating budget of $1.5 million, it moved from the SBS to the Secretary of the Presidency, bringing it in direct and regular contact with the executive.[47] The move revealed the DESCOM's disorganization and mismanagement while under the SBS. Archival records provide several examples of unpaid bills from SBS DESCOM projects that local coordinators now wished to bill to the Secretary of the Presidency, such as the rent, electric, and water bills for the local office in Jalapa, and an unpaid bill for the repair of a DESCOM tractor.[48] To remedy these problems, the national government issued an accord in 1966 that mandated that all expense reports and receipts for even the most mundane operations like oil changes be sent for approval to the DESCOM's central office at the Secretary of the Presidency.[49] Not only did this effectively streamline budgetary records but it also permitted the executive branch to more closely monitor local DESCOM expenditures and activities. Personnel changes accompanied this shift, with the removal of Molina and Hernández and the appointment of Martínez to DESCOM director.[50]

Martínez served as DESCOM director during the Méndez Montenegro presidency, and in 1974, he published a book where he reflected broadly on the central issues confronting Guatemala's development. Calling out the injustice inherent in Guatemala's social structure and the violence confronting the population, Martínez insisted on a revision of Guatemala's governmental hierarchies in a way that gave more direct representation to people from the country's 8,442 villages (*aldeas* and *caseríos*) by further breaking down the lowest level of governance—the municipality—into *aldeas centrales*, or central villages. He also called for gradual land reform that would reorganize the means of production and foster the emergence of what he called the "third sector of the economy," rooted in peasant cooperatives and businesses. These two measures, he believed, would allow for greater popular participation and pluralist solutions to socioeconomic problems that recipients would find appropriate for local cultures but that would still promote national unity. Progressive but centrist, publishing this critique of Guatemala's social structure and ineffectiveness of the government in the midst of a repressive military dictatorship in 1974 was certainly a bold move on Martínez's part and demonstrates yet another level of disconnect between the intentions of the DESCOM creators and the various layers of its bureaucracy.[51] When I interviewed him in 2016 and directly asked if he believed development functioned as a tool to fight the Cold War, he captured the complexity of the situation by stating that "it was used in various ways, by some for counterinsurgency; other people and institutions of goodwill worked openly and transparently and without double interests."[52]

Unlike Martínez, the highest levels of the Guatemalan government saw community development as a convenient way to gain resources for its counterinsurgency effort, and it quickly expanded the DESCOM from the western department of Chimaltenango to the war-torn eastern departments of Zacapa and Izabal, the site of the guerrilla insurgency. USAID supported this initiative, granting $280,000 in the spring of 1967 for community development in this region. The Guatemalan government nearly matched this amount, contributing the equivalent of $257,000. Between the two, nearly half a million dollars financed this project designed to bring more teachers, agricultural extension agents, and programs for crop diversification and cooperative formation to this war-torn area.[53] The Izabal-Zacapa project, a collaboration between the USAID, INTA, DESCOM, and the military's Civic Action program, was an effort to thwart political unrest.[54] State department official Charles Burrows made this goal explicit when he wrote that this development project was "of the utmost urgency. The aim in Izabal, of course, is to weaken both passive and active support of insurgents by carrying out a number of impact projects that will decrease unemployment."[55]

USAID supported the DESCOM with financial, material, and technical support, always striving to achieve the delicate balance of having the United

States properly recognized for its "humanitarian" assistance while channeling most money through Guatemalan institutions so as not to appear imperialistic. The USAID Special Development fund provided a convenient way to finance DESCOM projects while still de-emphasizing the role of the United States, instead giving the appearance of the Guatemalan government's active involvement in helping rural communities. The Guatemalan USAID office awarded funding to projects that aligned with U.S. national interests, fit within Guatemala's national plan for development, and did not overlap significantly with other U.S.-funded projects.[56] USAID continued to fund DESCOM's projects largely through the Special Development Fund, often steering Guatemalans who requested foreign aid to local DESCOM staff in an attempt to centralize efforts and reinforce the importance of this institution.

USAID records are replete with DESCOM requests that the Special Development Fund filled. In 1968 alone, the Guatemalan branch of USAID funded potable water projects, the construction of health centers, bridge repair and construction, training courses, video projectors, and financial assistance to cooperatives.[57] Individuals also directly petitioned USAID, the U.S. Embassy, and even the president for financial assistance, and all requests were funneled through the Special Development Fund. These requests fit within a longer historical tendency of Guatemalans to directly petition authority figures for favors and assistance, so these letters should not be considered extraordinary in that regard.[58] They do, however, demonstrate the range of these requests and the failure of USAID to fully hide its involvement in development projects, as ordinary Guatemalans were clearly aware of the type of financing that the U.S. government provided to Guatemala, as the following examples elucidate.

In 1975, Jesus Espinoza Guerra wrote to the U.S. ambassador, asking for financial assistance or clothes for his four-year-old triplets, whom he had proudly named Edgard, Allan, and Stuard after the three U.S. American astronauts who had landed on the moon as part of the 1971 Apollo 14 mission.[59] Another man, Bartolomé de la Cruz, requested that the U.S. government provide him with an accordion because he loved music but could not afford his own instrument.[60] Orlando Valladares Menéndez wrote to the Ambassador from San Luis Jilotepeque, first carefully explaining that he wished to be a professor and loved reading about U.S. history and "its eminent men." However, his poor vision prevented him from accomplishing this goal, so he requested that USAID send him sunglasses and medicine. He concluded his letter by stating that he was quoting Benjamin Franklin, who had declared, "All men were created equal, they were given by their creator certain unalienable rights, that among these are: life, liberty and the pursuit of happiness."[61]

Through these three examples, it is clear that Guatemalan social services and development assistance were not meeting basic needs nor were the objectives of USAID clear, as one petitioner asked for a nonessential item—an accordion. While programs like the DESCOM might be helping build new bridges and infrastructure, on an individual level, the effects were failing to meet the most basic needs, like medical treatment and clothing. In other words, existing programs failed to change structural conditions that would have made it possible for individuals to have access to more resources and thus cover their basic needs. Two of the three writers expressed clear loyalty to the United States, demonstrating their understanding of the goals of hemispheric solidarity. And all three recognized the money the U.S. government was investing in Guatemala, and they thought it plausible enough that they might receive assistance to spend the time and money on writing and mailing these letters.

Roberto Perdomo, the coordinator of the Special Development Fund in Guatemala, denied all three individual requests, carefully explaining that the fund supported projects of a communal, self-help nature, not individual requests. In each case, he referred the petitioner to the DESCOM and other appropriate Guatemalan institutions. What USAID, and by extension, the DESCOM, failed to address was that most Guatemalans did not have the resources to invest in these "self-help" projects. Addressing social inequality and the underlying causes of poverty were not within the realm of possibilities that these institutions were willing to introduce, as it would jeopardize the existing status quo. At the highest level, both USAID and the DESCOM remained committed to ostensibly framing program objectives in terms of democracy while actually using development to attempt to socially engineer predictable, controllable, and modernized citizens. A closer look at one place where the DESCOM operated demonstrates that the intended recipients were anything but passive blank slates, available for the state to inscribe values and meaning. This local history also reveals disjuncture between the intentions of the DESCOM's leadership and the practices of local staff. There was no blanket acceptance of modernization nor a resulting homogeneous citizenry but rather more mixed results that did not neatly fit within the state's development plan.

The DESCOM in Tactic

By July 1970, the DESCOM had centers in thirty-four municipalities across the departments of Quetzaltenango, Chimaltenango, Huehuetenango, San

Marcos, Alta Verapaz, Baja Verapaz, and Jalapa.[62] In 1971, the DESCOM inaugurated its Local Center No. 10 in the municipality of Tactic amid the recent and reportedly fraudulent election of Colonel Carlos Arana Osorio and the state of siege that he immediately declared in the country. Simultaneously, the Guatemalan countryside experienced an escalation of development projects, with the DESCOM operating in regions where there was not yet a significant guerrilla presence and leaving projects in war-torn areas to the military's Civic Action programs. These new regions of operation were also departments with larger Indigenous populations, indicating the state's growing racialized fear of Indigenous revolutionary potential—or at least its belief in the possibility that leftist organizers might easily manipulate these populations.[63] Based on 1964 census records, these departments had an Indigenous population of greater than 50 percent, with the exception of Jalapa (44 percent). Of the remaining fifteen departments, only four had majority Indigenous populations; by 1972, the DESCOM was also working in three of these (Sololá, Totonicapán, and Quiché).[64]

Like elsewhere in Guatemala, Tactic's DESCOM team had five members: an adult educator who was also the team coordinator (Emilio Vásquez Robles), a nurse (Magda Morales de Vásquez, Vásquez's wife), a home educator (Gladys Gamboa), a social worker (María Elena Márquez), and an agronomist (Carlos Milián Cantorál). The team also worked closely with three bilingual promoters who accompanied them to villages to translate both language and cultural norms. These promoters, like IING ethnographers, enjoyed relative prestige in these communities.[65] Their assistance validated the DESCOM for local people, who, according to oral histories, were wary of outsiders.[66] Additionally, Vásquez worked with local priest Father Ricardo Terga and together they wrote a monograph on the municipality in 1975, carefully recording ethnographic and ethnohistorical information that municipal residents shared with them.[67]

On June 19, 1971, members from DESCOM's Local Center No. 10 met with the municipal leadership, local military commissioners, and *alcaldes auxiliaries*, or representatives from Tactic's aldeas.[68] Indigenous leaders voluntarily held the position of alcalde auxiliar for a year, serving in this post as a part of the cargo system's structure of rotating local leadership.[69] In this way, similar to the IING, DESCOM staff members received permission from all levels of local governance before beginning their work in order to mitigate any conflicts.[70] In this July meeting, participants created the Municipal Committee of Programming, which prioritized community requests and established the DESCOM's schedule of projects.

Miguel Peláez Morales, who served as mayor during the DESCOM's tenure, recalled that the alcaldes auxiliaries welcomed the DESCOM's assistance; he attributed this ease of entry to the relationships that the PMIT had established with these same villages a little over a decade earlier. Although he noted that the DESCOM enjoyed much more financing and governmental support than the PMIT, he argued that the PMIT's positive reputation paved the way for the DESCOM, an institute that functioned locally in much the same way.[71] The DESCOM operated in this fashion in Tactic until 1981, when the local center was transferred north to Lanquín, closer to sites of guerrilla activity and military violence.[72]

Because a central goal of community development was to empower communities to utilize their own resources, DESCOM leaders deferred daily oversight of projects to local committees called Community Improvement Committees (*Comités Pro-Mejoramiento*) that would present proposals to the DESCOM. While the DESCOM's hope was that these would be standing committees, in at least one village, a former member recalled that they would create a new committee for each project and would dissolve it once completed.[73] This difference reflects the possibility that the DESCOM's planners failed to recognize the time constraints that rural Guatemalans faced and the different understandings of what collective organizing required.

While the DESCOM central office in Guatemala City, the National Economic Planning Council, and the U.S. State Department viewed community development as a way to counteract rising global leftist insurgency, local DESCOM staff did not frame their work in this international political context. Vásquez claimed that DESCOM staff never talked about political parties, elections, or politicians because if they had, residents would not have accepted their assistance. He also insisted that cordial relations always existed between program staff and participants, as he and his team made clear that "we hadn't come to alter the community's way of life but rather had come to bring some help from the government to the community, in order to improve their community, in order to develop their community."[74] Gamboa's recollections only slightly revised Vásquez's claim of political neutrality, as she remembered that around both the 1974 and 1978 presidential elections, the incumbent party's campaigns would use DESCOM vehicles to visit villages and spread propaganda. The team members could not prevent this from happening because the DESCOM was directly under the office of the president and their vehicles were state owned. Beyond these few episodes, however, she claimed that the DESCOM avoided any political affiliation or activities of a partisan nature.[75]

Importantly, multiple local participants also emphasized that from their perspective, the local DESCOM was neither clientelist nor corrupt like more recent development initiatives. This critique was likely accurate but also reflective of the contemporary context of my interviews, which took place in the wake of 2015 corruption scandals that ultimately resulted in President Otto Pérez Molina's resignation.[76] Still, this claim by DESCOM staff that they did not meddle in local politics but rather sought active collaboration with the villages where they worked is a sentiment that recipients shared. Through careful coordination, thoughtful preliminary study, and regular meetings with local leaders, DESCOM staff brought, from both project staff's and recipients' perspectives, humanitarian help from the central government, thus extending its reach, for better and for worse, into rural Guatemala.

In Tactic's municipal records, the first request for DESCOM assistance came from the village of Pasmolón for building a school. Though primary school attendance was compulsory, many families avoided sending their older children because they needed their labor and because schools were in disrepair. Heriberto Isem, a Pasmolón resident, remembered how he had to wake early to work for a few hours before classes.[77] DESCOM staff member Carlos Milián described the current one-room school as being in "extremely dangerous conditions" and resident Alberto Bin recalled that he used corn kernels, beans, and rocks to do mathematics lessons.[78] On July 25, 1971, program staff met with parents of students and the Pasmolón teacher and discussed the construction logistics. Through a local translator, parents expressed their inability to offer economic help but their willingness to provide labor; the municipal alcalde pledged to hire a carpenter and a mason. After discussion in Poqomchi', parents agreed to each provide Q5 in addition to labor to demonstrate their commitment to the project.[79] In contrast with development experts' belief that rural people needed to "be awakened" and were intrinsically incapable of identifying realistic solutions to their collective problems without outside intervention, Pasmolón residents demonstrated their capacity for planning and action while highlighting that the only reason they had not built their own school was a lack of material resources.

Just over six months later, DESCOM staff, the municipal committee, school personnel, parents, and students celebrated the Pasmolón school's inauguration, complete with speeches and the singing of the national hymn.[80] A larger ceremony took place in September, and in addition to the same local attendees, the assistant director of the DESCOM as well as the director of the Chimaltenango Regional Center attended to give congratulatory speeches and award diplomas of service to participants.[81] Ceremonies and certificates created new rituals and underscored the DESCOM's hope for a psychological transformation, and the attendance of high officials indicates that the Pasmolón school exemplified the type of projects that the DESCOM praised. The DESCOM later supported school construction in the municipal villages of El Manantial and Chacalté as well.[82]

However, Vásquez and Terga's ethnography, written in 1975, still indicated widespread resistance to school attendance throughout the municipality. New schools did not solve the labor shortage issue, provide parents with extra economic resources to mitigate the cost of school supplies, or address parental hesitance to send female students to schools with male teachers. Building primary schools also did not address the lack of secondary or higher education opportunities for students in Tactic's villages. Because the majority of residents could never afford to send their children for additional schooling outside the community, despite their reported desire to do so, they saw little benefit in primary education.[83] While providing essential infrastructure, DESCOM schools could not address deeper issues that affected access to education.

In addition to school construction, potable water systems were infrastructure projects that villages often requested. When the DESCOM began working in Tactic, beyond the municipal center, only the village of Tampó had potable water available in town; in all the other villages, women walked to water sources and hauled it in buckets back to their houses.[84] In April 1972, Chiacal organized an improvement committee with the explicit goal of "realizing distinct activities of a socio-cultural character for the development of the aldea so that they can foster a better means of life."[85] For this town, development meant the acquisition of a higher standard of living, but on their own terms. Importantly, they also recognized that development initiatives were cultural, as they could potentially alter daily practices and interpersonal relationships and exchanges. In 1974, the Chiacal committee proposed a potable water project because the people only had open water wells that collected rainwater and runoff, and the water remained stagnant until used, posing high contamination risks. The closest spring was located on Rubén Milián's privately owned finca, and he prohibited community access.[86] The local committee requested DESCOM's assistance in negotiating with Milián to allow residents to construct a piped water system from his property; DESCOM staff members successfully secured this permission, and they provided the concrete pipes while residents provided the labor.

Rogelio Bin Quej, who in 2016 was the only living member of the local committee, proudly recalled his town's efforts to solve the problem that had long plagued people's health. Another resident of Chiacal, Enrique Tun, narrated a similar experience; his uncle served alongside Bin on the local committee. For months, work crews rotated every eight days so that everybody contributed to the project while still having time to tend to their crops and complete household tasks. Men dug ditches and placed pipes while women provided food and drink. Upon completion, the piped water filled several closed tanks in the village center, replacing the open wells. This system served Chiacal residents until it was replaced in the early 2000s with an updated system that brought water to every home.[87]

On June 6, 1974, the DESCOM sponsored an inauguration ceremony for the project and awarded all participants with a diploma of service, a simple certificate that Bin has carefully guarded and proudly displayed to me. Similar to the school projects, potable water systems did meet a tangible, immediate need. Unacknowledged, however, was the fact that the DESCOM had secured permission from a local landowner and provided the expensive piping, two critical components that townspeople could not do. It was not a lack of confidence or ability to do collective work that had impeded Chiacal residents from obtaining potable water prior to June 1974; it was their lack of political and financial capital. The DESCOM could not remedy that structural condition.

Townspeople in Pasmolón also organized to construct a potable water system. Heriberto Isem recalled that in the 1970s, residents did not have electricity or piped water. As in Chiacal, residents collaborated with the DESCOM to pipe water from a mountain spring located two miles away to ten closed water tanks. The committee later decided to pipe the water to individual homes, but only 36 of the approximately 200 homes received a water spigot, and the local improvement committee determined which families obtained this valuable resource, prioritizing their family members. Isem referred to this moment as a "major blow" [*"gran golpe"*] for the committee's credibility because residents felt that since all had collaborated in the project, they should receive equal access to the resource, and eventually the committee members resigned. To help solve this dilemma and restore faith in community development, the new committee secured assistance in expanding the water project to all homes.[88] As seen here, development's intended recipients were anything but passive, and they actively shaped the process and the outcomes of development as they, at times, competed over limited resources and exhibited favoritism. When projects did not equally benefit all residents, some expressed outrage and implied that they would not support future development initiatives if the matter went unresolved. Through exerting their agency, recipients again proved their ability to ensure the success or failure of development.

The DESCOM's intended recipients also shaped projects geared toward agricultural modernization and crop diversification. Globally, Malthusian fears of overpopulation and insufficient food supplies generated the Green Revolution, a collection of efforts to figure out ways to feed the world through improved agricultural techniques, modified seeds and crop varieties, and more efficient transportation.[89] Because U.S. foreign policy focused on creating healthy agricultural entrepreneurs, modernization's success hinged on the ability to form a rural middle class. As seen in the prototype of Juan Chapín and in the case of the INCAP's nutrition project in Magdalena, the state connected health and production and had prioritized the improvement of nutrition for some time. The Juan Chapín primer engaged in contemporary (and historical) debates about the merits of producing for a domestic market versus growing crops for export, and some Guatemalan experts did recognize the crucial role that Indigenous farmers played in cultivating consumables for the national population.[90] However, the Chapín primer, and then the DESCOM thirty years later, portrayed subsistence agriculture and monoculture as a negative, poverty-inducing practice rather than one that could be sustainable with more equitable land distribution, and it linked this form of agriculture to Indigeneity. Discursively coding subsistence agriculture in this way ignored how it challenged the structuring of society in terms of the capitalist market. It also ignored how subsistence agricultural practices might allow for individuals to allocate time for other communal and cultural activities instead of pursuing the cultivation of excess produce. In turn, this investment of time could strengthen ethnic identities in the face of modernization's homogenizing tendencies. This turn away from promoting subsistence and the cultivation of food staples, then, was a drastic departure from earlier national agrarian priorities and in line with international trends instead of national needs.

While top-down DESCOM assumptions racialized subsistence agriculture as backward Indigenous practices and hindrances to national progress, these assumptions did not reflect realities nor DESCOM staff opinions in Tactic. Vásquez noted that women sold various fruits, flowers, chickens, eggs, turkeys, chiles, and ground coffee alongside corn and beans at market.[91] He also detailed the typical diet as consisting of corn tortillas and beans and various herbs and vegetables. Families also consumed fruits, meat, and cheese, particularly on Sundays and holidays.[92] However, he also specified that insufficient land was the key problem confronting socioeconomic development and that this issue was racialized; he indicated that non-Indigenous families were "in a better situation," as many owned land. In contrast, Indigenous families held only a few *cuadras* (1 *cuadra* equals roughly 188 square feet) for both their homes and property. As a result, Indigenous tactiqueños had to seek employment as wage laborers or resident laborers, but locally, this was becoming increasingly difficult as landowners were transforming cultivated land into pastureland for cattle ranching. This transition also raised the cost of renting land beyond the reach of many campesinos, thus resulting in increased seasonal migration.[93] Further, land shortage affected rural families' ability to obtain sufficient staples for familial consumption; they typically had enough corn for half the year and had to acquire the rest at the local market. INDECA, the National Institute of Agricultural Commercialization, built silos in Tactic and sold corn at lower prices (Q0.04 per pound), but to obtain this corn, women had to stand in line starting at midnight and could only purchase five pounds at a time.[94] So, despite this generalized call by development experts to diversify agriculture, land tenure patterns in Tactic made such lofty goals rather impractical.

Martínez Ferraté, the national DESCOM director in the late 1960s, remarked in his 1974 book that private property should serve a social function; until Guatemala could overcome its "anachronistic" social structure based on unequal land tenure, development would be untenable. Using the 1965 Constitution, he challenged the notion that agrarian reform by definition was revolutionary and left leaning, instead arguing that it could be done in a gradual way that aligned with the constitution, one that the military government itself had created.[95] He, alongside other contemporaries and later scholars, remarked on the colonization efforts along the southern coast in Nueva Concepción y La Máquina in the 1960s that had attempted to integrate the small farmer in a way that would not upset the status quo. However, insufficient resources, poor planning, constantly changing objectives, and lack of collaboration with local authorities severely hampered the efficacy of the initiative.[96] But voices like Martínez Ferraté's were in the minority. Instead of recognizing structural inequality and in turn enacting sweeping agrarian reform and land redistribution, most contemporary development experts largely focused on a racialized version of agricultural modernization, blaming Indigenous campesinos' "traditional" cultivation methods as the reason for insufficient harvests and their supposed reliance on corn as the root cause for malnutrition.

Despite these critiques from both the national and local leadership of the DESCOM, project staff were limited to the types of projects that the national government approved, as it was under the direct jurisdiction of the presidency.

Accordingly, the DESCOM in Tactic adhered to this agricultural modernization model although local staff recognized the deeper issues that prevented
the countryside's widescale transformation. Training materials informed
DESCOM staff that agriculture could be considered "developed" when farmers
were simultaneously completing three economic functions: that of worker, administrator, and capitalist, thus modeling the "permitted Indian's" economic
practices.[97]

U.S. development experts and the government wholeheartedly supported
this objective. A secret memorandum providing comments of the 1970
Guatemalan Country Analysis and Strategy Paper remarked that for development to be successful, the Guatemalan government needed to "[aid and pro-
mote] the formation of government and private institutions necessary for
rural modernization and national integration" and train rural leaders in community development tactics. It also called for the incorporation of rural peasants and small industries into the national market and for the "acceleration of
national integration of [the] indigenous (Indian) population through [the]
above as well as education and other social opportunity."[98] This report high-
lighted how the absence of a rural middle class and the failure to integrate rural
campesinos into national markets prevented an overall improvement in living
standards, portraying the peasantry as a "demographic time bomb."[99] It continued applying the double condition of "backwardness" to Indigenous campesinos,
explaining their marginalization both in class and in racial terms.

The concept of modernized agriculture and a class of economically productive farmers was designed to improve livelihoods just enough to make
revolution unattractive but not enough to alter social hierarchies. As mentioned, the emphasis on commodity exports was not entirely a rupture with
the past, as Indigenous farmers had long grown coffee and other commodity
exports alongside agricultural staples. However, the more widespread emphasis on export crops did transform and urbanize the countryside, increase
costs of agricultural production, and for some people, cause a shift from agriculture to other economic sectors.[100] Elites found this model of agricultural
modernization palatable because it did not threaten land tenure patterns.
Again, like all the DESCOM's agenda, this model of agricultural modernization was not unique to Guatemala but was put into practice across the world
and ever so slightly adjusted for local contexts.[101]

Municipal residents remembered DESCOM efforts to shape local agrarian practices. Archival records indicate that village authorities supported
these initiatives. For example, in a September 1971 meeting, the DESCOM
staff reported positive feedback from a community survey about installing a

Center for Integral Development that would provide training in adult literacy, various manual skills, and home economics, including preparation and preservation of food.[102] At a lengthy afternoon meeting in October 1972, participants approved agricultural diversification projects for the villages of Cuyquel, Guaxpac, Chiacal, Pasmolón, and Tampó, which reportedly had been unanimously approved in each local committee.[103] In 1972, the DESCOM implemented its village garden and crop diversification programs in Tampó, Pasmolón, and Chiacal, and recipients remembered the introduction of new crops such as carrots, wheat, and cabbage.[104] Social promoters and DESCOM's home economics instructors taught local women new recipes that used these unfamiliar vegetables in an attempt to improve rural nutrition. Rogelio Bin recalled that during this time, he began growing mandarin tomatoes that he sold at the municipal market, thus increasing his family's income. Alberto Bin and Heriberto Isem remembered the community garden and the beehives that the DESCOM oversaw in Pasmolón, recounting that gardening was part of the school curriculum so students could take produce home. The DESCOM's agricultural expert taught alternative cultivation methods, distributed hybrid seeds, and introduced chemical fertilizers, insecticides, and herbicides. When local residents allowed DESCOM staff to use a portion of their land, the staff planted experimental fields to demonstrate how modern agricultural practices could provide higher yields.[105]

However, not all attempts at agricultural modernization were quickly accepted or utilized. DESCOM staff member Gladys Gamboa remembered that although people received seeds and insecticides for free, they hesitated to abandon their own cultivation techniques. Rogelio Bin recalled that women in Chiacal did not participate in agricultural initiatives because they were unfamiliar with other types of vegetables and were wary of outsiders.[106] Former mayor Miguel Peláez stated: "To change the mentality of the people with regard to monoculture was extremely difficult. There was a lot of conformity. They said, 'Well, if we survive with corn and beans then for what reason then should we complicate our life?' so they didn't accept these programs."[107] However, he also attributed the DESCOM's efforts with the reason why Tactic today is a wholesaler of agricultural products for the region, a commentary that possibly reflects on the status of municipal landowners rather than the reality of the majority of residents.

Another former mayor, Carlos López, recounted that the DESCOM respected the sacredness that Maya culture attributed to corn. He detailed how project staff did not try to change farmers' practices of erecting altars in their fields and praying for blessings for the harvest. However, he also remembered that DESCOM efforts to change agricultural practices had mixed results. For example, DESCOM staff encouraged diversification and tried to teach farmers to plant their crops in rows rather than digging holes for individual seeds.[108] Vásquez learned about the sacredness that Indigenous tactiqueños attributed to corn, as he detailed the planting ceremony in his ethnography.[109] Even though project staff understood the spiritual significance of the corn planting, they promoted alternative crops in the hope that farmers would prioritize the potential for higher yields over sacred traditions, thus reflecting different developmental priorities. While some farmers did accept these suggestions, others maintained that years of experience had convinced them that their methods were best.[110]

Farmers also remembered their reticence to adopt agricultural modernization. Enrique Tun from Chiacal said that initially they used the synthetic fertilizers that the DESCOM provided; however, they quickly realized that these fertilizers harmed the soil, so they abandoned this practice.[111] Historian David Carey Jr.'s fieldwork in Tecpán and San José Poaquil revealed similar hesitation on the part of Kaqchikel Maya farmers to widely use synthetic fertilizers, not because of any unwillingness to adopt new technologies but because of the accompanying environmental and health problems.[112] Though local staff were aware of the interconnectedness that Poqomchi' recipients recognized between the environment and human well-being, the DESCOM program as a whole did not and continued promoting projects that recipients deemed incompatible with their values. Recipients were more prone to accept projects they requested, like potable water, while remaining more ambivalent about those which the DESCOM gently imposed, revealing discrepancies in development theorization and development praxis.

Alberto Bin recognized that these projects did provide some assistance, but he recalled how they did nothing to solve the larger issue of access to land. Even if they had adopted these agricultural techniques, they did not actually have any land to cultivate. He explained that renting land was incredibly expensive and beyond the financial reach for most residents. Furthermore, the only land available to him was of a poor quality, located high on the mountain, about which he stated, "Damn, (*púchicas*), we could cultivate that, but how?"[113] Like Bin, many recipients—as well as some project staff—only saw DESCOM agricultural programs as a short-term alleviation to a much larger, structural problem.

Like responses to agricultural projects, the DESCOM's public health efforts also saw mixed results. In an episode similar to what INCAP anthropologists noted in the 1950s in Magdalena Milpas Altas, Terga and Vásquez wrote that tactiqueños hid their children from "Amigos de las Américas" volunteers who tried to measure and weigh them for a nutrition study. Reportedly, both Indigenous and non-Indigenous residents feared that "the 'gringas' were weighing and measuring the children because they were going to take the fattest ones to the United States to eat."[114] And as Rodríguez noted during his time with the PMIT two decades earlier, tactiqueños still showed little interest in receiving vaccines or injections, pills, or other medications, instead favoring local healers. Practically, utilizing a healer required less time than visiting the clinic and was more cost-effective.[115] Vásquez never questioned healers' knowledge or abilities nor indicated any desire for residents to stop using their services. Instead, the DESCOM simply tried to complement the use of healers with vaccination campaigns, establishment of health clinics, and midwife training, one project that does seem to have met some success, as twenty-six midwives that Vásquez describes as "Indigenous, illiterate, and monolingual" completed the training program that his wife conducted.[116]

Two contemporary issues also contributed to the DESCOM's lack of success in public health initiatives in Tactic. First, in the mid-1970s, the Association for Family Welfare (APROFAM) chose Tactic as its pilot program, perhaps because of the state's perception of the DESCOM's success in the municipality. As another state institution, the DESCOM had to indirectly support APROFAM programs, and Father Terga believed it possible that some residents conflated the two despite their different focuses. Terga recalled that he did not support APROFAM because it violated church principles, and many residents feigned participation in order to gain material benefits but threw away the birth control pills. Because of the temporal overlap and governmental sponsorship of both programs, Terga presumed that the DESCOM lost some of its credibility after APROFAM arrived in 1975.[117] In fact, Gladys Gamboa worked for APROFAM after the DESCOM left Tactic, and she contrasted residents' acceptance of the DESCOM with their rejection of APROFAM's family planning initiatives.[118] Fidelina Xuc Buc, a Poqomchi' bilingual educator from Tactic, also briefly worked for the APROFAM, not with their family planning initiatives (she was only seventeen at the time) but with their home economics programs, and she also recalled that women accepted these aspects but rejected family planning.[119] Again, we see different ideas of development at play here; DESCOM planners and Western public health experts in general measured development in statistical terms—slower population growth rates, lower infant mortality, higher life expectancies, greater caloric intake per capita, and so on. While not inherently problematic, for many recipients, these numbers did not capture their unwillingness to change or compromise religious and cultural practices for the sake of slightly altering statistics.

Second, an event early in the DESCOM's presence in Tactic also perhaps shaped negative perceptions of public health initiatives. In a municipal meeting on August 3, 1971, DESCOM staff met with municipal leaders and the auxiliary alcaldes to discuss a troubling radio news report out of Guatemala City that Tactic was suffering from epidemic typhus, a disease spread through lice. Tactic's leadership accused the DESCOM of spreading this rumor. Trying to repair their tenuous relationship, Vásquez explained that the local DESCOM had been doing a delousing campaign but did not have the proper insecticide, so it had requested it from the Ministry of Public Health. He surmised that an individual within the ministry had wrongfully spread the notice of epidemic typhus based on that request, and he assured his audience that he had already taken steps to publish additional press releases denying the epidemic and clarifying the DESCOM's activities in Tactic. Existing evidence does not capture the report's language or tone but given Tactic's predominant Indigenous population and contemporary stereotypes that Indigenous communities were more disease prone, it is likely that the employee who spread this rumor did so based on racialized assumptions. After an hour of discussion (which the archival record did not detail), municipal leadership seemed appeased and ended the meeting noting the overall benefits of the DESCOM's campaigns.[120] In calling out the local DESCOM staff for this unfortunate event, Tactic's leadership signaled that it would not tolerate slander or violations of local trust.

How, then, should we evaluate the decade of work that the DESCOM did in Tactic? Both Poqomchi' and non-Indigenous tactiqueños praised the DESCOM's efforts in their oral histories, even if they recognized that some efforts were not as successful as planners had hoped. No Poqomchi' interviewee critiqued the DESCOM for trying to change their culture, instead dating that to the imposition of civil patrols and required community service in some aldeas in the 1980s.[121] In fact, Onofre Bin even recalled that in 1974, his village held Maya ceremonies asking for the blessing of DESCOM initiatives.[122] At the planning level and in the mentalities of development experts and politicians, the DESCOM fit their racialized model of modernization. But in practice in Tactic, it appears to have been a program that provided flexibility for recipients to participate as they chose and dictate the projects they wished to prioritize, although limited by what the program made possible. As a result, both program staff and beneficiaries alike rightly critiqued the DESCOM for its inability to address the structural foundations of Guatemala's highly inequitable society.

Comparisons with Contemporary Development Initiatives

It is difficult to know the extent to which Tactic's experiences with the DESCOM are representative of efforts across the country because no institutional archive of the DESCOM remains. And obtaining a glimpse into local perspectives of the program, as I have done for Tactic, requires sources such as oral histories or municipal records, sources that in Guatemala are not easy— and sometimes not possible—to obtain. The following examples of state-sponsored community development initiatives from both the DESCOM and other contemporary programs parallel the ambivalent results that occurred in Tactic, and while this likely points to the ability of beneficiaries to leverage program resources to their own ends, future research is needed to analyze local agency in a deeper fashion.

In 1968, USAC student Marina Figueroa Arriola completed the fieldwork for her social work degree in the Kaqchikel village of San Rafael el Arado, a newly formed (1960) aldea of Sumpango in the department of Sacatepéquez. She analyzed the efforts of the DESCOM in San Rafael from 1966 to 1968, detailing the key problems that local DESCOM staff identified and explaining if and how such issues were resolved. Projects mirrored many of those the DESCOM pursued in Tactic: school construction, latrine and stove distribution to houses, agricultural modernization, literacy, road improvement, and potable water programs. Yet in San Rafael, Figueroa rarely attributed success to any projects, blaming these failures on residents' unwillingness to change their attitudes. In her conclusion, she writes the revealing and racist critique: "The *indígena* isn't a useless and despicable being; he only needs to be stimulated, so that he can come out of the lethargy in which he has lived and be able to convert himself into a useful and capable member of his country."[123]

Buried within her descriptions of each project, we can glimpse the actual reasons projects often failed to materialize. The DESCOM in San Rafael heavily relied on financial assistance from outside institutions, and this funding rarely seemed to materialize. Further, the DESCOM regional center failed to send promised supplies for the local school, generating distrust. A local landowner refused to donate land for road widening and the municipal government did not intervene. Additionally, agricultural diversification projects included impractical programs like fish tanks for carp harvesting or cypress tree plantings for village beautification, projects that did nothing to address land tenure or seasonal migration issues. And the one project that Figueroa claimed the community enthusiastically supported and requested—a potable water system—did not make it onto the DESCOM's agenda.[124] Though this thesis provides just one perspective into DESCOM activities in San Rafael, and a highly racialized one at that, it does suggest that the relationship between local teams and intended recipients significantly varied across the country, impacting both the efficacy of DESCOM initiatives and the continued circulation of portrayals of Indigenous Guatemalans as unmodern, incapable, and in need of outside intervention. In other words, for individuals like Figueroa and possibly the local DESCOM team in San Rafael, only through the actions of non-Indigenous outsiders could Guatemala's Indigenous population be transformed into what they considered to be permitted modern Indigenous citizens.

Private non-governmental organizations also collaborated with state institutions to provide community development projects. For example, U.S. doctor Carroll Behrhorst established the Chimaltenango Development Project in 1962, which worked in predominantly Kaqchikel Maya communities. In his 1974 report to the Christian Medical Commission, he asserted that outside experts had to work *with* local populations instead of imposing projects. Detailing an example where his team wished to treat children for diarrhea, team members instead asked the village's women what they wanted, who in turn requested chickens for a protein source and apples to grow as a cash crop. In providing these items, they developed a positive rapport in the village. Later in the report, he also emphasized the project's emphasis on land redistribution, as his team had recognized that without addressing this structural issue, no public health initiatives would ever resolve existing inequalities.[125]

Another private organization that collaborated with the Guatemalan state was the Guatemalan Movement for Rural Reconstruction (GMRR), which began operating in Jalapa in 1965 and closely collaborated with the DESCOM to organize producer and consumer cooperatives. In 1974, the GMRR reported the completion of a series of educational seminars that 770 people attended. Themes included agricultural techniques, committee organizational strategies, accounting basics, and community development theory, indicating the clear understanding of development as linked to capitalist economic growth.[126] Eventually expanding to Escuintla, GMRR helped coffee growers form the Las Brisas Coffee Cooperative and financed the construction of a factory to process and package beans for export. In 1973, the cooperative paid off a $30,000 debt and ended the season with $9,000 in its bank account, which GMRR promoted as a success story.[127]

Intended recipients also carefully navigated other development intrusions beyond the DESCOM, demonstrating parallels to the experiences of Poqomchi' tactiqueños. Based on years of fieldwork in San Pedro Necta, anthropologist

Nicholas Copeland examined how Mam Maya farmers participated in the General Directorate of Agricultural Services, or DIGESA programs. They utilized the "controlled empowerment" discourse that this initiative allowed to challenge classism and racism by participating in the capitalist market through cultivating export crops and utilizing new technologies.[128] Scholar Edgar Esquit's local history of the Kaqchikel municipality of Comalapa does not focus on a specific development program, but he argues that throughout the 1970s, Kaqchikel leaders utilized various development initiatives to challenge ladino power and structural racism, eventually gaining control of the municipal government. However, the military state viewed these actions as subversive, and by the early 1980s, almost all municipal leaders had been assassinated or disappeared.[129] Clearly, recasting development initiatives to challenge the ideology of modernization and alter the status quo became increasingly dangerous to do.

Together, these examples indicate that the goal of creating a rural middle class through self-help initiatives and local organizing figured centrally in development initiatives across the Guatemalan countryside. Though some accounts detail outright racism while others point more to racialized assumptions, all believed intended recipients to require guidance, training, and supervision, and like the DESCOM's foundational principle, to need awakening to the opportunities that state-defined modernization provided. In other words, the work race did in the counterinsurgency state's development programs was to continue solidifying the notion of permitted and expected behaviors of Guatemalan Indigenous citizens, while at times unintentionally providing spaces and opportunities at the local level for the contestation of these racialized norms and the expression of alternative ideas about development and Indigeneity.

Conclusion

The DESCOM did succeed in meeting some material needs; throughout the country, new roads, schools, bridges, potable water systems, and other communal infrastructure were built. Like the other contemporary development initiatives briefly analyzed here, the DESCOM's adoption of a universal understanding of modernization was simply not compatible with Guatemala's diversity. The state only saw capitalist development as the end goal, foreclosing other routes to improved well-being that did not coincide with notions of Western modernization. While the DESCOM's director and project staff did not necessarily share this view, the range of possible actions they could take was directly limited by this definition of what community development should entail. When the DESCOM operated in predominantly Indigenous regions, its key focal areas by the 1970s, planners positioned outsiders as the architects of the "permitted Indian." Based on racialized assumptions about Indigenous people's inability to participate without outside guidance, self-help projects became a stopgap by meeting a few material needs without actually altering the status quo or addressing longer histories of racialized exploitation.

The self-help structure of the DESCOM intended to foster collective acceptance of modernization. But as this chapter has argued, many development experts did not factor in local agency, mistakenly believing recipients to be malleable and passive. Instead, participants accepted elements of the DESCOM programs they believed would improve their lives and rejected aspects they deemed culturally incompatible or practically ineffective. On-the-ground project staff members occupied an uncomfortable intermediary role, as they sought to bring meaningful and helpful change to rural communities. However, like Martínez and Vásquez, many refused to force participants to comply and recognized the limited efficacy that their efforts could have if unaccompanied by structural change. Particularly Martínez took great risks in criticizing the existing regime for its ineffectiveness in rural development, perhaps a factor in his decision to move to Costa Rica by the mid-1970s. As the next chapter will show, challenging the status quo, particularly in the midst of an increasingly violent civil war infused with Cold War ideology, would bring horrific results and clearly indicate the boundaries for behaviors that the state found acceptable of its Indigenous citizens.

CHAPTER SIX

A Little Cuba in the Ixcán Jungle, 1968–1982

After traveling from his hometown of Ixtahuacán San Ildefonso to Santa Cruz Barillas, then trudging through knee-deep mud for three more days, José Sales Ramírez arrived at the plot of land the Maryknoll priests had promised him.[1] Insects buzzed incessantly, replacing the village commotion to which Ramírez was accustomed with the jungle's deafening roar. Sales surveyed this overgrown land, wondering how his family could grow corn and beans in this hot and humid environment. But arduous physical labor was nothing new for Sales and the other Mam Maya campesinos who accompanied him on this journey. They had regularly migrated seasonally to coffee and cotton plantations, where they worked for obscenely low wages performing backbreaking labor in dangerous conditions. Never able to accrue enough money to buy sufficient land, these Indigenous campesinos scraped by year after year.[2]

In the early 1960s when the diocese in Huehuetenango first started radio announcements about the possibility of migrating to the Ixcán, many Indigenous campesinos like Sales were skeptical. Some feared that this was just another ploy by ladinos to fool them and steal their money, and others hesitated to leave their communities of origin. However, it was not the landowners' corrupt middlemen making these offers but rather the Maryknoll priests, who had a reputation for community-driven engagement. Furthermore, the INTA had approved the project, promising legal title for these uncultivated lands.

The land that the INTA allocated was situated between the Ixcán and Xalbal Rivers, bordered to the north by Mexico and to the south by privately owned fincas. Despite a difficult first few years, the colony eventually flourished, forming a profitable cooperative and exporting cash crops such as cardamom and coffee.[3] Indigenous campesinos from various Maya ethnic groups migrated, thus creating diverse and multilinguistic towns throughout the colony. By the early 1970s, the Ixcán Grande project seemed to be a wild success, one perfectly in line with the national government's plan to develop rural Guatemala through agricultural colonization schemes. But by mid-decade, the Guatemalan military had occupied the region, "disappeared" several colonists, and severely impeded the autonomy of the cooperative. When Ixcán Grande's leadership refused to allow mineral and petroleum companies to extract resources from the colony, the military state deemed the colony to be antagonistic toward national development interests. And when the *Ejército Guerrillero de los Pobres* (Guerrilla Army of the Poor) began clandestine operations in the region in 1972, the military state labeled the region a "little Cuba" and all its Indigenous campesinos as subversive, thus racializing the violence through indiscriminately targeting Indigenous people. The Ixcán became a site of increased military presence, surveillance, and suspicion, culminating in state-sponsored massacres and scorched earth policy in the early 1980s.

This chapter argues that this state-approved development project, in just six years, came to be seen as subversive and as a key site of racialized violence. Because its development model deviated from the state-sanctioned path of modernization in some ways, this peripheral, borderland region found itself at the center of the state's national security agenda. The military state racialized these alternate practices of development to homogenize Ixcán Grande's diverse Indigenous population as singularly dangerous, and thus expendable. This chapter first analyzes the agrarian reform of the 1960s and contextualizes Maryknoll's presence in Guatemala. Then, it moves into a discussion of the Ixcán Grande project and examines its transformation from sanctioned to subversive and what ramifications these categorizations had for its residents.

1960s Colonization and Agrarian Reform

Maryknoll's Ixcán Grande project was not Guatemala's first experiment with internal colonization to resolve unequal land tenure. President Arévalo had sponsored a short-lived, costly, and failed colony in the Petén in 1945, and in 1955, Castillo Armas launched small-scale colonization projects in nineteen rural development zones along the southern coast, using $14 million in U.S. aid.[4] Yet by 1962, only 25,000 people had gotten land; in comparison, Arbenz's agrarian reform affected between 200,000 and half a million people in just two years.[5] Unlike the 1952 agrarian reform, colonization did not aim for structural change to landholding patterns. Rather, it simply intended to place unused government land into a few lucky hands and modernize agricultural methods in the process. As John R. Hildebrand, an agricultural economist for International Development Services, wrote, "The machete-corn-patch operation may be picturesque, but without change, the future of Guatemala will not be bright."[6]

Even the 1962 *Decreto 1551 Law of Agrarian Transformation* recognized the failure of Castillo Armas's project, as the law's first sentence declared that this previous effort did not achieve the desired results among Guatemala's campesinos. Decreto 1551 founded the INTA, a centralized entity that controlled

all land redistribution efforts and whose leadership the president directly selected.[7] The 1962 land reform law called for the state's redistribution of vacant
lands (*tierras baldíos*), national land, and uncultivated land from fincas larger
than 100 hectares, exempting forestlands and mining zones. Importantly, the
1962 reform remained highly centralized unlike the 1952 agrarian reform,
which had established local agrarian committees and allowed campesinos to
denounce large landholdings. Instead, the 1962 law dictated that only the
INTA could expropriate and redistribute land.[8]

According to Decreto 1551, the INTA would only redistribute land in the form
of the *patrimonio familiar*, or family unit land holdings. To qualify, the family
needed a property holder that was a national citizen, male, between eighteen
and sixty years old, and physically and mentally capable. These farmers had to
aspire to participate in the market economy, reflecting anthropologist Liza
Grandia's astute argument that colonization schemes in Guatemala served as a
way to eliminate subsistence agriculture.[9] The INTA provided provisional titles
and required recipients to pay for the land at reduced rates. It also reserved the
right to reclaim land from recipients who abandoned, sold, or rented their land,
failed to follow good cultivation practices (i.e., only practiced subsistence agriculture), defaulted on loan payments, or expressed "bad conduct putting in
danger one's neighbors."[10] These caveats allowed the INTA to force a certain
conception of the modern citizen upon rural farmers. By designating the male-
led family as the desired social unit, the Guatemalan government gendered development by projecting a strictly Western notion of acceptable gender roles
and social organization. The INTA also forced farmers into the capitalist economy by requiring them to accept loans and sell at markets, thus altering local
economic practices. And in compelling recipients to change their cultivation
practices, the government transformed the historical relationship that farmers
had to land and time, a relationship closely tied to spiritual beliefs and social
relations.[11]

From its inception, Guatemalans questioned the utility of the INTA and
the latest rendition of agrarian reform. Supporters argued that the law systematically, and not rashly, studied land to determine its availability for expropriation and then carefully selected recipients. For example, a 1965
newspaper article actually praised the lengthy procedures required to expropriate and retitle land, arguing that the Alliance for Progress's "peaceful
revolution" enacted change too quickly and only served international political interests instead of fostering national stability.[12] Along these lines,
another journalist wrote that by not quickly handing out free land to campesinos, the INTA was fostering a "new man of the fields," one that did not expect

government handouts but instead developed a sense of personal ambition and drive to achieve change.[13]

However, critics argued that Decreto 1551 was nothing more than a means to "fill a requirement demanded by the Alliance for Progress, so that their country can obtain funds and that is all."[14] When newspaper articles proudly announced titling ceremonies and redistribution efforts, critics maintained that these formalities were simply propaganda efforts for the military regime to foster public support and political clientelism. One editorial even argued that the INTA was really "giving them a bit of porridge with a finger (*darles atole con el dedo*)" because recipients received provisional titles and loans to cultivate the land and thus only acquired crippling debt. While certainly criticizing the INTA, this depiction also disparages campesinos in extremely paternalistic language. By using the analogy of children being weaned through eating porridge from their mothers' fingers, the author quite literally equates campesinos with small, helpless children, incapable of accomplishing anything without the state's assistance.[15]

The INTA's work fit squarely within the emphasis on colonization as a means of resolving the land tenure issue without structural change or resource distribution, in essence refusing to recognize that both were direct effects of unequal power relations.[16] Guatemala's National Development Plan for 1965–1969 prioritized the modernization of its agriculture sector as second only to transportation, to be achieved namely through "massive agrarian colonization of national lands."[17] So when the Maryknoll Catholic order proposed a colonization project in the Ixcán to provide land for parishioners, the INTA supported this venture, believing it dovetailed nicely with national development priorities.

The Maryknoll Order in Guatemala

Established in 1911, Maryknoll focused its mission efforts on East Asia for thirty years but in the aftermath of World War II shifted to a new mission field—Latin America.[18] Fathers Arthur Allie and Clarence Witte arrived in Guatemala in 1943 and began collaborating with the archbishop to determine what locations were best suited to mission work, eventually settling on the department of Huehuetenango in the western highlands.[19] Huehuetenango only had three priests for around 200,000 people, the majority of whom were Indigenous and considered among Guatemala's most marginalized populations.[20] Thus, Huehuetenango provided an excellent space for relatively autonomous mission work in an underserved region in both civil and religious respects.

By October 1952, Maryknoll had twenty-two priests living and working in eight parishes across Huehuetenango.[21] Priests and nuns founded cooperatives and developed socioeconomic projects, increasingly inspired by the social gospel of liberation theology. The Maryknoll hospital in Jacaltenango became nationally recognized as an exceptional center for rural health, with a U.S. diplomat's wife even describing Jacaltenango as a "small paradise of civilization."[22] Father Thomas Melville established a lime (calcium) production cooperative, an important ingredient in the corn tortillas that highlanders consumed at nearly every meal, and members used the proceeds to start a technical school.[23] The San Mateo Ixtatán parish began harvesting wheat and established a production cooperative under Father Arthur Nichols. Father Ronald J. Potter wrote from San Andres Cuilco that his parish's agricultural cooperative had successfully built community cohesion. Father Arthur Melville, Thomas's brother, created a parish credit union, a rabbit-raising program, and a cooperative vegetable garden in La Libertad, although he clearly noted in his diaries that without meaningful land reform, none of these smaller projects would "do much in itself." Father William Woods helped form a wood-carving cooperative in Santa Cruz Barillas.[24] And in Brother Felix Fournier's 1963 report about Maryknoll's projects, he referenced the 1944 Revolution, noting, "The buds of another Spring are out."[25]

While military repression raged in eastern Guatemala during the 1960s, in the western highlands, Maryknoll priests were cautiously optimistic that their efforts could bring meaningful change for their parishioners. These efforts differed from the state-sponsored community development projects such as the DESCOM initiatives. Maryknoll priests did not apply a universal model to distinct local contexts but rather organically implemented ideas that originated due to active collaborations between priest and community. Further, the majority of Maryknoll's projects took the form of cooperatives, allowing local leaders to assume positions of authority via these new institutions and collectively and democratically make decisions.

Maryknoll's work drew the attention of the U.S. State Department. In a 1962 embassy report, Gerald P. Lamberty, the second secretary of the U.S. Embassy in Guatemala, reported that Maryknoll's socioeconomic development programs had successfully begun to change the psychology and daily practices of the Indigenous population in the region, helping to develop "new conceptions of his role in the universe." This position underscores the way that U.S. politicians racialized their understandings of development in predominately Indigenous regions, firmly rooting their understanding of Indigeneity within the discourse of degeneration but with the belief that outside influences, especially U.S. American priests, could regenerate the Indigenous population. Lamberty recognized that priests' understanding of local cultures had resulted in more successful programs than either state-led Guatemalan or official U.S. efforts. As living conditions improved, Lamberty noted that the level of political consciousness also increased, indirectly suggesting that Maryknollers were guiding local voting citizens to choose democracy but also reminding his audience of his real fear of the revolutionary potential of Indigenous peasants if left unguided.[26] In other words, to use historian Julie Gibbings's concept, once the Guatemalan state abandoned the "politics of postponement" and recognized the historical agency of Indigenous people, it also surrendered its ability to control expressions of citizenship.[27] Thus, for Lamberty, monitoring the structure of development projects was imperative for ensuring that the social engineering he believed to be taking place fit with the acceptable confines that the Guatemalan state and the United States had established. That Indigenous people might dictate the terms of their own participation in development initiatives remained quite beyond his comprehension.

Not all Guatemalans were as enthusiastic about Maryknoll efforts as the U.S. Embassy. The order's prominent presence in Huehuetenango had grown so much that the bombastic editor of the daily *La Hora*, Congressman Clemente Marroquín Rojas, published an article under the pseudonym of Friar Canuto Ocaña that referred to Huehuetenango as *"una república marinolesca* (a Maryknoll republic)." Here, he expressed his concern that foreigners were essentially governing an independent republic, acting autonomously in this remote region and taking advantage of the impoverished situation of "the Indian" to "communize them [*comunizarlos*], perhaps without using the word 'communism.'"[28]

These trepidations occurred because in December 1967, Maryknoll priests and brothers Thomas and Arthur Melville, along with Sister Marian Peter, quietly left Guatemala after the student organization that they sponsored became directly involved in the guerrilla movement. Soon thereafter, the national press published several articles about the "Melville Affair" that protested the political engagement of these religious actors.[29] Marroquín Rojas even wrote that "I don't know why the hell the government is waiting to kick all of the famous Maryknolls out of the country . . . a legion of preachers, not of the faith, but of communism."[30] However, the Guatemalan government did not expel all Maryknollers, perhaps recognizing their critical services to the rural population.

While most priests did not condone the armed insurgency, they did realize, in the words of Father William Mullan, that all their development projects were "just a Band-Aid" for a much deeper wound.[31] Maryknollers recognized that, to quote Brother Marty Shea, "land was equal to life," as it was a Guatemalan campesino's most valuable commodity. Without it, one could not overcome poverty and exploitation.[32] Every day these priests witnessed the telling statistic from the 1964 agrarian census that 87.4 percent of Guatemala's farms were too small to provide work and food for a campesino family, and these small farms only covered 18.6 percent of Guatemala's arable land.[33] Recognizing that the Guatemalan government would not enact any meaningful or significant agrarian reform, Maryknoll priests began to think of alternative ways that they might help their parishioners acquire land.

The Ixcán Grande Colony's Early Years

In the mid-1960s Maryknoll decided to launch a colonization project in the Ixcán jungle to help overcome the problem of insufficient land and seasonal migration. According to a study by the University of Wisconsin's Land Tenure Center in 1968, a farmer from Huehuetenango earned an average gross annual income of only Q108.05, compared to a highland average of Q207.55. And while nonmigratory families had an average family income of Q161.23, migratory families only made a meager Q85.13.[34] Oral histories illustrate the dismal story to which these incomes allude. Those without adequate access to land had to migrate to find work, despite this being a dismal option that would bring neither prosperity nor stability. For example, a man from Soloma spent four months seeking seasonal employment, working first in Escuintla cutting sugarcane, then in Mazatenango picking coffee, and finally in Retalhuleu picking cotton. When he returned home with nothing but fifty cents' worth of bread, he decided to migrate to the Ixcán Grande project.[35] Two of the first colonists of the Ixcán Grande project, Rafael Pascual and Mariano Martín Pablo, recalled the hardships on the fincas. Martín had migrated for seven consecutive years to cotton fincas, so when he heard about the Ixcán Grande colonization project, he decided that the risk of traveling to the jungle with the possibility of acquiring land was a better option than continued migration.[36] Another resident of Mayalán, a Mam Maya man from Todos Santos Cuchumatán named Vicente Carrillo, recounted that his family traveled to the coast every two to three months looking for work, stating that the family's life was extremely hard.[37]

In March 1965, Maryknoll approved the plan for the Ixcán Grande project, placing Edward Doheny, a priest and a pilot, in charge. Despite the 1967 Melville Affair, the Ixcán Grande project still received state support, in part because it released the state from the financial burden of the project and because it was precisely the kind of initiative that the Guatemalan government saw as an acceptable alternative to agrarian reform. Father Doheny adopted a gradual, methodical approach to colony development. During the planning process, he worked closely with INTA director Leopoldo Sandovál, an agricultural engineer who had years of experience with the Inter-American Institute for Cooperation on Agriculture, the FAO, the DESCOM, and the SFEI.[38] Together, these two men designed the project in accordance with Decreto 1551, maintaining the colony's structure around the patriarchal family unit and reinforcing the citizen's vertical relationship with INTA authorities, and subsequently, the state.[39]

In 1966, the first group of colonists, all from Todos Santos Cuchumatán, moved with Doheny to the Ixcán, and a second group from Ixtahuacán San Ildefonso arrived soon after.[40] The land they encountered was tropical lowlands, a complete contrast from the colonists' cool, mountainous homes. María Matías Pavo was three years old when she arrived in 1967, and she wistfully remembers the region's beauty, stating, "Here there was a really grand jungle, it was a virgin jungle with all of its wild animals . . . like tigers, leopards . . . big birds, wild turkeys. It was a beautiful place, gorgeous, the rivers were so clean, so beautiful, crystalline, the rocks . . . it was all very beautiful for me."[41] With the help of an engineer, Doheny measured four circular centers and divided them each into forty-acre familial plots arranged as slices of a pie. Residents built a church, school, health center, and soccer field in the center of each town. In this way, families lived in proximity to one another, fostering community and providing protection from wild animals. Doheny chose this circular model based on Sandovál's suggestions, as the latter had traveled to Israel and learned about the kibbutz model, a planned agricultural community that became a key component of the Israeli state's counterinsurgency and development initiatives along its disputed Palestinian border.[42]

Despite building six centers in two years, migrants struggled to survive. Vicente Carrillo, who moved to the Ixcán with his wife and two children, described how strenuous the labor of survival was and how difficult it was to acquire basic commodities, such as salt and sugar. The closest town was Santa Cruz Barillas, several days away by foot, and colonists had no choice but to make the trek and carry in all their supplies. Despite these challenges, Carrillo emphasized that it was better than their prior life, as they were working to improve their own land and community, not that of the finca owner.[43]

To help new arrivals adjust, the cooperative established a mentorship program. Newcomers found a sponsor that had been living in the colony, and they worked alongside this sponsor family for six months. In this way, new families learned the colony's rules and regulations and acquired the necessary skills to prosper in this new environment. After the designated time, the male head of household could become a cooperative member and receive his own plot of land, paying Q70 for surveying fees and necessary infrastructure projects. By 1969, Ixcán Grande residents had surveyed over 18,000 acres and were using 6,000 acres in the ten centers they had established under Doheny's leadership.[44]

Unexpected change literally blew through the colony in the late 1960s. One day, while Doheny was giving afternoon mass, a strong wind caused a large tree branch to fall through the church's thatched roof. The branch landed directly on the altar, hitting Doheny in the head.[45] After receiving medical attention, he returned to the United States on furlough. During this respite, Doheny left the priesthood, married, and died a few years later of cancer. For a few months, the Ixcán Grande project had no priest, and all surveying work halted in Doheny's absence. In 1969, Maryknoll reassigned Father William Woods to the Ixcán region. Also a pilot, Woods began pastoring the nearly 250 families living in the colony.[46]

Born in 1931, Woods joined Maryknoll in 1958 and was assigned to work in Guatemala. Because he was a pilot and had created a small colonization project called *Palestina* in his Santa Cruz Barillas parish, the regional superior believed Woods to be a qualified replacement for Doheny.[47] Affectionately referring to him as Willie, Woods's fellow priests often invoked his Texan heritage to explain his grandiose ideas and fondly recalled that he always wore a cowboy hat and boots and carried a revolver. To Ixcán Grande residents, he was Padre Guillermo, *nuestro finado Padre* (our beloved Father).[48]

Woods worked tirelessly for the cooperative, constantly flying his 1969 Cessna A-185E, appropriately named the TG-TEX, delivering supplies, taking people to get medical attention, bringing in volunteers, and sending the cooperative's agricultural products to market. Whereas Doheny had been systematic and rigidly followed every regulation and law, Woods was the complete opposite, constantly finding loopholes in bureaucratic procedures and ignoring rules that he believed inhibited progress toward his primary goal—acquiring legal title to the Ixcán Grande lands. He also reconfigured the vertical power relationship that had existed between priest and colonists by allowing them to meet independently, collectively make decisions, and guide the colony's future.[49] Woods believed that soon, Guatemala's elite would buy this fertile land with the hope of discovering petroleum or minerals, thus causing land prices to skyrocket. From Woods's perspective, the best option

FIGURE 6.1 An Ixcán Grande center. (Fr. J. Towle, M.M., Fr. Bill Woods, M.M./ Maryknoll Mission Archives.)

was to quickly colonize all the land the INTA had unofficially allotted to the colony and press the institute to disseminate legal titles.[50]

Through analyzing the space and structure of Ixcán Grande, it is apparent how residents modified the state's high modernist vision in a way that fit their needs and realities. Space is neither fixed nor passive but rather serves as a text through which we can analyze efforts of institutions and individuals as they interacted with it to "fix" it, give it meaning, control, and modify it.[51] Town layouts reveal how ideas about modern cities and citizens influenced colonists and priests alike, especially in terms of layout and access to amenities (see figure 6.1). Family homes reflect components of the construction patterns that development experts promoted, though at times these plans did not match reality due to impracticality or insufficient resources.

INTA engineers drafted the blueprint for the residential homes, a model likely shared with multiple agricultural colonies. The model home's blueprint indicated that the structure was to be one large room that measured eight by eight feet. The walls had screened windows to ventilate the space while keeping out disease-carrying insects and had doors to prevent animals from entering. The blueprint delineated clearly designated spaces: a closet separated the large sleeping area from the rest of the home, the kitchen included a table and chairs, and the living room featured two couches. This design contrasted with the colonists' former highland homes, where domestic activities revolved around the central wood-burning stove, which was essential for warmth. The Ixcán's hot and humid tropical climate rendered this custom physically unnecessary, but it would have also affected daily social practices. In this modern rural home, each space's purpose theoretically regulated behaviors and shifted the way that families and neighbors interacted. Finally, the blueprints also included latrines, in accordance with modern hygiene practices. However detailed these blueprints were, it is difficult to know how closely colonists actually abided by them. One U.S. American volunteer who lived in Ixcán Grande in the late 1970s recalled that no homes had screens or latrines, as these were cost prohibitive and considered nonessential.[52] Thus these blueprints demonstrate the INTA's vision for Ixcán Grande more so than the homes colonists actually constructed, indicating a disconnect between the state's modernizing plan and its implementation in the Ixcán.[53]

Analyzing the meanings colonists attributed to the constructed infrastructure gives insight into their notions of development and citizenship. Every center featured a meetinghouse that doubled as the cooperative's store. Here men and women regularly discussed issues and democratically made decisions and elected the cooperative's leadership. This process mirrored that which the state promoted through the DESCOM, though notably without its multiple layers of oversight. Still, development experts' goal of fostering local democracy was a clear success in Ixcán Grande, but this is what would eventually render it a dangerous space in the military state's eyes.

Likewise, through the store, the state's objective of integrating rural Indigenous people into the capitalist economy also came to fruition. Here the cooperative sold necessities like salt, sugar, soap, and oil, bringing in these products from regional markets. Using national currency, residents purchased these goods and sold the cash crops they grew, which included cardamom and sugar.[54] Former migratory workers effectively became active members of a local capitalist economy that had direct ties to major national exporters of agricultural products, allowing them to accumulate wealth and reinvest in their enterprises. These Indigenous farmers, in just a few years, had become part of the capitalist sector that the state desired to establish among campesinos.

These new agricultural entrepreneurs also prioritized having access to Western medicine. Residents built health centers where they received available vaccines and medicines (see figure 6.2). Because no state health promoters worked in the area, Maryknoll doctors from the Jacaltenango hospital trained interested locals in basic medicine. José Sales Ramírez recalls how

FIGURE 6.2 Community health clinic. (Puig, Selwyn/Maryknoll Mission Archives.)

Doctor Juana, a Maryknoll sister, taught him how to administer vaccines and first aid and how to treat common ailments like intestinal parasites and fevers. While some residents certainly continued to utilize natural medicinal practices, this coexisted alongside Western medicine, aligning with the state's plan for modernizing the countryside.

Finally, colonists valued formal education, so in 1975, residents from the Ixcán Grande villages of Mayalán, Xalbal, and La Resurrección each petitioned USAID for funding to complete their school building projects. In these nearly identical applications, a school building committee asked for $1,000 from USAID's Special Development Fund to cover the costs of metal roofing, window screens, cement, and hardware for the doors, the only materials the colonists were unable to acquire from available natural resources.[55] In order to meet USAID's requirement of self-help projects, each committee detailed how residents had contributed $1,700 to cover labor and local supplies. Woods would transport the requested supplies by plane; residents simply needed a small grant to complete these projects within the designated six months. The school committees submitted INTA blueprints for a model rural school in their USAID applications, perhaps hoping this would increase the likelihood of funding. This school mirrored the style for which development experts had long advocated. Instead of being open-air or one-room schools, these buildings measured 192 square feet and had three classrooms, complete with walls, several screened windows, roofs, and doors. The Xalbal school application reported that colonists were currently using a "shed with a thatched roof" as the educational building for more than 200 students. These projects were not only necessary; they were urgent.[56]

USAID agreed to fund the schools, and Roberto Perdomo, the general coordinator of the Special Development Fund, wrote his own recommendation on all three applications: "The people of the colonization has been working [*sic*] in the area since 1970. The community has already built a landing strip, a health center, and a market building. This project would serve not only to provide improved educational activities but also to encourage pioneering efforts in this region. I recommend approval of this project for Q1000."[57] In each file, the project is noted as completed by the end of 1975, well within the proposed time frame.[58]

The physical infrastructure in Ixcán Grande shows how colonists accepted certain tenets of modernization but prioritized projects and adjusted provided plans according to their collective logic and reasoning. Recognizing the importance that access to health care would have for their survival against tropical disease, residents almost immediately built health centers and requested that Woods fly in doctors to train local health promoters.[59] Formal education, while valued, was not as pressing. As a result, colonists did not construct adequate school facilities for nearly a decade. The colony's early years showcase the dynamic relationship between modernization and communitarian development and the creative ways that individuals fashioned a form of development that resonated with them, drawing upon aspects from both models.

Despite these infrastructure advancements, the INTA was slow to fulfill its promise of land titles. Initially, Maryknoll had acquired a loan from MISE-REOR, the German Catholic bishop's socioeconomic development program, to provide the Huehuetenango diocese with $100,000 to buy the land. The diocese then donated the land to the INTA, which was supposed to title it in the cooperative's name.[60] However, this process proved difficult because in the land registry office, the titles to this region were a mess. The government had given out most titles in the early twentieth century, and since then, it had reallocated some titles and revoked others with no clear paper trail, making it difficult for INTA officials to determine whether these lands were national lands, and if not, to determine who the owners were.[61]

Further complicating this process was the change in the titling procedures. While Doheny had requested individual titles, Woods felt it would be more secure to issue a collective title in the cooperative's name because individuals would be unable to sell their plots and divide the cooperative's land. Additionally, this approach would also expedite the titling process for the entire region, as surveyors could title a measured plot under the cooperative even if a colonist did not yet occupy it. In his rush to settle the land before others could buy it, Woods also changed the format of the plots; instead of the circular model, surveyors measured rectangular plots that were slightly bigger, forty-three acres instead of forty. This style of measuring was quicker, and Woods was willing to sacrifice careful planning for efficient relocation of people to the Ixcán.[62]

It is unclear whether Woods unilaterally made the decision to title land in the cooperative's name or if he consulted the colonists. Woods's custom of regularly meeting with members of Ixcán Grande's leadership and granting them autonomy suggests that the titling change was likely a collective decision. Regardless, this decision was controversial, and it caused confusion among residents. Every month, colonists made payments on the diocese's loan, and though Ixcán Grande leadership explained this system to all new colonists, some feared that the Church was taking advantage of them. As the INTA continuously delayed issuance of the land title, tensions rose.

The 1970s saw a rapid influx of Indigenous highlanders relocating to the region, and the general public grew more aware that the Ixcán's land was actually well suited for agriculture, not barren as many had believed. Woods feared that the INTA's hesitation to title the land might stem from its desire to keep valuable land out of the hands of Indigenous campesinos. Foreseeing a land grab, Woods worked to acquire and settle land quickly, and the changes he implemented facilitated this, though they increased intercommunal tensions.

Thus, in its formative years, the Ixcán Grande colony mirrored many of the "acceptable" behaviors that the state desired of the Indigenous population. As residents built new lives in the jungle, they integrated themselves into the national economy and sought to become the rural middle class the state desired. However, their relative autonomy began to raise the suspicions of state authorities, and combined with new contingencies in the early 1970s—the entrance of an armed guerrilla movement and the discovery of petroleum—the state increasingly viewed the colony as a threat to the Guatemalan nation and, more broadly, to the hemisphere.

From Sanctioned to Subversive: Local Rivalries and Cold War Geopolitics

Nineteen seventy-one was a tough year for the Ixcán Grande colony, as some of the centers' leaders grew disgruntled with the change in titling and surveying procedures and the quick admission of new colonists. Unbeknownst to Woods, a delegation traveled to Guatemala City to inquire at INTA offices about the status of the promised land titles. When Woods learned of this, he proposed to remove these delegates from leadership; every center who had a delegate on this trip agreed to depose its leader except for Centro 2.[63] Complicating these problems with Centro 2 was the INTA's involvement with another nearby colonization project. In 1970, the INTA, with the support of USAID, had begun working with a new colony, Kaibil Balam, located across the Xalbal River from Ixcán Grande.[64] These colonists quickly received their individual titles, so some Centro 2 residents grew concerned that the promised collective title would never materialize. To protest the decision to pursue a collective title, this Centro 2 group formed its own consumer cooperative and traded directly with merchants in the municipal capital of Santa Cruz Barillas, thus bypassing the project's cooperative.[65] They also met secretly with leaders from Kaibil Balam and considered blockading the landing strip so that Woods could not return to Ixcán Grande. In essence, this small group of disgruntled colonists wanted to expel Woods from the colony and instead work directly with the INTA to gain private titles for their parcels.[66] Despite these troubles, Woods managed to acquire more land for the cooperative in 1972, and because of these internal divisions, the INTA became more involved in overseeing the cooperative, which Woods hoped would expedite titling procedures.[67]

A decision about personnel further exacerbated tensions with Centro 2. In 1972, educators from Centro 2 traveled to the capital to attempt to obtain certification from the Ministry of Education that would appoint them as the cooperative's state appointed teachers, and again they visited the INTA to inquire about their land titles. When the cooperative's leadership in Mayalán learned about this, they expelled several families and the head teacher, Miguel Ortíz, from Centro 2.[68] These families relocated to lands that bordered Mexico and the eastern bank of the Ixcán River, founding a new town called Ixtahuacán Chiquito.[69] However, this land was within the boundaries of what the INTA had promised to Ixcán Grande; it just had not yet been settled. To strengthen its claim to this disputed territory, the Ixtahuacán Chiquito group used its political capital with the mayor of Santa Cruz Barillas, the municipality under whose jurisdiction Ixcán Grande fell, and municipal officials began to spread dangerous rumors about Ixcán Grande.[70]

In 1973, Mayor Gregorio D. Reyes wrote to the departmental governor, Colonel Juan Baltazar Martínez, to report that Ixcán Grande was taking all matters of justice into its own hands, acting like a "state independent of our Republic."[71] Governor Baltazar quickly replied, reporting that he had asked the bishop of Huehuetenango to sort out the issues with these people who are "under the orders of Padre Guillermo Woods," but that if the bishop failed, he would appeal to the president, because he could not permit anarchy.[72] In another appeal to Governor Baltazar just a few months later, Mayor Reyes admitted that he supported the Ixtahuacán Chiquito faction, revealing his bias against Woods and Ixcán Grande. He requested that the INTA interfere on behalf of Ixtahuacán Chiquito by giving its people lands that Woods was parceling out to Ixcán Grande members.[73] Ixtahuacán Chiquito's alliance with the municipal mayor proved instrumental in raising government suspicion of the Ixcán Grande project.

In the same year, a few Ixcán Grande board members asked the municipal government to send an official to the colony to complete the civil registry instead of making all residents travel to the distant municipal capital. The municipal officials insulted the Ixcán representatives and rejected their petition, going as far as suggesting that in the Ixcán, the residents were "forming a *Cuba chiquita*," a little Cuba, referencing the 1959 Cuban Revolution and Cuba's subsequent efforts to support similar revolutionary movements elsewhere in the hemisphere and in the world.[74] National officials also deployed this label. In 1974, INTA director Armando Sandoval Alarcón threatened the cooperative leaders, stating that they were turning the region into a little Cuba.[75] Beyond his role at INTA, Sandovál's brother Mario was Guatemala's vice president and a self-described fascist. He had been secretary general of the far-right political party, the *Movimiento de Liberación Nacional* (MLN) and had also financing the *Mano Blanca* death squads of the 1960s.[76] Colonists would have known not to take his threats lightly. Clearly, the Guatemalan government was becoming increasingly uneasy about the autonomy and community-driven organization of the Ixcán Grande project.

This telling accusation reveals the power that charges of communism held against political opponents and the awareness that rural Guatemalans had of international rivalries and Cold War politics. The example of Cuba functioned as a model of the possible for revolutionaries and right-wing regimes alike, serving as inspiration for the former and as a dire warning for the latter.[77] Guatemala remained a key theater of the Cold War after the 1954 coup, as both the Guatemalan government and the United States believed that communism would hold wide appeal to the peasantry and working classes.[78] Guatemala had become a "counterinsurgency state" that remained authoritarian and willingly utilized the "institutionalized apparatus created and imposed by the United States in the 1960s to prevent 'another Cuba.'"[79]

FIGURE 6.3 Father Woods distributing land titles. (Personal File Fr. Bill Woods/ Maryknoll Mission Archives.)

Despite these rumors of subversion, and perhaps in an attempt to win colonist support for the government, on May 30, 1974, President General Carlos Arana Osorio issued a title for 8,098 hectares (~20,000 acres) of land between the Xalbal and Ixcán Rivers in the name of the *Cooperativa Agrícola de Servicios Varios "Ixcán Grande" R.L.* A notarized decree from the *Sección de Tierras* dated April 15, 1974, accompanied the title, and this required the INTA to accept additional lands that Woods had purchased and add them to the cooperative. The title functioned as a collective title, and the cooperative was not able to divide, sell, or mortgage the land for twenty years. Additionally, the cooperative could not abandon the land and had to avoid monoculture, implement new technologies and cultivation techniques, and respect national forest laws, which prohibited slash-and-burn agricultural methods.[80] In a long-awaited ceremony, Woods distributed titles of co-ownership to 389 farmers (see figure 6.3).[81]

Although the cooperative had finally obtained a sense of security, its troubles did not end. Beginning in 1974, Ixtahuacán Chiquito residents cultivated lands they believed to be nationally held and available for expropriation. In actuality, these lands belonged to a private finca that Woods had purchased for Ixcán Grande.[82] In December 1974, matters escalated nearly to the point of violence when 600 residents from Ixcán Grande traveled to the disputed territory, armed with machetes and their land title, to defend it against Ixtahuacán Chiquito's incursions. Luckily, the two sides decided to meet to settle the dispute peacefully.[83]

Despite this peaceful resolution, Ixtahuacán Chiquito residents reported to a national newspaper that Woods and INTA authorities were conniving to seize their cultivated land for Ixcán Grande. In response, INTA director Sandovál Alarcón explained that Woods had purchased the lands and the INTA, like all citizens, had to respect private property. Rebuking Ixtahuacán Chiquito, he dramatically stated, "We are not magicians, nor do we possess extraterrestrial powers to give a solution to situations that have to be framed within legal precepts." In another article, Sandovál reminded readers that Ixcán Grande leadership had expelled Ixtahuacán Chiquito for breaking the cooperative's rules. Despite his conviction that Ixcán Grande was a "little Cuba," Sandovál reported that Woods had followed legal procedures by purchasing and donating land to the INTA for distribution to Ixcán Grande.[84] Shortly thereafter, and despite Woods's vehement protest, the INTA granted Ixtahuacán Chiquito nearly 4,500 acres of land that encompassed part of the disputed territory in an effort to foster peace between Ixtahuacán Chiquito and Ixcán Grande.[85] As these internal divisions challenged Ixcán Grande, new external factors also brought changes and difficulties to the colony, further cementing the state's categorization of the region as subversive.

The Franja Transversal del Norte

In August 1970, the Guatemalan government issued *Decreto 60–70*, declaring the region called the *Franja Transversal del Norte* (FTN) an agrarian development zone and designated all "vacant" land national property, placing it immediately under the INTA's control.[86] The FTN, which spread across the departments of Huehuetenango, El Quiché, Alta Verapaz, and Izabal, and included the Ixcán, was known for its natural resources, including minerals, petroleum, hardwoods, and fertile land.[87] Prior to the official designation of the FTN as a development zone, national governments had remarked on the possibility of natural resource reserves in the Ixcán. For example, Castillo Armas's 1955 Petroleum Code, drafted with the direct assistance of representatives from U.S. petroleum companies, gave concessions for exploratory drilling throughout the FTN. *El Estudiante*, a student journal, critiqued the code, arguing that it would transform Guatemala into a "vile Yankee colony."[88] Although companies periodically conducted exploratory drilling, no efforts were successful until the 1970s.[89]

In March 1975, the Shenandoah Oil Company found oil in four wells and predicted a potential yield of 10,761 barrels a day. These wells were located in the FTN but to the east of Ixcán Grande, closer to Rubelsanto and Chisec, Alta Verapaz. Shenandoah, along with Basic Resources International Limited and Saga Petroleum S.A., agreed to give the Guatemalan government 51 percent of the selling price. In return, they received a twenty-year extension to their forty-year concession, permission to construct an oil pipeline, and contracts to develop highways throughout the FTN. Reports even called Guatemala the Kuwait of America, indicating the degree to which this discovery quickly entered the public imagination in exaggerated ways.[90] These reports exacerbated the land grab in the FTN, as the Guatemalan elite eagerly acquired holdings they formerly viewed as wild, desolate, and unprofitable jungle.

Occurring simultaneously in the mid-1970s, Guatemala's civil war began to escalate once again in the countryside. The military had largely contained the guerrilla uprising in the east, but new organizations emerged in the west, seeking to build alliances with Indigenous campesinos. State-sponsored death squads continued to "disappear" and assassinate anyone suspected of leftist political tendencies, guerrilla activity, or popular organizing. The successive authoritarian governments of Colonel Carlos Arana Osorio (1970–1974) and General Kjell Laugerud García (1974–1978) enabled other military leaders to join the ranks of the country's elite, and the FTN became what was popularly coined the "Zone of the Generals." Military officials used familial connections in the INTA to acquire the best available land in this agrarian development zone. General Kjell Laugerud García and his vice president, Mario Augusto Sandovál Alarcón, each had personal connections to the FTN. As mentioned, the INTA director was Mario Sandovál's brother Armando, and the INTA's vice president was Hans Laugerud García, the president's brother.[91] Hans Laugerud also managed the FTN development project, including its finances and all its road-building initiatives. In February 1977, President Kjell Laugerud appointed his defense minister, General Romeo Lucas García, as coordinator for the development of the FTN, a region where the latter's family owned land and had commercial ties to Shenandoah Oil and International Nickel.[92] Otto Spiegler, defense minister under Lucas García once the latter became president in 1978, also held land in the region, estimated by some to be over 700,000 acres.[93] It is impossible to trace exactly how much land the INTA redistributed to military elite, as many INTA records have been destroyed and land was not always titled in the name of the military officer but rather under a family member's name or under a corporation. However, one surviving INTA document, although incomplete, lists property registries for landholdings in

Alta Verapaz, including several properties registered to General Romeo Lucas García and to a company called *Agropecuaria Yalpemech, S.A.* Yalpemech was the name of one of General Lucas García's largest fincas and became a site of oil drilling in the 1980s.[94]

These supposedly petroleum-rich lands that the INTA was classifying as vacant lands were not actually uncultivated but rather were sites of spontaneous campesino colonization, with many of the residents being Indigenous campesinos from Alta Verapaz.[95] The INTA, often with military assistance, evicted these residents, granting some families plots further to the west in the Ixcán region. Using the successful models of Ixcán Grande and its own Kaibil Balam colony, the INTA established similar colonization projects in the region, such as Polígono 15 and 16, Valle de Candelaria, and San José la 20.[96] US-AID financed these projects, justifying this resettlement in terms of agricultural development.[97] Supporters of these projects emphasized that the FTN included Guatemala's richest regions, full of possibilities that could strengthen the national economy and reduce Guatemala's dependence on imports. However, critics argued that these projects only allowed the state to populate the region with poor farmers who could serve as cheap labor for extractive industries. As on coastal plantations, they believed that campesinos' cheap or coerced labor would build the infrastructure for agroindustry, petroleum extraction, and mining, only benefiting the landed elite.[98]

FTN development affected campesinos in Alta Verapaz much more directly than those in the Ixcán, but the Ixcán Grande project still felt the effects of this project.[99] In 1974, the Shenandoah Oil Company began cutting a road with assistance from the army's Engineering Battalion that would cross the cooperative's lands in order to transport crude oil first to Cobán, then to Atlantic ports and to the Cementos Novella plant in El Progreso.[100] General Lucas García had holdings to the west of the cooperative's land, and he bragged that by crossing Ixcán Grande, this road would connect his estate to the oil fields to the east.[101] He also visited Mayalán in 1976, and he reportedly told residents that "Mayalán is sitting on top of gold," referencing the black gold of petroleum, revealing the interest he and the state had in these reserves.[102] In 1974, company workers also began drilling exploratory wells throughout the cooperative, chopping down trees and uprooting harvests. As residents like Jiménez Pascual recall, the region was heavily militarized, so the cooperative protested but did not initially try to halt the oil company's work.[103] However, Ixcán Grande residents vehemently protested the proposed road, insisting that their legal title prohibited the oil company from crossing through privately owned land without their authorization.[104] This action antagonized the military and positioned Ixcán Grande as subversive and oppositional to what the government perceived as national development.

Woods tried to combat the elite land grab in the FTN by purchasing, surveying, distributing, and titling as much land as possible around the colony.[105] In April 1975, he solicited $1 million from MISEREOR for these tasks, justifying this high amount: "I think we can do a lot for a lot of people right now, I also see that every day more and more good land is being bought and worked by big land holders."[106] MISEREOR did not provide $1 million, but in June 1975 it did wire him 100,000 Deutsch marks, the contemporary equivalent of $41,356.[107] Woods actively sought out private finca owners and made offers on their land while fundraising. By 1976, the cooperative's population had increased to 10,000, and it had five centers, but residents continued to face challenges to their security and autonomy.[108]

The Entrance of the EGP in the Ixcán

The entrance of the Guerrilla Army of the Poor (EGP) exacerbated the tense situation in the Ixcán and significantly raised the stakes of accusations of communism and subversion. In 1972, a group of sixteen Guatemalan men crossed the border from Mexico into Guatemala and entered the Ixcán jungle. For three years, they lived there clandestinely, working to build a popular base of support among the campesino communities in the region.[109] Though contemporaries did not yet realize it, this organization of the EGP would mark the beginning of a second major wave in Guatemala's civil war.

Rumors of guerrilla operations circulated in the Ixcán prior to the EGP's entrance. In November 1969, residents told Woods that there were guerrillas in nearby San Luis Ixcán. Woods decided it best to alert the military to avoid any accusations that Ixcán Grande supported the guerrillas, so he radioed the base in Santa Cruz del Quiché.[110] For several months, Woods and colonists heard of almost daily helicopter bombings of San Luis Ixcán and perhaps regretted their decision to notify the military.[111] Through this experience, they also recognized just how violently the military would respond to reports of guerrilla activity, proven or rumored.

Colonists in Ixcán Grande debated how to respond. Some joined the EGP in the mid-1970s, but the majority worked to appease both sides, often using the opportunities that strategic alliances with one side could provide to pursue personal goals. EGP members began visiting towns to foster support, and almost always, they told town leaders to radio the military after giving the guerrillas a few hours' head start. This way, residents did not suffer the military's wrath, but they also did not betray the EGP, another dangerous position to take.[112] However, remaining neutral quickly became impossible, especially after June 1975, when the EGP publicly declared its existence through the *ajustificación* (justified killing) of notoriously exploitative finca owner Luis Arenas Barrera, a wealthy, politically connected landowner popularly known as the Tiger of the Ixcán.[113] Mayalán resident Jiménez Pascual described Arenas as a brutal employer who forced employees to work twelve-hour days.[114]

Throughout 1975, reports of guerrilla and army interference in Ixcán Grande significantly increased, and in his year-end report, Woods detailed how quickly tensions had escalated. In March 1975, Woods received word that students from the national university were holding clandestine meetings on the outskirts of the cooperative's land to recruit campesinos for the EGP. While the letter did not explicitly state where these meetings took place, oral testimonies that priest and anthropologist Ricardo Falla collected indicated that the guerrillas were operating near Ixtahuacán Chiquito and the Ixcán Grande communities of Los Angeles, La Resurrección, and Cuarto Pueblo.[115] Just two months later, and a week before the EGP's public declaration, a murdered colonist from Ixtahuacán Chiquito was found buried in a shallow grave in the same area. Rumors circulated that the EGP had killed him due to reports that he was a military informant. However, another rumor alleged that the deceased man's wife had an affair with the local cooperative's president, so the husband had collaborated with the government in order to take revenge on his wife's lover, not for political reasons.[116]

Within a few days of the death of this colonist and the aforementioned death of Arenas, Woods reported that the Guatemalan army sent four planes of paratroopers and two helicopters, beginning the militarization of the region. Woods estimated that around 100 soldiers were now stationed in the Ixcán, with their headquarters near the Ixcán Grande town of Xalbal, located near Arenas's finca.[117] Upon their arrival, detentions, interrogations, and "disappearances" of colonists began occurring at irregular intervals during the night, keeping colonists in constant fear.[118] In late June 1975, the military "disappeared" fourteen men from Xalbal based on a list that the military had acquired of suspected guerrillas. Rumors spread that the wife of the murdered colonist from Ixtahuacán Chiquito had provided the army with the list, using this as an opportunity to exact revenge on her personal enemies. Woods wrote, "Immediately there were people who became very friendly with the soldiers and rumor has it that their enemies were also picked up by the Army."[119] Given the colony's deep internal divisions, particularly with Ixtahuacán Chiquito, it is not surprising that some individuals used the political climate for personal gain, though they never could have anticipated the scale of repression that was to come over the next decade.

Health promoter Miguel Sales Ordóñez was one of the Xalbal residents that the army took. When he never returned, Woods pressed the military commanders for information about Sales and the other missing colonists, despite being told by the bishops of El Quiché and Huehuetenango that he should "have nothing to do with the situation." Woods enlisted the help of a Guatemalan lawyer, who suggested that Sales's wife file a habeas corpus with a judge in Santa Cruz del Quiché, the location of the nearest military base. As a foreigner, Woods could not file a formal complaint; only Guatemalan citizens could do so. Woods met with Xalbal leaders and explained their options, pledging his help.[120] Instead of remaining neutral as instructed, Woods visited the base in Santa Cruz del Quiché, where he spoke with the second in command, who told him to "mind my own buissness [*sic*] and preach the love of God to the people."[121]

Finally, Woods decided to leverage his U.S. citizenship and connections in the United States and in Guatemala City to generate public awareness about the kidnappings. He asked the missing colonists' wives to write telegrams, which he planned to send to U.S. and Guatemalan newspapers. When he flew to Santa Cruz del Quiché to send these telegrams, he received an order that Civil Aeronautics had suspended his pilot's license and had ordered all the cooperative's planes to be immediately grounded because they were "a danger to lives and property."[122] Even though Woods got the order revoked within a few days, largely through his personal friendship with Julio Maza, the president's secretary, his protests had fostered increased animosity and suspicion of the zone's military commanders.

Miguel Sales Ordóñez's wife, María Gómez Pérez, inquired about her missing husband. While Woods was recuperating from hepatitis in the United States during September and October 1975, she requested an audience with the president, traveling ten days by foot and then riding a bus for fifteen hours to finally arrive in the capital, a city she had never previously visited. Speaking to journalists through an interpreter, Gómez explained how the military had taken thirty Xalbal residents over the last six months, leaving their families destitute. She was now raising her eight children alone, and she had lost their harvest and faced extreme economic difficulties in her husband's absence. National newspapers printed her story, further raising awareness about military abuses. What this publicity also served to do, however, was to unintentionally position the Ixcán Grande cooperative as subversive.[123]

The military used the increased guerrilla presence to justify its occupation of Ixcán Grande, establishing encampments in every center by the end of 1975. Residents recall that soldiers kidnapped people almost daily and demanded that colonists carry identification cards and receive permission to travel outside their communities. Colonists even faced danger just going to their fields to work, as soldiers accused them of holding clandestine meetings or of providing supplies to the guerrillas.[124] Then, in early 1976, the military limited Woods's flights to trips to perform his priestly duties or personal business, and the military carefully monitored his every move.[125] Because Ixcán Grande residents had no other means to transport their products to the markets in Guatemala City, the Guatemalan Air Force (FAG) began providing this service. A 1977 military publication entitled "Operación Ixcán" reported the great success of the program, citing the large quantities of agricultural products that the FAG transported out of the region, reprinting photographs of President Laugerud visiting the cooperatives for various ceremonies and community celebrations, and listing the medical services that FAG provided to residents.

The Air Force placed Colonel Fernando Castillo Ramírez in charge of this operation. In 2014, he published a book about his experience because he believed it erroneous to categorize the military's role in providing "humanitarian" assistance to the Ixcán campesinos as part of a brutal counterinsurgency campaign.[126] When I interviewed him in 2016, Castillo explained that the guerrillas "were not interested in the wellbeing of the country, they said and offered many things, they offered a better life, they offered better living conditions, but they never gave these to them, and everything that they offered was a lie."[127] From his perspective, it was the FAG that rescued Ixcán residents from "subversion," providing them with security and the necessary services to economically prosper, bypass middlemen, and receive social services. A 1977 newspaper article shared Castillo's mentality, reminding residents, "The Guatemalan soldier is your brother. He is just as Indian as you all; he is here to protect you. The Guatemalan soldiers are your brothers, they are your countrymen; you see us in uniform, but we are all equal and we are here to help you."[128] In perpetuating the racialized stereotype of Indigenous people as easily duped and categorizing Ixcán Grande colonists as such, the military lessened their humanity, denied their agency, and justified its own role as paternalistic protector.

However, these perspectives gained little credence with Ixcán residents who daily witnessed Guatemalan soldiers taking away their neighbors and family, butchering their animals, monitoring their masses and meetings, inspecting all their shipments, and constantly accusing them of guerrilla collaboration.[129] Aside from the atrocities that the military committed in the name of security, the FAG's services were not reliable, with planes often not arriving at scheduled times. Colonists remember large shipments of crops rotting in warehouses while awaiting transport and people suffering because they were unable to get timely transportation to a hospital.[130] It was an inadequate replacement for Woods's services and only furthered the state's ability to control the colony.

On November 20, 1976, Woods left Guatemala City at 10:01 A.M. in the TG-TEX to make the fifty-five-minute flight over the mountains and into the Ixcán.[131] Four passengers accompanied him: Selwyn Puig, a reporter and photographer for the *Maryknoll Magazine*; John Gauker, also affiliated with Maryknoll; and Ann Kerndt and Dr. Michael Okada, both of the Direct Relief Foundation. Kerndt and Okada decided to fly with Woods despite a warning from Colonel Roberto Salazar just two weeks prior to "dissociate . . . from Bill, since linking [ourselves] with him suggests that [we] are party to his one-man rule in the Ixcán in opposition to the authorities in this country."[132]

Late that afternoon, John's wife, Phyllis Gauker, called Father Ronald Hennessey, the Maryknoll regional superior, to ask if the plane had arrived in the Ixcán. Every community except one, Belén, had functioning radios and always reported Woods's safe arrival, yet Hennessey had not received a call. Hennessey tried to calm Gauker, explaining how Belén was their first stop, and on occasion, either engine trouble or bad weather prevented Woods from leaving Belén and thus from informing the office of his arrival. Hennessey stayed on the radio late into the night, slept a few hours, and then resumed listening and calling at 5:00 A.M. At 6:45 A.M., he received word from one of the Ixcán centers that the plane had never arrived.[133]

By seven in the morning, Guatemala's Civil Aeronautics office informed Hennessey that Woods's plane had crashed in San Juan Cotzal just north of Santa Cruz del Quiché, killing all passengers immediately upon impact. By evening, the Guatemalan Air Force had transported the victims' remaining dismembered body parts to a Guatemala City funeral home, where friends and family attempted to identify the victims using distinguishing clothing and physical features. All that remained of Father Woods was a severed arm, still dressed in his denim jacket.[134] Ixcán Grande residents grieved the death of their priest and advocate. As colonist Mariano Martín Pablo recalled, "We were left like orphans."[135]

From the outset, the plane crash was shrouded in mystery, generating rumors about what really transpired, which I have analyzed at length elsewhere.[136]

Civil Aeronautics investigator Natzul René Méndez cited poor weather conditions and dangerous piloting as the reasons for the crash, despite it being the dry season in Cotzal.[137] Although the Civil Aeronautics' Weather Division report noted only a slight wind, unlimited visibility, and no precipitation, Méndez maintained that "local topographical conditions in the locale of the accident" created conditions that were "not good to carry out a visual flight."[138] Rather curiously, Méndez had not been an investigator for very long; previously, he had been the Civil Aeronautics gardener. Nor did he actually visit the crash site; rather, he completed his report based on aerial observations from a helicopter.[139]

Father Hennessey traveled to San Juan Cotzal in early December to conduct his own unofficial investigation. He found the bad weather explanation questionable, because when he had visited the town immediately after the crash to get the death certificates, no one had mentioned inclement conditions. What he learned on this December visit confirmed his doubts. The local priest, Father Axel Mencos Méndez, told Hennessey that he had left Cotzal at 11:00 A.M. and there had been no clouds. His parishioners confirmed that it had not clouded over or rained the entire afternoon. Another pilot, Guy Gervais, later confirmed that he also made several trips that day through the same area, and the weather was clear. Finally, and seemingly prophetically, Woods himself had written to his family just a few months prior, explaining that it was precisely in this area, where the plane would dip down into the valley after crossing the mountains and be within clear view of the military base, where anyone could shoot him down. He had predicted that if the military wanted to kill him, this was the exact location where it would be easiest to do so.[140] Although Hennessey had serious doubts about the supposedly accidental nature of Woods's crash, he also felt that there was not sufficient evidence to suggest foul play. And he was also acutely aware that at any moment, the Guatemalan military government could expel all foreign priests from the country. In order to not jeopardize Maryknoll's future in Guatemala, Hennessey stopped investigating the crash. As he wrote to one of the victim's family members, "If there was sabotage only a drunken or bragging tongue will tell. And for this we must wait."[141]

With the death of Bill Woods, Ixcán Grande lost one of its strongest advocates and its direct link to the international community. The colony was essentially an occupied space, with the FAG completely taking over all transit in and out of the region and the military establishing bases in each of the major centers. Woods's death and the disappearances of the Xalbal settlers the year before showcase the military's strategy at the time of using telling examples to warn others about the tremendous cost of challenging the state development project. When General Romeo Lucas García became president in 1978, his regime's scorched earth policy would depart from this systematic assassination approach and unleash broader terror in the Ixcán, turning it into one of the bloodiest theaters of Guatemala's genocidal civil war. This final section explores how competing visions of modernity and citizenship informed these horrific actions and shaped the ways that involved individuals—perpetrators and victims—made sense of what happened.

State-Sponsored Genocide in the Ixcán

As historians have shown, analyzing the nature of violence and how it changes over time matters, as it allows for the characterization of the relationship between involved parties and the motivations and desired outcomes of those involved as they coalesce within specific historical contingencies.[142] The reader should be forewarned that this section contains a few detailed examples of the violence that Ixcán Grande residents faced at the hands of the military state. I have included these graphic scenes not in any way to sensationalize violence but to show the reader "the reality of the unimaginable" and to communicate the trauma that civilians experienced—and still do live with as daily reality.[143] The inclusion of these episodes underscores the gruesome and personal ways that the Guatemalan military terrorized the civilian population and showcases the military state's desire to completely eradicate a population it viewed as "prohibited Indians." The disappearing of the Xalbal colonists and Bill Woods's death mark a change in the type of violence the military enacted against Ixcán residents, as it transitioned to more indiscriminate, extreme forms after 1976. By 1981, the EGP largely controlled the Ixcán Grande region. The Guatemalan army abandoned its outposts in the five cooperative centers after guerrilla attacks, but not without an ominous warning. As one lieutenant told Xalbal residents, "We will return, but in another form."[144]

In March 1982, the Guatemalan military fulfilled this horrible promise, and over the next six months soldiers completely destroyed towns and massacred inhabitants of the five centers of Ixcán Grande: Cuarto Pueblo, Pueblo Nuevo, Xalbal, Mayalán, and Los Angeles.[145] In the aftermath of the violence, two independent truth commissions—the United Nations' *Comisión de Esclarecimiento Histórico* (CEH) and the Archbishop of Guatemala's *Oficina de derechos humanos del arzobispado de Guatemala* (ODHAG)—collected oral interviews from eyewitnesses to the violence, and these sources provide important insight into the nature of the violence throughout the nation. These reports detail how in Xalbal, soldiers locked civilians in a house and burned them alive. In Cuarto Pueblo, soldiers massacred townspeople for an entire week and completely destroyed the cooperative, including crops and livestock. Upon hearing about the state violence in Xalbal and Cuarto Pueblo, residents in Pueblo Nuevo and Mayalán fled. Still, the military destroyed these towns, burning all houses and buildings, destroying cultivated fields, cutting down fruit trees, and slaughtering livestock.[146]

José Sales Ramírez, whose experience of arriving in the Ixcán began this chapter, recalled how mistaken he and his neighbors were when they believed that the military would not reenter Ixcán Grande. While he considers himself and his family fortunate that they were able to escape, he recounted how they fled "with only the clothes that they were wearing," eating corn from fields that the military had not yet destroyed as they traveled for two weeks to the Mexican border. On the way, they encountered other survivors, including children whose parents had been killed. One little girl hid while watching soldiers tie her father to a tree and force him to watch them take turns raping her pregnant mother, eventually killing them both. A boy told Sales that he had seen soldiers tie a man to a post and behead him. They also killed the man's pregnant wife, cutting her unborn child from her womb and replacing it with her husband's severed head. As Sales described these atrocities to me, he remarked, "I don't know how to cry. I don't know why. I never cried for any problem, I never cry. But that time yes, I began to cry."[147] Another individual told ODHAG that during the Cuarto Pueblo massacre, he lay face up on the ground, pretending to be dead; from that vantage point, he witnessed soldiers rape women and slaughter people as they gathered for market day, including the elderly and children.[148] Another ODHAG testimony on the violence in Cuarto Pueblo reported how the military massacred an entire family whose head of household was a catechist; before killing him, however, they forced him to watch the torture and burning of his three-year-old child and the rape and death of his wife.[149] The state-sponsored violence that Ixcán Grande residents suffered had transformed from "disappearing" key leaders to attempting to completely eradicate the entire civilian population and destroying the colony. By the early 1980s, the military no longer saw a few individuals as guerrilla sympathizers but had racialized all Indigenous people in the region as subversive, despite their diversity and intercommunal conflicts and differences. The historical context of continued racism against Indigenous people coupled with anti-communism and the colonial legacy facilitated the military state's labeling of the Ixcán population as dangerous insurgents for their efforts to improve their material realities and their organizational strategies that were rooted in collective decisions instead of state-orchestrated programs.[150]

Once again, ideas about Indigeneity were revisited, revised, and redeployed within the context of the Ixcán Grande project.[151] Colonists hailed from different Maya communities and spoke several Maya languages, and once established in the Ixcán, many retained their cultural practices (language use, clothing, kinship networks) while also establishing new ties and new notions of the self and the collective. Though the intracolony conflicts discussed in this chapter dispel any romanticized notions of a harmonious utopian community, the predominant identity in the colony centered on being Indigenous campesinos, ascribing to both a race and class-based identity. Colonists valued the collective but also exercised their individual rights as Guatemalan citizens with decision-making power, as evidenced in their resistance to the FTN development plan and in varied interactions with the EGP. Through seizing the opportunity at landownership that Maryknoll provided and creating their own communities, colonists challenged structural inequalities in the state's development plans and demanded a reconfiguration of Guatemalan society.

The military elite, on the other hand, became increasingly preoccupied with the colony, especially with its autonomy and success, as this meant that the state had lost its ability to fully manage and control the direction of the colony's development. To deal with these anxieties, the counterinsurgency state homogenized this diverse population and racialized its members as "prohibited Indians," which it defined as a unitary group that was incapable of properly exercising its citizenship and unable to resist the allure of the guerrillas.[152] Using extreme violence, it sought to destroy the colony's communal relations and networks through genocide and through destruction of all infrastructure.[153] Visual evidence of this homogenization and direct targeting of Ixcán Grande exists in the military's designation of the region as a "red zone" on a color-coded map that detailed the counterinsurgency plan, designating it as enemy territory.[154] One survivor who fled to a refugee camp in Mexico told a journalist, "I guess the government does not want any more of the Indian race."[155]

The CEH reported that between March 1981 and March 1983, the Guatemalan army committed seventy-seven massacres in the Ixil and Ixcán regions, totaling 3,102 victims.[156] The CEH designated the Ixcán region as one of three regions most targeted by the military for being considered enemy territory. The other two regions were northern Huehuetenango, where most Ixcán Grande colonists originated, and the Ixil region of El Quiché, where international reports and even a Guatemalan court have since ruled that genocide occurred.[157] The CEH report briefly explores why Ixcán Grande experienced such cruel and comprehensive state violence despite neighboring sites of state-sponsored development that international agencies such as USAID funded. The report findings conclude, "The area of the cooperative Ixcán Grande had its own development, with much suspicion from the State and its institutions."[158] Colonists refused to remain under the state's direction and instead pursued a more autonomous model that rejected aspects of the state's plan that colonists did not find beneficial, such as the road construction project.

The Maryknoll order, on the other hand, did not conduct a multiyear truth commission, though some of its priests like Brother Marty Shea did live with Ixcán Grande refugees in camps in Mexico and others remained connected to the region, offering key support in the aftermath of the war as residents began to return home. A 1981 article in *Maryknoll Magazine* sought to explain how Ixcán Grande transitioned so rapidly from being a state-sanctioned project to one the military state considered a threat to national stability, quoting the following Jesuit manifesto: "Such options for the poor which stress individual rights are in opposition to national security policies which abrogate human rights. The resulting clash explains why the Our Father, advocating that God's kingdom of justice be established on earth, has become such a dangerous prayer."[159]

As scholars Marianne Schmink and Charles H. Wood argue, plans are "never innocent . . . [they] either reinforce or challenge existing social and economic arrangements."[160] From Maryknoll's perspective, the Ixcán Grande project succeeded in changing the status quo in providing resources and opportunities for residents to empower themselves through development on their own terms. But the counterinsurgency state viewed the only acceptable form of development as one that would provide superficial fixes without changing structural conditions that caused a reconfiguration of power relations. In other words, it left the status quo intact and it preserved the vertical hierarchy that rendered intended recipients as passive and submissive. Both the CEH and Maryknoll understood the violence to be a horrific consequence of Ixcán Grande residents' successful revision of the state's development project and the redefinition of the terms of their inclusion and participation in the nation.

Popular interpretations of the motivations behind the violence echo these institutional statements, as evidenced in testimonies that survivors gave to ODHAG. One testimony suggested that the government had made a decision to "exterminate all of the campesinos who had organized in cooperatives" and that to prevent future violence, the government "has to respect our culture, our right to opinion" and recognize and respect them as Indigenous people.[161] Another echoed this sentiment, maintaining that the violence took place because poor people and the guerrillas had dared to claim equality with the rich.[162] One pointed directly to the fact that Ixcán Grande residents had sought to solve their own problems by acquiring land *before* there was oil and interest from elite Guatemalans. In remarking on this chronology, the interviewee thus implied that their refusal to sell their land to speculators and wealthy landowners had led the government to view them all as guerrillas because they prioritized their community over the state's perceived national interest.[163] Survivors clearly understood how their pursuit of a better life outside the acceptable confines of state development projects had antagonized the state and how the historical contingencies of oil discovery and the entrance of the EGP into the region had coalesced to define them as subversive in the state's eyes.

Conclusion

As seen in the initial years of the Ixcán Grande project, some Guatemalans were able to use development to shape their futures as they wished. The modern development that Ixcán Grande residents pursued fit within the state's modernization in some respects, as communities often sought to implement aspects of Western medicine, education, democratic governance, and market economics into their daily lives. By the mid-1970s, the Ixcán Grande project was central to the state's development plans and security concerns, particularly given the FTN Development Plan. But Indigenous colonists ventured beyond the acceptable confines of the state's development plan when they organized their own communities and cooperative and dictated the terms of their development and degree of adhesion to the state's modernization project. Their actions challenged the status quo by threatening to shift local seats of power away from landowners and political elite and instead root power in the collective decision-making apparatus of the cooperative. Not only did they exacerbate tensions with the national government but they also earned Ixcán Grande the reputation for being a "little Cuba in the jungle," a categorization that had violent repercussions. This label, in tandem with the EGP entrance and the FTN petroleum discoveries, caused the military state to see the colonists' efforts as antithetical to Guatemala's security, and it unleashed horrific violence upon these newly formed communities. The Guatemalan military brutally suppressed colonists' efforts to use development to define and pursue a better life on their own terms, in the process racializing them as "prohibited Indians." Even in the aftermath of genocide, the military state continued to use development programs as a tool of counterinsurgency, enabling it to control the processes of change and shape the limits of the possible in a community. At the same time, survivors of the violence continued to take the extraordinary risk of pursuing development on their own terms as they rebuilt their lives. It is these dual uses of development that the next chapter explores.

CHAPTER SEVEN

Photographing Development
A Visual Analysis of War-Torn Guatemala, 1982–1996

Before sunrise, residents in the model village of Acul gathered for their morning flag ceremonies. These Indigenous campesinos were internally displaced people, as their communities of origin had been destroyed during the military's 1982 *Plan de Victoria 82*, a revamping of the scorched earth policies from the late 1970s. Like Ixcán Grande, the military had identified the Ixil region in northern El Quiché as subversive and as a region of guerrilla insurgency, and in the genocidal campaign's aftermath, researchers estimated that 90 percent of the surviving population was displaced.[1] Having accepted the Guatemalan army's offer of amnesty, some people had relocated to Acul, where the army promised them land and a new home.[2] On this morning and every other, Acul's residents stood shoulder to shoulder in orderly rows, with hands across hearts, singing the national hymn and pledging loyalty to the nation. Solemnly, they listened to the military official's lecture on patriotism and civics before lining up to receive breakfast, provided by the United Nations Development Program. After breakfast, residents joined their work crews or their civil patrol units to begin the day's work, under the military's watchful eye.[3]

Less than one hundred miles away, other internally displaced Indigenous people experienced a very different morning routine. Living in hiding as *Comunidades de población en resistencia* (CPR), these residents had also experienced the violent destruction of their communities and the massacre of their neighbors.[4] Women awoke at 2:00 A.M. to cook tortillas so that the cover of night would hide the smoke that their fires generated.[5] The rest of the CPR rose at dawn, ate a meager breakfast, and then worked from 7:00 A.M. to 3:00 P.M. in collective foraging and cultivation, leaving the remaining daylight hours for taking care of personal needs like washing clothes and preparing food. Without access to markets or urban centers, residents had to creatively rely on available natural resources or take great risks to acquire material basics. Constantly, CPR residents scoured the horizon for military troops and attentively listened for the sound of helicopters, ready in an instant to hide in the large holes they had dug as bomb shelters or to abandon their homes once more and flee from violence.[6]

When Efraín Ríos Montt assumed the presidency after a successful coup in 1982, Guatemala had been embroiled in civil war for twenty-two years and under uninterrupted military rule for over a decade. General Ríos Montt escalated the military presence in the countryside when he launched Plan Victoria 82, originally named Operation Ashes. According to Ríos Montt, this scorched earth policy sought to "dry up the human sea in which the guerrilla fish swim" through completely destroying all human life and infrastructure in zones believed to be the guerrilla base.[7] Between April and December 1982, communities like those in Ixcán Grande suffered horrific massacres, as described in the previous chapter. While many military officers, both then and at the time of research in 2016, did not deny the violence, they understood it to be "unfortunate but necessary . . . in their justified campaign strategy to destroy the guerrillas."[8] And while they did not deny military responsibility for some massacres, they argued that guerrilla organizations and the military were equally responsible for the violence.[9] However, most scholarship and studies by international organizations give a very different interpretation of the violence, condemning the widespread human rights abuses and extrajudicial killings the military was perpetuating against civilians.[10] In fact, the United Nations Truth Commission later reported that 200,000 people died during the thirty-six-year conflict, approximately 83 percent of whom were Indigenous. Further, the report stated that the Guatemalan military was responsible for 93 percent of these atrocities and had specifically targeted Indigenous populations, thus committing what the UN called state-sponsored genocide.[11]

These different interpretations of culpability and the nature of the violence itself frame understandings of the use of community development as a tool of counterinsurgency, or as a practice of governance, and as a tool of survival, or as a practice of politics in 1980s Guatemala. As survivors fled the scenes of massacres, they faced three primary options: flee across the Mexican border to refugee camps, remain in hiding in Guatemala and perhaps join a CPR, or relocate to a Pole of Development. Here, I analyze the diametrically opposed development models that emerged in the Poles of Development and in the CPRs, arguing that the counterinsurgency state used a modernization model of development to consolidate its strategic position while the CPR members used a communitarian understanding of development to resist and survive state violence. Additionally, the differences in these two models also reflects competing understandings of Indigenous agency and place in the nation.

My purpose here, as throughout the book, is not to evaluate the success or the failure of either of these projects. Nor do I aim to provide a comprehensive history of either the Poles of Development or the CPRs. Instead, I am concerned with the different significances that historical actors attributed to these projects and how ideas about the utility and very meaning of community development shaped the structure of each project and framed individual, collective, and institutional goals. There has been no moment in twentieth-century Guatemalan history where the differences between top-down, modernizing development and bottom-up, communitarian development have been so clear. The Poles of Development illustrate the extreme measures that the Guatemalan state took to force the Indigenous population into becoming "permitted Indians"; the CPRs exemplify the extreme conditions that some Indigenous people endured to continue pursuing development on their own terms.

The Utility of Photographs as Historical Sources

As discussed in the introduction, I limited oral history interviews to a couple of military officials who held high-level positions in military development initiatives and one civilian tasked with overseeing the Poles of Development in order to avoid interviewing individuals about the trauma they had experienced when their perspectives have been well documented elsewhere by themselves and by scholars and activists with long-term engagement with these populations. Photographs provide another vehicle into this past, and they serve as my central means to analyze these histories. The indexical nature of the photograph and its claims to truth, though disputed, do document an instant in time. Through the camera, the photographer documents "what was," yet at the same time, the event of photography is not closed but is an "open encounter" between subject, photographer, and viewer.[12] This open and ongoing interaction involves all participants in what Ariella Azoulay terms the "citizenry of photography" and binds them in a "civil contract" in which no member ever holds complete authority over another, even when the photograph was made in moments of extremely repressive conditions.[13]

Photographs allow one to "catch a glimpse of the past under construction," quite literally in the case of the photographs discussed in the chapter.[14] In them, we can analyze what Kevin Coleman refers to as the process of self-forging, or the idea that the photographed subject can use the medium of the camera to capture and present a version of oneself to the spectator. Certainly, there are instances when the power relations between photograph and subject are highly unbalanced, yet Coleman reminds us that the subject is always capable of acting and of mediating this encounter, even in small ways. We can extend this concept of self-forging to that of the collective, as communities represented a particular version of themselves to the citizenry of photography.[15]

As spectators, then, our participation within the citizenry of photography is not passive; we should not merely look at images but "watch them," bridging the actual moment in which the camera shutter closes with the present moment of viewing.[16] Ethical spectatorship—this participation in the citizenry of photography—requires the viewer to recognize what Nicholas Mirzoeff calls the countervisuality in the image, or the attempt to denaturalize and destabilize the power relationships at play. Doing so allows for the photographed subjects to demand the right to look and to be seen on their terms, calling for the viewer to recognize their existence and the ways in which they actively challenged authority.[17] Through an empathetic viewing of these images, one can understand how photographs can both serve to reinforce existing power hierarchies, as the image works "as a means of surveillance, discipline, and classification," and function as a means for photographed subjects to forge their own subjectivities and engage the viewer in ways the photographer perhaps did not anticipate and cannot control.[18] In the images analyzed in this chapter, the reader will watch two distinct types of settlement projects and through them better understand and recognize the existence of two competing visions for the reconstruction of the Guatemalan nation and corresponding forms of citizenship.

A personal archive provides the photographic source base for my analysis of the Poles of Development. Engineer and businessman Rolando Paiz Maselli was one of the directors of the *Programa de Ayuda para Vecinos del Altiplano* (Aid Program for Highland Communities, PAVA) in 1982 and volunteered with the Poles of Development, giving his time and considerable financial resources to help the military design and implement model villages.[19] Paiz Maselli was also an amateur photographer. To document his service with the Poles of Development, he regularly photographed the progress of the construction projects in different villages, over time printing these images and creating personal albums of each model village. Organized chronologically, the photographs convey a sense of linear progress, starting with images of destruction and ending with celebratory photographs at the village's inauguration ceremony. Few images have captions, but those that are present clarify Paiz Maselli's own interpretation of the photograph. Over time, these albums have been damaged, and individual photographs were in too fragile a condition to permit reproduction for their inclusion in this book.[20] Thus, I have selected several images to discuss, and I have provided the reader with a description of the content and form of the image alongside my visual analysis.[21] Despite this drawback, these images remain an important and fascinating historical source for analyzing the material and ideological work of the Poles of Development.

A very different kind of visual archive frames my analysis of the CPRs. Out of fear for their lives, these mobile communities did not publicly announce their existence until September 7, 1990, after living in hiding for nearly a decade.[22] After this announcement, the CPRs received more open support from national and international organizations and used photojournalism to document life in the CPRs. Two of these archives provide the source base for the second half of this chapter: images from the archive of the *Comité Holandes de Solidaridad* (Dutch Committee of Solidarity, CHS) and the photography of Jonathan Moller, a U.S. American documentary photographer who worked with the National Coordinating Office for Refugees and Displaced of Guatemala.[23] The dissemination of their work, in tandem with international press coverage, brought further awareness to the existence of the CPRs and of ongoing human rights abuses. Moller later published many of his images in *Our Culture Is Our Resistance: Repression, Refuge, and Healing in Guatemala*, a book that powerfully combines his photographs with testimonials, essays, and poetry to tell the stories of the photographed subjects.[24] Thus, unlike Maselli's albums, which he created for personal recollection, these photographers engaged in solidarity work and created these images for a public audience. The photographs' indexical quality proves to Guatemalans and to the international community that internally displaced people had survived the violence and continued to place demands, as citizens, upon the state. At the same time, these photographs demand that the viewer recognize the precarity facing CPR residents, as they struggled to forge self and community in the midst of ongoing violence. These images allow for an analysis of the communitarian structure of the CPRs, underscoring the ways in which Indigenous campesinos defined development as they wished.

Photographs as historical sources are analytical tools to explore the ways in which discourses of development shaped the reconstruction of war-torn Guatemala. The visual medium of the photograph, then, does not just mechanically reproduce what was. It also communicates existence; it reveals ongoing struggle; and even in the most desperate of circumstances, it engages subject, photographer, and viewer in a relationship that demands that each see and recognize the existence of the other. These visual artifacts reveal the contestations over racialized identity and nation and the ways that community development factored heavily in the pursuit of these competing visions for a future Guatemala.

Development in the Model Villages

During the early 1980s, the Guatemalan military's scorched earth campaign was one side of a two-pronged military strategy called *Fusiles y Frijoles*, or Bullets and Beans. First the military attacked towns it had labeled as subversive and destroyed infrastructure; then, it implemented its "beans" strategy of providing immediate assistance to survivors through relocating them to one of several Poles of Development, allegedly for their own safety. The Plan of Assistance to Areas of Conflict (PAAC) within the military's Office of Civil Affairs utilized community development to ensure the success of the counterinsurgency campaign. Though the PAAC itself was a new military department, it continued the trend of state-led modernization and the use of development projects as counterinsurgency tactics.[25] In the Poles of Development, the PAAC called for a strategy named the 3Ts—*Techo, Trabajo, y Tortilla* (roof, work, and tortilla)—providing internally displaced people with food and shelter in exchange for labor, essentially disciplining the labor force.[26] The military believed that providing development assistance would gain residents' loyalty and provide a surveillance apparatus that justified an extensive militarized presence.

Although the first stage for the resettlement of internal refugees began in late 1982, it was not until June 1984 under President and General Oscar Humberto Mejía Víctores that the Guatemalan government institutionalized the Poles of Development.[27] *Decreto-Ley 65–84* established four poles, two in El Quiché (Ixil region and Playa Grande), one in Huehuetenango (Chacaj), and one in Alta Verapaz (Chisec). The military later formed two more poles, Senahú in Alta Verapaz and Yanahí in El Petén. Several model villages comprised each pole, and the law tasked the military with overseeing all movement and activity.[28]

The Guatemalan government based the Poles of Development on the strategic hamlet program that the United States and the Republic of Vietnam implemented in the late 1950s, a project that Bernard Fall called the "most mammoth example of 'social engineering' in the non-Communist world."[29] Presented as a form of nation building, the strategic hamlet program, like the Agroville Program in South Vietnam, relocated rural communities into new, militarized villages that effectively combined surveillance with high modernist development and worked to "administer, protect, and control the population."[30] The U.S. and South Vietnamese militaries assigned peasants to work teams and local militia battalions, hoping that "'traditional' loyalties to family and formerly isolated, largely autonomous villages would be replaced by 'modern' identification with a specifically South Vietnamese nation-state."[31] Importantly, it also placed military officials, instead of regional leaders, in charge of these new villages, firmly linking rural Vietnam to the central government in Saigon.

Guatemala adopted what 1983 Civil Affairs director Colonel Mario Paiz Bolaños called the "*gringo* war policy" and mirrored its Poles of Development on the strategic hamlet program, constructing villages in the departments hardest hit by Victoria 82: El Quiché, Huehuetenango, and Alta Verapaz.[32] Touted as a bottom-up, decentralized development model, in reality the structure of the Poles of Development aligned more with already established practices of midcentury developmentalism, or state-run development projects, like the DESCOM and INTA colonization programs. This model combined public and private efforts, and as historians like Amy Offner and J. T. Way argue, this neoliberal project was not a complete rupture with the past but rather implemented similar ideas and frameworks.[33] The Poles of Development were designed to allow the military state to pacify and rebuild the countryside on a shoestring budget through collaboration with state and nonstate institutions. Under the auspices of decentralization, the state created the *Coordinadores Interinstitucionales* (CCII) that operated at the national, departmental, municipal, and local levels.[34] But similar to the structure of the DESCOM, this decentralized system was actually tightly controlled, as any type of local project by a public or private institution or individual had to be approved and operate through the CCII. In other words, the CCII existed as a counterinsurgency apparatus that served to "smuggl[e] militarism into the new body politic" through a militarized nationalism.[35] Importantly, a military commander oversaw each level of coordination, from the director of civil affairs of the National Defense Department to the local military authority at the local level. The military justified this structure by arguing that the "subversion" capitalized on perceived "administrative disorder," so a hierarchical system would gain the trust of the people and ensure the effectiveness of development efforts.[36]

In 1983, President Mejía Víctores traveled to the Ixil Maya town of Acul in El Quiché to see the destruction the community had experienced in April 1982, which the military attributed to the guerrillas. General Eduardo Wohlers Monroy, an air force officer, remembered hearing Mejía Víctores's speech to the survivors on the radio, where the president promised to build them a new town in one hundred days. After impulsively making this commitment, Mejía Víctores tasked the Office of Civil Affairs, where Paiz Bolaños served, and the Committee of National Reconstruction, where Wohlers Monroy worked, with accomplishing this goal.[37] Already, the military was establishing poles of development in Playa Grande and Chisec but without coordinating efforts through the CCII; Acul would be the pilot project for this new organizational hierarchy.[38]

With few financial resources, and no engineering experience, Colonel Paiz Bolaños questioned how his office could possibly proceed with this monumental task. He called his nephew, Rolando Paiz Maselli, an engineer and businessman, and asked for his assistance. Immediately Paiz Maselli agreed to personally hire an architect and an engineer to help the military design this model village, and he enthusiastically committed to help oversee the project.[39] Not only that, but he took along his camera and carefully documented the reconstruction of Acul through this technological medium. Just under the one-hundred-day goal, on December 22, 1983, Mejía Víctores returned to inaugurate the new Acul.[40] From the military's perspective then, the Poles of Development accomplished their twofold mission of separating the civilian population from the guerrillas and rebuilding the Guatemalan countryside under the military's direction. The process of reconstructing Acul, as depicted through Paiz Maselli's photographs, demonstrates how the military used the logic of modernization in designing the new Acul as part of its counterinsurgency efforts.

In two spiral hardcover, self-adhesive photo albums simply titled "Acul I" and "Acul II," Paiz Maselli carefully arranged his printed photographs to tell a narrative about his experiences working in the Poles of Development in this particular place. In roughly chronological order, he grouped similarly themed photographs, showing the process by which residents, the military, and the various participating institutions rebuilt this town. Paiz Maselli wrote captions for some of the images, carefully cutting cardstock rectangles in which he inscribed his short descriptions in neat, block handwriting. Through the albums' narrative, Paiz Maselli inscribed his version of the Poles of Development history and a personal account of his own self-forging through this experience.

As described in the opening anecdote, residents in the Poles of Development gathered every morning for a civics lesson, and the album includes an image of this daily scene. On the photograph's left-hand side, two lecturing military officials stand on a tower of wooden pallets, extending their gaze downward toward their subjects, clearly demonstrating the hierarchy of power in the model village. Below them, internal refugees appear as a huddled mass of blurred figures that are nearly indistinguishable from one another. Though mud and stacked wooden boards occupy the foreground of the image, the photograph emphasizes the people, overexposing the surrounding mountains to erase them from the scene, much as the Poles of Development project wished to remove the history of the war from the landscape and from the memory of the people themselves. These daily reeducation lessons attempted to create a loyal, pliable, and homogeneous citizenry of "permitted Indians," flattening diversity and any prior personal or collective identities that the listeners held. In 1984, a teacher from one of the model villages described the importance of these assemblies in the following way: "We have to work them, to raise their consciousness. OUR WORK IS LIKE ERASING AN OLD CASSETTE TAPE AND RECORDING SOMETHING NEW" (emphasis in original).[41] Paiz Maselli confirmed the 6:00 A.M. meetings, stating that everyone stood neatly in lines while listening to the military's fifteen-minute lecture, after which all participants left in their assigned groups to start their workday.[42]

The album contains many images of work crews, and these continue evincing the theme of teamwork. Yet two of these images also inadvertently reveal the military's presence in overseeing the reconstruction. In one blurry photograph of men hauling mud for brickmaking, a soldier appears along the edge of the cornfield that frames the image's background, nearly blending in with the landscape. He stands at attention in full uniform with his hands on his rifle, overseeing the work crew and ensuring that no one enter or exit through the tall rows of corn. And in an image of work crews cutting boards on the nearby road, on the right-hand edge of the photograph's frame is an armed soldier, carefully overseeing the work. Soldiers rarely appear in the album, and most photographs focus on the laborers alone or depict them collaborating with outside experts, effectively erasing the presence of the military in carefully overseeing the process. Thus, the blurred soldier on the edges of these photographs appears almost by accident, as a part of the hazy background, not as the central subject of the image. Yet the indexical nature of the photograph records his presence and, by extension, the omnipresent element of state surveillance, reminding the viewer that this project is taking place during a time of war.

The Poles of Development project reiterated the Guatemalan state's long history of portraying labor as patriotic duty.[43] Paiz Maselli emphasized his belief that collective work fostered patriotism through documenting the labor of work crews accomplishing different tasks through group efforts. In one photograph, a work crew of approximately ten men hauls a large tree trunk to the construction site. They used rope to strap smaller branches across the top that they then held and used to lift each end of the trunk. Five neatly dressed men wearing wide-brimmed hats appear in the foreground of the image, together holding one of the branches and lifting the front half of the heavy trunk. A small toddler sits nonchalantly upon the log, apparently along for the ride. Despite carrying this load for an unknown distance, the men appear laughing and conversing, with most directing their gazes either to the child or to one another, and only one directly engages the camera. What is mechanically reproduced in this photograph is a moment of smiles; what is omitted is any sense of individual history or broader context. Importantly, however, this photograph and its handwritten caption provide Paiz Maselli's interpretation. Glued just above the image, on a cut piece of lined cardstock, reads the caption of "They begin to work together," revealing the belief that Acul's residents needed guidance in learning how to work together, a position likely shared by many of the project supervisors. From their perspective, any abilities on the part of Ixiles—or Mayas more generally—to engage in relations of reciprocity had been destroyed during the war and thus the military state needed to help reconstruct these collective bonds. Like the philosophies undergirding the DESCOM's self-help principles, the Poles of Development architects believed rural Indigenous Guatemalans to be capable of collectively harnessing their abilities and energies toward a common goal, but only when given expert outside guidance, and they sought to channel these solidarities in a way they deemed appropriate.

Not all images of residents communicate joy, performed or real. One image shows two young Ixil women posing in front of a tall stack of bricks. They sit on a shorter brick stack angled slightly toward one another, with their hands neatly folded in their laps. Wearing the red *corte* from the Nebaj region, these women directly return the photographer's gaze without smiling. Their eyes serve as what Roland Barthes calls the punctum, or the point that pricks the viewer and refuses to be forgotten.[44] Revealing a profound grief and wariness coupled with bravery and resistance, they directly and intensely stare at the man taking their photograph, demanding that he and all future participants in the citizenry of photography see them as individuals, despite the state viewing them collectively as rehabilitating subversives. And they sit against a wall of bricks that is evidence of the labor residents performed, as these bricks, made on-site, became the building blocks of the new Acul.

The album contains images of the process of brickmaking. One photograph depicts hundreds of bricks neatly lined on the ground in the sun to bake. The photograph's structure follows a reverse diagonal, with the rows of bricks tracking from the bottom right corner toward the center of the frame, each brick identical in color and size. These rows of newly molded bricks function as a metaphor for the rows of residents at the morning meetings. The uniform rows demonstrate the military's understanding of progress as based upon homogeneous, rigid standards. Just as these bricks were crucial components of the new buildings being constructed in the Poles of Development, the military saw the residents as a critical part of molding the new Guatemalan nation, but only if they were transformed into "permitted Indians." In a Guatemala with a robust Maya movement and with youth cultures challenging the traditional racial dichotomy that never actually defined Guatemalan society but was institutionalized through law, census categories, and popular discourse, the military's modernization sought a social integration where Indigenous people complied with maintaining the status quo.[45] It desired for all Guatemalans to be wholly committed to a militarized nationalism that would define their sense of self, interpersonal relationships, daily life, and ways of conceptualizing self and society. As a part of neoliberal multiculturalism, it racialized Indigeneity to define the appropriate expressions of culture, the acceptable patterns of belief, and it rendered inauthentic, or impermissible, any autonomous modes of being.[46]

Paralleling the limited definition of racialized Indigeneity that the Poles of Development project planners sought to impart, outside experts also dictated all plans and decisions regarding urban design, ensuring that these new communities would follow the state's modern urbanization plan. The military believed that the dispersed nature of Indigenous villages was "isolated" and easily susceptible to what they called guerrilla "subversion." This isolation, in turn, made the Indigenous population "aliens to modernity" who "represented a particular threat to the nation."[47] Paiz Maselli shared this perspective, arguing that "living dispersed isn't proper" as it made the extension of services like electricity, water, and roads more expensive and difficult. He felt that it hindered educational and economic opportunities and, critically, made families vulnerable to guerrilla intrusion.[48] Thus, as a solution, project planners developed a centralized organization for the model villages that relocated residents into town centers where they would not only be "safe" but also available to receive the military's instruction that would transform them into the state's version of modern Indigenous citizens. In a scene not unlike the layout of U.S. suburbia, though certainly not as pompous, the model villages' identical houses were compactly built on small lots laid out on an urban grid of major and minor roads.

Model villages had access to potable water and electricity, and while both technologies did help to simplify daily life, they also connected residents to national utility services, thus incorporating them into the national economy. Now, instead of obtaining water at public *pilas*, or water taps, a common meeting space, residents now just walked to nearby spigots to obtain safe drinking water. Project designers located these spigots near city centers to permit the close monitoring of public gatherings and conversations, increasing the visibility of all residents. While still communal, these spaces were now under the military's watchful gaze. Likewise, the town's streets were lined with bright lights, at once making nighttime travel safer but also easier to supervise. One photograph showcases the streetlights, featuring the main entrance to Acul and its two-lane road as its main subject, centered in the middle of the frame. Along both sides of the road stand tall utility poles painted a bright white along the bottom with wires and streetlights at the top. Cornfields are planted on each side of the road, and the viewer can see the buildings of Acul in the distance, with the mountains as their backdrop. The lights illuminate not only the town but also the fields and the road, making it difficult to enter Acul undetected. With the compact arrangement of the village and the illumination of its streets, residents could discern each other's movements, as could the soldiers stationed to guard the village. These modern conveniences made unauthorized meetings, ceremonies, or even personal trysts much more difficult to hide. They rendered daily life visible to the state, which in the eyes of the project planners was a positive improvement and mode of protection.

Long a counterinsurgency strategy, agricultural modernization remained central to the Poles of Development project as a tool of social engineering.[49] Just as the project planners mapped the new Acul onto the landscape as they wished, they also chose the crops and methods for cultivation. An Inforpress journalist reported that the military required residents to grow crops other than corn, even going to the extreme of cutting down any planted corn. However, the presence of cornfields in several of Paiz Maselli's photographs would suggest that this was not a regular practice, or at least did not continuously occur in Acul. With funding from USAID's 520-T Rural Modernization program, the military implemented agricultural programs to grow commercial crops such as brussels sprouts, broccoli, and spinach, acting as a middleman to sell these products to foreign markets.[50] Images of Taiwanese experts appear in the album, showing how they taught cultivation methods, implemented

irrigation systems, and led demonstration classes in which residents were expected to participate. Additionally, the military required the use of new
strains of seeds and fertilizers, demonstrating the state's continued reliance
on expert opinion over local knowledge.[51] By drawing residents into the market economy through these specific agricultural practices, the state codified
these behaviors as modern, rendering all else anachronistic and harmful for
national progress.

The final pages of Paiz Maselli's Acul album depict the inauguration ceremony of December 22, 1983, discursively situating it as the celebratory grand
finale to this intense period of labor. One photograph is spatially divided hor-
izontally, with the upper half of the image showing the mountains in the
background and the lower half depicting the crowd of people gathered in
the public park for the inauguration events. Along the horizon line is a simple
wooden building upon which hangs a large Guatemalan flag. In the foreground, men, women, and children have gathered for the occasion and seem
to be casually conversing with one another. The carefully orchestrated public
events sent clear messages to the national and international press—and to the
new community itself—about the meaning of acceptable Indigeneity under
this militarized nationalism. The Guatemalan flag flew high in many locations, reminding attendees that this project was part of the effort to reconstruct a war-torn Guatemala and once again incorporate Indigenous people
as "permitted Indians" into the Guatemalan nation. It also served to signify
that while the discourse and ideology of modernization certainly transcended
the boundaries of the nation-state, its implementation was very much a national
project.

For military officials, not only was the new town complete but so were
their efforts to de-Indianize the population and reconstruct Indigeneity according to the state's ideal. Parades opened the day's activities, and Indigenous women dressed in ceremonial *traje* walked through the street alongside
members of the *cofradías*, or civic-religious organizations. Publicly displaying
these symbols of Indigenous identity indicated the state's approval of these
cultural behaviors as symbols that the government could appropriate to represent a broader Guatemalan national identity. These parades illustrated the
concept of the "permitted Indian," serving to "preserve forms of tradition
that emanate from the past in pristine ways; that performance of stasis is the
condition of possibility for being accorded status as proper Indians."[52] This
practice of selecting what it perceived to be picturesque, authentic, and romanticized notions of Indigeneity, stripping them of any deeper meaning,
and appropriating them as a national symbol continued to characterize the

state's definition of integration. It erased any notion of "Indigenous specific-ity" and instead reduced all things Maya to a singular, folkloric identity.[53]

Included in the numerous photographs of Acul's inauguration ceremonies are several of parades. For example, one image shows the participation of co-fradías alongside state authorities to depict the convergence of traditional and local authorities with the modern and national state authorities. The photograph's subjects stand in a horizontal line, and in between the male Ixil Maya authorities is a representative from the Banco Nacional de Vivienda, wearing a dark suit. He appears smiling while the cofradía leadership main-tain more solemn, serious expressions. In placing these groups together, the image gives the appearance of cooperation, equality, and mutual respect. These inauguration events also served as the military state's way of challeng-ing accusations of genocide by publicly demonstrating how military officials allowed Ixil Maya cultural traditions in the new Acul. But this inclusion was limited; like the state-sanctioned indigenismo that historian Julie Gib-bings describes for the 1930s, the counterinsurgency state's practice of defin-ing the acceptable confines of Indigeneity "fixed Mayas in the past in folkloric traditions and rendered other aspects of Maya culture threatening in the pre-sent."[54] The photograph shows us the state's practice of allowing the use of ceremonial traje within the context of a national celebration as a symbol of Guatemalan nationalism and folkloric heritage. What the photograph ex-cludes, however, is any context relating to the limitations that the militarized state placed upon cofradía ceremonies or the persecution that Indigenous au-thorities endured during the civil war and its aftermath. Again, the expres-sions on the faces of the Ixil participants pierce the viewer, asking for the citizenry of photograph to consider how the state was appropriating Ixil cul-ture for its own purposes and thus attempting to divorce the meanings and values from these cultural signifiers.

These inauguration ceremonies symbolized what the authoritarian state considered to be the rebirth of rural Guatemala. It is not surprising that these photographs serve as the bookend for Paiz Maselli's album; after all, he viewed the construction of the model villages as his most patriotic accom-plishment, so it seems only fitting that he ended with images he interpreted as celebratory. In reading his album, we can literally see that through the Poles of Development, the state hoped to transform the landscape it viewed as a nonmodern, wild, and dangerous place that fostered isolation and guerrilla infiltration to a space that was orderly, urbanized, secure, and easy to surveil. The Poles also worked to transform those the state believed to be "prohibited Indians" into "permitted Indians" who adopted a Guatemalan national identity and strong loyalty and commitment to the state's civilizing mission. As the Paiz Maselli album showcases authoritarian modernization at work in model villages and his interpretation of that process, by reading the album as part of the citizenry of photography, we are also compelled to see alternative narratives that coexisted and tell histories of self-forging not just by Paiz Maselli but by development's intended recipients, amid challenging circumstances.

Development in the CPRs

In May 1996, a survivor of the war and CPR member gave an oral testimony to a member of the ODHAG Truth Commission. After surviving the 1982 Xalbal massacres, she and others formed a CPR nearby, thus maintaining a connection to the land they had received in the Ixcán Grande colonization project. They suffered from ongoing military violence, including the murder of the interviewee's sister and two children by two soldiers in 1983. At the time of the ODHAG interview in the CPR, this community had existed over thirteen years. When asked about her vision for Guatemala's future, the interviewee replied, "We don't want more violence and death from the armies. We want peace and the ability to reconstruct our cooperatives. For this reason, we are here as a CPR, both returned people and displaced people in our own cooperatives."[55] As this testimony elucidates, some internally displaced people viewed the CPR as a site of resistance. Despite the violence they had suffered, they stayed near their homes "because of love for the *patria* and for our land." Instead of living under military control, they "opted for a new style of life with a lot of sacrifice and strength."[56] Many people died in the CPRs, either from health complications or military violence, but the CPRs survived despite the military's constant attempt to eliminate them.

CPRs formed in three geographic areas: the Sierra Mountains of El Quiché, the Ixcán jungle, and western Petén. A pamphlet that the *Asamblea Permanente de Grupos Cristianos* published in the early 1990s described the CPRs as an opportunity "to live in liberty and . . . not be subjected by the Army to civil patrols, poles of development, model villages and re-education centers."[57] And in their own words, CPR residents explained this decision to avoid the Poles of Development in a 1993 newspaper interview, declaring, "Neither did we want to be in the model villages because they are nothing more than concentration camps where they take our brothers as if they were hens. We are human beings."[58] When the Mexican government, in collaboration with the Guatemalan army, moved its refugee camps farther away from the border in May 1984, some refugees returned to Guatemala and joined a CPR.[59] According to priest and anthropologist Ricardo Falla, who lived in the CPRs, returnees anticipated living in CPRs for a long period of time, not temporarily.[60] Thus, they recognized the importance of establishing a functioning communal structure in an effort to find some type of stability and security amid ongoing repression.

CPR residents organized a community committee with several commissions: one for work, production, health, education, vigilance, social life, and resources. Additionally, they maintained contact with other regional CPRs, taking great risks to regularly meet and collectively make decisions. For example, the CPR Ixcán had an overarching authority called the *Comité de Parcelarios*, and each community sent representatives to this entity's meetings. Importantly, women participated alongside men at each level of CPR governance.[61] Grassroots organizing and a democratic political system were cornerstones of the CPR development model.

In 1991, a journalist estimated that 20,000 people were residing in CPRs, enduring ongoing repression and hardships.[62] The military maintained that the CPRs were guerrilla outposts, so they constantly bombed areas where they believed the CPRs to be located, always looking for signs of life such as clothes drying in the sun or planted fields.[63] For example, several ODHAG testimonies discuss a military massacre of an estimated fifty CPR members near China Tzejá, where military patrols fired at residents and threw grenades into their bomb shelters.[64] To protect themselves from persecution, members worked collectively to survive and formed sentry units to watch for military patrols.[65]

In addition to constantly fearing military reprisals, on a bodily, daily level, residents confronted illness and hunger. One ODHAG interviewee recalls how the CPR collectively planted fields that had corn, orange trees, and rice. However, the military cut down these crops annually from 1984 to 1986, leaving residents only roots and bananas to eat. Others recalled that CPR residents starved; lived exposed to the elements; and did without basic items such as salt, soap, and clothes. Orphaned infants died because there were no milk substitutes for them to have; as one interviewee recalled, children died at a rate of one to two per day in the beginning due to disease, hunger, and psychological trauma.[66] Despite these challenges, CPR residents forged new selves that were deeply rooted in the collective experience of surviving devastation. In doing so, they used their own perceptions of history to define their way of "being-in-time" and thus reject the state's notions of permitted Indigeneity.[67]

Despite the danger and tremendous hardships they faced each day, CPR residents considered themselves to be "an example and a seed of a new society—the hope of the poor people of Guatemala."[68] This vision and sense of collective purpose directly related to how CPRs defined development. Their position reveals an alternative to modernization, and though it did share some of the same material goals, at its core it was fundamentally different in its egalitarian structure. As a 1996 statement from the CPR Ixcán's General Assembly explained, what they sought was "a better life for everyone. We understand that community development is not just wellbeing but also access to education, health, recreation, and cultural activities." They believed land should be collectively titled and worked in order to keep it out of the hands of the rich and the petroleum companies, and they viewed it as their responsibility to take care of the earth and "maintain ecological equilibrium."[69]

The patterns of social organizing within the CPRs exemplified their understanding of democracy and serve as a juxtaposition to the authoritarian nature of Guatemala's government and the restrictions that the populace faced. Though both the Poles of Development and the CPRs emphasize collective efforts, in the former it was top-down and rigid whereas in the latter it was flexible and community driven. In 1991, residents of the CPR Ixcán issued their first public letter, and in it they explained the practice of democracy in the CPR, stating, "We all have made our laws of coexistence and we resolve our problems with good ideas and not with jails. Among us there is no repression or discrimination, there is democracy because there is equality, we all give our opinions and we all have the right to all the services. . . . We all work voluntarily and consciously in the production and in all the services of the community, no one receives pay, there is no exploitation among us. . . . The distribution of resources that arrive to our communities is just and collective."[70] This statement reflects the alternative to top-down modernization that communitarian development provided in the CPRs. Residents practiced a similar model of localized organizing to that which state programs such as the 1950s CALs and the PMIT advocated, yet what is distinctive about the CPR structure was that the end goal was not the penetration of capitalism into these communities or integration into a state version of homogenous nationalism. Because the CPRs existed outside the purview of the state, participants in these communities did not have to navigate outside impositions upon their lives but rather could organically and democratically forge their communities in a way that reflected local realities and beliefs.

Just as photographs depicted the modernizing, authoritarian structure of the Poles of Development and the state's permitted Indian model, they also

FIGURE 7.1 Distributing the day's catch. (Comité Holandés de Solidaridad con Guatemala Collection. Courtesy of CIRMA.)

reveal how CPR residents challenged the state's racialized modernization project. They developed an alternative understanding of modernity and of Indigeneity by practicing development in a communitarian way. Through the following reading of several images from the Moller and CHS archives, a conflicting sense of a state of exceptionalism and normalcy is conveyed, as residents engaged in everyday activities that only seem out of place when the viewer considers the historical context. This visual archive depicts four key themes: labor and work, the construction of infrastructure, the provision of public services, and the process of community building, and each in turn contributes to an overarching reconfiguration in the way CPR members defined the practice of development.

In CPRs, labor relations were based on reciprocity, adaptability, and prioritization of the community over the individual, as women and men foraged for food, built homes, and developed cultural programs. Some CPRs planted and cultivated small cornfields, but the military constantly conducted aerial surveillance of these regions, making it dangerous to clear large swaths of land. The military regularly burned fields they encountered in order to cut off CPRs and guerrilla forces—which they erroneously equated as one and the same—from food supplies.[71] Thus, CPR residents had to search for alternative food sources, such as fish, roots, and herbs. Figure 7.1 reveals the common practice of equitably distributing gathered food among residents, who

FIGURE 7.2 Man washing clothes, CPR Petén. (Jonathan Moller Collection. Courtesy of CIRMA.)

often prepared and consumed meals together. It mirrors the biblical parable of multiplying a few fish to feed a multitude, as men and children gather around a tarp with the day's catch. While the three men focus on counting and sorting the small, silvery fish before them, the children direct their gazes at the camera, reminding the viewer that they, too, were the target of military violence. And through their participation in counting fish, they are internalizing the politics of redistribution and recognizing an ethos other than the accumulation of wealth.

Within the CPRs, understandings of democracy took on new and practical meanings, leading to a breakdown of gender- and age-defined labor roles. Because massacres destroyed family units, it is plausible that survivors had to adopt the tasks that their deceased family members had previously done. Figure 7.2 presents a departure from traditional gender roles, as it features a

FIGURE 7.3   Hiding metal roofs with leaves. (Comité Holandés de Solidaridad con Guatemala Collection. Courtesy of CIRMA.)

man washing clothes, a job that women typically undertook. He is standing in a stream, naked from the waist up, and he maintains his gaze on his work as if ignoring the camera. Large, flat rocks line a fallen log, and the man uses one of these as a washboard, carefully scrubbing his white shirt with soap. Though he appears alone in the image, the presence of multiple rocks indicates that washing was often a communal practice. The arrangement of the flat rocks parallels similar images of lines of pilas found in village squares where women would have gathered to wash clothes and socialize. Thus, the image compels the viewer to recognize that ordinary tasks, like laundry, remained a social experience, and CPR residents replicated it as best they could while living in hiding. Labor was not just utilitarian in nature; it was integral to community formation.

Second to obtaining food, building town infrastructure and providing residents with public services like health care were central components of CPR life. Figure 7.3 depicts a CPR house with cane walls and a metal roof whose overhang provided a small porch area. To prevent the sun from reflecting against the roof and revealing its location to aerial surveillance, residents have covered it with leaves. Building houses not only provided immediate shelter but also grounded members in the reality that they had survived state efforts to eradicate them. Unlike the model villages, CPR residents did not build homes according to an outside logic and imposed plan. These were not

FIGURE 7.4 Hugo carrying palm leaves to construct his roof, CPR Petén. (Jonathan Moller Collection. Courtesy of CIRMA.)

cinderblock houses with screened windows and doors; they did not have cement floors and neat patios, gardens, and animal pens. Nor were they neatly aligned on grid-like rows of intersecting streets. Instead, CPR members used natural camouflage and built homes in spatial arrangements that made sense for social relations and security tactics.

Though the photographs do not provide this information, it is reasonable to assume that building a house would be one of the first steps a new CPR member would take, as it would provide shelter and a sense of normalcy in a moment of devastation. Perhaps this is the task that Hugo, the subject of figure 7.4, has set for himself, as he hauls palm leaves for his house's roof in the CPR Petén. It is not clear if he is embarking on this task alone or if other community members are assisting him. Either way, Hugo likely benefited from community support in other ways, such as shared food, provision of meals, and protection from local patrols. In this image, Hugo directly returns the camera's gaze, pausing from his hard labor to ensure that the camera captures his efforts and more importantly, himself. Hugo's presence depicts the military's failure to end all forms of communitarian development; he defiantly exercises his right to be seen and demands that the citizenry of photography recognize and respect his ability to define development on his own terms.

In addition to building infrastructure, CPR members prioritized certain public services, namely education and health care. Despite living in hiding, they wanted children to attend school, so in 1982 CPRs began naming local teachers to provide instruction for children and adults alike. Teachers utilized whatever resources they had for student instruction, as Ramírez Pedro, a teacher in the CPR Ixcán, described:

> We began to work without notebooks or pencils, crayons, chalkboards, erasers. We made wooden planks for each student and with a little piece of charcoal they would start writing. We used the remains of burned corrugated metal as our chalkboards. Because the children couldn't handle the humidity, the cold, the mud, the mosquitos, so many illnesses, we couldn't study all day. At the beginning we didn't even have a roof. We had to work amidst these limitations. . . . Creating new things was costly, we had to think, reflect, amid a really hard situation, on top of all this were the bombings, shelling, the constant persecution by the Army.[72]

Despite exposure to the elements, disease, military violence, and inadequate resources, teachers courageously held classes, imparting a style of popular education that infused academic lessons with local values rooted in the experience of resistance.[73] Unlike the literacy campaigns of the revolutionary period, education in the CPRs emphasized values as dictated by the community itself, rather than those the state wished to impose upon its citizenry.

Figure 7.5 demonstrates this creative pedagogy. Here, two boys proudly pose for the camera, demonstrating a biology lesson about the digestive and respiratory systems. Using their bodies as a textbook, the teacher outlined their stomachs, lungs, and intestines with a marker, educating the students about different organs and biological functions. The two boys took obvious delight in the lesson; the camera captured them widely smiling while posing with their arms around each other, partners in this interactive educational experience. The student on the left side of the image sheepishly gazes just off camera, as if reacting to the playful jests and encouragement from onlooking classmates. Through the image, the spectator can almost see the photographer in this classroom, watching students gleefully learn about complex subjects like human biology while fully recognizing that their bodies remained

FIGURE 7.5 Biology class. (Comité Holandés de Solidaridad con Guatemala Collection. Courtesy of CIRMA.)

targets of state-sponsored violence. Yet for a moment, that fear seems suspended amid children's laughter and fascination with the new concepts they are learning.

For Ramírez and other popular teachers, learning content without also acquiring a strong sense of ethics and morality was futile, so CPR schools emphasized the intellectual and moral development of students and an understanding of Indigenous history and culture, alongside content and skill mastery.[74] Teachers continued practicing their vocation despite being outside of a national school system and no longer receiving a salary for their work (figure 7.6). In other words, education was not standardized, nor did teachers exchange their labor for wages. Instead, they considered it to be their contribution to the CPR, and they regularly held classes that taught students literacy skills in Spanish while also relaying the importance of using Indigenous languages. Teachers also held adult literacy classes, indicating that CPR members prioritized formal education and wanted to be literate in the national language.[75] The education system within CPRs should not be understood as an outright rejection of the model espoused through modernization, a model that centered Western knowledge and pedagogies. Rather, educators accepted elements they deemed appropriate, such as discussing biology systems or Spanish grammar, while adapting and integrating additional content within it. According to Ramírez, this style of popular education differed from the

FIGURE 7.6 Teacher preparing lessons, CPR Petén. (Jonathan Moller Collection. Courtesy of CIRMA.)

official curriculum in that it was holistic and taught residents' histories as part of Guatemalan history.

Figure 7.7 captures the essence of the popular education taught within CPRs, as Moller exposed this image to focus on the daily lesson presented on the makeshift chalkboard. In this dirt-floor school, built with cane and a thatched roof, a young boy sits with his notebook reading and copying the lesson written on the tarp. First, the lesson announces the simple fact that "today is Monday, November 15, 1993." Though a simple date for the student, for the spectator it is an important marker of time; it indexes this moment and embeds it within a historical context. Over a decade after the genocidal violence of the early 1980s, at the end of 1993, people like this young student are still internally displaced, living in fear of the violence their government wishes to enact upon them.

FIGURE 7.7 Today is Monday, CPR Sierra. (Jonathan Moller Collection. Courtesy of CIRMA.)

The teacher, though physically not present in the photograph in bodily form, appears abstractly; his hat hangs next to the chalkboard, and his written words communicate important lessons to his students. His text's subject is always plural, referring interchangeably to the family, to the CPR of the Sierra, to the workers, and to Indigenous Guatemalans, reflecting the emphasis on the collective subject as the foundation of society. First, the lesson explains that good nutrition is important for the family's health and proudly conveys the self-sufficiency of the CPR. In doing so, the text presents the idea of subsistence as positive and emblematic of sustainability, whereas the ideology of modernization positioned it as negative and as a sign of poverty. This self-sufficiency is made possible, the lesson continues, because all the workers have united "to fight for our rights as *indígenas* and as Guatemalans." Though demographic statistics for CPR residents do not exist, based on its location, members of the CPR of the Sierra likely came from both Ixil and K'iche' Maya communities (and perhaps others), yet here the lesson clearly communicates a broader sense of Indigenous identity. It also communicates a shared class identity as workers. Importantly, it argues that these identities are neither incompatible with each other nor with a national identity but rather can be simultaneously held and equally privileged. The lesson communicates that CPR residents manifest this struggle for their rights as Indigenous citizens through their resistance to "all the injustice that Indigenous Guatemalans now endure," clearly including Indigenous history as a central part of Guatemalan history and calling attention to structural oppression. Here, race functions as a self-ascribed identity of collective strength through historical struggle rather than as an imposed category that connotes subversion and the need for rehabilitation. Like the designers of the Poles of Development, CPR members also sought to create a new Guatemala, but one that was communitarian in nature, free from racism and discrimination, and dictated from below, not from above.

Alongside education, health services were key to the survival of CPR residents, and however rudimentary the facilities, communities utilized whatever human resources and medical supplies they could acquire to help treat illnesses and injury. Several years after the CPRs were established, CPR health promoters began attending training sessions to learn how to treat residents for health conditions such as anemia, dysentery, diarrhea, skin rashes, and infections.[76] Figure 7.8 shows a health promoter using a stethoscope to examine an infant in a one-room clinic that is empty except for a makeshift table. The presence of the baby symbolizes innocence while simultaneously reminding the citizenry of photography that the military state categorized this child as subversive and thus an intended target of repression. Yet this child exists, demanding recognition that he has survived, despite tremendous odds, and that he represents the next generation of Indigenous citizens who will continue the struggle for equality. The baby also reminds the spectator that for the survivors of military violence, life still continued, people procreated, children were born, and in these clandestine towns, adults experienced the joys and challenges of raising families.

In the same vein, CPR residents emphasized the maintenance of cultural and social traditions. Certainly, the majority of each day was spent trying to survive, and residents were constantly vigilant, ready to hide or flee at a moment's notice from military violence. Still, they continued traditions such as religious ceremonies and weddings, held recreational events such as dances and soccer games, and started new families. CPR residents intentionally worked to strengthen social bonds and create moments of joy amid incredible struggle

FIGURE 7.8 Health promoter, CPR Sierra. (Jonathan Moller Collection. Courtesy of CIRMA.)

and tragic loss, prioritizing interpersonal relationships, relaxation, and collective celebration as part of the communitarian development model.

In viewing images showcasing celebrations and recreation, it is easy to forget their context, as the subjects tend to communicate joy and a carefree attitude, acting as agents of their own future, not as defeated victims. Figure 7.9 depicts a moment of recreation, as several teenaged boys play an impromptu soccer game. The photograph captures the soccer ball suspended in the air, caught between the two opposing teams. One must wonder, from where did the CPRs obtain a soccer ball? All possessions not found in the natural surroundings had to be carefully carried to the CPRs, so the presence of this soccer ball indicates that someone made the effort—and took the risk—to acquire it, inflate it, and bring it safely to the community. This soccer game re-

FIGURE 7.9 Soccer game in the CPR. (Comité Holandés de Solidaridad con Guatemala Collection. Courtesy of CIRMA.)

veals the prioritization of recreation, thus promoting some kind of normalcy amid extraordinary circumstances.

Beyond the more typical forms of recreation, CPR residents built community through celebrating life's major moments, such as the wedding seen in figure 7.10. The bride's white veil, like the soccer ball, indicates that someone acquired and transported it safely to the village. On this day, residents donned their best clothes and joined in celebrating a marriage, reminding the viewer that traditions continued in hiding and that individuals did not put their life moments on hold but rather persevered and sought to create new communities in the CPRs for however long would be necessary.

While they held celebrations of major life moments and participated in recreational events, CPR communities also emphasized the collective memory of their struggle. Just as they refused to be made invisible by the Guatemalan military's denial of their existence, they also refused to forget the atrocities they had endured and the people whom they had lost. In figure 7.11 Don Nicolas, an Indigenous priest, holds a cross upon which he has written a series of units of time: 40 years, 50 years, 5 years, 25 years, 6 years, 3 years, 7 months. Each inscription of the passage of time measures the length of one human life, a life cut short during the war. And each life referenced on this cross was a family member that Don Nicolas had lost. These numbers have been inscribed at the intersection of the cross's two beams, referencing the

FIGURE 7.10 Wedding day in the CPR Sierra. (Jonathan Moller Collection. Courtesy of CIRMA.)

crucifixion of Jesus Christ and thus marking the parallels between their sacrifices and indicating the innocence of his family members. The word "*baleados*" (shot) appears inscribed above their ages, identifying the military as the perpetrators of this unfathomable and indiscriminate violence. Staring directly into the camera, Don Nicolas's expression is one of solemn anger and profound grief. His stare is this image's punctum, wounding the viewer with the story of his massacred family and demanding that the spectator return his gaze in a way that commits to recognizing his loss and remembering the lives of the deceased. Yet his demands go beyond the act of recognition; as his gaze pierces that of the viewer, he mandates that the citizenry of photography respond and prevent future atrocities such as this one.

Though Moller foregrounded Don Nicolas in framing this photograph, he also intentionally chose a wider depth of field that also kept the immediate

FIGURE 7.11 Baleados, CPR Sierra. (Jonathan Moller Collection. Courtesy of CIRMA.)

background in focus. Don Nicolas stands in a walled structure made from inter-locking logs; surrounding him are dozens of inscribed crosses. The image does not tell us who bears these crosses, but it does communicate that Don Nicolas's story is not exceptional, nor is he alone. Perhaps all CPR members made com-memoratory crosses for the family they lost, and together they remember and grieve while reconstructing their lives. The photograph makes evident how CPR residents embedded historical memory into the fabric of the community, pursuing a development model that emphasized emotion and spiritual well-being alongside material development. Commemorations like this underscore that the community did not want to erase the violence of the past but allowed it to continue to fuel their struggle against injustice.

These photographs of the CPRs speak to the past, providing glimpses of what was and what happened. They also transcend time and speak to the present and future, as the intervention of the camera allows for the possibility of a conversation of sorts between photographer, photographed subject, and spectator. This communication offers much in terms of making sense of the past, in this case, aiding in an understanding of the alternative that CPR members created to revise state-imposed development by modernization. Importantly, CPR members did not fully reject the model of modernization, as they prioritized Western education and health care, constructed single-family homes, and pursued a democratic political system. At the same time, the community was not organized in a hierarchical fashion but rather one that was more communal, one where the individual was subordinated to the collective, one that was not profit driven, and one that emphasized sustainability and celebration of diversity. This development model also worked to condone an Indigenous subjectivity marked by agency, self-determination, and collective autonomy. But the conversation among members within this citizenry of photography does not end with a discussion of the past and of understandings of development and citizenship. It continues into the present, into this moment of spectatorship, obliging us, as spectators now part of this citizenry of photography, to reflect and to act.

Conclusion

The visual archive makes clear that between the military campaigns of the early 1980s and the 1996 Peace Accords, two distinct models of community development emerged in efforts to rebuild the Guatemalan nation. On the one hand, the military state continued to use community development, coupled with the ideology of modernization, as a tool of counterinsurgency, initiating the Poles of Development project as a way to gather the displaced Indigenous population into highly centralized, controllable towns. The structured life in the model villages served as a practice of governance designed to impart a sense of national identity, an understanding of the state's ever-present gaze, an integration into the market economy, and a clear sense of the type of political participation the state deemed acceptable.

On the other hand, the CPRs depict a communitarian style of development rooted in collective decision-making and autonomy. What CPR residents rejected about the state's model was not the opportunities provided but rather the ideologies and top-down structure that undergirded this model. They demanded a decentralized yet collective organizational structure, as they believed this to be truly democratic and the best means for ordinary Guatemalans to directly participate in determining the nation's future.[77] They wanted local committees to collectively make decisions, not officials in government offices or military bases. And they believed in communal autonomy to either revise or reject any outside impositions deemed inappropriate or irrelevant for the collective. In designing development in this way, the CPRs called for a modernity based on a model of inclusivity that rejected the bifurcated categorization of Indigenous citizens as either "permitted" or "prohibited." Amid civil war, the differences between these two projects were incredibly stark and made clear how development could simultaneously be used to support the state's counterinsurgency project as a practice of governance and challenge state's authority through the practice of politics.

Additionally, the two projects presented drastically different ideas about Indigeneity and Indigenous subjectivity. The Poles of Development project revised and reinforced the dichotomy of the permitted and prohibited Indian models, with the former remaining subservient, assimilating to the state's notion of citizenship, and exhibiting cultural practices only as national folklore. The military state categorized the latter, on the other hand, as subversive and in need of elimination, as seen in the previous chapter's discussion of the violence that the state enacted upon the Ixcán and across the country. The CPR project rejected this dichotomy and characterization of acceptable Indigenous citizenship as fully compliant with the state's dictates. Instead, it maintained that Indigenous people were historical actors and citizens capable of political engagement and decision-making on their own terms. As Indigenous Guatemalan citizens, CPR residents insisted that their long-term, collective struggle, of which the civil war was only the latest chapter, was the foundation for their collective strength, and they insisted that recognition and inclusion as equals was exactly what Guatemala needed in order to reestablish peace and improve standards of living.

Protagonists in Guatemala's Development

This book began with Hélida Cabrera's historic visit in 1955 to San Carlos Alzatate, a Poqomam Maya and Xinca municipality in the eastern department of Jalapa. Although other IING staff as well as regional politicians had racialized residents as backward and dangerous, outside modernity and not worthy of the state's attention, Cabrera immediately recognized that the town welcomed the potential state resources she could connect them to, as long as they could request items and programs they desired and thus retain their sense of autonomy. This theme has resonated throughout this book, as Indigenous Guatemalans did not outright reject development but rather fashioned and pursued alternatives to the ideology of modernization, even against the possibility of violent repercussions. In doing so, they challenged the racism embedded within many development initiatives that sought to control expressions of Indigeneity and shape the contours of citizenship.

The history of rural development in Guatemala underscores the importance of analyzing development as a dialectical and multilayered process, one that considers not only project goals and intended outcomes but also the ways in which the recipients interacted with, challenged, and appropriated these projects. In the history this book recounts, the majority of intended recipients were Indigenous Guatemalans, as it was this population that the state wished to convert into "permitted Indians." Local intermediaries and recipients helped decouple the idea of ladinization from integration, suggesting instead that Indigeneity was compatible with modernity and that both should be defined at the local level rather than imposed from above. Internationally constituted discourses of development framed national ideas about the place of people categorized as Indigenous within the Guatemalan nation, shaping Guatemala's engagement with hemispheric notions of indigenismo and reconfiguring problems confronting Indigenous people as socioeconomic rather than innate or cultural, though some indigenistas continued to racialize material signs of poverty, like illiteracy, as Indigenous. As Guatemala's own devastating civil war expanded against the backdrop of the global Cold War, state notions of Indigenous citizenship became more deeply embedded in discourses of modernization and anti-communism, and the authoritarian state increasingly saw individuals who deviated from this linear model of development as subversive and antithetical to national progress and security. To reiterate this book's first main argument, development simultaneously served multiple functions as it reinforced state attempts to control, surveil, simplify, and racialize but also allowed for access to resources and a means to challenge racism and forge alternative identities.

This complex history spans political ruptures ranging from democratic revolution to genocide, yet along the way it is clear time and time again that community development projects served multiple purposes and reinforced different agendas. All the while, the discourse of development gave individuals a common language to frame their demands and actions, even if the meanings attributed to concepts such as modernity and development drastically differed. As we have seen, individuals used these concepts to further inscribe racialized notions of inferiority, backwardness, and even subversion upon people classified as Indigenous while others created alternative meanings that allowed them to contest racism and project understandings of modernity that were compatible with how they defined Indigeneity and that did not fully subscribe to modernization. Furthermore, in seeking to "make the Indian walk," project planners and experts often sought to reinforce a political agenda, first as a way to foster support for the Revolution's widespread social reforms and after the 1954 Counterrevolution as a means for U.S. foreign policy makers to "peacefully" contain communism and for the Guatemalan military state to consolidate its authoritarian rule. However, through their experiences working in rural communities, project staff, such as the IING ethnographers, the local DESCOM team, or Maryknoll priests often recognized that the modernization model was not an effective way to address the structural issues they confronted. The actual implementation of development was often less of an imposition and more of an active collaboration and series of compromises and thus, a mixed bag of successes and failures.

Most importantly, framing community development as a dialectical, highly complex process emphasizes this book's second overarching argument, that is, development's intended recipients—in this case, Indigenous Guatemalans—operated as central protagonists, as active contributors, and as historical agents. Experts and politicians often viewed Indigenous recipients as malleable and passive and as blank slates upon which to inscribe modernized behaviors and practices. Their project proposals and reports tended to relegate the recipients to the margins by focusing on the physical infrastructure they built or dehumanized the recipients by reducing them to a series of statistics and numbers. Local staff members functioned as intermediaries who sought to relay program objectives and implement projects, and many learned to recognize the necessity for local collaboration, adjusting not only to programming but to the very epistemological foundation upon which projects were based. Recipients themselves repeatedly demonstrated their ability to negotiate proposed projects and use opportunities to pursue their own interests and deromanticize notions of Indigenous communities as singularly minded and harmonious, instead showcasing complex competing interests, strategic alliances, and processes of negotiation. These practices shaped the past and the histories this book recounts, and development's dialectical nature continues to operate in the present, providing Guatemalans with opportunities and obstacles.

Development in Postwar Guatemala

On December 29, 1996, as Guatemalans and international observers wildly celebrated in the central plaza of downtown Guatemala City, government officials and representatives from the guerrilla movements signed the final piece of the Peace Accords. Negotiations between the Guatemalan state and the *Unidad Revolucionaria Nacional Guatemalteca* (URNG) were protracted throughout the early 1990s.[1] For over five years, delegates discussed a series of issues and signed agreements that culminated in the final accord of December 1996, formally ending the thirty-six-year armed conflict that left approximately 200,000 people dead and 1.5 million internally displaced, and beginning the long (and unfinished) process of truth and reconciliation.[2]

   One significant component of the negotiations was the *Agreement on Identity and Rights of Indigenous Peoples*, which took nine months to write and carried the potential to redefine the Guatemalan nation.[3] In this agreement, both parties agreed that members of the diverse population in Guatemala were "protagonists in its [Guatemala's] development, in all senses," clearly recognizing the agency of Indigenous people in actively participating in development projects and no longer positioning them as mere objects to be "made to walk," as expressed at the 1940 Pátzcuaro conference. The document, which ordered signees to "promote a reform of the Constitution," called for a form of municipal autonomy that would allow Indigenous communities "to determine their own development priorities, particularly in the fields of education, health, culture, and the infrastructure." Furthermore, it mandated that the Guatemalan government allow communal landholding, recognize customary law and traditional authorities, title Indigenous lands, assist internally displaced people and returning refugees in reclaiming land the military seized after the scorched earth campaign, and obtain permission from Indigenous communities *before* beginning any exploitation of natural resources in these areas.[4] However, the agreement failed to invite Indigenous people to participate in the negotiating process in an open and serious way despite contemporary efforts by Maya revolutionaries to study and address how to reconstruct Guatemala in a more equitable way.[5] Neither did the agreement address the possibility of regional autonomy and only vaguely hinted toward abstract notions of implementation rather than actual legislation.[6] Despite these serious shortcomings, clearly expressed in this agreement is the recognition of alternative models of development as valid, legitimate, and acceptable, signaling an erosion of the dichotomy of the permitted and prohibited Indian models and an acceptance of all Indigenous Guatemalans as citizens capable of—and entitled to—determining their own futures.

The agreement also committed the Guatemalan government to promote the congressional ratification of the International Organization of Labor's 1989 Convention 169, the *Indigenous and Tribal Peoples Convention*, the document upon which Guatemala's own *Agreement on Identity and Rights of Indigenous Peoples* was based. The Guatemalan Congress ratified International Organization of Labor (ILO) 169 on June 5, 1996, but did subordinate it to the Guatemalan Constitution, at once theoretically strengthening the government's commitment to Indigenous rights but also introducing a significant loophole that could potentially allow for noncompliance.[7] ILO 169 obliges states not only to recognize Indigenous communities' right to order their development priorities but also to actively participate in project planning, implementation, and evaluation.[8] Furthermore, ILO 169 acknowledges structural oppression and calls for socioeconomic development initiatives to remedy this issue but importantly, "in a way that is compatible with their [Indigenous Peoples'] aspirations and way of life." In many ways, the model that ILO 169 employs parallels earlier moments of collaborative development efforts such as the PMIT or the Ixcán Grande project. The difference is that in 1996, the Guatemalan state officially condoned this model of development, if only on paper, rather than abruptly shutting down projects or violently targeting program participants.

The 1996 final Peace Accords integrated all previously signed agreements, including the *Agreement about Identity and Rights of Indigenous Peoples* discussed above. Further, some of its central concepts dealt directly with socioeconomic development and Indigeneity.[9] For example, points five and six deem Guatemala to be a multiethnic and pluricultural state and call for "participatory socioeconomic development oriented on the common good" and based upon social justice and sustainability. Additionally, the Peace Accords designated the Guatemalan state as responsible for ensuring such a development transpired, one rooted in the "social investment" of the country and based on providing basic education, health services, and employment to all Guatemalans. And finally, the Peace Accords mandated that a key focal area of this development plan address the ongoing inequitable land tenure system.

Though vague and abstract, the type of development that signers of the Peace Accords agreed to in December 1996 is important in two aspects. One, it designated Guatemala as multiethnic and pluricultural. Formally defining the nation in this way ended official programs of homogenization or de-Indianization and defined integration as rooted in diversity. Indigenous people, some indigenista figures, and even some local program staff had long recognized this national reality now formally stated in the Peace Accords. This language and its underlying concepts had the capability of reorienting power relations *if* acted upon; it was an attempt to do away with the racial privilege Guatemalan ladinos had historically enjoyed and instead deem any attempts to prioritize one worldview or one subset of the population as superior to another as antithetical to the very foundational principles of the nation. Second, in formally recognizing ethnic and racial difference, the Peace Accords also acknowledged the legitimacy of and the need for alternative models of development. Outlined in points six through nine of the Peace Accords is not another rendition of modernization but rather a more abstract, open-ended call for collaboration in improving the lived realities of all Guatemalans in ways that are sustainable, equitable, empowering, and rooted in social justice. To accomplish this, the state would have to pursue models of development based on local demands, as expressed by local actors. It would allow for development models that might adhere in some ways to modernization but would also leave space for vernacular modernisms.[10]

Taken together, these three documents reflect how debates about the nature and necessity of socioeconomic development played a central role in discussions about Indigenous rights and in the transition to peace in Guatemala. Embedded within these documents is the state's acceptance that all Guatemalans—and explicitly Indigenous people, given the long history of oppression and recent genocide—could and should be the architects of their own development and able to define and pursue a version of modernity *if* they wanted to and how they desired. In theory, it erased the racialized dichotomy of the permitted/prohibited Indian based on a conception of modern/

premodern and developed/underdeveloped, instead allowing for diversity and difference. Given this vision presented in the Peace Accords, many Guatemalans were hesitantly hopeful that long histories of oppression, racism, and material poverty might finally begin to slowly erode and be replaced by a more equitable future.

Development in Post-Peace Guatemala

Any initial optimism about these reforms' potential for remaking Guatemala quickly faded, as they only encouraged constitutional changes that the Guatemalan Congress either never ratified or gave little resources toward their effective implementation and oversight. Efforts to create constitutional amendments repeatedly stalled and fell victim to political infighting. Finally, the Guatemalan Congress combined the constitutional reforms that related to the Peace Accords alongside others and repackaged them into four broad themes: (1) redefining the nation and social rights, (2) legislative branch, (3) executive branch, and (4) judicial branch. These four categories, into which the Congress collapsed over fifty reforms, was what the Guatemalan public voted for in a simple yes or no vote in May 1999. The referendum became increasingly politicized within the context of upcoming national elections, and a massive campaign against ratification drew on racist fears about Indigenous empowerment and equality. Coupled with an extremely poor voter turnout (only 18.5 percent of eligible voters participated), the *Consulta Popular* (popular referendum) failed to get the majority vote needed to ratify the constitutional amendments that the Peace Accords had dictated.[11] In this moment, Guatemala experienced, in the words of Kaqchikel scholar and activist Demetrio Cojtí Cuxil, a "crisis of public legitimacy" for the Peace Accords and in the struggle for Indigenous rights.[12] As scholars have rightly pointed out, Guatemalans confronted (and continue to face) a "war by other means," or the ways that explanations of past injustice and ways of remembering can continue to wreak violence on the present moment.[13]

Discourses and practices of development continue to shape social categories and lived experiences amid the ongoing struggle to fulfill the promises made in the Peace Accords. Neoliberal economic policies allowed the Guatemalan state to divest itself of its responsibility to provide services for Guatemalans through handing off this responsibility to private entities. As a result, NGOs poured into Guatemala, bringing with them money, brokering new types of power relations and, in some cases, new assaults on Indigenous cultures and practices. In some cases, this aid bonanza also connected people and formed new solidarities, redistributed resources, and at times leveraged international attention to ongoing issues of injustice, once again highlighting development's complexities, opportunities, and pitfalls.[14] Erin Beck's insightful "agent-based approach" comparative study of two NGOs operating in Guatemala's western highlands shows the complexity of the social construction of different development models by explaining the various ways involved actors defined success and the different forms of agency for which each model allowed.[15] Micha Rahder's analysis of conservation organizations in the Petén demonstrates how state employees, like those of the *Consejo Nacional de Áreas Protegidas* (National Protected Areas Council), continue to function as intermediaries who navigate different knowledges, intense webs of local politics and dangers, and challenging circumstances in an attempt to mitigate harmful situations for people and the environment.[16] In post-peace Guatemala, intermediaries still hold important and complicated roles in development initiatives, and the blend between the public and private continues to be murky as actors navigate this landscape in pursuit of better—and community-defined—opportunities.

But in other cases, historical divisions and unequal power relations continue to manifest themselves within these new contexts, reminding us not to romanticize rural peoples and mistakenly assume harmonious relations exist at the local level. For example, as Matilde González-Izás has argued, in the K'iche' municipality of San Bartolomé Jocotenango, the postwar "improvement committees" simply allowed former military members and civil patrol leaders a new institution through which to retain power over their fellow townspeople, a power that relied on instilling fear through terror.[17] Nicholas Copeland's ethnographic fieldwork in San Pedro Necta traces how in post-peace Guatemala, political parties utilize development projects as a clientelist means to garner votes. He also found that rural Guatemalans frame discrimination in discourses of development rather than in overtly racist ways and that the state continues to enact counterinsurgency violence and control upon the population through ensuring ongoing precarity and scarcity of resources.[18] Further, Indigenous Guatemalans continue to face direct challenges to their ability to own and maintain their land, as state concessions to large megaprojects such as mining, agro-export plantations, and hydroelectric dam projects facilitate violent evictions of rural communities, environmental contamination, and persecution of activists, all of which can cause ruptures within the community.[19] For example, Q'eqchi' Maya activist Bernardo Caal Xol has been imprisoned since January 2018 after being sentenced to serve seven years for protesting the construction of the Oxec hydroelectric plants, for which his community received no prior consultation, as legally mandated.[20] Extractive industries like Oxec dams, in tandem with the Guatemalan state, regularly violate the mandate of ILO 169 of the right to consultation prior to the implementation of extraction, instead violently evicting and terrorizing Indigenous campesinos.[21] Many of these practices and the impunity that their perpetrators often receive are simply a refashioning of the state-sponsored violence during the armed conflict.

In terms of local development, a 2002 law implemented the nationwide system of the Development Councils, a decentralized but vertically hierarchical schema of organizations intended to create development initiatives from the ground up in the name of "efficiency," "intercultural harmony," and "cultural respect." At the local level, these *Consejos Comunitarios de Desarrollo Urbano y Rural* (COCODE) serve to fulfill the mandates of the Peace Accords and ILO 169 of permitting Indigenous communities to dictate their development priorities, petition the state for funding, and make decisions on a collective and popular basis.[22] The COCODEs do provide the potential for allowing alternate models of development, and they are an important institution for non-elite Guatemalans to voice their ideas and concerns. As localized institutions, they also can act based on local conditions, needs, and belief systems. And at every level within the development council system, Indigenous representatives comprise part of the membership of each committee, as do representatives from campesino and labor organizations, student groups, NGOs, and women's organizations. The legal institutionalization of the COCODE system and its linkage to the fulfillment of the Peace Accords provides Indigenous actors with a framework inside the confines of the state apparatus through which to advocate for development in ways that make sense for their communities; in fact, that is the very stated intention of the law.[23] No longer do struggles for communitarian development have to be clandestine, like in the CPRs, and no longer should requests to deviate from the modernization model of development be met with defunding or violent hostility, as in the PMIT and the Ixcán Grande cooperative. Legally, these initiatives should be viewed as consistent with the new Guatemala and new ties of citizenship across ethnic divisions that the Peace Accords outlined, thus allowing Indigenous Guatemalans to join their fellow citizens as, to paraphrase the *Agreement on Identity and Rights of Indigenous Peoples*, protagonists in the nation's development and future.[24]

But in some ways, the COCODE system is not a complete departure from the past.[25] Once again, we see how midcentury developmentalism laid the groundwork for this neoliberal model of decentralized development. The

DESCOM operated in much the same way, establishing local community improvement committees that would then channel requests through the DESCOM local center, then through the regional center, and finally to the national offices. Similarly, the CCII system in the Poles of Development mirrors the COCODE structure, as local actors had some flexibility in designing initiatives but were still accountable to several layers of hierarchical oversight, all the way to the office of the president. The COCODE system allows for some flexibility in defining Indigenous identity, but it still positions participation within this structure as the "permitted" means to pursue development in contrast to more radical cries for Indigenous autonomy that would operate outside of the state's control. While some of the actors are new, and while there are more opportunities within the context of democratic governance in which the COCODE operates, as opposed to the military authoritarianism of the CCII and the DESCOM, it is important to recognize the continuities, or at least the parallels and the influences of the past.

Amid this dismal scenario of post-peace Guatemala, there are glimpses of hope as Indigenous Guatemalans continue their struggle to pursue development based on their own definitions, according to their own priorities, and enacted in their own ways. Despite the limited application of the Peace Accords and their related articles, these documents did bring a new discourse of development to the public sphere, one centered on the acceptance of different paths to alternate modernities, the agreement to recognize and honor different project priorities and implementation plans, and the willingness to acknowledge Indigenous citizens on their own terms. Opportunities within the COCODE structure, the infusion of development discourse with human rights, local organizing and resistance, usage of extrastatal spaces to acquire resources and foster new forms of collaboration all present exciting possibilities for the pursuit of a more equitable socioeconomic development model for Guatemala. Glimpses from histories of past actors and projects who attempted to do similar things can guide those in the present to learn from their successes and their failures and their intended and unintended consequences.

IN OCTOBER 2018, K'iche' Maya activist, journalist, and anthropologist Irma Alicia Velásquez Nimatuj penned an open letter to President Donald Trump to offer her understanding of the structural issues behind the most recent wave of Central American migration to the United States. Writing as a large migrant caravan was traveling northward, Velásquez suggests that the reason for this decision to leave one's home was due to the failure of their respective governments to "create decent opportunities so that they can stay and fulfill their own dreams." She argues that Central American governments were not meeting the basic human conditions for survival because they had failed to support the creation and maintenance of critical infrastructure, provide basic health and educational services, and structure the economy and systems of taxation in ways that would lead to greater distribution of wealth. Under these conditions, Velásquez suggests, anyone would make the gut-wrenching choice to seek a better life elsewhere.

Velásquez's letter is a direct critique of the state's failure to provide for all its citizens and of its refusal to understand practices of socioeconomic development as instrumental for stability. It is also a pointed claim that the United States is complicit through its support of corrupt and violent regimes of the past and the present. She calls for the United States to use financial aid to Central American countries, including her home country of Guatemala, to foster the building of "states at the service of their citizens." She concludes with the mandate that "it is urgent to invest in all its inhabitants and not the few. It is urgent to invest in its people, recognizing their diversity, and it is urgent to create institutions that generate stability and promote the sharing of wealth." As she suggests, doing so would require the United States to channel development aid not through the upper echelons of government but through local and regional leaders who could more effectively invest and utilize that money based on their knowledge of local realities and needs. Although her scholarship reveals her full awareness of episodes of discord and competition for scarce resources at the local level, she still argues that an organic form of aid dispersal would be more effective than aid packages to corrupt regimes. And, she demands that the United States reckon with its long history of harmful foreign policies toward Central America, policies that this book has argued often promoted development programs that functioned as a tool of authoritarian control rather than a model of development that intended to empower communities and individuals, on their own terms.[26]

This book is my attempt to elucidate the history of a complex subject—community development—in the hopes that it would not only shed light on the harmful things done in its name but also allow us to question why initiatives throughout the twentieth century have failed to improve standards of living in Guatemala (and elsewhere), effectively contributing to the impossible choices that individuals like Central American migrants have to make on a daily basis today. The model of development and the act of recognition that Velásquez is proposing is not new but rather part of a historical demand to transform the status quo and reconfigure power relations through redefining development and modernity. As historian Jeremy Adelman observed, "Despite its many disasters and disappointments . . . the idea of 'development' remains amazingly resilient."[27] Our task, then, seems to be reckoning with its past failings and applying the lessons that history proffers in future initiatives.

At various stages in this project, friends, colleagues, family, and even interview subjects asked me if I felt that all development efforts were "bad," did good intentions count for anything, and did I think that the solution was just to do nothing if an initiative could not solve everything or avoid every pitfall. Was reducing illiteracy not a good thing? Were initiatives aimed at curbing malnutrition and lowering infant mortality rates not positive for a society? Should we really view building new houses and health clinics as harmful? As *On Our Own Terms* has shown, these are actually not simple questions, and there are no easy answers. While this book is not a blueprint for development initiatives, it should cause us to carefully consider the ways we seek to make a difference in our world. It has shown that development practices and priorities have to come from the desires of development's intended beneficiaries. It has emphasized the importance that a more equitable distribution of land has for any type of meaningful social change in Guatemala. And it has explained certain uses and abuses of development so that we can take care to be vigilant against them in our own endeavors.

This history shows that there are always hierarchies of power at play within development projects. Development practitioners must be aware of power configurations, both past and present, and be informed of histories and cultures of the places where they work, recognizing that universal or even widely applicable models of development are a harmful myth. Even well-intentioned actions can perpetuate darker histories of subjugation and can objectify, essentialize, and paternalize people. Thus, the outside expert needs to step aside and allow those whose lives development will directly affect to take charge and dictate the plans and implementation strategies, helping to facilitate the access of needed resources. In the examples discussed in this book, efforts that ceded as much control as possible to intended beneficiaries seemed to result in active collaborations to enact change, though these at times were messy and fraught with tension. Pursing a type of development based on permanent redistribution of resources in accordance with the demands of recipients can begin to introduce structural changes versus temporary, surface-level fixes. As we have seen, development is a powerful political tool; practitioners must actively reflect on whose agenda and initiatives they serve, upon whose values and norms a project is based, and what conditions it imposes upon host communities and if beneficiaries have willingly and freely accepted them. If the answers to these questions do not directly point to intended recipients, then history clearly warns against the consequences of such projects.

On Our Own Terms has offered an analysis of what development looked like in practice in Guatemala, showing along the way how the Cold War impacted everyday lives and the construction of race, citizenship, and modernity. While policy makers and experts often attempted to impose a development model based on modernization and sought to homogenize the citizenry through defining acceptable forms of Indigeneity, Indigenous Guatemalans insisted on the pursuit of their own versions of development that did not necessarily exclude all aspects of modernization but called for a reconfiguration of power, a recognition of Indigenous rights, cultures, and histories, and the right to determine their own futures. Because development initiatives became such a widely used tool in the Cold War for attempting to reshape rural peoples' mentalities and actions in order to minimize the appeal of leftist insurgency, rural Indigenous Guatemalans, like rural and Indigenous Peoples across the globe, regularly negotiated and navigated these outside impositions into their lives. Their actions shaped the Cold War, and their stories elucidate the contingencies and complexities this so-called peaceful means of fighting the Cold War wrought in Latin America and around the globe.

Notes

Introduction

1. I have followed Gregory Younging's guidance in *Elements of Indigenous Style: A Guide for Writing By and About Indigenous Peoples* (Edmonton, Canada: Brush Education Inc., 2018) in deciding what terms and capitalization patterns to use in this book. Thus, I capitalize Indigenous and Indigeneity to convey an understanding that these terms are rooted in broad histories of colonization. I use the phrase Indigenous Peoples to refer collectively to distinct Indigenous nations and societies. I use "Indigenous people" to broadly refer to individuals who identify or are identified as Indigenous. In the Guatemalan context, the Guatemalan state does not consider the different Indigenous groups living within the national borders to be autonomous political entities nor sovereign nations. Thus, in this context, "Indigenous people" or "the Indigenous population" is the terminology I employ to broadly refer to Indigenous individuals living in Guatemala while still recognizing the many ethnic groups that comprise this general categorization. Whenever possible, I refer to an individual or distinct community's ethnic identity.

2. Cabrera did not remember the exact date of this fieldwork assignment, but she did recall the name of the minister of education, who served under the Castillo Armas regime (mid-July 1954–1957). She spent most of 1956 working on a textile project, and she resigned from the IING later that year, so I have concluded that this visit to San Carlos Alzatate likely took place in 1955.

3. Taracena Arriola, et al., *Etnicidad, estado y nación en Guatemala, 1808–1944*, vol. 1,384; Handy, *Revolution in the Countryside*, 149–50.

4. Hélida Esther Cabrera, Interview by author, September 9, 2015. All interviews by the author unless otherwise specified; all translations are mine. Cabrera *Vivencias inolvidables*, 81–84.

5. Cabrera, Interview, September 24, 2015.

6. Cabrera, *Vivencias inolvidables*, 84–85, 88.

7. Cabrera, *Vivencias inolvidables*, 92–98.

8. Cabrera, Interview, September 19, 2015.

9. Dillingham, *Oaxaca Resurgent*, 24.

10. "Estudiantes voluntarios llegaron a Alzatate; Trabajarán Plan de Desarrollo de la Comunidad," *El Imparcial*, November 9, 1965.

11. "Nueva carretera se pondrá al servicio en S. Carlos Alzatate," *El Imparcial*, March 10, 1967; "San Carlos Alzatate B," *El Imparcial*, February 15, 1967.

12. Scott, *Seeing Like a State*.

13. Ferguson, *Anti-Politics Machine*, xiv; Erin Beck, *How Development Projects Persist*, 212; Vrana, *This City Belongs to You*, 6.

14. Martí, "Autores Americanos Aborígenes" in *Obras Completas de José Martí*, 336–37.

15. *Boletín Indigenista* 1, no. 1 (August 1941): 2.

16. Burkhart, *Holy Wednesday*; Lockhardt, *Nahuas after the Conquest*; Lovell, *Conquest and Survival*; Tilley, *Africa as a Living Laboratory*; Kramer, *Blood of Government*; Pérez, *Cuba in the American Imagination*.

17. Larson, *Trials of Nation Making*; Sattar, "*Indígena* or *Ciudadano*?

18. Guardino, *"The Time of Liberty"*; Howe, *A People Who Would Not Kneel*; Gould, *To Die in This Way*; Yannakakis, *The Art of Being In-Between*; Tutino, *Making a New World*.

19. Here I follow Odd Arne Westad's conceptualization of the global Cold War in Westad, *The Global Cold War*, 3–4.

20. Beck, *How Development Projects Persist*, 10.

21. Cullather, "Development? It's History," 642.

22. Immerwahr, *Thinking Small*, ix; Engerman, "Development Politics and the Cold War," 2; For literature about the long history of development, see Rist, *History of Development*; Macekura and Manela, "Introduction," in *The Development Century: A Global History*, ed. Macekura and Manela, 3.

23. Latham, *Modernization as Ideology*, 17.

24. Government of Guatemala (GOG), *Sexto censo de población 1950*, 1, 239.

25. Sackley, "Village as Cold War Site," 481–504.

26. Immerwahr, *Thinking Small*; Cullather, *Hungry World*.

27. Latham, *Modernization as Ideology*; Escobar, *Encountering Development*; Gilman, *Mandarins of the Future*; Engerman, et al., *Staging Growth*; Friedman, *Shadow Cold War*; Brazinsky, *Winning the Third World*; Latham, *Right Kind of Revolution*.

28. Cullather, *Hungry World*; Sayward, *United Nations in International History*; Palmer: *Launching Global Health*; Macekura, *Of Limits and Growth*; Thornton, *Revolution in Development*.

29. Chastain and Lorek, "Introduction," in *Itineraries of Expertise*, eds. Chastain and Lorek.

30. Hines, "Power and Ethics of Vernacular Modernism," 228–29; Gow, *Countering Development*, 4; Hines, *Water for All*, 15.

31. Rosemblatt, *The Science and Politics of Race*, 11.

32. Joseph and Nugent, "Popular Culture and State Formation in Revolutionary Mexico," in *Everyday Forms of State Formation*, ed. Joseph and Nugent, 12.

33. Rus, "The 'Comunidad Revolucionaria Institucional,'" in *Everyday Forms*, ed. Joseph and Nugent, 291.

34. Taylor, "Between Global Process," 145.

35. Joseph and Nugent, "Popular Culture," 20.

36. Taylor, "Between Global Process," 147.

37. Way, *Mayan in the Mall*, 3.

38. Harmer, *Allende's Chile*, 6; Joseph, "What We Now Know and Should Know," in *In from the Cold*, ed. Joseph and Spenser, 17. See Grandin and Joseph, eds., *Century of Revolution*, for scholarship that historically contextualizes the violence of the twentieth-century in Latin America as distinctly related to the Global Cold War.

39. Adams, "Guatemalan Ladinization and History," 527–43.

40. de la Cadena, *Indigenous Mestizos*, 6–7.

41. López, *Crafting Mexico*, 9, 131.

42. Carey Jr., "Rethinking Representation and Periodization," in *Out of the Shadow*, ed. Gibbings and Vrana, 145–74.

43. Coy Moulton, "Counter-Revolutionary Friends"; Galeano, *Guatemala: Occupied Country*.

44. U.S. Congress, House of Representatives, Committee on Foreign Affairs, Special Study Mission to Central America on International Organizations and Movements, 84th Congress, 1 session, rpt. 1155, 1955, 16, quoted in Streeter, *Managing the Counterrevolution*, 137.

45. Ronald Reagan Presidential Library, "Remarks in San Pedro Sula, Honduras, Following a Meeting with President José Efraín Ríos Montt of Guatemala," December 4, 1982. https://www.reaganlibrary.gov/archives/speech/remarks-san-pedro-sula-honduras-following-meeting-president-jose-efrain-rios-montt

46. Gotkowitz, "Introduction," in *Histories of Race and Racism*, ed. Gotkowitz, 10–11.

47. Mallon, "A Postcolonial Palimpsest," in Gotkowitz, *Race and Racism*, 322, 335.

48. Applebaum, Macpherson, and Rosemblatt, "Introduction: Racial Nations," in *Race and Nation*, eds. Applebaum, Macpherson, and Rosemblatt, 2, 7–8.

49. Gotkowitz, "Introduction," 11.

50. I place quotes around "the Indian" to make clear I am referring to the historical construct.

51. Barragán, "The Census," in *Race and Racism*, ed. Gotkowitz, 117; Martínez, *Genealogical Fictions*; Knight, "Racism, Revolution, and *Indigenismo*," in *The Idea of Race*, ed. Graham, 75; Wade, *Race and Ethnicity*, 38; Quijano, "Coloniality of Power," 219.

52. Earle, *Return of the Native*; Saldaña Portillo, *Indian Given*, 52.

53. Stepan, *"The Hour of Eugenics,"* 13, 136.

54. Chambers, "Little Middle Ground," in *Race and Nation*, 33.

55. Wade, *Race and Ethnicity*, 87, 154.

56. Taracena Arriola, et. al, *Etnicidad, Estado y Nación*, vol. 1, 37; McCreery, *Rural Guatemala*, 7; Grandin, *The Blood of Guatemala*, 83–84.

57. Barragán, "The Census," 113.

58. González Ponciano, "The *Shumo* Challenge," in *War By Other Means*, ed. McAllister and Nelson, 307–29; Hale, "Neoliberal Multiculturalism," 10–28; Warren, *Indigenous Movements*.

59. Gibbings, "Mestizaje in the Age of Fascism," 214–36; Adams y Bastos, *Las relaciones étnicas*, 36; Casaús Arzú, "La metamorphosis del racismo," in *Racismo en Guatemala?* eds. Arenas Bianchi et al.; Cojtí Cuxil, *Runa'oj Ri Maya' Amaq'*, 22–23.

60. Gotkowitz, "Introduction," 8.

61. Taracena Arriola, "From Assimilation to Segregation," in *Race and Racism*, ed. Gotkowitz, 104–107; Esquit, *La superación del indígena*, 33.

62. Grandin, *Blood of Guatemala*; Gibbings, "Shadow of Slavery"; Carey Jr., *Engendering Mayan History*, 150.

63. Grandin, *Blood of Guatemala*, 140; Esquit, *La superación del indígena*, 22–24.

64. When the prose does not make clear that I am talking about the model and construct of "the Indian," the "permitted Indian," or the "prohibited Indian," I add quotation marks to indicate this usage of these terms.

65. Hale and Millamán, "Cultural Agency and Political Struggle," 297–98; Hale, "Rethinking Indigenous Politics," 16–20.

66. Schirmer, *The Guatemalan Military Project*, 115–16.

67. Offner, *Sorting Out the Mixed Economy*.

68. Saldaña-Portillo, *The Revolutionary Imagination*, 27.

69. Grandin, *The Last Colonial Massacre*, 17, 180–81.

70. Scott, *Degrees of Freedom*, 6.

71. López, *Crafting Mexico*, 200.

72. Esquit, *La superación del indígena*, 33.

Chapter One

1. "Discurso del Señor Ministro de Educación Pública, Profesor Manuel Galich," *Boletín IING* 1, no. 1 (October–December 1945): 14; "Incorporación Indígena: Convención de maestros indígenas en Cobán," *Boletín IING* 1, no. 1 (October–December 1945): 41–42.

2. Gotkowitz, *Revolution for Our Rights*, 44.

3. Garrard-Burnett, "Indians Are Drunks"; Nelson, *Finger in the Wound*, 86–90; González Ponciano, *Diez años del indigenismo*. See Knight, "Racism"; the essays in Laura Giraudo and Juan Martín-Sánchez, eds. *La ambivalente historia del indigenismo* and in *Latin American Perspectives* 39, no. 5 (September 2012); and Dillingham, *Oaxaca Resurgent*, for examples of this revisionist scholarship.

4. Dawson, *Indian and Nation*, xiv–xv; Lewis, *Rethinking Mexican Indigenismo*, 7.

5. Way, *Mayan in the Mall*, 5; Esquit, *Comunidad y estado*, 95.

6. Gibbings, "Mestizaje," 224.

7. Esquit, *La superación del indígena*, 128; Taracena Arriola, "From Assimilation to Segregation," in *Histories of Race and Racism*, ed. Gotkowitz, 110–11.

8. Casey, *Indigenismo*, 199–200.

9. Gotkowitz, *Revolution for Our Right*, 160–61.

10. Cárdenas Escobar, *Reconcile the Indian*, 21.

11. Kiddle, *Mexico's Relations with Latin America*; Rosemblatt, *Science and Politics of Race*, 98.

12. Archivo General de Centroamérica (AGCA), *Memoria de la Secretaría de Relaciones Exteriores del Año de 1940*, 383; Kiddle, *Mexico's Relations*, 154–56.

13. Casaús Arzú, "La generación del 20," in *Las redes intelectuales*, eds. Casaús Arzú and García Giráldez, 257–58; Quintana, *La generación de 1920*, 426.

14. Casaús Arzú, "La generación del 20," 270–71. Asturias, *Sociología Guatemalteca*; Juárez Muñoz, *El Indio Guatemalteco*; Barrientos Batres, *El olvido de los gobernados*; Taracena Arriola, *Etnicidad, estado y nación*, vol. I, 376–79.

15. Stepan, *"Hour of Eugenics,"* 66, 84–85; Grandin, *Blood of Guatemala*, 230.

16. Gibbings, "Mestizaje," 216.

17. Casaús Arzú, "El indio, la nación," in *Las redes intelectuales*, 227–51; Mendoza, *Ensayos sobre pensamiento antropológico*, 43–44.

18. Appelbaum, et al., "Introduction," 7–8.

19. Lewis, *Rethinking Mexican Indigenismo*, 3; Dawson, *Indian and Nation*, xv.

20. "David Vela dio vida a La Chalana," *Prensa Libre*, February 24, 2017. http://www.prensalibre.com/hemeroteca/biografia-de-david-vela.

21. AO, David Vela, Interview by Edgar S. G. Mendoza, Guatemala City, October 25, 1990. All interviews conducted by Mendoza. With collaboration from Mendoza and the

working group Cátedra Joaquín Noval, I had the interviews digitized and transcribed, available online: http://antropologiadeguatemala.tumblr.com/autores.

22. Jorge Mario Garcia Laguardia, Interview, September 9, 2015.

23. AGCA, *Memoria de la Secretaría de Relaciones Exteriores del año de 1938*, 15, 133; "Breve Historial," *Boletín IING* 1, no. 1 (October–December 1945): 7; RRP, [23:8 (Box:Folder)], "Minutes of the Meeting of the Policy Board," February 4, 1942.

24. RRP [23:8], "Minutes of the Meeting."

25. RRP, [23:8], Oscar L. Chapman to Nelson Rockefeller, November 7, 1941; "Office of Indian Affairs to Work with the Inter-American Indian Institute," *Hispanic American Historical Review* 21, no. 3 (1941): 506–7. The Office of Indian Affairs became the Bureau of Indian Affairs in 1947.

26. Rosier, *Serving Their Country*, 73–84; Cárdenas Escobar, *Reconcile the Indian*, 67, 76–77.

27. RRP, [23:8], "Minutes of the Meeting of the Governing Board of the Inter-American Indian Institute," Mexico City, March 25, 1942.

28. Vela, *Orientación y recomendaciones*, 10.

29. Vela, *Orientación y recomendaciones*, 12.

30. Congreso Indigenista Interamericano, *Actas finales*, 60, 32, 36–37; Vela, *Orientación y recomendaciones*, 113, 52–53.

31. See Vela, *Orientaciones y recomendaciones*, for a full description of the discussions and resolutions from the Pátzcuaro conference.

32. AO, Vela.

33. Manuel Gamio to David Vela, December 7, 1944, expediente "David Vela," AIII, Mexico City. I am indebted to Raquel Escobar for sharing the Guatemala materials she gathered at this archive.

34. Kiddle, *Mexico's Relations*, 164.

35. Dawson, *Indian and Nation*, 114.

36. RRP, [23:8], "Minutes of the Meeting of the Policy Board"; "Observará los adelantos en la campana contra la filaria," *El Imparcial*, December 16, 1941.

37. "Agrupación para trabajar por la idea indigenista," *El Imparcial*, December 19, 1941; "Se realizará labor indigenista bajo entusiasta auspicios," *El Imparcial*, December 22, 1941.

38. III, *Boletín Indigenista* 2, no. 1 (March 1942): 7.

39. Castilho, *Slave Emancipation*, 15; Sieder, "Rethinking Democratisation," 106–8.

40. Dawson, *Indian and Nation*, xix; Taracena Arriola et al., *Etnicidad, estado y nación*, vol. 1, 175.

41. Here I follow Richard Rothstein's differentiation between *de jure* and *de facto* practices from his history of housing segregation. See *Color of Law*, vii–viii.

42. "Se realizará labor indigenista bajo entusiasta auspicios," *El Imparcial*, December 22, 1941.

43. AO, Vela.

44. Taracena Arriola et al., *Etnicidad, estado y nación*, vol. 1, 176; Grandin's *Blood of Guatemala* and Esquit's *La superación del indígena* discuss how Indigenous elites revised ideas about nationalism to include themselves as important intermediary figures, and while these historical actors did successfully challenge racist stereotypes, they also perpetuated the marginalization of lower-class Indigenous people.

45. III, *Boletín Indigenista* 3, no. 4 (December 1943): 225.

46. RRP, [37:7], Department of State press release, February 14, 1942.

47. III, *Boletín Indigenista* 3, no. 4 (December 1943): 225–26; III, *Boletín Indigenista* 1, no. 2 (November 1941): 32–33; III, *Boletín Indigenista* 1, no. 1 (August 1941): 9.

48. AO, Vela.

49. Penny, "From Migrant Knowledge," 388.

50. "Discurso del Señor Ministro de Educación, Profesor Manuel Galich," *Boletín IING* 1, no. 1 (October–December 1945): 12.

51. Carlos Guzmán Böckler, Interview, August 28, 2015; See González Ponciano, "The 'Indigenous Problem,'" in *Out from the Shadow*, eds. Gibbings and Vrana, for an interpretation of U.S. anthropology as imperialist.

52. Cullather, *Hungry World*, 27; Immerwahr, *Thinking Small*, 56–59; Redfield, *Chan Kom*; Redfield, *Tepoztlán*.

53. Rubinstein, *Doing Fieldwork*.

54. Rubinstein, *Doing Fieldwork*, 128, 131–32.

55. The following letters detail these relationships and can be found in STP, [89:8 (Box:Folder)]: Tax to Alfredo Méndez Domínguez, August 1976; Roberto Rosales to Tax, November 24, 1978; handwritten note by Tax that reports asking Flavio Rojas Lima to give R. Rosales money for rebuilding his home; Marta Rosales to Tax, September 6, 1971; Tax to Marjorie Bedoukian, April 18, 1972; Bedoukian to Tax, May 8, 1972; Tax to Bedoukian, May 16, 1972; Marta Rosales to Tax, May 29, 1972; Tax to Bedoukian, June 19, 1972; Bedoukian to Tax, June 24, 1972; Tax to Bedoukian, June 30, 1972.

56. STP, [81:4].

57. Adams, "El indigenismo guatemalteco," in *La ambivalente historia*, eds. Giraudo and Martín-Sánchez, 104. See Adams, "Antonio Goubaud Carrera," in *After the Coup*, eds. Smith and Adams, 17–48, for biographic analysis of Goubaud and his significance to Guatemalan anthropology.

58. Rubinstein, *Doing Fieldwork*, 45.

59. A. Adams, "El indigenismo guatemalteco," 116; RRP, [11:2], Goubaud to Redfield, May 14, 1942; RRP, [37:7], Redfield to Vela, August 3, 1942.

60. Mendoza, *Antropologistas y antropólogos*.

61. Tax, "Action Anthropology," 514–17; Stapp, "Introduction," in *Action Anthropology and Sol Tax*, 2, 8; Bennett, "Applied and Action Anthropology," S23–S53; Nash, "Applied and Action Anthropology," 68–69.

62. Smith, "Beyond Collaboration," in *Action Anthropology*, ed. Stapp, 82–83, 79.

63. Goubaud Carrera, *Food Patterns and Nutrition*; RRP, [11: 3], Redfield to Goubaud, June 24, 1943.

64. A. Adams, "El indigenismo guatemalteco," 116.

65. RRP, [11:2], Goubaud to Redfield, March 3, 1942, Goubaud to Redfield, March 24, 1942, Tax to Redfield, March 31, 1942, Goubaud to Redfield, March 24, 1942.

66. RRP, [11:2], Redfield to Goubaud, March 9, 1942, Goubaud to Redfield, March 24, 1942.

67. STP, [83:1], Sol Tax to Juan Comas, May 7, 1943.

68. STP, [89:3], Emma Reh to Tax, January 14, 1947.

69. STP, [85:1], Goubaud to Tax, May 11, 1944; STP [86:6], Tax to Alfred Kidder, October 9, 1943.

70. STP, [85:1] Tax to Goubaud, December 26, 1944.

71. STP, [89: 3], Reh to Tax, March 4, 1948; "Guatemala: Investigation on Nutrition," *Boletín Indigenista* 4:4 (December 1944): 291–93.

72. STP, [89:3], "A Study of Diet in Central America" FAO Report by Emma Reh. Reh sent Tax this report on March 2, 1951; STP, [89:3], Tax to Reh, March 25, 1951.

73. STP, [89:3], "A Study of Diet," 7.

74. STP, [89:3], Reh to Tax, November 22, 1946; STP, [89:3], "A Study of Diet," 8, 14–15.

75. STP, [85:1]: Goubaud to Tax, November 6, 1944, Goubaud to Tax, November 26, 1944, Goubaud to Tax, December 3, 1944, Goubaud to Tax, December 10, 1944.

76. Martínez Peláez, *Motines de Indios*.

77. Handy, "Sea of Indians," 194.

78. Adams, "Ethnic Images and Strategies in 1944," in *Guatemalan Indians and the State*, ed. Smith, 142–43.

79. Carey, Jr. *Our Elders Teach Us*, 187–88; and Carey Jr., *Engendering Mayan History*, 133–58, for Kaqchikel perspectives on Patzicía. See Rodas and Esquit, *Élite ladina-vanguardia indígena* for analysis of the massacre's historical antecedents to the massacre; Rodas and Esquit, *Élite ladina-vanguaurdia indígena*, 195.

80. RRP, [11:4], Goubaud to Redfield, January 29, 1945.

81. García Laguardia, *Constitución*, 192.

82. Taracena Arriola, et al., *Etnicidad, estado y nación*, vol. 1, 175–76; Esquit, *La superación del indígena*, 47.

83. García Laguardia, *Constitución*, 75–76.

84. García Laguardia, *Constitución*, 79.

85. República de Guatemala, *Diario de las Sesiones de la Asamblea Constituyente de 1945*, 138.

86. GOG, *Constitución de la República de Guatemala*, March 11, 1945, Artículo 9.

87. República de Guatemala, *Diario de las Sesiones*, 313.

88. República de Guatemala, *Diario de las Sesiones*, 428–30.

89. García Laguardia, *Constitución*, 142–43; Jorge Mario García Laguardia, Interview, September 9, 2015.

90. García Laguardia, *Constitución*, 53–55.

91. García Laguardia, *El estatuto indígena*, 57.

92. García Laguardia, *El estatuto indígena*, 46.

93. García Laguardia, *El estatuto indígena*, 46.

94. García Laguardia, *El estatuto indígena*, 75.

95. García Laguardia, Interview.

96. RRP [11:4], Goubaud to Redfield, February 24, 1945.

97. "Breve historial," *Boletín IING* 1, no. 1 (October–December 1945): 8; GOG, *Acuerdo Presidencial*, August 28, 1945. https://es.unesco.org/sites/default/files/guatemala_acuredo_28_08_1945_spa_orof.pdf

98. Lewis, *Rethinking Mexican Indigenismo*, 42.

99. Dawson, *Indian and Nation*, 114.

100. Existing documentation does not detail how the government selected teachers, nor have I found a full attendee list but instead rely on newspaper accounts and published reports about the meeting.

101. Ángel Ramírez, "La Escuela Rural Guatemalteca Debe Servir y Desarrollar Programas para el Niño Campesino," *El Imparcial*, September 11, 1963; "Cobán se anima en vísperas del congreso indigenista," *El Imparcial*, July 5, 1945; "Problemas del Indígena," *El Imparcial*, July 5, 1945; "Incorporación Indígena: Convención de maestros indígenas en Cobán," *Boletín IING* 1, no. 1 (October–December 1945): 41–42; RRP, [4:11], Goubaud to Redfield, July 24, 1945.

102. "Plagas que minan la salud del indígena," *El Imparcial*, July 12, 1945.

103. "Problemas del indígena debe ayudarse a resolverlos por el indígena mismo," *El Imparcial*, July 10, 1945.

104. RRP, [4:11], Goubaud to Redfield, July 24, 1945.

105. GOG, Acuerdo Presidencial, August 28, 1945. https://es.unesco.org/sites/default/files/guatemala_acuredo_28_08_1945_spa_orof.pdf; "Se crea el Instituto Indígena de Guatemala," *Mediodia*, August 29, 1945.

106. STP, [85:1], Tax to Goubaud, October 3, 1945.

107. "Discurso del Señor Ministro de Educación, Profesor Manuel Galich," *Boletín IING* 1, no. 1 (October–December 1945): 10, 7, 16.

108. "Conferencia del Director del Instituto, Licenciado Antonio Goubaud Carrera," *Boletín IING* 1, no. 1 (October–December 1945): 22, 27, 25.

109. AO, Francisco Rodríguez Rouanet, February 26, 1990.

110. "Fundación e inauguración," *Boletín IING* 1, no. 1 (October–December 1945): 9.

111. *Boletín IING* 1, no. 1 (October–December 1945): 2.

112. "Trayectoria de la Vida del Instituto," *Boletín IING* 1, no. 1 (October–December 1945): 38; RRP, [4:11], Goubaud to Redfield, September 14, 1945; RRP, [4:11], Goubaud to Redfield, December 15, 1945; RRP, [4:11], Goubaud to Redfield, January 15, 1945.

113. Francisco Rodríguez Rouanet, Interview, August 6, 2015; Pérez Molina, "Desarrollo de la antropología guatemalteca," 183–84; AO, Rodríguez Rouanet.

114. Dillingham, *Oaxaca Resurgent*, 8.

115. Robert Redfield, "Ethnic Groups and Nationality," *Boletín Indigenista* 5, no. 3 (September 1945): 245.

116. González Ponciano, "'Indigenous Problem,'" 111–12.

Chapter Two

1. Portions of this chapter were previously published in an earlier version in Foss, "'Una obra revolucionaria': *Indigenismo* and the Guatemalan Revolution, 1944–1954," in *Out of the Shadow: Revisiting the Revolution from Post-Peace Guatemala*, ed. Julie Gibbings and Heather Vrana (Austin: University of Texas Press, 2020), 199–221. Many thanks to the University of Texas Press for its kind permission to utilize this material here.

2. Brintnall, *Revolt Against the Dead*, 26.

3. STP, [91:11], Rosales's Diario de Aguacatán, September 3, 1944.

4. Brintnall, *Revolt*, 112.

5. STP, [91:11] Rosales's Diario de Aguacatán, October 20, 1944.

6. STP, [91:11] Rosales's Diario de Aguacatán, October 25, 1944; Brintnall, *Revolt*, 97.

7. Taracena et al., *Etnicidad, estado y nación*, vol. 1, 142–43, 152–53.

8. Goubaud Carrera, "El grupo étnico indígena: criterios para su definición," *Boletín IING* 1, nos. 2–3 (March–June 1946): 14–15.

9. Goubaud Carrera, "El grupo étnico indígena," 14.

10. Goubaud Carrera, "El grupo étnico indígena." The article includes several oversized tables.

11. Goubaud Carrera, "El grupo étnico indígena," 29.

12. AGCA, Sexto Censo de Población, 1950, 39; Quick, *Guatemala*, 6; CIRMA, MP-YC, Doc. 004, "Algunos rasgos de la realidad agraria en Guatemala," 5; Pernet, "Between Entanglements and Dependencies, 107.

13. Scott, *Seeing Like a State*, 2.

14. Scott, *Seeing Like a State*, 4.

15. Way, *Mayan in the Mall*, 42–43.

16. Rodríguez Rouanet, Interview, August 6, 2015.

17. May, "Retrospective View," 151.

18. Price, "Subtle Means and Enticing Carrots," 382; Price, *Cold War Anthropology*, 248–54.

19. Murdock et al., *Guía para la investigación etnológicas*.

20. IING, *Boletín del IING* 2, no. 2 (March 1947): 60–102.

21. Beck, "How Development Projects Persist," 23.

22. Dillingham, *Oaxaca Resurgent*, 178.

23. Cabrera, Interview, September 24, 2015.

24. Rodríguez Rouanet, Interview, August 12, 2014.

25. President Arbenz cancelled the SCIDE's contract in 1950; it returned to Guatemala under the Castillo Armas administration. See Way, *Mayan in the Mall*, 64.

26. IING, *Santo Domingo Xenacoj*, Publicación Especial No. 7, (Guatemala: Ministerio de Educación Pública, 1947), iii.

27. Griffith, "A Recent Attempt," 179–80, 186.

28. Esquit, *Otros poderes*, 210.

29. AGCA, Hemeroteca, paquete 13, *Alfabetización higiénica*, Publicación del Servicio Interamericano de Salud Pública en Guatemala 10:1 (July 1947): 2.

30. STP, [88:10], Tax to Lauriston Sharp, March 16, 1948.

31. Rodríguez Rouanet, Interview, August 12, 2014.

32. Grandin, *Blood of Guatemala*, 51; Esquit, *La superación del indígena*, 49.

33. Rahder, *Ecology of Knowledges*, 190.

34. The IING also published monographs on Chuarrancho, San Juan Sacatepéquez, Chinautla, Parramos, San Antonio Aguas Calientes, Santa Catarina Barahona, and Santo Domingo Xenacoj.

35. IING, *San Bartolomé Milpas Altas: síntesis socio-económico de una comunidad indígena guatemalteca*, publicaciones especiales del Instituto Indigenista Nacional No. 9 (Guatemala: Ministerio de Educación Pública, 1949), insert prior to preface.

36. GOG, *Sexto Censo de Población*, 1950, 9. The census reported the population as 900, lower than the ethnographers' calculations.

37. IING, *San Bartolomé*, vi–viii.

38. IING, *San Bartolomé*, 18–19.

39. IING, *San Bartolomé*, 10.

40. IING, *San Bartolomé*, 13.

41. Juárez Muñoz, *El Indio Guatemalteco*; Carey, Jr., "Drunks and Dictators"; Garrard-Burnett, "Indians Are Drunks."

42. IING, *San Bartolomé*, 14–15.

43. Gibbings, *Our Time Is Now*, 134–35; 269.

44. Nelson, *Who Counts?*

45. Thornton, "'Mexico Has the Theories'" in *The Development Century*, eds. Macekura and Manela, 264.

46. Tim Golden, "Juan José Arévalo is Dead at 86; Guatemala President in Late 40's," *New York Times*, October 8, 1990, 10. https://www.nytimes.com/1990/10/08/obituaries/juan-jose-arevalo-is-dead-at-86-guatemala-president-in-late-40-s.html; "Arévalo Bermejo, Juan José (September 10, 1904)," in *A Dictionary of Political Biography*, ed. Dennis Kavanagh and Christopher Riches (Oxford: Oxford University Press, 2009). http://www.oxfordreference.com/view/10.1093/oi/authority.20110803095423667.

47. Arévalo, *Escritos Políticos*, 200.

48. Black, *Garrison Guatemala*, 13.

49. Arévalo, "A New Guatemala," trans. Weld, in *Guatemala Reader*, 210.

50. Arévalo, "A New Guatemala," 306.

51. Vaughan, *Cultural Politics in Revolution*; Lindo-Fuentes and Ching, *Modernizing Minds*; Glenn, *American Indian/First Nations Schooling*.

52. Appelbaum et al., "Introduction," in *Race and Nation*, ed. Appelbaum et al., 6.

53. See Taracena Arriola et al., *Etnicidad, estado y nación*, vol. 1, chapter 3, "Educar para civilizar."

54. Carey, *Engendering Mayan History*, 181–82.

55. "Instituto Indígena en Jalapa," *La Hora*, May 30, 1946.

56. "Hay que alfabetizar," *El Imparcial*, August 13, 1945.

57. "Primero es la letra: Promesas y alcances de la campaña de alfabetización," *El Imparcial*, December 28, 1945.

58. Esquit, *La superación del indígena*, 33.

59. "El Analfabeto es una Vergüenza Nacional!" *El Imparcial*, December 13, 1945.

60. Cueto, *Cold War, Deadly Fevers*, 17; "Ejército de Alfabetización Nacional," *El Imparcial*, April 5, 1945; "Llamado al Aporte en pro de la campaña de la alfabetización," *El Imparcial*, April 12, 1945; "Censo Escolar de 1946" *El Imparcial*, November 2, 1945.

61. Cabrera, Interview, September 22, 2015.

62. AGCA, Biblioteca, Reg. 6132, "Campaña Nacional de Alfabetización, Instructivo General," (Departamento y Comité Nacional de Alfabetización, Guatemala: Junio 1948): 1–2, 5–7.

63. Vargas R., *En buen camino*, 4–6.

64. Piedra Santa, *Alfabetización y poder*, 68–69.

65. Streeter, *Managing the Counterrevolution*, 156.

66. "Inaugura Hoy la Campaña de Alfabetización" *El Imparcial*, April 9, 1945; "Plan general de la segunda campaña de alfabetización en el país," *El Imparcial*, September 15, 1945.

67. AGCA No. 1365, *A.B.C.*

68. Gibbings, *Our Time Is Now*, 194–95.

69. AGCA No. 1365, *A.B.C.*, 1945.

70. AGCA No. 6138, Vargas R., *Nuevo día*.

71. Vrana, *This City Belongs to You*, 150.

72. Juan Chapín also appears in *A.B.C.*, but there, his wife is named María and his children are named José and Lolita.

73. Vargas R., *Nuevo día*, 28.

74. AGCA Biblioteca, Reg. 6543, Geiger, *Communism versus Progress*.

75. Cullather, *Hungry World*, see chapter 1.

76. Servicio Cooperativo Interamericano de Salud Pública, *Alfabetización Higiénica* 1, no. 11 (August 1947): 23–27.

77. Cueto, *Cold War, Deadly Fevers*, 102.

78. AGCA Biblioteca, doc. 8383, *3ra campaña regional de alfabetización*, 1952.

79. *3ra campaña regional*, 19; *A.B.C.*

80. Vargas R., *Nuevo día*, 37.

81. Vargas R., *Nuevo día*, 46.

82. Vargas R., *Nuevo día*, 33.

83. Grandin, *Blood of Guatemala*, 114.

84. Vargas R., *Nuevo día*, 39, 29.

85. Gibbings, *Our Time Is Now*, 161.

86. Vargas R., *Nuevo día*, 53, 40, 28.

87. Vargas R., *Nuevo día*, 28.

88. Carey, *Engendering Mayan History*, 123, 99; Annis, *God and Production*.

89. Vargas R., *Nuevo día*, 54.

90. Vargas R., *Nuevo día*, 58.

Chapter Three

1. RAP, Richard Adams Field notes, March 6, 1951, 1:1 (Box:Folder). Unless otherwise noted, all future citations are field notes, with the author indicated; RAP, Hannstein, April 29, 1951, 1:1.

2. RAP, Díaz, February 21, 1953, 1:2.

3. RAP, Díaz, July 22, 1953, 1:2.

4. Gibbings, *Our Time Is Now*, 150. Gibbings's analysis of El Q'eq as a formative part of Q'eqchi' history shaped my reading and interpretation of Lobos's conquest narrative.

5. RAP, Raymond Amir, April 17, 1951, 1:4.

6. Stone, "Delimitation of the Area," 376.

7. Lutz, *Santiago de Guatemala*; Asselbergs, *Conquered Conquistadors*.

8. Stone, "Delimitation of the Area," 376.

9. Way, *Mayan in the Mall*, 43.

10. V.C. Fowke, "George Edwin Britnell, 1903–1961," *The Canadian Journal of Economics and Political Science / Revue canadienne d'Economique et de Science politique* 28:2 (May 1962): 286.

11. George E. Britnell to Eugene R. Black, letter dated June 15, 1951. http://documents .worldbank.org/curated/en/835191468751555135/pdf/multiopage.pdf.

12. IBRD, *Economic Development of Guatemala*.

13. Britnell, "Factors," 112.

14. Britnell, "Factors," 112.

15. *Foreign Relations of the United States* (FRUS), Guatemala, 1952–1954, eds. Susan Holly and David S. Patterson. Doc. 12. https://history.state.gov/historicaldocuments/frus1952 -54Guat/d12.

16. IBRD, *Economic Development of Guatemala*, 7.

17. Jacobo Arbenz was one of the leaders of the 1944 October Revolution and Arévalo's minister of defense. In 1949, Arbenz helped prevent one of several political coups against Arévalo, but this one resulted in the mysterious death of Colonel Francisco Javier Arana, head of the military, an opponent to Arévalo, and a presidential candidate. Arbenz easily won the election, although not without accusations of involvement in Arana's death. See Gleijeses, chapter 3, "The World of Jacobo Arbenz," in *Shattered Hope*.

18. Pacino, "Constructing a New Bolivian Society," 25–56. Soto Laveaga, "Bringing the Revolution to Medical Schools"; Berth, *Food and Revolution*.

19. Cullather, *Hungry World*, 8.

20. Cullather, *Hungry World*, 14–15; Aguilar-Rodríguez, "Cooking Modernity," 179–80; Olsson, *Agrarian Crossings*; Pernet, "Between Entanglements and Dependencies."

21. Escobar, "Power and Visibility," 434.

22. Richard Adams, Interview, August 10, 2014. See "The Goubaud Affair" in the John P. Gillin Papers, Box 10, Folder 13, Peabody Museum of Archaeology and Ethnology Archives for a detailed explanation of Goubaud's death. Official Guatemalan police report deemed his death a suicide, but family and friends feared foul play given recent tensions between Goubaud and the Arévalo administration in the months before his sudden death.

23. "Los orígenes del INCAP," *El Imparcial*, October 5, 1967. By 1954, Panama, Costa Rica, and Nicaragua had also joined; Scrimshaw, "Origins and Development of INCAP," 5.

24. "El Instituto de Nutrición (INCAP)," *El Imparcial*, September 28, 1967; "Función perenne del INCAP en Centroamérica quedó acordada," *El Imparcial*, December 19, 1959; CIRMA, Recortes de Prensa, La Morgue, Ramo—Salud, Folder INCAP—Instituto Nutrición su historia. "El INCAP y su historia" typed mimeograph, August 1954. INCAP was also under the direction of the Pan-American Sanitary Office, which in turn was a dependency of the World Health Organization.

25. "Tabla sobre composición de alimentos," *El Imparcial*, July 16, 1952.

26. RAP, *Censo de población 1950, tabulaciones preliminares*, May 9, 1951, 1:3. This does not appear to be an official census record but rather a document that one of Adams's students compiled in 1951 using the census categories and table.

27. RAP, Adams, February 17, 1951, 1:10.

28. Cueto, *Cold War, Deadly Fevers*, 13; Lewis, *Rethinking Indigenismo*, 83.

29. Adams, "Social Anthropology in INCAP," 153; RAP, Adams, March 6, 1951, 1:1; RAP, Berta Pineda, March 6, 1951, 1:1; RAP, Ana Díaz, February 7, 1951, 1:1; RAP, Pineda, March 6, 1951, 1:1.

30. RAP, Rosalio Saquic, April 27, 1951, 1:13.

31. Adams, Interview, August 10, 2014. See Foss, "*Una obra revolucionaria*," in *Out of the Shadow*, ed. Gibbings and Vrana, for further discussion of IING involvement and anthropologists' mediation of misunderstandings in Magdalena Milpas Altas.

32. RAP, Amir, April 17, 1951, 1:4.

33. RAP, Adams, February 17, 1951, 1:10.

34. RAP, Adams, February 2, 1951, 1:1; RAP, Adams, February 12, 1951, 1:1; RAP, Díaz, February 18, 1951, 1:1; RAP, Adams, February 20, 1951, 1:1.

35. RAP, Adams, February 20, 1951, 1:1; RAP, Hannstein, April 29, 1951, 1:1.

36. RAP, Adams, February 20, 1951, 1:1.

37. Carey Jr., *Our Elders Teach Us*, 195–97.

38. RAP, Adams, September 5, 1951, 1:13; RAP, Adams, August 5, 1951, 1:13.

39. RAP, Hannstein, June 30, 1952, 1:6.

40. RAP, Adams, August 30, 1951, 1:13.

41. RAP, Adams, September 9, 1951, 1:13.

42. RAP, Adams, February 17, 1951, 1:10.

43. RAP, Saquic, August 16, 1951, 1:13.

44. RAP, Adams, August 26, 1951, 1:11.

45. RAP, Adams, September 5, 1951, 1:12.

46. RAP, Saquic, July 21, 1951, 1:14.

47. RAP, Saquic, July 21, 1951, 1:14; RAP, Adams, August 5, 1951, 1:11.

48. RAP, Díaz, July 23, 1951, 1:2.

49. Freije and Nolan, "Interpretative Challenges in the Archive," 2.

50. Carey Jr., "Rethinking Representation," in *Out of the Shadow*, ed. Gibbings and Vrana.

51. RAP, Adams, February 6, 1951, 1:1.

52. RAP, Díaz, June 13, 1951, 1:2.

53. RAP, Díaz, June 13, 1951, 1:2.

54. RAP, Saquic, July 12, 1951, 1:14.

55. RAP, Saquic, August 14, 1951, 1:14; RAP, Díaz, August 13, 1951, 1:2.

56. RAP, Saquic, August 15, 1951, 1:14.

57. RAP, Díaz, August 14, 1951–August 19, 1951, 1:2.

58. RAP, Saquic, August 19, 1951, 1:14.

59. RAP, Díaz, September 4, 1951, 1:2.

60. RAP, Adams, September 3, 1951, 1:11.

61. RAP, Adams, February 17, 1951, 1:10.

62. RAP, Amir, April 28, 1951, 1:4.

63. RAP, Adams, February 17, 1951, 1:10.

64. RAP, Díaz, November 13, 1951, 1:2.

65. Saldaña-Portillo, *Revolutionary Imagination*, 27.

66. RAP, Díaz, November 30, 1951, 1:2.

67. Grandin, *Last Colonial Massacre*, 65.

68. RAP, Hannstein, June 20, 1952, 1:6; RAP, Hannstein, September 2, 1951, 1:6

69. RAP, Díaz, February 25, 1953, 1:2.

70. RAP, Hannstein, February 21, 1951, 1:6.

71. RAP, Hannstein, August 28. 1952, 1:7.

72. RAP, Hannstein, September 2, 1952, 1:7.

73. RAP, Hannstein, June 2, 1952, 1:6.

74. RAP, Díaz, January 29, 1951, 1:2.

75. RAP, Díaz, July 22, 1953, 1:2.

76. Dawson, *Indian and Nation*, 114.

77. Adams, *Joaquín Noval*, 15–16. José García Noval, Interview, October 16, 2015.

78. See Cátedra Joaquín Noval, comp. *Joaquín Noval* for a compilation of Noval's published and unpublished work.

79. Adams, *Joaquín Noval*, 16.

80. Adams, *Joaquín Noval*, 17; Noval, "Guatemala," 7; Grandin, *Last Colonial Massacre*, 120.

81. Archivo de Joaquín Noval, "Situación económica actual de los indígenas de Guatemala," (1965):1,13,5.https://docs.google.com/file/d/0BzFMOr10EFD0ZHZYZmk3RzZXUmc /edit.

82. IING, "La tenencia de la tierra en las regiones indígenas," *Boletín IING* 1, nos. 1–4, 2nd época (1957): 69.

83. Jaime Búcaro Archive, Doc. 61, IING, *Las migraciones indígenas internas en Guatemala* (Guatemala: Ministerio de Educación Pública, 1961), 16, 35–36, 42–44, 2.

84. Noval, "Actividades antropológicas, 112–13; Noval, "Informe del Instituto Indigenista Nacional de Guatemala: 1950," *Boletín Indigenista* 11 (1951); Joaquín Noval, "Informe del Instituto Indigenista Nacional de Guatemala: 1952," *Boletín Indigenista* 13 (1953).

85. Adams, *Joaquín Noval*, 17.

86. IBRD, *Economic Development of Guatemala*, 26, quoted in Gleijeses, *Shattered Hope*, 156.

87. Juan de Dios Rosales, "El crédito rural frente al problema indígena," *Boletín IING* 2, nos. 1–4, 2nd época (1960): 35.

88. De Dios Rosales, "El crédito rural," 36–37.

89. Handy, *Revolution in the Countryside*, 93.

90. CNPE, *Planificación económica*, 6.

91. Gleijeses, *Shattered Hope*, 150.

92. Gleijeses, *Shattered Hope*, 145.

93. Personal correspondence with José García Noval, February 18, 2018. I am grateful to Dr. García Noval for contacting Edgar Ruano Najarro, who interviewed Fortuny in Mexico in the 1980s about the possibility of Noval's involvement in the writing of Decree 900. Ruano confirmed that Noval was part of a second generation of PGT leadership and had more influence in the 1960s.

94. Grandin, *Last Colonial Massacre*, 52–53.

95. GOG, *Decreto 900*, June 17, 1952.

96. Handy, *Revolution in the Countryside*, 82, 89.

97. Way, *Mayan in the Mall*, 63.

98. Way, *Mayan in the Mall*, 150.

99. Chassé, "The Coastal Laboratory," in *Out of the Shadow*, ed. Gibbings and Vrana.

100. Handy, *Revolution in the Countryside*, 90.

101. Esquit, *Comunidad y nación*, 77.

102. Boyer, *Becoming Campesinos*, 20–23; Gould, *To Lead as Equals*, 7.

103. Foss, "Land and Labor Relations"; Forster, *Time of Freedom*; Handy, *Revolution in the Countryside*, 120–32; Grandin, "State Decomposition."

104. Gleijeses, *Shattered Hope*, 151–52; AGCA Hemeroteca, *Boletín Agraria*, año 1, no. 1 (August 1953); Grandin, *Last Colonial Massacre*, 54.

105. *Informe del ciudadano presidente de la república, coronel Jacobo Árbenz Guzmán* (1953), 9–10, quoted in Handy, *Revolution in the Countryside*, 92.

106. Handy, *Revolution in the Countryside*, 94. Handy bases this calculation on his extensive reviews of all the *Decreto 900* records. Piero Gleijeses references secondary literature and cites the larger number, 1.4 million acres, *Shattered Hope*, 155–56.

107. Gleijeses, *Shattered Hope*, 158–59; Handy, *Revolution in the Countryside*, 95.

108. AGCA Hemeroteca, *Boletín Agraria*, año 1, no. 2 (September 1953).

109. Gleijeses, *Shattered Hope*, 211–12.

110. Clemente Marroquín Rojas, "El case del diputado José Luis Arenas R.," *La Hora*, February 27, 1954, quoted in Gleijeses, *Shattered Hope*, 216.

111. Untitled advertisement, *El Imparcial*, June 5, 1952, quoted in Handy, *Revolution in the Countryside*, 100.

112. Guardino, *Peasants, Politics*.

113. GOG, *Sexto censo*, 8–10.

114. GOG, *Censo agropecuario 1950*, Tomo III, 153.

115. San Jacinto is located in Chimaltenango, right along the departmental border with Sacatepéquez. Santa María de Jesús, the town under whose jurisdiction the finca fell and from which other petitioners came, is located in Sacatepéquez.

116. AGCA, *Decreto 900*, Sacatepéquez, "Nacimiento El Hato," 2:5 (Paquete:Expediente). All AGCA records in this section come from the Decreto 900, Sacatepéquez records.

117. "Nacimiento el Hato."

118. Esquit, *Otros poderes*, 194–95.

119. Antonio Goubaud Carrera, "Las vitrinas de la alimentación indígena en el nuevo museo," *El Imparcial*, January 10, 1948; Carlos Soza Barillas, "Nuestro grave problema combatir la tuberculosis," *El Imparcial*, August 20, 1945.

120. José C. Díaz Duran, "La subsistencia del trabajador rural," *El Imparcial*, August 21, 1945.

121. Díaz Duran, "La subsistencia."

122. Carey Jr., "'Heart of the Country.'"

123. AGCA, El Portal, 1:10.

124. CIRMA, DOC DES 92, AMEmbassy Guatemala to Dept. of State, Despatch #75, "Mass Arrests of 'Communist' Peasant Leaders," July 29, 1954.

125. AGCA, La Azotea, 2:4.

126. Gibbings, *Our Time Is Now*, 343–51; Foss, "Land and Labor Relations," 11–12; Handy, *Revolution in the Countryside*, 123; Esquit, *Comunidad y estado*, 54.

127. The figure of sixty-five properties is referenced in a JAD report for El Tigre y Pachali, 4:1. In the file for Finca Los Tulipanes, records from the Dirección General de Rentas indicate the Herrera Hermanos held properties in Sacatepéquez, Chimaltenango, El Quiché, Guatemala, Escuintla, and Huehuentenango. 1A:9.

128. AGCA, Las Flores, 3:4.

129. AGCA, El Tigre y anexos Pachali, 4:1.

130. AGCA, El Pilar, 4:12.

131. AGCA, San Francisco Las Flores, 2:2.

132. See Olsson, *Agrarian Crossings*, for a discussion of transnational collaborations in agricultural modernization schemes.

133. AGCA, Florencia, 3:1.

134. AGCA, Los Tulipanes, 1a:9.

135. AGCA, Rejón #4, 4:5.
136. AGCA, Monte María, 1:7.
137. AGCA, El Naranjo, 4:4.
138. AGCA, San Rafael, 1:3.

Chapter Four

1. CIRMA, DOC DES 92, Foreign Service Despatch from AmEmbassy, Guatemala to Department of State, Despatch No. 75. July 29, 1954. Subject: Mass Arrests of "Communist" Peasant Leaders; Stokes Newbold, "Receptivity to Communist Fomented Agitation."

2. Adams, *Joaquín Noval*, 36.

3. Adams, *Joaquín Noval*, 36; Adams, Interview, August 10, 2014; García Noval, Interview, October 22, 2015. Adams asserted that it was Skinner Klee who arranged Noval's release due to their friendship despite drastic political differences. García Noval could not confirm, but he did find the possibility plausible, as he said that Noval always strived to maintain courteous relationships with colleagues of all political persuasions.

4. Cátedra Joaquín Noval, *Joaquín Noval: una antología*.

5. Schlesinger and Kinzer, *Bitter Fruit*; Cullather, *Secret History*; Gleijeses, *Shattered Hope*; Immerman, *CIA in Guatemala*.

6. Taracena Arriola, *Etnicidad, estado y nación*, vol. II, 55–56; Pérez Molina, "Desarrollo de la antropología guatemalteca," 175; Dary, "El estado y los indígenas," 120–21; Adams y Bastos, *Las relaciones étnicas*, 157.

7. Vrana and Gibbings, "Introduction," in *Out of the Shadow*, ed. Gibbings and Vrana, 8, 17.

8. Grandin, *Last Colonial Massacre*, xv.

9. Grandin, *Last Colonial Massacre*, 70.

10. Chastain and Lorek, eds., *Itineraries of Expertise*; Birn and Necochea López, eds., *Peripheral Nerve*.

11. Black, *Garrison Guatemala*, 17.

12. Immerman, *CIA in Guatemala*; Cullather, *Secret History*.

13. Handy, *Revolution in the Countryside*, 94.

14. Schlesinger and Kinzer, *Bitter Fruit*, 19–20.

15. Despite this use of a pen name, rumors circulated in Guatemala (and continue to do so) that Richard Adams worked for the Central Intelligence Agency. There is no evidence to support this, and Adams believes these rumors to be based on the fact that he helped to conduct this study and because he held a diplomatic visa at the time. Adams, Interview, August 10, 2014. My thanks to Marc Becker for pointing out the significance of "Stokes Newbold."

16. Newbold, "Receptivity to Communist Fomented Agitation," 361.

17. CIRMA, DOC DES 92, Foreign Service Despatch, from AmEmbassy, Guatemala, to Department of State. Despatch Number 75. July 29, 1954. Subject: Mass Arrests of "Communist" Peasant Leaders. Emphasis in original.

18. Murray Li, *Will to Improve*, 10; Buckley, *Technocrats and the Politics of Drought*, 6.

19. CIRMA, DOC DES 69, Office Memorandum, July 8, 1954, ARA Mr. Holland to ARA Robert F. Woodward, "Methods of Encouraging Democratic Government in Guatemala."

20. Grandin, *Empire's Workshop*; Streeter, "The Failure of 'Liberal Developmentalism'" 386.

21. Pacino, "Constructing a New Bolivian Society," 33–37; Larson, "Capturing Indian Bodies."

22. Streeter, *Managing the Counterrevolution*, 139–41.

23. Black, *Garrison Guatemala*, 2.

24. CIRMA, DOC DES 135. Memorandum of Conversation between Mr. Samuel Waugh, Henry Holland, and Robert L. Garner, September 10, 1954.

25. CIRMA, DOC DES 143, Thomas Mann to Raymond G. Leddy, September 17, 1954.

26. GOG, *Plan de Desarrollo Económico 1955–1960*, 2.

27. CIRMA, DOC DES 367, Memorandum of Conversation dated April 24, 1956. Subject: Guatemala: IBRD and Klein & Saks Missions.

28. Streeter, "Failure of 'Liberal Developmentalism,'" 393; CIRMA, DOC DES 367, Memorandum of Conversation, Subject: Guatemala: IBRD and Klein & Saks Missions, April 24, 1956; CIRMA, DOC DES 362, Memorandum of Conversation, Subject: Guatemala: Relations between Klein & Saks Mission and American Embassy, April 24, 1956.

29. CIRMA, DOC DES 362, Memorandum of Conversation, April 24, 1956, Subject: Guatemala: Relations between Klein & Saks Mission and American Embassy.

30. GOG, *Plan de Desarrollo Económico 1955–1960*, 8–9. See Way, *Mayan in the Mall*, 99–104, for a detailed analysis of the highway project.

31. GOG, *Plan de Desarrollo*, 18, 24; NARA, RG 59, 1955–1959 Central Decimal File, Box 4212, Despatch, Subject: Plans of INFOP and the Banco Nacional Agrario, dated February 18, 1955, 814.20/2-1855; NARA, RG 59, 1955–1959 Central Decimal Files Box 4215, Despatch, February 1, 1957, Subject: Guatemalan Official Emphasis on Social Problems: the "Arenas Affair," 814.40/2-157.

32. NARA, RG 59, 1955–1959 Central Decimal File, Box No. 4211, 814.16/8-2857. Despatch by Oscar M. Powell, Subject: Memorandum of Conversation with Acting President Luis Arturo Gonzalez Lopez of Guatemala on Rural Resettlement Program, August 28, 1957.

33. NARA, RG 59, 1955–1959 Central Decimal File, Box 4215, Memorandum of Conversation, June 9, 1958. Subject: Interview with Minister of Public Health of Guatemala, Participants—Dr. Mariano López Herrarte (minister), Mr. William A. Wieland, Director, Office of Middle America Affairs, Mr. Bayard King, Guatemala Desk officer, ARA Mr. Henry A. Hoyt. 814.55/6-958.

34. III, "Informe de Guatemala," *Boletín del Instituto Indigenista Interamericano* 15 (1955): 56. I am indebted to Professor Roberto Melville of CIESAS in Mexico City for gaining access to the archives of the III and transcribing all the *informes* from Guatemala for 1945–1960.

35. IING, "Un dictamen favorable," *Boletín IING* 1, nos. 1–4, 2a época (1957): 23–24. This boletín was written in 1955 but went unpublished until 1957.

36. IING, "Reorganización del Instituto," *Boletín IING* 1, nos. 1–4, 2a época (1957): 23–24.

37. Carey Jr., *Oral History in Latin America*, 105.

38. Carey argues that oral life history allows for narrators to "think about change over time," (Carey Jr., *Oral History in Latin America*, 170). Over the course of many hours of both guided and more open interviews with Don Francisco and Doña Hélida, it became clear that taken together, the series of interviews fit this categorization of life history, as they

wove personal stories alongside details of their professional work. Thus, in this section, I have analyzed them as such.

39. Portelli, *Death of Luigi Trastulli*, 2.

40. Rodríguez Rouanet, Interview, August 12, 2014; Rodríguez Rouanet, Interview, July 31, 2015; Rodríguez Rouanet, Interview, September 18, 2015.

41. Cabrera, Interview, September 21, 2015.

42. James, *Doña María's Story*, 152.

43. FRRA, *Una Vida*, unpublished memoir, 1999, with an addition in 2006; Rodríguez Rouanet, Interview, August 6, 2015; Rodríguez Rouanet, Interview, August 28, 2015.

44. IING, "Reorganización del Instituto," 28.

45. Cabrera, Interview, September 19, 2015; Cabrera, Interview, September 20, 2015.

46. IING, "Reorganización del Instituto," 28.

47. Rodríguez Rouanet, Interview, August 12, 2014.

48. Way, *Mayan in the Mall*; Streeter, *Managing the Counterrevolution*.

49. Cullather, *Hungry World*, 77.

50. Cullather, *Hungry World*, 77–79; Immerwahr, *Thinking Small*, 52. Chapter 1 of Immerwahr traces the early roots of community development initiatives in urban American areas.

51. Immerwahr, *Thinking Small*, 54.

52. Murray Li, *Will to Improve*, 12.

53. Girón Cerna, *Aldeas de cristal*, 131.

54. Terga and Vásquez Robles, *Tactic "el corazón del mundo,"* 47.

55. Terga and Vásquez Robles, 46–47.

56. Jaime Búcaro Moraga, "Por el mejoramiento integral de las comunidades indígenas," *El Imparcial*, August 11, 1959.

57. FRRA, Francisco Rodríguez Rouanet, "Proyecto de Mejoramiento Integral de Tactic, Alta Verapaz (PMIT)," April 2002, 3.

58. Dary, "El estado y los indígenas," 124; Pérez Molina, "Desarrollo de la Antropología Guatemalteca," 178–79.

59. FRRA, Rodríguez, "Resumen de las actividades del PMIT durante la permanencia del Jefe de Planificación e Investigaciones Técnicas como Coordinador Interino, en Tactic, Alta Verapaz," November 29, 1958.

60. AMT, 4:26 (Libro:Acta), July 29, 1955.

61. FRRA, Rodríguez, "PMIT," 2002, 6.

62. AMT, 4:14, May 20, 1955.

63. AMT, 5:3, February 7, 1958.

64. The municipal record details these measurements in varas and cuadras, with the school lot being 1 cuadra of 30 varas and the communal land plot being 3 cuadras of 26 varas. The square foot equivalent is approximately 6,757 square feet and 15,480 square feet, respectively.

65. Paz Lemus, *Enacting Youth*, 51.

66. AMT, 4:14, May 20, 1955.

67. AMT, 5:49, September 30, 1958.

68. IING, "Plan de mejoramiento integral de una comunidad indígena," *Boletín del IING* 2, nos. 1–4, 2a época (1960): 76–77.

69. Margarita Wendell, "En torno a un programa de alfabetización bilingüe: un año en el proyecto de Tactic," *Guatemala Indígena* 2, no. 3 (1962): 129, 132; Juan de Dios Rosales, "Informe del Instituto Indigenista Nacional de Guatemala: 1959," *Boletín Indigenista* 20 (1960).

70. Wendell, "En turno a un programa," 133, 139.

71. Carey Jr. notes this trend for Kaqchikel girls and school attendance in *Engendering Mayan History*, 178.

72. Wendell, "En torno a un programa," 134–35.

73. Both the 1945 and the 1956 Constitution designated Spanish (and only Spanish) as the national language; Maxwell, "The Path Back to Literacy," in *After the Coup*, ed. Smith and Adams, 118.

74. Dawson, *Indian and Nation*, 35.

75. FRRA, Field notes, May 20, 1957.

76. FRRA, Field notes, May 17, 1957, May 19, 1957. One entry reported how discord between the two local schools prevented effective collaboration in raising funds for the Red Cross. When one school hosted a sports exhibition to raise funds, the other school refused to collaborate and even kept students in school late so that they could not attend the program.

77. FRRA, Field notes, April 24, 1957.

78. FRRA, Field notes, May 1, 1957; Rodríguez Rouanet, Interview, September 8, 2015.

79. For sources on latrine construction, see FRRA, Rodríguez, "PMIT," 14; Francisco Rodríguez Rouanet, "Resumen . . . ," 6; FRRA, Field Notes, May 20, 1957. For sources on midwife training, see AMT, 5:28, July 22, 1957; AMT, 5:31, August 23, 1957; AMT, 5:17, April 30, 1958; Carey Jr., *Engendering Mayan History*, 44.

80. Carey Jr., *Engendering Mayan History*, 45.

81. See Reverby, "Ethical Failures and History Lessons"; and Crafts, *Mining Bodies*; Rodríguez Rouanet, Interview, September 8, 2015; FRRA, Field Notes, April 14, 1957.

82. Rodríguez Rouanet, Interview, September 19, 2015.

83. Rodríguez Rouanet, Interview, September 8, 2015.

84. FRRA, Field notes, April 29, 1957.

85. FRRA, Field notes, April 24, 1957, April 29, 1957.

86. FRRA, Field notes, May 30, 1957.

87. FRRA, Field notes, May 28, 1957, May 17, 1957.

88. FRRA, Field notes, April 24, 1957.

89. FRRA, "Resumen . . . ," 2; FRRA, Rodríguez, "PMIT," 13.

90. Carey Jr., "Guatemala's Green Revolution"; Chassé, "The Coastal Laboratory," in *Out of the Shadow*, ed. Gibbings and Vrana.

91. Ministerio de Economía, *Política Económica del Gobierno de Liberación*, 22.

92. Streeter, *Managing the Counterrevolution*, 155. Streeter cites this report as the "Minotto Briefing" from 1956 to 1959.

93. Lewis, *Rethinking Mexican Indigenismo*, chapter 4.

94. FRRA, Field notes, May 11, 1957.

95. FRRA, Field notes, May 11, 1957.

96. FRRA, Field notes, May 17, 1957.

97. In 2016, I did several oral histories with older residents in Tactic, but none remembered the PMIT project, as they had been very young children at the time.

98. AMT, 5:59, January 12, 1959.

99. "Proyecto de Tactic," *El Imparcial*, May 15, 1959.

100. Jaime Búcaro Moraga, "Por el mejoramiento integral de las comunidades indígenas II," *El Imparcial*, August 12, 1959.

101. FRRA, Rodríguez, "PMIT," 12.

102. FRRA, Rodríguez, "PMIT," 13.

103. Archivo Legislativo del Congreso de la República de Guatemala, *Diario de Sesiones del Congreso de la República de Guatemala*, October 29, 1958, 8–11.

104. FRRA, Rodríguez, "PMIT," 13.

105. AMT, 5:33, June 24, 1960; 5:34, June 28, 1960.

106. Miguel Peláez Morales, Interview, Tactic, September 1, 2016.

107. MinEd, *Memoria del Segundo Congreso Nacional de Educación*, October 22–30, 1956, Guatemala City (1957): 45–46.

108. MinEd, GOG, *Memoria de Labores* (July 1966–June 1967): 2.

109. MinEd, GOG, *Memoria de Labores* (July 1971–June 1972): 28.

110. MinEd, GOG, *Memoria de Labores* (July 1970–June 1971): 76–77. The Guatemalan Quetzal was 1:1 with the U.S. dollar at the time.

111. MinEd, GOG, *Memoria de Labores* (July 1970–June 1971), 77.

112. MinEd, GOG, *Memoria de Labores* (July 1970–June 1971), 77.

113. NARA, RG 286, P 376 Container 29, Folder "Social and Institutional Development FY 1969," Report by Mr. Robert E. Culbertson, Director, "Possible Use of Excess FY 70 Funds," March 6, 1970.

114. MinEd, GOG, *Memoria de Labores* (July 1966–June 1967): 51; MinEd, GOG, *Memoria de Labores* (July 1971–June 1972): 61; MinEd, GOG, *Memoria de Labores* (July 1974–June 1975): 161.

115. MinEd, GOG, *Memoria de Labores* (July 1978–June 1979): 119.

116. CNPE, *La planificación en Guatemala*.

117. Cueto, *Cold War, Deadly Fevers*, 9.

Chapter Five

1. An earlier version of a portion of this chapter was published as Foss, "Community Development in Cold War Guatemala: Not a Revolution but an Evolution," *Latin America and the Global Cold War*, ed. Thomas C. Field Jr., Stella Krepp, and Vanni Pettinà (Chapel Hill: University of North Carolina Press, 2000), 123–47. Many thanks to The University of North Carolina Press for its kind permission to utilize this material here.

2. Dillingham, *Oaxaca Resurgent*, 26.

3. Sackley, "Village as Cold War Site," 482.

4. "Trabajos en Chimaltenango y en Parte de Sacatepéquez," *El Imparcial*, November 12, 1964.

5. Sackley, "Village as Cold War Site," 490.

6. Gibbings, *Our Time Is Now*, 4–5.

7. Latham, *Right Kind of Revolution*.

8. Keller, *Cuba, the United States*; Harmer, *Allende's Chile*; Sarzynski, *Revolution in the Terra do Sol*; Brands, *Latin America's Cold War*.

9. Adolph Berle, *Navigating the Rapids, 1918–1971: From the Papers of Adolf A. Berle* (New York: Harcourt Brace Jovanovich, 1973), 729, quoted in Rabe, *Most Dangerous*, 22.

10. JFK, Papers of John F. Kennedy, Presidential Papers, President's Office Files, Countries, Guatemala: General, 1962, letter from Ydígoras Fuentes to Kennedy, July 4, 1962.

11. JFK, White House Central Subject Files, Series 7: Countries, Box 57, Folder Co: Guatemala (CO 97): Executive, cable, Ydígoras to Kennedy, October 29, 1962.

12. José R. Castro, "Desarrollo de la Comunidad," *El Imparcial*, December 6, 1965; "Declaration of Punta del Este: August 17, 1961," *Inter-American relations*, compiled by Sklar and Hagen. http://avalon.law.yale.edu/20th_century/intam15.asp; Ministerio de Gobernación de Guatemala, *Decreto Ley 296*, November 24, 1964.

13. JFK, Papers of Arthur M. Schlesinger Jr., White House Files, Classified Subject Files, Box 40, Folder: Latin America General, 1962, "Guidelines for Policy and Operations in Latin America," Department of State, May 1962.

14. JFK, "Address at a White House Reception for Members of Congress and for the Diplomatic Corps of the Latin American Republics," March 13, 1961. https://www.jfklibrary .org/archives/other-resources/john-f-kennedy-speeches/latin-american-diplomats -washington-dc-19610313. For contemporary examples of similar initiatives, see Immerwahr, *Thinking Small*, especially chapters 3 and 4 for a discussion of the Etawah project and the Filipino community development program, respectively; Sackley, "Village Models; Pribilsky, "Development and the 'Indian Problem.'"

15. JFK, Papers of John F. Kennedy, Presidential papers, President's Office Files, Countries, Guatemala: General 1961, "Consideraciones y respuestas del Gobierno de Guatemala, C.A. al discurso del Excelentísimo señor John F. Kennedy, pronunciado el 13 de abril de 1961, exponiendo su "Plan Kennedy," para el Desarrollo y Modernización de la América Latina." The date in this title is incorrect; the speech actually took place on March 13, 1961.

16. John F. Kennedy, "JFK Address at the UN General Assembly," September 25, 1961.

17. JFK, George W. Ball Papers, Box 5, Folder Guatemala March 15, 1962–March 19, 1962.

18. CIRMA, DOC DES, No. 734, Memorandum to Mr. McGeorge Mundy, Subject: "Guatemala," January 21, 1963; JFK, Papers of President Kennedy, National Security Files, Countries, Box 101a, Folder: Guatemala: General January 1963–March 1963, Telegram from Guatemala City to Secretary of State, March 15, 1963.

19. JFK, Papers of President Kennedy, National Security Files, Countries, Box 101a, Folder: Guatemala: General January 1963–March 1963, Telegram from Guatemala City to Secretary of State, March 15, 1963; US Embassy cable from March 31, 1963; JFK, National Security Files, Countries, Box 101a, Folder: Guatemala, General April 1963–July 1963, outgoing telegram from State to AMEmbassy Guatemala.

20. Rabe, *Most Dangerous Area*, 73–76.

21. CNPE, *La planificación en Guatemala*, 16, 21, 10.

22. NARA, RG 59, A5730, Bureau of Inter-American Affairs/Office of Central American Affairs, Records Relating to Guatemala, 1956–1975, Container 16, Folder "Action Plan for Guatemala 1968–1969," Action Memorandum for the Administrator, from James R. Fowler, Deputy U.S. Coordinator, Alliance for Progress.

23. NARA, RG 59, AI 5730, Container 12, Folder "Economic Affairs (gen) Land Reform Guatemala 1966," letter from Charles R. Burrows to Lincoln Gordon, Subject "Rural

Development in Guatemala," October 7, 1966. Gordon had just returned from serving as ambassador to Brazil; in 1967, he became president of Johns Hopkins University.

24. NARA, RG 59, A1 5730. Bureau of Inter-American Affairs/Office of Central American Affairs, Records Relating to Guatemala, 1956–1975, Container #13, Folder - General Reports, Statistics, Background, Guatemala 1966, *Secret - Summary and Conclusions*.

25. Way, *Mayan in the Mall*, 91.

26. NARA, RG 286, P367 Container 2 Guate: Subject Files, Folder: Community Development, Ernest F. Witte, "Community Development in Selected Countries," *Community Development Review. Special Issue: 1962 International Conference of Social Work, from the Community Development Division of USAID* 7, no. 1 (June 1962): 1–2, 8–9.

27. See Offner, *Mixed Economy*, chapter 3 for a detailed analysis of self-help housing initiatives throughout the Americas.

28. NARA, RG 286, P367 Container 2 Guate: Subject Files, 1961–63, Folder: Community Development, J. Sheldon Turner, "The Fifth Freedom," *Community Development Review. Special Issue: 1962 International Conference of Social Work, from the Community Development Division of USAID* 7, no. 1 (June 1962): 64.

29. SBS, *Programa Integral de Desarrollo de la Comunidad para Guatemala de la Jefatura de Gobierno*, #3 Colección Bienestar Social y Desarrollo de la Comunidad (Guatemala: 1964), 19.

30. NARA, RG 59, A1 5730. Bureau of Inter-American Affairs/Office of Central American Affairs, Records Relating to Guatemala, 1956–1975, Container #13, Folder - General Reports, Statistics, Background, Guatemala 1966, Secret - Summary and Conclusions.

31. GOG, *Decreto-Ley Número 296*, November 24, 1964.

32. Foss, "Community Development in Cold War Guatemala"; Simpson, *Economists with Guns*; Field, *From Development to Dictatorship*; Leacock, *Requiem for Revolution*.

33. NARA, RG 286, P367, Guate: Subject Files, 61–63, Container 2, Folder: Community Development, Letter from Taylor Peck (Acting Public Affairs Officer) to USIA, June 7, 1962.

34. Way, *Mayan in the Mall*, 79.

35. "Homenaje a Elisa de Stahl se prepara en Quezaltenango," *El Imparcial*, June 10, 1960; "Un discurso de Elisa Molina de Stahl, Hija predilecta de Quezaltenango," *El Imparcial*, December 18, 1953; "Doble homenaje de simpatía a la señora Elisa Molina de Stahl en un gesto de reconocimiento," *El Imparcial*, October 3, 1959.

36. León Aguilera, "Mujer fuerte de la Biblia," *El Imparcial*, January 8, 1960; Romelia Alarcón Folgar, "Doña Elisa Molina de Stahl o las hadas existen," *El Imparcial*, February 2, 1964.

37. Poston, *Democracy Speaks Many Tongues*, 1.

38. Arcadio Ruiz Franco, "Personajes inolvidables—Doctor Salvador Hernández Villalobos," *El Imparcial*, January 11, 1972.

39. Rodolfo Martínez Ferraté, Interview, November 21, 2016.

40. SBS) Departamento Personal, Planillas de Sueldos, January–June 1965; SBS, Departamento Personal, Planillas de Sueldos, April–June 1966.

41. "Actos en San Martín Jilotepéque en la inauguración del centro local acción conjunta para el desarrollo de la comunidad," *El Imparcial*, February 5, 1965; "400 centros de alfabetización de adultos por la acción conjunta," *El Imparcial*, July 17, 1965; "Acción conjunta en

Joyabaj," *El Imparcial,* December 1965; "Acción conjunta en Chiatá," *El Imparcial,* September 6, 1965.

42. Martínez Ferraté, Interview.

43. "Guatemala encabeza desarrollo de la comunidad en América; constancias en la II Reunión Regional," *El Imparcial,* June 21, 1965.

44. "Colaboración mutual en mes," *El Imparcial,* February 24, 1966.

45. Dunkerley, *Power in the Isthmus,* 448–49.

46. Beckett, *Modern Insurgencies and Counterinsurgencies,* 172; National Security Archive, NSA Electronic Briefing Book No. 11, *U.S. Policy in Guatemala, 1966–1996* by Kate Doyle and Carlos Osorio, Document 4, U.S. Department of State, Intelligence Note, October 23, 1967, "Guatemala: A Counter-Insurgency Running Wild?" https://nsarchive2.gwu.edu /NSAEBB/NSAEBB11/docs/doc04.pdf.

47. GOG, *Decreto-Ley 1642,* November 3, 1967; AGCA, Secretaría de Asuntos Sociales, Dirección Administrativo, Paquete 1, Tomo 4, "Cuadro Comparativo de Presupuesto para 1966," Año 1964–1968; SBS, Departamento Personal, Planillas de Sueldos, January–June 1965; Ministerio de Gobernación de Guatemala, Acuerdo Gubernativo de November 3, 1967. The Quetzal was pegged 1:1 to the U.S. dollar during this time.

48. AGCA, Secretaría de Asuntos Sociales, Dirección Administrativo, Paquete: No. 2, "Dirección Administrativa, 1965–68, Oficios, Providencias, Documentación Miscelánea," Emigdio Falla González to Dirección del SBS, November 22, 1968; Emigdio Falla González to Directora de Bienestar Infantil y Familiar, August 29, 1968; Emigdio Falla González to Dirección de SBS, May 28, 1968; Emigdio Falla González to the Dirección del SBS, May 29, 1969; Emigdio Falla González to the Jefe del Departamento Administrativo, May 8, 1968. These records are uncatalogued at the AGCA.

49. AGCA, Secretaría de Asuntos Sociales, Dirección Administrativo, Paquete: No. 2, "Dirección Administrativa, 1965–68, Oficios, Providencias, Documentación Miscelánea." Untitled document referencing this Acuerdo Gubernativo from February 24, 1966.

50. Columbia University Special Collections, International Institute for Rural Reconstruction (IIRR), 26:920, "Unificarán esfuerzos con Bienestar Social," *Prensa Libre,* August 9, 1966; IIRR, "Del Manejo de Fondos en Bienestar Social," *Prensa Libre,* August 9, 1966.

51. Rodolfo Martínez Ferraté, *Una política rural para el Desarrollo* (Solidarios: Dominican Republic, 1974).

52. Martínez Ferraté, Interview.

53. NARA, USAID Records, RG 286, Entry # P376: Guatemala Central Subject Files: 1964–1978, Container #19, Department of State Air Pouch - from AmEmbassy Guatemala - Economic Summary - Guatemala - First Quarter 1967.

54. NARA, RG 286, P383 Subject Files: 1963–1981, USAID Mission to Guatemala/Program Office, Container #7, Folder PRM - 187 Rural Comm. Leadership and Modernization - ProAgs, FY 1967, Project Agreement 67–7, Project Title: Rural Community Leadership and Modernization (Rural Development, Zacapa and Izabal), April 6, 1967.

55. NARA, RG 59, Bureau of Inter-American Affairs/Office of Central American Affairs, A1 5730: Records Relating to Guatemala, 1956–1975, Container #12, Folder: Economic Affairs (gen) Land Reform Guatemala 1966, Letter from Charles R. Burrows to Lincoln Gordon, Subject "Rural Development in Guatemala," October 7, 1966.

56. NARA, RG 286, P 376: Guatemala Central Subject Files: 1964–1978, Container 19 Folder called PRM 7-2 International Organizations, FY 67, Airgram, Department of State, to AID Circular, Subject: Final AID Appraisal of Requested United Nations Development Programs/Special Fund Projects.

57. NARA, RG 286, P 383 Subject Files 1963–1981, Container 9, Folder PRM Special Development Fund.

58. McCreery, *Rural Guatemala*, 220; Esquit, *Otros poderes*, 212; Taracena Arriola, et al., *Etnicidad, estado y nación*, vol. 1, 286–87.

59. NARA RG 286, P 591, Project Files: 1975–1978, USAID Mission to Guatemala/Program Office, Container #7, Folder - Social and Institutional Development, FY 1976, Letter from Jesus Espinoza Guerra to US Ambassador, August 5, 1975. Espinoza is referring to Edgar Mitchell, Alan Shepard, and Stuart Roosa.

60. NARA, RG 286, P 591 Project Files 1975–1978 Container #4, Folder: SOC: Social and institutional Development, letter from Bartolomé de la Cruz R. to US Ambassador, December 9, 1974.

61. NARA, RG 286, P 591 Project Files 1975–1978 Container #4, Folder: SOC: Social and institutional Development, letter from Orlando Valladares Menéndez to US Ambassador, January 15, 1975.

62. Rodas Pineda, *Estudio del municipio de Jacaltenango*, 46.

63. Based on 1964 census records, all these departments had an Indigenous population greater than 50 percent, with the exception of Jalapa (44 percent). The only department with a majority ladino population where the DESCOM would expand by 1981 was El Progreso.

64. GOG, Departamento de Estadística, Censo de 1964, 104.

65. Gladys Gamboa de Fernández, Interview, September 1, 2016; Emilio Vásquez Robles, Interview, September 3, 2016.

66. Rogelio Bin Quej, Interview, September 24, 2016.

67. Terga and Vásquez, *Tactic*.

68. AMT, Libros de Actas, 8:252 (Book:Acta), June 19, 1971. All AMT records from the Libros de Actas.

69. Terga and Vásquez, *Tactic*, 83.

70. Vásquez, Interview.

71. Miguel Peláez Martínez, Interview, September 2, 2016.

72. Vásquez, Interview; Martínez Ferraté, Interview; Gamboa, Interview. The informant is uncertain about this date, but other interviews confirmed that the DESCOM's work diminished in the early 1980s due to the civil war and then left Tactic by the mid-1980s.

73. Bin Quej, Interview.

74. Vásquez, Interview.

75. Gamboa, Interview.

76. Heriberto Isem, Interview, September 24, 2016; Alberto Bin, Interview, September 24, 2016.

77. Isem, Interview; Terga and Vásquez, *Tactic*, 82.

78. AMT, 9:17, September 3, 1971; Bin, Interview.

79. AMT, 9:2, July 25, 1971.

80. AMT, 9:8, February 15, 1972.

81. AMT, 9:41, September 12, 1972.

82. Terga and Vásquez, *Tactic*, 82–83; AMT, 9:17, September 3, 1971.

83. Terga and Vásquez, *Tactic*, 82–83.

84. Terga and Vásquez, *Tactic*, 77.

85. AMT, 9:16, April 13, 1972.

86. Rogelio Bin Quej, Interview by Aracely Cahuec, September 2016.

87. Bin Quej, Interview; Enrique Tun, Interview by Aracey Cahuec, September 2016; "592 Obras Realizadas por Desarrollo de la Comunidad," *El Imparcial*, April 16, 1975.

88. Isem, Interview. Isem did not recall exactly when this decision took place, but later stated that he was around nineteen years old, dating this conflict to the mid-1970s. No other interviewees from Pasmolón recalled this conflict, and there are no pertinent records in the municipal archive.

89. Cullather, *Hungry World*, 8.

90. Carey Jr., "'Heart of the Country.'"

91. Terga and Vásquez, *Tactic*, 69.

92. Terga and Vásquez, *Tactic*, 78.

93. Terga and Vásquez, *Tactic*, 63–65.

94. Terga and Vásquez, *Tactic*, 65.

95. Martínez Ferraté, *Una política rural*, 7, 14, 97–118.

96. Copeland, "Greening the Counterinsurgency," 985–86; Martínez Ferrate, *Una política rural*, 126; JFK, Collection 184: Returned Peace Corps Volunteer Collection, Series 035, Box 37, Folder: Guatemala: 1968–1970 Windrem, Peter.

97. Smith and Foster, *Los Aportes de la Sociología*, 20–21.

98. NARA, RG 59 Department of State, Bureau of Inter-American Affairs/Office of Central American Affairs, Entry #A1 5730 Records Relating to Guatemala 1956–1975, Container #14, Folder IRG/COIN (April–June) 1968 Guatemala, Secret Memorandum, from Richard Bernhart to Mr. Albert L. Brown, dated April 22, 1968.

99. Copeland, "Greening the Counterinsurgency, 986.

100. Way, *Agrotropolis*.

101. See Olsson, *Agrarian Crossings*, Buckley, *Technocrats and the Politics of Drought*.

102. AMT, 9:9, September 25, 1971.

103. AMT, 9:44, October 17, 1972.

104. Carlos Salomon López Cantoral, Interview, September 2, 2016; Isem, Interview, Otilia Isem Cir, Interview, September 23, 2016.

105. AMT, 9:44, October 17, 1972; Gamboa, Interview; Lesli Magdalena Guzmán, Interview, September 1, 2016; López, Interview; Isem, Interview; Otilia Isem Sierra, Interview, September 23, 2016; Bin, Interview; Bin Quej, Interview; María Hercilia Cantoral Hernández, Interview, September 24, 2016.

106. Bin Quej, Interview by Cahuec.

107. Peláez Martínez, Interview.

108. López, Interview.

109. Terga and Vásquez, *Tactic*, 64.

110. López, Interview.

111. Tun, Interview by Cahuec.

112. Carey Jr., "Guatemala's Green Revolution."

113. Bin, Interview.

114. Terga and Vásquez, *Tactic*, 79.

115. Terga and Vásquez, *Tactic*, 75.

116. Terga and Vásquez, *Tactic*, 55–56.

117. Ricardo Terga, Interview, February 27, 2017.

118. Gamboa, Interview.

119. Fidelina Xuc Buc de Elías, Interview, September 24, 2016.

120. AMT, 9:4, August 3, 1971.

121. Isem, Interview; Bin, Interview.

122. Onofre Bin, Interview by Aracely Cahuec, September 2016.

123. Figueroa Arriola, *San Rafael el Arado*, 58.

124. Figueroa Arriola, *San Rafael el Arado*, 28–56.

125. RAC, RG 1.7 Project Files, Series 319, Box 1035, Folder 7033, Carroll Behrhorst, "The Chimaltenango Development Project, Guatemala," *Contact 19*, 1974.

126. RAC, RG 1.7 Project Files, Series 319, Box 1035, Folder 7032, "Movimiento guatemalteco de reconstrucción rural," February 2, 1974.

127. RAC, RG 1.7 Project Files, Series 319, Box 1035, Folder 7032, Interviews, SWA, Subjects: Guatemalan Rural Development, February 8, 1974.

128. Copeland, "Regarding Development," 424, 433.

129. Esquit, *La superación del indígena*, 314.

Chapter Six

1. A small portion of the background information on the Ixcán Grande colony appears in Foss, "Rumors of Insurgency and Assassination in Ixcán, Guatemala," *Journal of Social History* 55, no. 1 (Fall 2021): 105–26. Many thanks to Oxford University Press and the journal for their kind permission to utilize this material here.

2. José Sales Ramírez, Interview, October 12, 2016.

3. Alan Riding, "Guatemala Opening New Lands, but Best Goes to the Rich," *New York Times*, April 5, 1979.

4. Grandia, *Enclosed*, 45–46; Gleijeses, *Shattered Hope*, 45; Handy, *Revolution in the Countryside*, 80; Hildebrand, "Guatemalan Colonization Projects," 42–43; Hildebrand, "Farm Size," 51; Andersson, "Arévalo's Tomorrowland," in *Out of the Shadow*, ed. Gibbings and Vrana.

5. Streeter, *Managing the Counterrevolution*, 152. Jim Handy estimates that closer to 500,000 people benefited from *Decreto 900*, *Revolution in the Countryside*, 94.

6. Hildebrand, "Guatemalan Rural Development Program," 68.

7. CIRMA, DOC DES No. 708, Airgram from the AmEmbassy Guatemala to Department of State, "Banco Nacional Agrario Opposes Agricultural Reform Bill pending in Congress," August 22, 1962.

8. GOG, Decreto Numero 1551, "Ley de Transformación Agraria," October 11, 1962.

9. Grandia, *Enclosed*, 48.

10. CIRMA, DOC DES No. 725, "Summary of Agrarian Reform Law," airgram from U.S. Embassy in Guatemala to Department of State, November 8, 1962; Decreto 1551.

11. Gibbings, *Our Time Is Now*, 2020. See especially chapter 3.

12. "Reforma Agraria," *El Imparcial*, July 16, 1965.

13. "Echan bases de organización que afirme la Reforma Agraria," *El Imparcial*, January 19, 1968.

14. CIRMA, DOC DES No. 716, Letter to Mr. Edwin M. Martin, Assistant Secretary of State, from Victor C. Folsom, Vice President and General Counsel for the United Fruit Company, October 4, 1962.

15. "Cultivar la tierra es vestirla de Gala, dijo Arana al entregar 4 mil hectáreas," *El Imparcial*, October 31, 1972; "Tierra para el que trabaja, porvenir del país en laborar su suelo, expresó Arana," *El Imparcial*, September 30, 1972; "302 Títulos de Tierra en propiedad en La Ranchería," *El Imparcial*, November 17, 1972; "En San Gil de Morales, Izabal, Hoy," *El Imparcial*, October 30, 1972; "75 familias más dueñas de tierras," *El Imparcial*, February 28, 1972; "I.N.T.A. un año de labores—contribución al progreso de Guatemala," *El Imparcial*, July 3, 1971; F. Rubén Gonzales Rivera, "Interrogantes ante el INTA," *El Imparcial*, November 10, 1972.

16. Dillingham, *Oaxaca Resurgent*, 76.

17. CNPE, *La planificación en Guatemala*, 12.

18. Egan, *Maryknoll in Central America*; William Mullan, Interview, August 22, 2016; Hernández Sandoval, *Guatemala's Catholic Revolution*; Fitzpatrick-Behrens, "From Symbols of the Sacred."

19. Egan, *Maryknoll in Central America*, 2; Allie, Arthur Papers, Diary, October 16, 1944 (36/1), MFBA, MMA, Maryknoll, New York. All priests' papers from MFBA unless otherwise noted.

20. Egan, *Maryknoll in Central America*, 3, 6.

21. Egan, *Maryknoll in Central America*, 22–23.

22. Shea, Interview, August 22, 2016; Jane C. Corrigan, "Un milagro en las montañas de Los Cuchumatanes, Huehuetenango," *El Imparcial*, August 1, 1964.

23. Melville, Thomas Papers, Diary, February 1963, (26/5), MMA.

24. Nichols, Arthur Papers, Diary, June 1963, (23/13), MMA; Potter, Ronald J. Papers, Diary, October 1965, (26/9), MMA, Emphasis in original; Melville, Arthur G. Papers, Diary, December 1963 (27/3), MMA; Woods, William J. Papers, Diary, March 1966, (23/18), MMA; McLeod, Daniel Papers, Diary, August 1965 (23/18), MMA.

25. Fournier, Felix Papers, Diary, "Report 1963," (26/11), MMA.

26. CIRMA, DOC DES No. 730, Airgram, To Department of State, from U.S. Embassy, subject "U.S. Missionaries have own aid program in Guatemalan Indian Area," November 15, 1962, by Gerald P. Lamberty, A-296.

27. Gibbings, *Our Time Is Now*, 5.

28. Clemente Marroquín Rojas (pseud. Canuto Ocaña), "La republica marinolesca de Huehuetenango," *La Hora*, January 29, 1968.

29. Roy Centeno, "Noticia de El Imparcial sobre expulsión de religiosos se comprueba en N. York," *El Imparcial*, January 18, 1968; "Superior Maryknoll explica lo ocurrido con religiosos extrañados," *El Imparcial*, January 18, 1968; "Ocultos padres de sacerdotes obligados a salir de Guatemala," *El Imparcial*, January 20, 1968.

30. Marroquín Rojas (pseud. Canuto Ocaña), "Focos de rebelión en hermandades e Iglesias," *La Hora*, January 24, 1968.

31. Mullan, Interview.

32. Shea, Interview.

33. CIRMA, Inforpress, Doc. 2555, Shelton H. Davis and Julie Hodson, *Witness to Political Violence in Guatemala: The Suppression of a Rural Development Movement* (Oxfam America, 1982), 45.

34. George W. Hill and Manuel Gollas, *The Minifundia Economy and Society of the Guatemalan Highland Indian*, Working Paper No. 30, The Land Tenure Center, University of Wisconsin, July 1968, 25, 57–58.

35. Falla, *Ixcán*, 64–66.

36. Pascual, Interview, October 13, 2016; Mariano Martín Pablo, Interview, October 13, 2016.

37. Vicente Carrillo, Interview, October 13, 2016.

38. *In memóriam del Ingeniero Leopoldo Sandovál Villeda*, edición especial (Guatemala: Asociación de Investigación y Estudios Sociales, 2012), 13; Martínez Ferraté, Interview.

39. Central America Region (CAR), Ixcán Grande Project Files (IGPF), Edward Doheny, "The Ixcán Grande Colonization Project—Guatemala C.A.," (31/3), MMA.

40. Doheny, Edward Papers, Diary, September 1965, (26/16), MMA; CAR, IGPF, Doheny, "Ixcán Grande."

41. María Matías Pavo, Interview, October 12, 2016.

42. Jiménez Pascual José Jiménez, Interview, October 13, 2016; CAR, IGPF, Letter Bill Woods to General Spry at Wings of Peace, April 23, 1976, (30/5), MMA; Rayman, *Kibbutz Community*.

43. Carrillo, Interview.

44. José Jiménez, Interview; CAR, IGPR, Letter, Ed Doheny to John Breen, April 15, 1969, (30/5), MMA.

45. Matías Pavo, Interview; Carrillo, Interview; Sales, Interview.

46. CAR, IGPF, Morrissey, James A., "The Ixcán: Crucible for Change," 1985, (30/17), MMA, 8.

47. CAR, IGPF, "Proyecto de Colonización, Ixcán Grande," (30/3), MMA.

48. José Jiménez, Interview.

49. Mullan, Interview; Shea, Interview.

50. CAR, IGPF, Correspondence with James Morrissey, 1968–1972. Letter from Bill Woods, February 23, 1969, (30/9), MMA.

51. Craib, *Cartographic Mexico*, 3–8; Fernando Purcell, "Dams and Hydroelectricity: Circulation of Knowledge and Technological Imaginaries in South America, 1945–1970," in *Itineraries of Expertise*, ed. Chastain and Lorek, 222.

52. Lesley Miles, personal communication, February 20, 2020.

53. NARA, USAID RG 286, P591, USAID Mission to Guatemala, Project Files: 1975–1978, Container #5, Folder—School Construction, Mayalán, Ixcán Grande.

54. CAR, IGPF, Letter from Woods to General Spry (Wings of Peace), April 23, 1976, (30/5), MMA.

55. NARA, USAID, RG 286, Project Files: 1975–1978, Container 5, Folder: School Construction, Mayalán; NARA, USAID RG 286, Project Files: 1975–1978, Container 5, Folder: School Construction, La Resurrección, Ixcán Grande; NARA, USAID, RG 286, Project Files: 1975–1978, Container 7, Folder: School Construction, Xalbal, Ixcán Grande.

56. NARA, RG 286, USAID Mission to Guatemala/Program Office. Project Files: 1975–1978, Container 7. "Special Development Fund Project Submission Summary, Xalbal, Ixcán Grande," 1975.

57. NARA, RG. 286 USAID Mission to Guatemala Project Files: 1975–1978, Container 5, "Project Submission Summary—Mayalán," 1974.

58. NARA, RG 286, USAID Mission to Guatemala/Program Office. Project Files: 1975–1978, Container 7. "Special Development Fund Project Submission Summary, Xalbal, Ixcán Grande," 1975.

59. Sales, Interview.

60. Falla, *Ixcán*, 61; CAR, IGPF, Letter from Woods, March 15, 1973, (30/8), MMA.

61. "Tenencia de las tierras," *El Imparcial*, May 4, 1964; Grandia, *Enclosed*, 120.

62. Falla, *Ixcán*, 39.

63. Falla, *Ixcán*, 40.

64. Way, *Mayan in the Mall*, 126.

65. Falla, *Ixcán*, 41; CAR, IGPR, Letter, Bishop Gerbermann to Miguel Ortíz Jiménez and Sebastian Sales, July 16, 1971, (30/7), MMA.

66. Sales, Interview; CAR, IGPF, Morrissey, "The Ixcan," 16–20.

67. CAR, IGPF, Letter from Woods, November 10, 1972, (30/9), MMA.

68. CAR, IGPF, Morrissey, "The Ixcán," 18–20; Falla, *Ixcán*, 41.

69. Falla, *Ixcán*, 40–41; Morrissey, "The Ixcán," 417, 433–46; CAR, IGPF, Reports, 1971–1993, "Ixtacán Chiquito," (31:3), MMA.

70. CAR, IGPF, Letter, Gerberman to Miguel Ortiz Jimenez and Sebastian Sales, July 16, 1971, (30/7), MMA.

71. CAR, IGPF, Letter, Alcalde Gregorio D. Reyes, Santa Cruz Barillas, to Gobernador Coronel Juan Baltazar Martínez, Huehuetenango, May 23, 1973, (30/14), MMA.

72. CAR, IGPF, Letter, Gobernador Coronel Juan Baltazar Martínez, Huehuetenango to Gregorio D. Reyes, Santa Cruz Barillas, May 25, 1973, (30/14), MMA.

73. CAR, IGPF, Letter, Gregorio D. Reyes, Santa Cruz Barillas to Gobernador Coronel Juan Baltazar Martínez, Huehuetenango, August 18, 1973, (30/14), MMA.

74. CAR, IGPF, Letter, Directiva de la Cooperative Ixcán Grande to "whom it may concern," June 5, 1973, (30/7), MMA; Harmer, "Two, Three Many Revolutions?"; Martín Pablo, Interview.

75. Sales, Interview.

76. Norman Gall, "Slaughter in Guatemala," New York Review of Books, May 20, 1971. Accessed online April 3, 2017. http://www.nybooks.com/articles/1971/05/20/slaughter-in-guatemala/; Black, *Garrison Guatemala*, 22.

77. Brands, *Latin America's Cold War*, 27.

78. See Grandin, *Last Colonial Massacre*; García Ferreira, ed., *Guatemala y la Guerra Fría*.

79. Jonas, *Battle for Guatemala*, 116–17.

80. CAR, IGPF, Letter from Woods, April 20, 1974, (30/14), MMA; CAR, IGPF, *Título de Propiedad*, May 30, 1974, (30/16), MMA.

81. Falla, *Ixcán*, 42.

82. "Problema de Ixcán está siendo tomado muy en serio por la INTA," *El Imparcial*, July 9, 1975; "Comisión del INTA a Ixcán para Intervenir en Problemas," *El Imparcial*, May 9, 1975.

83. Falla, *Ixcán*, 50–51.

84. "Problema de Ixcán," *El Imparcial*, July 9, 1975.

85. CAR, IGPF, Letter, Bill Woods to Otto Valdimiro Sánchez, Jefe del departamento de colonización de INTA, July 28, 1975 (30/14), MMA; CAR, IGPF, Letter, Otto Vladimiro Sánchez, Jefe del departamento de colonización y desarrollo agrario, INTA, to the Directivo de la cooperativa La Resurrección, July 15, 1975, (30/16), MMA.

86. "Fueron declaradas por el Congreso: Zonas de desarrollo agrario," *El Imparcial*, August 21, 1970; *Decreto No. 60-70, El Guatemalteco: Diario oficial de la República de Guatemala*, September 16, 1970, no. 53.

87. "Zonas de Desarrollo Agrario," *El Imparcial*, August 21, 1970.

88. Piedra Santa Arandi, *El petróleo y los minerales en Guatemala*, Colección Problemas Socio-económicas No. 1, 2a ed. (Guatemala: Universidad de San Carlos, 1979), 17, 22; CIRMA, DOC DES No. 235, Memorandum of Conversation, February 7, 1955; CIRMA, DOC DES No. 236, Memorandum of Conversation, February 14, 1955; CIRMA, DOC DES No. 366, "Foreign Service Despatch, from AMEmbassy Guatemala to Dept. of State," May 2, 1956.

89. CIRMA, DOC DES No. 588, Foreign Service Despatch, September 29, 1959.

90. Piedra Santa, *El petróleo*, 39–40, 48.

91. "Problemas de Ixcán está siendo tomado muy en serio por la INTA," *El Imparcial*, July 9, 1975; Eduardo P. Villatorro, "Atacan al INTA quienes no se acercan a ver como se trabaja," *El Imparcial*, July 9, 1977.

92. Melville, *Through a Glass Darkly*, 403.

93. Solano, *Contextualización histórica*; Alan Riding, "Guatemala Opening New Lands, but Best Goes to the Rich," *New York Times*, April 5, 1979; Melville, *Through a Glass Darkly*, 403; CIRMA, Comité Holandes, Cartapacio 68, Doc. 39, "Nueva ofensiva: Contrainsurgencia en el Ixcán con dinero de la CE," *Suplemento de la ILA (Revista alemana sobre América Latina)* 125 (May 1989), 3.

94. CIRMA, Colección Anónima de Alta Verapaz, Caja 1, Paquete 1, "Proyecto de colonización de la faja transversal del norte de la república," n.d.; Luis Solano, "Development and/as Dispossession," in *War by Other Means*, ed. McAllister and Nelson, 127; Black, *Garrison Guatemala*, 54.

95. CIRMA, Colección Anónima de Alta Verapaz, Caja 2, Paquete 1, Ejército Guerrillero de los Pobres, "Mac'a chic li ve chok'lao li neba' mas ket cachab li pub rex colbal li cachoch," March 1980.

96. Manz, *Paradise in Ashes*; Santos, *El Silencio del Gallo*.

97. Santos, *El Silencio del Gallo*, 166–67.

98. CIRMA, MP-YC 9, "La política agraria de los gobiernos de Guatemala."

99. Grandin, *Last Colonial Massacre*.

100. Solano, *Guatemala: petróleo y minería*, 51; Solano, "Development and/as Dispossession," 127.

101. Ron Chernow, "The Strange Death of Bill Woods," *Mother Jones* (May 1979): 36.

102. Joel Simon, *The Rise and Fall of Guatemala's Ixcán Cooperatives, 1965–1989*, Thesis. Stanford University, 1989, cited in Solano, *Guatemala: petróleo y minería*, 80.

103. José Jiménez, Interview.

104. Sales, Interview.

105. Alan Riding, "Guatemala Opening New Lands."

106. CAR, IGPF, Letter, William Woods to Jaime Cordova of MISEREOR, April 13, 1975, (30/8), MMA.

107. CAR, IGPF, Letter, MISEREOR to Woods, June 18, 1975, (31/4), MMA.

108. CAR, IGPF, William Woods, Progress Report, April 1, 1976, (31/3), MMA.

109. Díaz-Polanco, "Prólogo: Etnicidad y autonomía," in *Los pueblos indígenas*, by Payeras, 8.

110. AHPN, Departamento de Investigaciones Criminológicas, Registro Maestro de Fichas, CUIT 458585, Dirección General de la Guardia Hacienda, December 1, 1969.

111. CAR, IGPF, Morrissey, "The Ixcán," 11.

112. Ricardo Falla, *Ixcán*, see chapter 5.

113. Payeras, *Los días de la selva*.

114. José Jiménez, Interview.

115. Falla, *Ixcán*, 233–35.

116. CAR, IGPF, W. Woods, "Report of Army Interference in Ixcán," January 14, 1976, (31/3), MMA.

117. Woods, "Report of Army Interference."

118. ODHAG, Interview no. 960, October 24, 1996: ODHAG, 5210, October 25, 1997. All ODHAG references are for interviews conducted as part of the Church's Truth Commission, identified by number and date.

119. Woods, "Report of Army Interference."

120. Sales, Interview.

121. Woods, "Report of Army Interference."

122. Woods, "Report of Army Interference."

123. CAR, IGPF, "Treinta campesinos desaparecen en Ixcán Grande, cunde el pánico," *La Nación*, January 9, 1976, (31/3), MMA; "APG pide investigar caso de desaparecidos de Ixcán," *El Imparcial*, February 3, 1976.

124. Sales, Interview; José Jiménez, Interview.

125. CAR, IGPF, Letter, Joseph M. Glynn (Maryknoll headquarters, NY) to Ronald W. Hennessey, April 15, 1976, (30/5), MMA; CAR, IGPF, Letter, Ronald Hennessey to Monseñor Martínez, July 29, 1976, (30/7), MMA.

126. Castillo Ramírez, *Ixcán en tiempos del conflicto*.

127. Fernando Castillo Ramírez, Interview, November 14, 2016.

128. Raúl González G., "En Ixcán por el presidente para cesar infundios," *El Imparcial*, May 14, 1977.

129. Sales, Interview; José Jiménez, Interview.

130. Falla, *Ixcán*, 87–91.

131. MMP, 14:7 (Box:Folder), English translation of untitled Aeronáutica Civil report, prepared by Natzul René Méndez H., Aircraft Inspector, on November 25, 1976, University of California San Diego Special Collections. All references to the Margarita Melville Papers come from this collection.

132. MMP, 14:7, Father Ronald W. Hennessey, Regional Superior of the Maryknoll Fathers to Father Raymond W. Hill, Superior General, "Report on the Plane Crash of Father

William H. Woods on November 20, 1976," December 27, 1976; MMP, 14:7, Patrick Ahern, "Meeting on Plane Crash," June 20, 1977.

133. Hennessey, "Report on the Plane Crash."

134. Hennessey, "Report on the Plane Crash."

135. Martín Pablo, Interview.

136. Foss, "Rumors of Insurgency and Assassination."

137. MMP, 14:7, translation of Méndez report.

138. MMP, 14:7, translation of Méndez report. The weather report was completed on November 22, 1976, by Carlos E. Saravia G.

139. MMP, 14:7. Armond V. Edwards, Aeronautical Safety Inspector, to Frank T. Taylor, Bureau of Accident Investigation, May 24, 1977, "Trip Report—Guatemala—Cessna 185 Accident"; MMP, 14:7, letter from Ronald M. Hennessey to Patrick Ahern, June 27, 1977.

140. Ron Chernow, "The Strange Death of Bill Woods," 32.

141. MMP, 14:7. Letter from Ronald W. Hennessey to Patrick Ahern, March 21, 1977.

142. Walker, *Tupac Amaru Rebellion*, 9–17.

143. Levenson, *Adiós Niño*, 16.

144. Falla, *Ixcán*, 506.

145. For a more detailed account of these massacres, see CIRMA, Comité Holandés, Cartapacio 68, Doc. 39, "Nueva ofensiva: Contrainsurgencia en el Ixcán con dinero de la CE," *Suplemento de la ILA (Revista alemana sobre América Latina)* 125 (May 1989): 4: Falla, *Ixcán*, 2015: CEH, *Guatemala: Memory of Silence, Tz'inil na'tab'al*, 12 vol. (February 1999); ODHAG, *Guatemala Nunca Más: Informe proyecto interdiocesano de recuperación de la memoria histórica* (Guatemala, ODHAG: 1998).

146. CEH, *Guatemala: Memoria del Silencio*, Tomo III (1999): 268–69.

147. Sales, Interview.

148. ODHAG, 452, May 12, 1996.

149. ODHAG, 453, January 1, 1996.

150. Esquit, *La superación*, 380; Annis, *God and Production*, 6.

151. Mallon, "Postcolonial Palimpsest," 322.

152. Mallon, "Postcolonial Palimpsest," 326; Miller, "Development, Space, and Counterinsurgency in *Development Century*, ed. Macekura and Manela, 151.

153. Grandin, *Blood of Guatemala*, 222.

154. Carmack, "Editor's Preface," in *Harvest of Violence*, xv.

155. Davis, "Introduction: Sowing the Seeds," in *Harvest of Violence*, ed. Carmack, 24.

156. Sanford, *Buried Secrets*, 157.

157. CEH, *Memoria del Silencio*, Tomo III, 396; Elisabeth Malkin, "Former Leader of Guatemala is Guilty of Genocide Against Mayan Group," *New York Times*, May 10, 2013.

158. CEH, *Guatemala: Memoria del Silencio*, Tomo III, 396.

159. CIRMA, Inforpress Centroamericana, Cartapacio 841:215. Frank Maurovich, "Option for poor angers the State," *Maryknoll* 4 (April 1981), 27.

160. Schmink and Wood, *Contested Frontiers in Amazonia* (New York: Columbia University Press, 1992), 51, quoted in Grandia, *Enclosed*, 175.

161. ODHAG, 706, December 10, 1995.

162. ODHAG, 7054, October 10, 1996.

163. ODHAG, 960, October 24, 1996.

Chapter Seven

1. Mack, "Assistance and Control," in *Guatemala Reader*, ed. Grandin et al., 421.

2. While military records and my interview sources insisted that relocation to a Pole of Development was completely voluntary, many other accounts claim that the military forced internal refugees into these villages as part of their pacification and reeducation campaigns.

3. CIRMA, Iglesia en Exilio (IGE), No. 26, "Guatemala, 'A New Way of Life': The Development Poles," *Guatemalan Church in Exile* 4, no. 5 (September–October 1984): 7; U.S. National Security Archive, No. 00794, Department of Defense Joint Chiefs of Staff Message Center, "Guatemala/Views of Coup Leader," April 7, 1982.

4. Communities of Population in Resistance of the Sierra, "We Are Civilians," *Guatemala Reader*, 428.

5. Moller, *Nuestra cultura*, 44.

6. Manz, *Paradise in Ashes*.

7. Michael Richards, "Cosmopolitan Worldview and Counterinsurgency in Guatemala," *Anthropological Quarterly* 58, no. 3 (July 1985): 95, quoted in Schirmer, *Military Project*, 45.

8. Schirmer, *Military Project*, 57.

9. Mario Enrique Paiz Bolaños, Interview, November 2, 2016; Eduardo Wohlers Monroy, Interview, November 10, 2016.

10. Organization of American States, Inter-American Commission for Human Rights, "Report on the Situation of Human Rights in the Republic of Guatemala," Doc. 21, rev. 2, October 13, 1981. https://www.cidh.oas.org/countryrep/Guatemala81eng/chap.2.htm; Manz, *Paradise in Ashes*; Sanford, *Buried Secrets*, 114–15.

11. CEH, *Memory of Silence, Conclusions and Recommendations*, 1999, 17, 85, 20. https://www.aaas.org/sites/default/files/migrate/uploads/mos_en.pdf.

12. Barthes, *Camera Lucida*, 4; Azoulay, *Civil Imagination*, 2–3, 17.

13. Azoulay, *Civil Contract of Photography*, 23.

14. Coleman, *Garden of Eden*, 21.

15. Coleman, *Garden of Eden*, see chapter 1, "Photography as a Practice of Self-Forging."

16. Azoulay, *Civil Imagination*, 73, 86.

17. Mirzoeff, *Right to Look*, 23–24, 6.

18. Coleman, *Garden of Eden*, 28; Grandin, "Can the Subaltern be Seen?"

19. AVANCSO, *Política institucional*, 9, 21; Solano, "Quiché en el contexto," *El Observador* 6, nos. 32–33 (2011): 94–95. https://issuu.com/observadorguatemala/docs/el_observador_32-33/94; Ejército Guatemala, Twitter Post, April 21, 2017, 11:48 A.M. https://twitter.com/Ejercito_GT/status/855463175709483008.

20. Those interested in viewing low-resolution versions of these images can consult my dissertation, *Until the Indian Is Made to Walk: Indigenismo and Development in Cold War Guatemala, 1940–1996*, PhD Diss., Indiana University, 2018.

21. Here I follow Ada Ferrer's insightful methodology in *Freedom's Mirror*, where she analyzes Antonio Aponte's book of paintings that no longer exists but that featured centrally in his interrogation. See chapter 7.

22. Moller, *Nuestra cultura*, 52.

23. See Moller's website at https://www.jonathanmoller.org/ to learn more about his other projects in Cuba, Peru, and elsewhere.

24. Moller, *Our Culture.*

25. Way, *Mayan in the Mall,* 144.

26. Schirmer, *Military Project,* 58; Irwin, "The 'Development' of Humanitarian Relief," in *The Development Century,* ed. Macekura and Manela, 55.

27. Myrna Mack, "Assistance and Control," *Guatemala Reader,* 424.

28. GOG, Recopilación de Leyes 103, Decreto Ley 65–84, June 26, 1984, 311–13; Ejército de Guatemala, *Polos de Desarrollo y Servicios,* "Acuerdo Gubernativo Número 801-84," September 12, 1984, 9–11.

29. Fall, *Two Viet-Nams,* 373, quoted in Latham, *Right Kind of Revolution,* 138.

30. Miller, "Development, Space, and Counterinsurgency," 165–67.

31. Latham, *Right Kind of Revolution,* 139.

32. Biggs, "Modernization," in *Quagmire,* 153–95; Paiz Bolaños, Interview.

33. Offner, *Mixed Economy;* Way, *Agrotropolis,* 61–62.

34. MPBA, "Palabras del Señor de división, Oscar Humberto Mejia Víctores, Jefe de Estado y Ministro de la Defensa Nacional a los honorables señores representantes a la Asamblea Nacional Constituyente," n.d. It is likely that this speech occurred around June 1984 when the Assembly voted on legislating the Poles of Development and the Interinstitutional Coordinators; GOG, *Decreto Ley Número 111-84,* November 26, 1984.

35. Way, *Agrotropolis,* 42.

36. MPBA, "Polos de Desarrollo y Servicios," June 19, 1984.

37. Wohlers Monroy, Interview.

38. Ejército de Guatemala, *Polos de Desarrollo,* 89.

39. Paiz Bolaños, Interview; Rolando Paiz Maselli, Interview, November 8, 2016.

40. Paiz Maselli, Interview; Wohlers Monroy, Interview. Paiz Maselli claimed that Acul's reconstruction took eighty-two days, while Wohlers Monroy stated that it took ninety days.

41. CIRMA, IGE No. 26, "Guatemala 'A New Way of Life': The Development Poles," 7.

42. Paiz Maselli, Interview.

43. Taracena Arriola, "From Assimilation to Segregation," 105–6.

44. Barthes, *Camera Lucida,* 26–27.

45. Warren, *Indigenous Movements;* González Ponciano, "*Shumo* Challenge," in *War by Other Means,* ed. McAllister and Nelson; Way, *Agrotropolis;* Charles R. Hale, "Mistados, Cholos," in *Race and Racism,* ed. Gotkowitz.

46. Hale, "Neoliberal Multiculturalism," 10–28.

47. Gibbings, *Our Time Is Now,* 368.

48. Paiz Maselli, Interview.

49. Way, *Mayan in the Mall,* 145–46.

50. CIRMA, Colección Inforpress, Serie: Documentos, No. 2364, "Información manuscrita sobre las Aldeas modelo y la represión en ellas," 1986; USAID, "Small Project Development: Project No. 520-0233 (Loan No. 520-T-026)," USAID/Guatemala, Audit Report No. 1-520-82-10, April 28, 1982.

51. Presidencia de la República, CRN, "Secreto: Directiva PAAC-002," December 1982; Presidencia de la República, CRN, "Instructivo 001 FERTICREDITO," May 24, 1983.

52. Rifkin, *Beyond Settler Time,* 6.

53. Saldaña-Portillo, *Indian Given,* 203.

54. Gibbings, *Our Time Is Now,* 269.

55. ODHAG, 1071, May 21, 1996.

56. CIRMA, Comité Holandés de Solidaridad (CHS), 23, CPR, 31, Asamblea Permanente de Grupos Cristianos, "Comunidades de Población en Resistencia—CPR-," 1.

57. CIRMA, Comité Holandés de Solidaridad (CHS), 23, CPR, 31, Asamblea Permanente de Grupos Cristianos, "Comunidades de Población en Resistencia—CPR-," 1.

58. CIRMA, CHS, 23, CPR, 51, Juan Castillo y Carlos Castañeza, "CPR: Nos acusan de guerrilleros para que los delitos queden impunes," *Siglo Veintiuno*, March 5, 1993.

59. Catherine L. Nolin Hanlon and W. George Lovell, "Flight, Exile, Repatriation, and Return: Guatemalan Refugee Scenarios, 1981–1998," in *The Maya Diaspora*, ed. Loucky and Moors, 40.

60. Falla, *Historia de un gran amor*.

61. CIRMA, CHS, 23, CPR, 94, Letter written from the Comité de Emergencia Ixcán to Estimados Señores, January 9, 1991, 4; CIRMA, CHS, 23, CPR, 78—"Declaración Política de la XV Asamblea General de las Comunidades de población en resistencia CPR-Ixcán, December 1995.

62. CIRMA, CHS, 23, CPR, 54: Guatemala, Voices from Silent Refuge, by Louise Edwards, Report on the Americas, Volume XXV, Number 1 (July 1991).

63. CIRMA, CHS, 23, CPR, 31, Asamblea Permanente de Grupos Cristianos, Comunidades de Población en Resistencia; ODHAG, 9689, November 30, 1996; ODHAG, 8019, September 27, 1996; ODHAG, 752, January 24, 1996; ODHAG, 1071, May 21, 1996; ODHAG, 720, December 25, 1995; ODHAG, 928, May 3, 1996; ODHAG, 483, January 10, 1996; ODHAG, 1133, November 7, 1996.

64. ODHAG, 8037, July 18, 1996; ODHAG, 5942, August 4, 1997; ODHAG, 1136, August 25, 1996.

65. CIRMA, CHS, 23, CPR, 31, Asamblea Permanente de Grupos Cristianos, "Comunidades de Población en Resistencia—CPR-," 58; CIRMA, CHS, 23, CPR, 104, "Apuntes sobre las CPR," 6.

66. ODHAG, 8037, July 18, 1996; ODHAG, 8001, May 23, 1996; ODHAG, 928, May 3, 1996; ODHAG, 1133, November 7, 1996.

67. Moller, *Nuestra cultura*, 88; Rifkin, *Beyond Settler Time*, 27–29.

68. CIRMA, CHS, 23, CPR, 94, Letter written from the Comité de Emergencia Ixcán, January 9, 1991, 6.

69. CIRMA, CHS, 23, CPR, 76 "Declaración Política Asamblea General Extraordinaria," Comunidad Primavera, CPR, Ixcán, March 23, 1996.

70. CIRMA, CHS, 23, CPR, 94, Letter from the Comité de Emergencia Ixcán, January 9, 1991, 4; CIRMA, CHS, 23, CPR, 76 "Declaración Política," CPR, Ixcán, May 23, 1996.

71. CIRMA, CHS, 23, CPR, 103, "Breve Informe de la Situación de la Población en Resistencia"; CIRMA, CHS, 23, CPR, 105 Comunidades de Población en Resistencia C.P.R., Ixcán Guatemala C.A., "Denuncia ante el público nacional e internacional," 1989.

72. CIRMA, CHS, 23, CPR, 82, "Entrevista con Ramírez Pedro, Maestro Popular y Miembro del Equipo de Educación Popular del Ixcán."

73. Huezo, *Resisting and Surviving*.

74. CIRMA, CHS, 23, CPR, 82, "Entrevista con Ramírez Pedro."

75. CIRMA, CHS, 23, CPR, 94, Letter from the Comité de Emergencia Ixcán, January 9, 1991, 5.

76. CIRMA, CHS, 23, CPR, 109, Comité de Unidad Campesina CUC, "Informe descriptivo de las Comunidades de Población en Resistencia," 4.

77. CIRMA, CHS, 23, CPR, 45, "Declaración política de la Asamblea General Extraordinaria de la CPR de la Sierra ante el pueblo y gobierno de Guatemala, ante los pueblos y gobiernos del mundo," 1996.

Conclusion

1. The URNG was formed in 1982 in the aftermath of the military's scorched earth campaigns as an attempt to bring cohesion to several leftist guerilla organizations under one organization. Members from the EGP, FAR, PGT, and ORPA formed the URNG.

2. For an in-depth analysis of the history of the peace negotiations and their immediate aftermath in Guatemala, see Jonas, *Of Centaurs and Doves*.

3. Jonas, *Of Centaurs and Doves*, 75.

4. *Agreement on Identity and Rights of Indigenous Peoples*, Mexico City, Mexico, March 31, 1995. https://www.usip.org/sites/default/files/file/resources/collections/peace_agreements/guat_950331.pdf; Sieder, "Rethinking Democratisation," 103.

5. Foss, "National Tomorrow"; Konefal, *For Every Indio Who Falls*.

6. Warren, "Pan-Mayanism and the Guatemalan Peace Process," in *Globalization on the Ground*, ed. Chase-Dunn, Jonas, and Amaro, 149.

7. International Labor Association, ILO Press Release ILO/96/20, "Guatemala Ratifies Convention Guaranteeing Indigenous Rights," June 13, 1996. https://www.ilo.org/global/about-the-ilo/newsroom/news/WCMS_008061/lang--en/index.htm#:~:text=The%20ratification%20formalises%20a%20commitment,their%20economic%20or%20social%20development.; Jonas, *Of Centaurs and Doves*, 77.

8. Consejo Nacional para el Cumplimiento de los Acuerdos de Paz Rajpop ri Ch'uch'ulen Taqanik, "Convenio 169 de la OIT sobre pueblos indígenas y tribales en países independientes," in *Cartilla de Derechos Indígenas: Selección de Artículos—Resumen* (Guatemala, 2011): 55–56.

9. These issues were also specifically negotiated as part of the May 1996 Agreement on Socioeconomic Aspects and Agrarian Situation.

10. *Acuerdos de Paz Firme y Duradera*, December 29, 1996. https://www.usip.org/sites/default/files/file/resources/collections/peace_agreements/guat_final_961229.pdf.

11. Jonas, *Of Centaurs and Doves*, 195–200; Bastos and Camus, "Difficult Complementarity: Relations between the Mayan and Revolutionary Movements," in *War by Other Means*, ed. McAllister and Nelson, 82.

12. Demetrio Cojtí Cuxil, "The Impact of the Popular Referendum on Compliance with the Indigenous Accord and on Democratization in Guatemala," in *The Popular Referendum (Consulta Popular) and the Future of the Peace Process in Guatemala*, Latin American Program, Working Papers #241, ed. Cynthia J. Arson (Washington, DC: Woodrow Wilson Center for International Scholars, 1999), 26.

13. McAllister and Nelson, "Aftermath," in *War by Other Means*, eds. McAllister and Nelson.

14. McAllister and Nelson, "Aftermath," 33–34; Way, *Mayan in the Mall*, 186–88.

15. Beck, *How Development Projects Persist*.

16. Rahder, *Ecology of Knowledges*.

17. González-Izás, "Labor Contractors to Military Specialists," in *War by Other Means*, eds. McAllister and Nelson.

18. Copeland, *Democracy Development Machine*.

19. Dougherty, "Global Gold Mining Industry"; Grandia, *Enclosed*; Solano, *Guatemala: petróleo y minería*; Irma Alicia Velásquez Nimatuj, "A Dignified Community Where We Can Live: Violence, Law, and Debt in Nueva Cajolá's Struggle for Land," in *War by Other Means*, eds. McAllister and Nelson. For analyses of the impact of hydroelectric dams in rural Guatemala, see Diane M. Nelson, "Water Power Promise: Revisiting Revolutionary DIY," in *Out of the Shadow*, eds. Gibbings and Vrana; and Batz, "La Lucha Contra Megaproyectos," in *Pensar Guatemala desde la Resistencia*, ed. Prensa Comunitaria, 89–122.

20. PBI Guatemala, "Bernardo Caal Xol, defender of the Cahabón River," https://pbi -guatemala.org/en/who-we-accompany/peaceful-resistance-cahab%C3%B3n/bernardo -caal-xol-defender-cahab%C3%B3n-river.

21. See Costanza, "Indigenous Peoples' Right," to better understand the denial of prior consultation and the creative legal mechanism Indigenous Guatemalans have begun to employ to challenge natural resource extraction on their land. See the legal cases *Choc v. Hud-Bay Minerals Inc.* and *Caal v. HudBay Minerals Inc.* about the human rights abuses conducted by Canadian mining companies; for collective resistance to mining, see Daniel Villatoro García, "La Puya: una comunidad en resistencia, una empresa insistente," *Plaza Pública*, July 1, 2016. https://www.plazapublica.com.gt/content/la-puya-una-comunidad-en-resistencia-una -empresa-insistente. These are but a few telling examples of repeated violations of ILO 169 and human rights abuses that have occurred in post-peace Guatemala in the name of national development.

22. Congreso de Guatemala, Decreto No. 11-2002, Ley de los consejos de desarrollo urbano y rural, March 12, 2002.

23. See Sieder, "Rethinking Democratisation," for further analysis of the disconnect between the intentions and the implementations of the law.

24. *Agreement on Identity and Rights of Indigenous Peoples*.

25. See Esquit, *La superación del indígena*, 414–17, for his analysis of the promises and problems with the COCODE system in Comalapa.

26. Irma Alicia Velásquez Nimatuj, "An Open Letter to President Donald J. Trump and the Government of the United States of America," Skylight Films Blog, October 22, 2018. https://skylight.is/2018/10/an-open-letter-to-president-donald-j-trump-and-the-govern ment-of-the-united-states-of-america/.

27. Adelman, "Epilogue: Development Dreams," in *The Development Century*, eds. Macekura and Manela, 327.

Bibliography

Archives

GUATEMALA

Archivo de la Oralidad (AO), Escuela de Historia, USAC
Archivo General de Centro América (AGCA)
Archivo Histórico de la Policía Nacional (AHPN)
Archivo Legislativo del Congreso de la República de Guatemala
Archivo del Ministerio de Educación Pública (MinEd)
Archivo Municipal de Tactic (AMT)
Archivo de la Oficina de Derechos Humanos del Arzobispado de Guatemala (ODHAG)
Archivo de la Secretaría de Bienestar Social (SBS)
Centro de Investigaciones Regionales de Mesoamérica (CIRMA)
    Colección Anónima de Alta Verapaz
    Comité Holandes de Solidaridad (CHS)
    Coordinadora Alemana
    Documentos Desclasificados (DOC DES)
    Fototeca
    Iglesia en Exilio (IGE)
    Inforpress
    INGUAT
    Instituto Indigenista (IING)
    Mario Payeras-Yolanda Colom (MP-YC)
Personal Archive of Francisco Rodríguez Rouanet (FRRA)
Personal Archive of Jaime Búcaro Moraga
Personal Archive of Mario Paiz Bolaños (MPBA)
Personal Archive of Rolando Paiz Maselli (RPM)

MEXICO

Archivo del Instituto Indigenista Interamericano (AIII), Mexico City

UNITED STATES

Columbia University Libraries Special Collections, New York, New York
    International Institute for Rural Reconstruction (IIRR)
Hanna Holborn Gray Special Collections Research Center, University of Chicago Library
    Robert Redfield Papers (RRP)
    Sol Tax Papers (STP)
John F. Kennedy Presidential Library (JFK), Boston, Massachusetts
Maryknoll Missions Archives (MMA), Maryknoll, New York

Nettie Lee Benson Latin American Collection, University of Texas Libraries, University of
    Texas at Austin
  Richard N. Adams Papers (RAP)
Peabody Museum of Archaeology and Ethnology Archives, Harvard University
  John P. Gillin Papers
Rockefeller Archive Center (RAC), Sleepy Hollow, New York
University of California San Diego Special Collections
  Margarita Melville Papers (MMP)
U.S. National Archives and Records Administration (NARA), College Park, Maryland
  RG 59: State Department
  RG 286: U.S. Agency for International Development
  RG 469: Foreign Assistance Agencies

Interviews

Adams, Richard; Panajachel
Bin, Alberto; Pasmolón
Bin Quej, Rogelio; Chiacal
Cabrera, Hélida Esther; Santiago Atitlán
Cantoral, María Hercilia; Tactic
Carrillo, Vicente; Mayalán
Castillo Ramírez, Fernando;
    Guatemala City
Gamboa de Fernández, Gladys; Tactic
García Laguardia, Jorge; Guatemala City
García Noval, José; Guatemala City
Guzmán Böckler, Carlos; San Lucas
    Sacatepéquez
Guzmán, Lesli Magdalena; Tactic
Isem, Heriberto; Pasmolón
Isem Cir, Otilia; Tactic
José Jiménez, Jiménez Pascual; Mayalán
López Cantoral, Carlos Salomon;
    Tactic

Martín Pavo, Mariano; Mayalán
Martínez Ferraté, Rodolfo;
    Guatemala City
Matias Pavo, María; Mayalán
Mullan, William; Guatemala City
Paiz Bolaños, Mario Enrique;
    Guatemala City
Paiz Maselli, Rolando; Guatemala City
Pascual, Rafael; Mayalán
Peláez Martínez, Miguel; Tactic
Rodríguez Rouanet, Francisco;
    Guatemala City
Sales Ramírez, José; Mayalán
Shea, Martin; Guatemala City
Tun, Enrique; Chiacal, Interview
    by Araceli Cahuec
Vásquez Robles, Emilio; Cobán
Wohlers Monroy, Eduardo;
    Guatemala City

Newspapers and Magazines

Alfabetización higiénica
Boletín Agraria
*Boletín del Instituto Indigenista
    Interamericano*
*Boletín del Instituto Indigenista Nacional
    de Guatemala*
Boletín Indigenista
El Imparcial

Guatemala Indígena
La Hora
Mother Jones
The New York Times
Prensa Libre
Salud es Vida
*Sololá: Revista monográfica
    y turista*

Published Primary Sources

Arévalo Bermejo, Juan José. *Escritos Políticos*. Guatemala: Tipografía Nacional, 1945.

Cabrera, Hélida Esther. *Vivencias inolvidables: abriendo brechas en el campo de la investigación social, 1951–1956*. Con la colaboración de Sandra E. Herrera Ruiz. Guatemala: Centro de Estudios Urbanos y Regionales, Universidad de San Carlos, 2006.

Comisión para la esclarecimiento histórico. *Guatemala: Memoria del Silencio*, 1999.

Congreso Indigenista Interamericano. *Actas finales de los tres primeros Congresos Indigenistas Interamericanos*. Ciudad de Guatemala: Editorial del Ministerio de Educación Pública, 1959.

Consejo Nacional de Planificación Económica. *Planificación económica en Guatemala*. Guatemala City: Tipografía Nacional, 1960.

———. *La planificación en Guatemala (su historia, problemas y perspectivas)*. Guatemala, 1969.

Doyle, Kate, and Carlos Osorio. National Security Archive. NSA Electronic Briefing Book No. 11. *U.S. Policy in Guatemala, 1966–1996*.

Ejército de Guatemala. *Polos de Desarrollo y Servicios*. Guatemala, 1984.

Government of Guatemala. *Sexto censo de población*, 1950.

———. *Censo agropecuario 1950*, 1955.

———. *Plan de Desarrollo Económico 1955–1960, Hacia la nueva vida*. versión resumida. Guatemala C.A.: Tipografía Nacional, 1957.

———. *Censo de 1964*.

Instituto Indigenista Nacional de Guatemala. *San Bartolomé Milpas Altas: síntesis socio-económico de una comunidad indígena guatemalteca*. Publicaciones especiales No. 9. Guatemala: Ministerio de Educación Pública, 1949.

———. *Santo Domingo Xenacoj*. Publicaciónes especiales No. 7. Guatemala: Ministerio de Educación Pública, 1947.

International Bank for Reconstruction and Development. *The Economic Development of Guatemala: The Report of a Mission (English)*. Washington, DC, 1951.

Ministerio de Economía. *Política Económica del Gobierno de Liberación: Reunión con los sectores de la iniciativa privada*. Ministerio de Economía: Guatemala, C.A., 1957.

Murdock, George, Clellan Ford, Alfred Hudson, Raymond Kennedy, Leo Simmons, and John Whiting. *Guía para la investigación etnológicas*. Translated by Radamés A. Altieri. Edición privada. Reprint from Publicación Número 250 del Instituto de antropología de la Universidad Nacional de Tucumán, Argentina (1939). Pátzcuaro, Mexico: Centro Regional de Educación Fundamental para la América Latina, 1952.

Oficina de Derechos Humanos del Arzobispado de Guatemala. *Guatemala Nunca Más: Informe proyecto interdiocesano de recuperación de la memoria histórica*. Guatemala: ODHAG, 1998.

Organization of American States. Inter-American Commission for Human Rights. "Report on the Situation of Human Rights in the Republic of Guatemala." Doc. 21. rev. 2. October 13, 1981.

Quick, Silvia. *Guatemala*. Country Demographic Profiles. Washington, DC: U.S. Department of Commerce, 1977.

República de Guatemala. *Diario de las Sesiones de la Asamblea Constituyente de 1945.*

Secretaría de Bienestar Social. *Programa Integral de Desarrollo de la Comunidad para Guatemala de la Jefatura de Gobierno.* Series "Colección Bienestar Social y Desarrollo de la Comunidad." Guatemala, 1964.

Sklar, Barry, and Virginia M. Hagen. Compilers. *Inter-American relations; collection of documents, legislation, descriptions of Inter-American organizations, and other material pertaining to inter-American affairs.* Washington, DC: U.S. Government Printing Office, 1972.

Smith, Lynn, and George Foster. *Los Aportes de la Sociología y de la Antropología para el Desarrollo de la Comunidad.* Series "Colección Bienestar Social y Desarrollo de la Comunidad." Guatemala, 1964.

Terga, Ricardo, and Emilio Vásquez Robles. *Tactic "el corazón del mundo": Un estudio histórico etnológico de un pueblo Pokomchí de Alta Verapaz.* 1976.

Vargas R., Gonzalo. *En buen camino.* Guatemala: Ministerio de Educación Pública. Campaña Nacional de Alfabetización, 1950.

Vargas R., Gonzalo. *Nuevo Día.* Guatemala: Ministerio de Educación Pública. Campaña Nacional de Alfabetización, 1946.

Vela, David. *Orientación y recomendaciones del Primer Congreso Indigenista Interamericano.* Ciudad de Guatemala: Publicaciones del Comité Organizador del IV Congreso Indigenista Interamericano, 1959.

Secondary Sources

Adams, Richard N. "Guatemalan Ladinization and History." *The Americas* 50, no. 4 (1994): 527–43.

———. *Joaquín Noval como indigenista, antropólogo y revolucionario.* Ciudad de Guatemala: Editorial Universitaria, Universidad de San Carlos, 2000.

———. "Social Anthropology in INCAP." *Food and Nutrition Bulletin* 31, no. 1 (2010): 152–60.

Adams, Richard y Santiago Bastos. *Las relaciones étnicas en Guatemala, 1944–2000.* La Antigua, Guatemala: CIRMA, 2003.

Aguilar-Rodríguez, Sandra. "Cooking Modernity: Nutrition Policies, Class, and Gender in 1940s and 1950s Mexico City." *The Americas* 64, no. 2 (October 2007): 177–205.

Annis, Sheldon. *God and Production in a Guatemalan Town.* Austin: University of Texas Press, 1987.

Applebaum, Nancy P., Anne S. Macpherson, and Karin Alejandra Rosemblatt, eds. *Race and Nation in Modern Latin America.* Chapel Hill: The University of North Carolina Press, 2003.

Asselbergs, Florine. *Conquered Conquistadors: The Lienzo de Quauhquechollan, a Nahua Vision of the Conquest of Guatemala.* Boulder: University Press of Colorado, 2008.

Asturias, Miguel Ángel. *Sociología Guatemalteca: el problema social del indio.* Edición e introducción Julio César Pinto Soria. Ciudad de Guatemala; Editorial Universitaria Universidad de San Carlos, 2008.

AVANCSO. *Política institucional hacia el desplazado interno en Guatemala.* Cuaderno de investigación No. 6. Guatemala: AVANCSO, 2008.

Azoulay, Ariella. *The Civil Contract of Photography*. Translated by Rela Mazali and Ruvik Danieli. New York: Zone Books, 2008.

———. *Civil Imagination: A Political Ontology of Photography*. Translated by Louise Bethlehem. London: Verso, 2012.

Barrientos Batres, Salomón. *El olvido de los gobernados: el indígena en el imaginario de nación de los intelectuales guatemaltecos de la década de 1920*. Guatemala: Centro Editorial Vile, 2013.

Barthes, Roland. *Camera Lucida: Reflections on Photography*. Translated by Richard Howard. New York: Hill and Wang, 1981.

Batz, Giovanni. "La Lucha Contra Megaproyectos en la región Ixil y las violaciones de los derechos indígenas." In *Pensar Guatemala desde la Resistencia: el neoliberalismo enfrentado*, edited by Prensa Comunitaria, 89–122. Guatemala City, Guatemala, F&G Editores, 2018.

Beck, Erin. *How Development Projects Persist: Everyday Negotiations with Guatemalan NGOs*. Durham, NC: Duke University Press, 2017.

Beckett, Ian F. W. *Modern Insurgencies and Counterinsurgencies: Guerrillas and Their Opponents since 1750*. London: Routledge, 2001.

Bennett, John W. "Applied and Action Anthropology: Ideological and Conceptual Aspects." *Current Anthropology* 37, no. S1 (February 1996): S23–S53.

Berth, Christiane. *Food and Revolution: Fighting Hunger in Nicaragua, 1960–1993*. Pittsburgh, PA: University of Pittsburgh Press, 2021.

Biggs, David. *Quagmire: Nation-Building and Nature in the Mekong Delta*. Seattle: University of Washington Press, 2010.

Birn, Anne-Emanuelle, and Raúl Necochea López, eds. *Peripheral Nerve: Health and Medicine in Cold War Latin America*. Durham, NC: Duke University Press, 2020.

Black, George. *Garrison Guatemala*. New York: Monthly Review Press, 1984.

Boyer, Christopher H. *Becoming Campesinos: Politics, Identity and Agrarian Struggle in Postrevolutionary Michoacán, 1920–1935*. Stanford, CA: Stanford University Press, 2003.

Brands, Hal. *Latin America's Cold War*, paperback edition. Cambridge, MA: Harvard University Press, 2012.

Brazinsky, Greg A. *Winning the Third World: Sino-American Rivalry during the Cold War*. Chapel Hill: The University of North Carolina Press, 2017.

Brintnall, Douglas E. *Revolt Against the Dead: The Modernization of a Mayan Community in the Highlands of Guatemala*. New York: Gordon and Breach, Science Publishers, Inc., 1979.

Britnell, G. E. "Factors in the Economic Development of Guatemala." *American Economic Review* 43, no. 2. Papers of the Proceedings of the Sixty-fifth Annual Meeting of the American Economic Association (May 1953): 104–14.

Buckley, Eve E. *Technocrats and the Politics of Drought and Development in Twentieth Century Brazil*. Chapel Hill: The University of North Carolina Press, 2017.

Burkhart, Louise M. *Holy Wednesday: A Nahua Drama from Early Colonial Mexico*. Philadelphia: University of Pennsylvania Press, 1996.

Carey, David, Jr. *Our Elders Teach Us: Maya-Kaqchikel Historical Perspectives*. Tuscaloosa: University of Alabama Press, 2001.

———. *Engendering Mayan History: Kaqchikel Women as Agents and Conduits of the Past, 1875–1970*. New York: Routledge, 2005.

———. "Guatemala's Green Revolution: Synthetic Fertilizer, Public Health, and Economic Autonomy in the Mayan Highland." *Agricultural History* 83, no. 3 (2009): 283–322.

———. "Drunks and Dictators: Inebriation's Gendered, Ethnic, and Class Components in Guatemala, 1898–1944." In *Alcohol in Latin America: A Social and Cultural History*, edited by Gretchen Pierce and Áurea Toxqui, 131–57. Tucson: University of Arizona Press, 2014.

———. *Oral History in Latin America: Unlocking the Spoken Archive*. New York: Routledge, 2017.

———. "'The Heart of the Country': The Primacy of Peasants and Maize in Modern Guatemala." *Journal of Latin American Studies* 51 (2019): 273–306.

Carmack, Robert M., ed. *Harvest of Violence: The Maya Indians and the Guatemalan Crisis*. Norman: University of Oklahoma Press, 1988.

Casaus Arzú, Marta Elena. "La metamorphosis del racismo en la elite de poder en Guatemala." In *Racismo en Guatemala? Abriendo el debate sobre un tema tabú*, edited by Clara Arenas Bianchi et al. 45–110. Ciudad de Guatemala: AVANCSO, 2004.

Casaus Arzú, Marta Elena, and Teresa García Giráldez, eds. *Las redes intelectuales centroamericanas: un siglo de imaginarios nacionales (1820–1920)*. Guatemala: F&G editores, 2009.

Casey, Dennis F. *Indigenismo: The Guatemalan Experience*. PhD diss., University of Kansas, 1979.

Castilho, Celso. *Slave Emancipation and Transformations in Brazilian Political Citizenship*. Pittsburgh, PA: University of Pittsburgh Press, 2016.

Castillo Ramírez, Fernando. *Ixcán en tiempos del conflicto armado interno: una guerra que se combatió con desarrollo, conozca la verdadera historia*. Guatemala: Palo de Hormigo, 2014.

Cátedra Joaquín Noval, comp. *Joaquín Noval: una antología*. Guatemala City: Editorial Universitaria USAC, 2018.

Chase-Dunn, Christopher, Susanne Jonas, and Nelson Amaro, eds. *Globalization on the Ground: Postbellum Guatemalan Democracy and Development*. Lanham, MD: Rowman & Littlefield Publishers, Inc., 2001.

Chastain, Andra B., and Timothy W. Lorek. *Itineraries of Expertise: Science, Technology, and the Environment in Latin America*. Pittsburgh, PA: University of Pittsburg Press, 2020.

Cojtí Cuxil, Demetrio. "The Impact of the Popular Referendum on Compliance with the Indigenous Accord and on Democratization in Guatemala." In *The Popular Referendum (Consulta Popular) and the Future of the Peace Process in Guatemala*, Latin American Program, Working Papers #241, edited by Cynthia J. Arson. Washington, DC: Woodrow Wilson Center for International Scholars, 1999.

———. *Runa'oj Ri Maya' Amaq': Configuración del Pensamiento Político del Pueblo Maya*, parte 1. Guatemala, C.A.: Cholsamaj, 2006.

Coleman, Kevin. *A Camera in the Garden of Eden: The Self-Forging of a Banana Republic*. Austin: University of Texas Press, 2015.

Copeland, Nicolas. "Greening the Counterinsurgency: The Deceptive Effects of Guatemala's Rural Development Plan of 1970." *Development and Change* 43, no. 4 (2012): 975–98.

———. "Regarding Development: Governing Indian Advancement in Revolutionary Guatemala," *Economy and Society* 44, no. 3 (2015): 418–44.

————. *The Democracy Development Machine: Neoliberalism, Radical Pessimism, and Authoritarian Populism in Mayan Guatemala*. Ithaca, NY: Cornell University Press, 2019.

Costanza, Jennifer N. "Indigenous Peoples' Right to Prior Consultation: Transforming Human Rights from the Grassroots in Guatemala." *Journal of Human Rights* 14 (2015): 260–85.

Coy Moulton, Aaron. "Counter-Revolutionary Friends: Caribbean Basin Dictators and Guatemalan Exiles against the Guatemalan Revolution, 1945–1950." *The Americas* 76, no. 1 (2019): 107–35.

Crafts, Lydia. *Mining Bodies: U.S. Medical Experimentation in Guatemala during the Twentieth Century*. PhD diss., University of Illinois at Urbana-Champaign, 2019.

Craib, Raymond B. *Cartographic Mexico: A History of State Fixations and Fugitive Landscapes*. Durham, NC: Duke University Press, 2004.

Cueto, Marcos. *Cold War, Deadly Fevers: Malaria Eradication in Mexico, 1955–1975*. Baltimore, MD: Johns Hopkins University Press, 2014.

Cullather, Nick. *Secret History: The CIA's Classified Account of its Operations in Guatemala, 1952–1954*. Stanford, CA: Stanford University Press, 1999.

————. "Development? It's History." *Diplomatic History* 24, no. 4 (Fall 2000): 641–53.

————. *The Hungry World: America's Cold War Battle against Poverty in Asia*. Cambridge, MA: Harvard University Press, 2010.

Dary, Claudia F. "El estado y los indígenas: del indigenismo al multiculturalismo." In *Guatemala: Historia Reciente (1954–1996). Tomo III, Pueblos indígenas, actores políticos*, edited by Virgilio Álvarez Aragón et al., 105–67. Ciudad de Guatemala: FLACSO, 2013.

Dawson, Alexander S. *Indian and Nation in Revolutionary Mexico*. Tucson: University of Arizona Press, 2004.

De la Cadena, Marisol. *Indigenous Mestizos: The Politics of Race and Culture in Cuzco, Peru, 1919–1991*. Durham, NC: Duke University Press, 2000.

Díaz-Polanco, Héctor. "Prologo: Etnicidad y autonomía en el pensamiento de Mario Payeras." In *Los pueblos indígenas y la revolución guatemalteca: Ensayos étnicos 1982–1992*, Mario Payeras, 7–15. Guatemala: Magna Terra esarro, 1997.

Dillingham, A. S. *Oaxaca Resurgent: Indigeneity, Development, and Inequality in Twentieth-Century Mexico*. Stanford, CA: Stanford University Press, 2021.

Dougherty, Michael. "The Global Gold Mining Industry, Junior Firms, and Civil Society Resistance in Guatemala." *Bulletin of Latin American Research* 30, no. 4 (2011): 403–18.

Dunkerley, James. *Power in the Isthmus: A Political History of Modern Central America*. London: Verso, 1989.

Earle, Rebecca. *The Return of the Native: Indians and Myth-Making in Spanish America, 1810–1930*. Durham, NC: Duke University Press, 2007.

Egan, Lawrence A. *Maryknoll in Central America, 1943–2011: A Chronicle of U.S. Catholic Missionaries*. Self-published, 2011.

Ekbladh, David. *The Great American Mission: Modernization and the Construction of an American World Order*. Princeton, NJ: Princeton University Press, 2010.

Engerman, David C. "Development Politics and the Cold War." *Diplomatic History* 41, no. 1 (2017): 1–19.

Engerman, David C. Nils Gilman, Mark H. Haefele, and Michael E. Latham, eds. *Staging Growth: Modernization, Development, and the Global Cold War*. Amherst: University of Massachusetts Press, 2003.

Escobar, Arturo. "Power and Visibility: Development and the Invention and Management of the Third World." *Cultural Anthropology* 3, no. 4 (November 1988): 428–43.

———. *Encountering Development: The Making and Unmaking of the Third World*, paperback reissue. Princeton, NJ: Princeton University Press, 2012.

Escobar, Raquel L. Cárdenas. *Reconcile the Indian, Reconcile the Nation: Transnational Indian Reform in the Era of Inter-American Politics, 1930–1960*. PhD diss., University of Illinois at Urbana-Champaign, 2020.

Esquit, Edgar. *Otros poderes, nuevos desafíos: relaciones interétnicas en Tecpán y su entorno departamental, 1871–1935*. Guatemala: Instituto de Estudios Interétnicos, USAC, 2002.

———. *La superación del indígena: la política de la modernización entre las élites indígenas de Comalapa, siglo XX*. Guatemala: Instituto de Estudios Interétnicos, USAC, 2010.

———. *Comunidad y estado durante la revolución: política comunal maya en la década de 1944 a 1954*. Guatemala: Tijaal Ediciones, 2019.

Falla, Ricardo. *Historia de un gran amor*. Guatemala: USAC Editorial Universitaria, 2006.

———. *Ixcán: El campesino indígena se levanta*. Vol. 3. Guatemala: AVANCSO, 2015.

Ferguson, James. *The Anti-Politics Machine: "Development," Depoliticization, and Bureaucratic Power in Lesotho*. Minneapolis: University of Minnesota, 1994.

Ferrer, Ada. *Freedom's Mirror: Cuba and Haiti in the Age of Revolution*. Cambridge: Cambridge University Press, 2014.

Field, Thomas C. *From Development to Dictatorship: Bolivia and the Alliance for Progress in the Kennedy Era*. Ithaca, NY: Cornell University Press, 2014.

Figueroa Arriola, Marina Esthela. *Estudio sobre el desarrollo de la comunidad de San Rafael el Arado*. Thesis, USAC, 1968.

Fitzpatrick-Behrens, Susan. "From Symbols of the Sacred to Symbols of Subversion to Simply Obscure: Maryknoll Women Religious in Guatemala, 1953–1967." *The Americas* 61, no. 2 (2004): 189–216.

Forster, Cindy. *The Time of Freedom: Campesino Workers in Guatemala's October Revolution*. Pittsburgh, PA: University of Pittsburgh Press, 2001.

Foss, Sarah. "Land and Labor Relations in Guatemala's 1952 Agrarian Reform: Rethinking Rural Identities." *Historia Agraria de América Latina* 1, no. 1 (April 2020): 1–21.

———. "Community Development in Cold War Guatemala: Not a Revolution but an Evolution." In *Latin America and the Global Cold War*, edited by Thomas C. Field Jr., Stella Krepp, and Vanni Pettinà, 123–47. Chapel Hill: The University of North Carolina Press, 2020.

———. "The National Tomorrow: The Utopian Vision of *Octubre Revolucionario* in the Aftermath of Genocide in Guatemala." *The Latin Americanist* 64, no. 4 (December 2020): 423–50.

———. "Rumors of Insurgency and Assassination in the Ixcán, Guatemala, 1968–1981." *Journal of Social History* 55, no. 1 (2021): 105–26.

Freije, Vanessa, and Rachel Nolan. "Interpretative Challenges in the Archive: An Introduction." *Journal of Social History* 55, no. 1 (2021): 1–6.

Friedman, Jeremy. *Shadow Cold War: The Sino-Soviet Competition for the Third World*. Chapel Hill: The University of North Carolina Press, 2015.

Galeano, Eduardo. *Guatemala: Occupied Country*. Translated by Cedric Belfrage. New York: Monthly Review Press, 1969.

García Ferreira, Roberto, ed. *Guatemala y la Guerra Fría en América Latina, 1947–1977*. Guatemala: CEUR, USAC, 2010.

García Laguardia, Jorge Mario. *El estatuto indígena en la Constitución guatemalteca de 1945*. Ciudad de Guatemala: Editorial Serviprensa, 2010.

———. *Constitución y Constituyentes de 1945 en Guatemala*. Guatemala City: Instituto de Investigaciones Jurídicas, 2012.

Garrard-Burnett, Virginia. "Indians Are Drunks and Drunks Are Indians: Alcohol and Indigenismo in Guatemala 1890–1940." *Bulletin of Latin American Research* 19, no. 3 (July 2000): 341–56.

Gibbings, Julie. "Mestizaje in the Age of Fascism: Interracial Sex, Germans, and Q'eqchi' Mayas in Alta Verapaz, Guatemala." *German History* 34, no. 2 (2016): 214–36.

———. "The Shadow of Slavery: Historical Time, Labor, and Citizenship in Nineteenth Century Alta Verapaz, Guatemala." *Hispanic American Historical Review* 96, no. 1 (2016): 73–107.

———. *Our Time Is Now: Race and Modernity in Postcolonial Guatemala*. Cambridge: Cambridge University Press, 2020.

Gibbings, Julie, and Heather Vrana, eds. *Out of the Shadow: Revisiting the Revolution from Post-Peace Guatemala*. Austin: University of Texas Press, 2020.

Gilman, Nils. *Mandarins of the Future: Modernization Theory in Cold War America*. Baltimore, MD: Johns Hopkins University Press, 2003.

Giraudo, Laura, and Juan Martín-Sánchez, eds. *La ambivalente historia del indigenismo: campo interamericano y trayectorias nacionales 1940–1970*. Lima: Instituto de Estudios Peruanos, 2011.

Girón Cerna, Carlos. *Aldeas de cristal: Conferencias y escritos*. Guatemala, C.A.: Litografías modernas, 1967.

Gleijeses, Piero. *Shattered Hope: The Guatemalan Revolution and the United States, 1944–1954*. Princeton, NJ: Princeton University Press, 1991.

Glenn, Charles Leslie. *American Indian/First Nations Schooling: From the Colonial Period to the Present*. New York: Palgrave Macmillan, 2011.

González Ponciano, Jorge Ramón. *Diez años del indigenismo en Guatemala (1944–1954)*. Thesis, Escuela Nacional de Antropología e Historia: México, D.F., 1988.

Gotkowitz, Laura. *A Revolution for Our Rights: Indigenous Struggles for Land and Justice in Bolivia, 1880–1952*. Durham, NC: Duke University Press, 2008.

———, ed. *Histories of Race and Racism: The Andes and Mesoamerica from Colonial Times to the Present*. Durham, NC: Duke University Press, 2011.

Goubaud Carrera, Antonio. *Food Patterns and Nutrition in Two Spanish-American Communities*. Master's Thesis, University of Chicago. 1943.

Gould, Jeffrey L. *To Lead as Equals: Rural Protest and Political Consciousness in Chinandega, Nicaragua, 1912–1979*. Chapel Hill: The University of North Carolina Press, 1990.

———. *To Die in This Way: Nicaraguan Indians and the Myth of Mestizaje, 1880–1965*. Durham, NC: Duke University Press, 1998.

Gow, David. *Countering Development: Indigenous Modernity and the Moral Imagination.* Durham, NC: Duke University Press, 2008.

Grandia, Liza. *Enclosed: Conservation, Cattle and Commerce Among the Q'eqchi' Maya Lowlanders.* Seattle: University of Washington Press, 2012.

Grandin, Greg. *The Blood of Guatemala: A History of Race and Nation.* Durham, NC: Duke University Press, 2000.

———. "Everyday Forms of State Decomposition: Quetzaltenango, Guatemala, 1954." *Bulletin of Latin American Research* 19, no. 3 (2000): 303–20.

———. "Can the Subaltern Be Seen? Photography and the Affects of Nationalism." *Hispanic American Historical Review* 84, no. 1 (2004): 83–111.

———. *Empire's Workshop: Latin America, the United States, and the Rise of the New Imperialism.* New York: Henry Holt and Company, 2006.

———. *The Last Colonial Massacre: Latin America in the Cold War.* Updated edition. Chicago: University of Chicago Press, 2011.

Grandin, Greg, and Gilbert M. Joseph, eds. *A Century of Revolution: Insurgent and Counterinsurgent Violence During Latin America's Long Cold War.* Durham, NC: Duke University Press, 2010.

Grandin, Greg, Deborah T. Levenson, and Elizabeth Oglesby, eds. *The Guatemala Reader: History, Culture, Politics.* Durham, NC: Duke University Press, 2011.

Guardino, Peter F. *Peasants, Politics, and the Formation of Mexico's National State.* Stanford, CA: Stanford University Press, 1996.

———. *"The Time of Liberty": Popular Political Culture in Oaxaca, 1750–1850.* Durham, NC: Duke University Press, 2005.

Hale, Charles R. "Rethinking Indigenous Politics in the Era of the 'Indio Permitido.'" *NACLA* 38, no. 1 (2004): 16–21.

———. "Neoliberal Multiculturalism: The Remaking of Cultural Rights and Racial Dominance in Central America." *Political and Legal Anthropology Review* 28, no. 1 (2005): 10–28.

Hale, Charles R., and Rosamel Millamán. "Cultural Agency and Political Struggle in the Era of the *Indio Permitido.*" In *Cultural Agency in the Americas,* edited by Doris Sommer, 281–304. Durham, NC: Duke University Press, 2006.

Handy, Jim. "A Sea of Indians: Ethnic Conflict and the Guatemalan Revolution, 1944–1952." *The Americas* 46, no. 2 (1989): 189–204.

———. *Revolution in the Countryside: Rural Conflict and Agrarian Reform in Guatemala, 1944–1954.* Chapel Hill: The University of North Carolina Press, 1994.

Harmer, Tanya. *Allende's Chile & The Inter-American Cold War.* Chapel Hill: The University of North Carolina Press, 2011.

———. "Two, Three Many Revolutions? Cuba and the Prospects for Revolutionary Change in Latin America, 1967–1975." *Journal of Latin American Studies* 45 (2013): 61–89.

Hernández Sandoval, Bonar. *Guatemala's Catholic Revolution: A History of Religious and Social Reform, 1920–1968.* Notre Dame, IN: University of Notre Dame Press, 2019.

Hildebrand, John R. "Farm Size and Agrarian Reform in Guatemala." *Inter-American Economic Affairs* 16, no. 2 (1962): 51–58.

———. "Guatemalan Rural Development Program: An Economist's Recommendations." *Inter-American Economic Affairs* 17, no. 1 (1963): 59–72.

———. "Guatemalan Colonization Projects: Institution Building and Resource Allocation." *Inter-American Economic Affairs* 19, no. 4 (1966): 41–52.

Hill, George W., and Manuel Gollas. *The Minifundia Economy and Society of the Guatemalan Highland Indian.* Working Paper No. 30. The Land Tenure Center. University of Wisconsin, July 1968.

Hines, Sarah. "The Power and Ethics of Vernacular Modernism: The Misicuni Dam Project in Cochabamba, Bolivia, 1944–2017." *Hispanic American Historical Review* 98, no. 2 (2018): 223–56.

———. *Water For All: Community, Property, and Revolution in Modern Bolivia.* Oakland: University of California Press, 2021.

Howe, James. *A People Who Would Not Kneel: Panama, the United States, and the San Blas Kuna.* Washington, DC: Smithsonian Institution Press, 1998.

Huezo, Stephanie Michelle. *Resisting and Surviving: Popular Education in El Salvador and Its U.S. Diaspora (1968–2018).* PhD diss., Indiana University, 2019.

Immerman, Richard H. *The CIA in Guatemala: The Foreign Policy of Intervention.* Austin: University of Texas Press, 1982.

Immerwahr, Daniel. *Thinking Small: The United States and the Lure of Community Development.* Cambridge, MA: Harvard University Press, 2015.

James, Daniel. *Doña María's Story: Life History, Memory, and Political Identity.* Durham, NC: Duke University Press, 2001.

Jonas, Susanne. *The Battle for Guatemala: Rebels, Death Squads, and U.S. Power.* San Francisco: Westview Press, 1991.

———. *Of Centaurs and Doves: Guatemala's Peace Process.* Boulder, CO: Westview Press, 2000.

Joseph, Gilbert M., and Daniel Nugent, eds. *Everyday Forms of State Formation: Revolution and the Negotiation of Rule in Modern Mexico.* Durham, NC: Duke University Press, 1994.

Joseph, Gilbert M., Daniel Nugent, and Daniela Spenser, eds. *In from the Cold: Latin America's New Encounter with the Cold War.* Durham, NC: Duke University Press, 2008.

Juárez Muñoz, J. Fernando. *El Indio Guatemalteco: ensayo de sociología nacional.* Vol. I. Guatemala: Tipografía Latina, 1931.

Keller, Renata. *Cuba, the United States, and the Legacy of the Mexican Revolution.* Cambridge: Cambridge University Press, 2015.

Kiddle, Amelia M. *Mexico's Relations with Latin America during the Cárdenas Era.* Albuquerque: University of New Mexico Press, 2016.

Knight, Alan. "Racism, Revolution, and *Indigenismo*: Mexico, 1910–1940." In *The Idea of Race in Latin America, 1870–1940,* edited by Richard Graham, 71–113. Austin: University of Texas Press, 1990.

Konefal, Betsy. *For Every Indio Who Falls: A History of Maya Activism in Guatemala, 1960–1990.* Albuquerque: University of New Mexico Press, 2010.

Kramer, Paul A. *The Blood of Government: Race, Empire, the United States & the Philippines.* Chapel Hill: The University of North Carolina Press, 2006.

Larson, Brooke. "Capturing Indian Bodies, Hearths, and Minds: The Gendered Politics of Rural School Reform in Bolivia, 1910–52." In *Proclaiming Revolution: Bolivia in Comparative Perspective,* edited by Merilee Grindle and Pilar Domingo, 32–59. Cambridge, MA: Harvard University Press, 2003.

———. *Trials of Nation Making: Liberalism, Race, and Ethnicity in the Andes, 1810–1910*. Cambridge: Cambridge University Press, 2004.

Latham, Michael E. *Modernization as Ideology: American Social Science and "Nation Building" in the Kennedy Era*. Chapel Hill: The University of North Carolina Press. 2000.

———. *The Right Kind of Revolution: Modernization, Development, and U.S. Foreign Policy from the Cold War to the Present*. Ithaca, NY: Cornell University Press, 2010.

Leacock, Ruth. *Requiem for Revolution: The United States and Brazil, 1961–1969*. Kent, OH: Kent State University Press, 1990.

Levenson, Deborah T. *Adiós Niño: The Gangs of Guatemala City and the Politics of Death*. Durham, NC: Duke University Press, 2013.

Lewis, Stephen E. *Rethinking Mexican Indigenismo: The INI's Coordinating Center in Highland Chiapas and the Fate of a Utopian Project*. Albuquerque: University of New Mexico Press, 2020.

Lindo-Fuentes, Héctor, and Erik Ching. *Modernizing Minds in El Salvador: Education Reform and the Cold War, 1960–1980*. Albuquerque: University of New Mexico Press, 2012.

Lockhardt, James. *The Nahuas after the Conquest: A Social and Cultural History of the Indians of Central Mexico, Sixteenth through Eighteenth Centuries*. Stanford, CA: Stanford University Press, 1992.

López, Rick A. *Crafting Mexico: Intellectuals, Artisans, and the State After the Revolution*. Durham, NC: Duke University Press, 2010.

Loucky, James, and Marilyn M. Moors, eds. *The Maya Diaspora: Guatemalan Roots, New American Lives*. Philadelphia: Temple University Press, 2000.

Lovell, George W. *Conquest and Survival in Colonial Guatemala: A Historical Geography of the Cuchumatán Highlands, 1500–1821*, 3rd ed. London: McGill-Queen's University Press, 2005.

Lutz, Christopher H. *Santiago de Guatemala, 1541–1773: City, Caste, and the Colonial Experience*. Norman, OK: University of Oklahoma Press, 1994.

Macekura, Stephen J. *Of Limits and Growth: The Rise of Global Sustainable Development in the Twentieth Century*. Cambridge: Cambridge University Press, 2015.

Macekura, Stephen J., and Erez Manela, eds. *The Development Century: A Global History*. Cambridge: Cambridge University Press, 2018.

Manz, Beatriz. *Paradise in Ashes: A Guatemalan Journey of Courage, Terror, and Hope*. Berkeley: University of California Press, 2004.

Martí, José. "Autores Americanos Aborígenes." In *Obras Completas de José Martí*, vol. 8, 336–37. La Habana, Cuba: Centro de Estudios Martinianos, 2001.

Martínez, María Elena. *Genealogical Fictions: Limpieza de Sangre, Religion, and Gender in Colonial Mexico*. Stanford, CA: Stanford University Press, 2008.

Martínez Ferraté, Rodolfo. *Una política rural para el Desarrollo*. Dominican Republic: Solidarios, 1974.

Martínez Peláez, Severo. *Motines de Indios: la violencia colonial en Centroamérica y Chiapas*, 2nd ed. Guatemala: F&G, 1991.

May, M. A. "A Retrospective View of the Institute of Human Relations at Yale." *Behavioral Science Notes* 6, no. 3 (1971): 141–72.

McAllister, Carlota, and Diane M. Nelson, eds. *War by Other Means: Aftermath in Post-Genocide Guatemala*. Durham, NC: Duke University Press, 2013.

McCreery, David. *Rural Guatemala, 1760–1940*. Stanford, CA: Stanford University Press, 1994.

Melville, Thomas R. *Through a Glass Darkly: The U.S. Holocaust in Central America*. Self-published through Xlibris Corporation, 2005.

Mendoza, Edgar S. G. *Ensayos sobre pensamiento antropológico (Guatemala y Brasil)*. Vol. I. Guatemala City: Escuela de Historia de la Universidad de San Carlos, 2009.

———. *Antropologistas y antropólogos: una generación*. Guatemala: Universidad de San Carlos de Guatemala, 2011.

Mirzoeff, Nicholas. *The Right to Look: A Counterhistory of Visuality*. Durham, NC: Duke University Press, 2011.

Moller, Jonathan. *Nuestra cultura es nuestra resistencia: repression, refugio y recuperación en Guatemala*. Spain: Turner Publications, 2004.

———. *Our Culture Is Our Resistance: Repression, Refuge, and Healing in Guatemala*. New York: Powerhouse Books, 2004.

Murray Li, Tania. *The Will to Improve: Governmentality, Development, and the Practice of Politics*. Durham, NC: Duke University Press, 2007.

Nash, Manning. "Applied and Action Anthropology in the Understanding of Man." *Anthropological Quarterly* 32, no. 1 (1959): 67–81.

Nelson, Diane M. *A Finger in the Wound: Body Politics in Quincentennial Guatemala*. Berkeley: University of California Press, 1999.

———. *Who Counts? The Mathematics of Death and Life After Genocide*. Durham, NC: Duke University Press, 2015.

Newbold, Stokes. "Receptivity to Communist Fomented Agitation in Guatemala." *Economic Development and Cultural Change* 5, no. 4 (1957): 338–61.

Noval, Joaquín. "Actividades antropológicas del Instituto Indigenista Nacional de Guatemala." *Boletín Bibliográfico de antropología americana*. Tomo XIV, no. 1 (1951): 112–13.

———. "Guatemala: The Indian and the Land." *Américas* 6, no. 3 (1954): 4–8; 41–43.

Offner, Amy C. *Sorting Out the Mixed Economy: The Rise and Fall of Welfare and Developmental States in the Americas*. Princeton, NJ: Princeton University Press, 2019.

Olsson, Tore C. *Agrarian Crossings: Reformers and the Remaking of the US and Mexican Countryside*. Princeton, NJ: Princeton University Press, 2017.

Pacino, Nicole. "Constructing a New Bolivian Society: Public Health Reforms and the Consolidation of the Bolivian National Revolution." *The Latin Americanist* 57, no. 4 (2013): 25–56.

Palmer, Stephen. *Launching Global Health: The Caribbean Odyssey of the Rockefeller Foundation*. Ann Arbor: University of Michigan Press, 2010.

Payeras, Mario. *Los días de la selva*. La Habana, Cuba: Casa de las Américas, 1980.

Paz Lemus, Lilian Tatiana. *Enacting Youth: Political Agency and Youth Subjectivities in Tactic, Guatemala*. PhD diss., Vanderbilt University, 2019.

Penny, H. Glenn. "From Migrant Knowledge to Fugitive Knowledge? German Migrants and Knowledge Production in Guatemala, 1880s–1945." *Geschichte und Gesellschaft* 43 (2017): 381–412.

Pérez, Louis A. *Cuba in the American Imagination: Metaphor and the Imperial Ethos*. Chapel Hill: The University of North Carolina Press, 2008.

Pérez Molina, Olga. "Desarrollo de la antropología guatemalteca: influencias intelectuales e institucionalidad en la década de los cuarenta y cincuenta del siglo XX." *Estudios* (2010): 161–86.

Pernet, Corinne A. "Between Entanglements and Dependencies: Food, Nutrition, and National Development at the Central American Institute of Nutrition." In *International Organizations and Development, 1945–1990*, edited by Marc Frey et al., 101–25. London, UK: Palgrave MacMillan UK, 2014.

Piedra Santa, Irene. *Alfabetización y poder en Guatemala, los años de la Guerra fría 1944–1984.* Guatemala: Proyecto de Desarrollo Santiago-PRODESA, 2011.

Piedra Santa Arandi, Rafael. *El petróleo y los minerales en Guatemala.* Colección Problemas Socio-económicas No. 1, 2a ed. Guatemala: Universidad de San Carlos, 1979.

Portelli, Alessandro. *The Death of Luigi Trastulli and Other Stories: Form and Meaning in Oral History.* Albany: State University of New York Press, 1991.

Poston, Richard W. *Democracy Speaks Many Tongues: Community Development Around the World.* New York: Harper & Row, 1962.

Pribilsky, Jason. "Development and the 'Indian Problem' in the Cold War Andes: *Indigenismo*, Science, and Modernization in the Making of the Cornell-Peru Project at Vicos." *Diplomatic History* 33, no. 3 (2009): 405–26.

Price, David H. "Subtle Means and Enticing Carrots: The Impacts of Funding on Cold War Anthropology." *Critique of Anthropology* 23, no. 4 (2003): 373–401.

———. *Cold War Anthropology: The CIA, the Pentagon, and the Growth of Dual Use Anthropology.* Durham, NC: Duke University Press, 2016.

Quijano, Aníbal. "Coloniality of Power and Eurocentrism in Latin America." *International Sociology* 15, no. 2 (2000): 215–32.

Quintana, Epaminondas. *La generación de 1920.* Ciudad de Guatemala: Tipografía Nacional, 1971.

Rabe, Stephen G. *The Most Dangerous Area in the World: John F. Kennedy Confronts Communist Revolution in Latin America.* Chapel Hill: The University of North Carolina Press, 1999.

Rahder, Micha. *An Ecology of Knowledges: Fear, Love, and Technoscience in Guatemalan Forest Conservation.* Durham, NC: Duke University Press, 2021.

Rayman, Paula M. *Kibbutz Community and Nation Building.* Princeton, NJ: Princeton University Press, 1981.

Redfield, Robert. *Cham Kom, a Maya Village.* Chicago: University of Chicago Press. 1962.

———. *Tepoztlán, a Mexican Village: A Study of Folk Life.* Chicago: University of Chicago Press, 1973.

Reverby, Susan M. "Ethical Failures and History Lessons: The U.S. Public Health Service Research Studies in Tuskegee and Guatemala." *Public Health Reviews* 34, no. 1 (2012): 1–18.

Rifkin, Mark. *Beyond Settler Time: Temporal Sovereignty and Indigenous Self-Determination.* Durham, NC: Duke University Press, 2017.

Rist, Gilbert. *The History of Development: From Western Origins to Global Faith.* 3rd ed. Translated by Patrick Camiller. London: Zed Books, 2011.

Rodas, Isabel, and Edgar Esquit. *Élite ladina-vanguardia indígena de la intolerancia a la violencia: Patzicía 1944.* Guatemala: Caudal, S.A., 1997.

Rodas Pineda, Belia Cota. *Estudio del municipio de Jacaltenango, Departamento de Huehuetenango y la proyección del Programa Nacional de Desarrollo de la Comunidad en el mismo*. Thesis. Universidad de San Carlos, 1974.

Rosemblatt, Karin Alejandra. *The Science and Politics of Race in Mexico and the United States, 1910–1950*. Chapel Hill: The University of North Carolina Press, 2018.

Rosier, Paul C. *Serving Their Country: American Indian Politics and Patriotism in the Twentieth Century*. Cambridge, MA: Harvard University Press, 2009.

Rothstein, Richard. *The Color of Law: A Forgotten History of How Our Government Segregated America*. New York: Liveright Publishing Corporation, 2017.

Rubinstein, Robert A. *Doing Fieldwork: The Correspondence of Robert Redfield and Sol Tax*. Rev. ed. Piscataway, NJ: Transaction Publishers, 2001.

Sackley, Nicole. "The Village as Cold War Site: Experts, Development, and the History of Rural Reconstruction." *Journal of Global History* 6 (2011): 481–504.

———. "Village Models: Etawah, India, and the Making and Remaking of Development in the Early Cold War." *Diplomatic History* 37, no. 4 (2013): 749–78.

Saldaña-Portillo, María Josefina. *The Revolutionary Imagination in the Americas and the Age of Development*. Durham, NC: Duke University Press, 2003.

———. *Indian Given: Racial Geographies across Mexico and the United States*. Durham, NC: Duke University Press, 2016.

Sanford, Victoria. *Buried Secrets: Truth and Human Rights in Guatemala*. New York: Palgrave Macmillan, 2003.

Santos Gurriarán, Carlos. *Guatemala: El Silencio del Gallo*. Barcelona, Spain: Random House Mondadori, S.A., 2007.

Sarzynski, Sarah. *Revolution in the Terra do Sol*. Stanford, CA: Stanford University Press, 2018.

Sattar, Aleezé. "*Indígena* or *Ciudadano*? Republican Laws and Highland Indian Communities in Ecuador, 1820–1857," in *Highland Indians and the State in Modern Ecuador*, edited by Kim Clark and Marc Becker, 22–36. Pittsburgh, PA: University of Pittsburgh Press, 2007.

Sayward, Amy L. *The United Nations in International History*. London: Bloomsbury Academic, 2017.

Schirmer, Jennifer. *The Guatemalan Military Project: A Violence Called Democracy*. Philadelphia: University of Pennsylvania Press, 1999.

Schlesinger, Stephen, and Stephen Kinzer. *Bitter Fruit: The Story of the American Coup in Guatemala*. Rev. ed. Cambridge, MA: Harvard University Press, 2005.

Scott, James C. *Seeing Like a State: How Certain Schemes to Improve the Human Condition Have Failed*. New Haven, CT: Yale University Press, 1998.

Scott, Rebecca. *Degrees of Freedom: Louisiana and Cuba after Slavery*. Cambridge, MA: Harvard University Press, 2005.

Scrimshaw, Nevin. "Origins and Development of INCAP." *Food and Nutrition Bulletin* 31, no. 1 (2010): 4–8.

Sieder, Rachel. "Rethinking Democratisation and Citizenship: Legal Pluralism and Institutional Reform in Guatemala." *Citizenship Studies* 3, no. 1 (1999): 103–18.

Simpson, Bradley R. *Economists with Guns: Authoritarian Development and U.S.-Indonesian Relations, 1960–1968*. Stanford, CA: Stanford University Press, 2008.

Smith, Carol A., ed. *Guatemalan Indians and the State, 1540–1988*. Austin: University of Texas Press, 1990.

Smith, Timothy J., and Abigail Adams, eds. *After the Coup: An Ethnographic Reframing of Guatemala 1954*. Urbana: University of Illinois Press, 2011.

Solano, Luis. *Guatemala: petróleo y minería en las entrañas del poder*. Inforpress Centroamericana, 2005.

———. "Quiché en el contexto del Desarrollo de la Franja Transversal del Norte: La repartición de los recursos naturales." *El Observador* 6, nos. 32–33 (2011): 83–106.

———. *Contextualización histórica de la Franja Transversal del Norte (FTN)*. Guatemala: Centro de Estudios y Documentación de la Frontera occidental de Guatemala, 2012.

Soto Laveaga, Gabriela. "Bringing the Revolution to Medical Schools: Social Service and a Rural Health Emphasis in 1930s Mexico." *Mexican Studies* 29, no. 2 (2013): 397–427.

Stapp, Darby C., ed. *Action Anthropology and Sol Tax in 2012: The Final Word? Journal of Northwest Anthropology, Memoir, 8*. Richland, WA: Northwest Anthropology, 2012.

Stepan, Nancy Leys. *"The Hour of Eugenics": Race, Gender, and Nation in Latin America*. Ithaca, NY: Cornell University Press, 1991.

Stone, Doris. "A Delimitation of the Area and Some of the Archaeology of the Sula-Jicaque Indians of Honduras." *American Antiquity* 7, no. 4 (1942): 376–88.

Streeter, Stephen M. "The Failure of 'Liberal Developmentalism': The United States's Anti-Communist Showcase in Guatemala, 1954–1960." *International History Review*, 21, no. 2 (1999): 386–413.

———. *Managing the Counterrevolution: The United States and Guatemala, 1954–1961*. Athens: Ohio University Center for International Studies, 2000.

Taracena Arriola, Arturo, Enrique Gordillo Castillo, Tania Sagastume Paiz, Carmén Álvarez Medrano, Soili Buska, Margarita López Raquez, Edelberto Torres Escobar, and Hugo Amador Us. *Etnicidad, estado y nación en Guatemala, 1944–1985*, Vol. II. Antigua, Guatemala: CIRMA, 2004.

Taracena Arriola, Arturo, Gisela Gellert, Enrique Gordillo Castillo, Tania Sagastume Paiz, and Knut Walter. *Etnicidad, estado y nación en Guatemala, 1808–1944*, Vol. I. Antigua Guatemala: CIRMA, 2009.

Tax, Sol. "Action Anthropology." *Current Anthropology* 16, no. 4 (1975): 514–17.

Taylor, William B. "Between Global Process and Local Knowledge: An Inquiry into Early Latin American Social History, 1500–1900." In *Reliving the Past: The Worlds of Social History*, edited by Olivier Zunz. Chapel Hill: The University of North Carolina Press, 1985.

Thornton, Christy. *Revolution in Development: Mexico and the Governance of the Global Economy*. Oakland: University of California Press, 2021.

Tilley, Helen. *Africa as a Living Laboratory: Empire, Development, and the Problem of Scientific Knowledge*. Chicago: University of Chicago Press, 2011.

Tutino, John. *Making a New World: Founding Capitalism in the Bajio and Spanish North America*. Durham, NC: Duke University Press, 2011.

Vaughan, Mary Kay. *Cultural Politics in Revolution: Teachers, Peasants, and Schools in Mexico, 1930–1940*. Tucson: University of Arizona Press, 1997.

Vrana, Heather A. *This City Belongs to You: A History of Student Activism in Guatemala, 1944–1996*. Oakland: University of California Press, 2017.

Wade, Peter. *Race and Ethnicity in Latin America*, 2nd ed. London: Pluto Press, 2010.

Walker, Charles F. *The Tupac Amaru Rebellion*. Cambridge, MA: Harvard University Press, 2014.

Warren, Kay B. *Indigenous Movements and Their Critics: Pan-Maya Activism in Guatemala*. Princeton, NJ: Princeton University Press, 1998.

Way, J. T. *The Mayan in the Mall: Globalization, Development, and the Making of Modern Guatemala*. Durham, NC: Duke University Press, 2012.

———. *Agrotropolis: Youth, Street, and Nation in the New Urban Guatemala*. Berkeley: University of California Press, 2021.

Westad, Odd Arne. *The Global Cold War: Third World Interventions and the Making of Our Times*. Cambridge: Cambridge University Press, 2007.

Yannakakis, Yanna. *The Art of Being In-Between: Native Intermediaries, Indian Identity, and Local Rule in Colonial Oaxaca*. Durham, NC: Duke University Press, 2008.

Index

CPSIA information can be obtained
at www.ICGtesting.com
Printed in the USA
LVHW041953100523
746640LV00005B/422